MARKETING CLASSICS

MARKETING CLASSICS
A Selection of
Influential Articles

3rd edition

Ben M. Enis
Keith K. Cox
University of Houston

Allyn and Bacon, Inc.
Boston · London · Sydney · Toronto

Printed in the United States of America

Library of Congress Cataloging in Publication Data

Enis, Ben M   comp.
  Marketing classics.

  Includes bibliographical references and index.
    1. Marketing—Addresses, essays, lectures. I. Cox,
Keith Kohn. II. Title.
HF5415.E67 1977   658.8'008   76-39910
ISBN 0-205-05715-2

Contributors

Lee Adler
Wroe Alderson
Ralph S. Alexander
Leo V. Aspinwall
Raymond A. Bauer
James A. Bayton
Neil H. Borden
Louis P. Bucklin
Donald F. Cox
Joel Dean
Peter F. Drucker
Foundation for Research on
    Human Behavior
John Kenneth Galbraith
Robert E. Good
Paul E. Green
Stephen A. Greyser
Mason Haire

Russell I. Haley
Stanley C. Hollander
John A. Howard
George Katona
Robert J. Keith
Philip Kotler
Robert F. Lanzillotti
Robert J. Lavidge
Theodore Levitt
Sidney J. Levy
Bruce Mallen
Phillip McVey
Edgar A. Pessemier
Jagdish N. Sheth
Wendell R. Smith
Gary A. Steiner
Frederick N. Sturdivant

Contents

Preface

When this book was conceived, we commented in the Preface:

> Marketing is that phase of human activity that produces economic want-satisfaction by matching consumers' needs and the resources of business firms. From the firm's point of view, consumer-satisfaction is the result of its marketing strategy. Strategy is based on marketing philosophy and is derived from the analysis of consumers and their functional interrelationships with such market forces as economic conditions, competitors' actions, institutional change, and other environmental factors. This volume is a compilation of articles that provide broad insight into the field of marketing.
>
> The authors consider these works to be among the classics of marketing literature. These articles are generally recognized by marketing scholars as being of enduring significance to marketing thought. They are widely quoted, have led to new directions in marketing research, and reflect the views of influential scholars. Consequently, these are works with which serious marketing students should be familiar, and to which they should have ready access. We believe the book will be a useful supplement to advanced undergraduate courses in marketing management and marketing strategy and to graduate courses in marketing fundamentals and marketing theory. The practitioner might also enjoy having these familiar works in his library.
>
> The articles in this volume were chosen on the basis of extensive research in marketing literature, and the authors were fortunate to obtain the suggestions of a number of colleagues. Nevertheless, it would be presumptuous to imply that we have compiled *the* classic works of marketing. Marketing is too rich, too complex, too diverse a discipline to be subsumed in one volume. Our selections reflect our own perceptions of and biases about marketing. . . .

The third edition of *Marketing Classics* reflects our continuing attempt to match this concept to the needs of marketing students. Responses to questionnaires sent to some adoptors of the second edition revealed that this anthology is used in a wide variety of courses, ranging from introductory marketing to doctoral-level seminars.

This edition includes several new articles that have stood the test of time, and deletes a few genuine *classics* that our research indicates are no longer frequently assigned to students for various reasons.

In addition, we have included several types of *comprehension aids.* These aids are described in the following section, "To the Reader."

Again, we are most grateful to the authors and publishers who granted permission to reprint their work. Our list of competent secretarial help includes Gwen Florence and Rebecca Davis on the first edition; Betty Wolfe and Marleen Vickers on the second edition; and Jelka Woodard in this third edition. In spite of all this assistance, errors of commission and omission no doubt appear in the anthology. We are, of course, responsible for these errors and would very much appreciate having them called to our attention.

BME
KKC

To The Reader

The purpose of a readings book is to present the work of various authorities in the field in convenient form. *Marketing Classics* represents, in our judgment, the best that the marketing discipline has to offer. To aid you in efficiently comprehending these articles, we have added the following material:

1. A suggested procedure for systematically evaluating an article
2. A key relating the articles to standard textbooks in marketing
3. Short introductions to each part of the book
4. Brief biographical sketches of each author
5. An index

Please make whatever use of these comprehension aids that you deem appropriate.

Critical Evaluation of an Article: A Suggested Procedure

1. *Who is the author?* (What are his qualifications for writing on this topic?)
   Scholarly achievements
   Business or administrative experience
   Other published work

2. *What is the author's message?*
   Major theme (in one sentence, if possible)
   Purpose of the message
   Author's viewpoint

3. *What evidence is offered to support this theme?*
   Three of four key points supported by references, facts, quotes, etc.

4. *How well is the argument presented?*
   Logical consistency
   Limitations and/or assumptions
   Completeness

5. *How does this article relate to other work in this area of marketing?*
   Other authorities (articles, books, etc.)
   Personal experience

6. *What is the significance of this article for marketing management?*
   Managerial usefulness of ideas presented
   Future direction of work in this area

Marketing Textbooks Correlated with Marketing Classics

Marketing Classics Article Number

Chapters in Text	Ennis[1]	McCarthy[2]	Boone & Kurtz[3]	Marcus[4]	Buskirk[5]	Stanton[6]	Kotler[7]	Staudt, Taylor, Bowersox[8]
1	4, 5, 7	2, 4	1, 2, 4, 18	1, 2, 3, 4	1, 2, 4, 7, 25	1, 2, 3, 4, 7	1, 2, 3, 4, 6, 7	1, 2
2	1, 2, 3, 18	1, 7	3, 5, 6	1, 7	8	18, 25		3, 4, 5
3	8	5	13, 14, 17	6, 8	19, 20	5, 19, 20	18, 25	25
4	24	18	19, 20	15	5	9, 10, 11	9, 10, 11, 12, 15	
5		8	9, 10, 11, 12, 15	9, 10, 11, 12	18, 21, 22, 23	15, 16, 22, 23		19, 20
6	17, 25	19, 20	16, 21, 22, 23	19, 20	9, 10, 11, 12, 15	12, 21		9, 10, 11
7	13, 14, 16		26		16, 26		19, 20	12, 15, 16
8	9, 10, 11, 12, 15	9, 10, 11, 12, 15	27, 28			26		
9	19, 20		24	17			21, 22, 23	
10	21, 22, 23, 26	3		13, 14	27, 28		16	21, 26
11	31, 32		29, 30		24	31, 32	26	
12	29, 30	26					31, 32	13, 14
13	27, 28			16, 26			24, 27, 28	22, 23 24
14		21, 22, 23	31					27, 28
15	6		32	29, 30		27		
16		27, 28	7, 8		31, 32	24	29, 30	29, 30

	[1]	[2]	[3]	[4]	[5]	[6]	[7]	[8]
17	24							
18	31, 32	18	17	7	6, 8			
19	16, 29	13, 14, 17		5, 8				
20	30						13, 14, 17	
21	31	28			29, 30		13, 14, 17	6, 8
22	32							
23	25	29, 30	17, 13, 14	3				
24	13, 14, 17	31, 32	27, 28	24	21, 22, 23	18, 25	5	7
25	6							
26								
27								
28		16, 29	30	31	32	25	13, 14, 17	6
29								
30								

[1] Enis, Ben, *Marketing Principles* (Goodyear Publishing, 1974).

[2] McCarthy, Jerome, *Basic Marketing*, 5th edition (Richard D. Irwin, 1975).

[3] Boone, Louis and David Kurtz, *Contemporary Marketing* (Dryden Press, 1974).

[4] Marcus, Burton, et al., *Modern Marketing* (Random House, 1975).

[5] Buskirk, Richard, *Principles of Marketing*, 4th edition (Dryden Press, 1975).

[6] Stanton, William, *Fundamentals of Marketing*, 4th edition (McGraw-Hill, 1975).

[7] Kotler, Philip, *Marketing Management: Analysis, Planning, and Control*, 3rd edition (Prentice-Hall, 1976).

[8] Staudt, Tom, Donald Taylor, and Donald Bowersox. *A Managerial Introduction to Marketing*, 3rd edition (Prentice-Hall, 1976).

PART
I

MARKETING PHILOSOPHY

Any discipline or area of human inquiry is based on a philosophy, a set of principles that provide the rationale for the existence of the discipline. The articles in Part I present a cross-section of the philosophy of marketing.

Levitt's article sets the stage. It vividly demonstrates the need for a broad interpretation of the marketing function and is perhaps the discipline's single best definitive statement. Levitt's thoughts on the continuing relevance of his paper are also included in this edition. Wroe Alderson, in his trenchant style, provides an overview of the marketing discipline. He envisions marketing discipline as based in the economics of imperfect competition, composed of the problem-solving activities of consumers and firms, and illuminated by concepts from the social sciences. The articles by Drucker and by Keith each illustrate Levitt's viewpoint and Alderson's framework. Drucker focuses on the macro, or societal, role that marketing performs in promoting economic growth and individual freedom. Keith's paper complements Drucker's. It emphasizes marketing's micro or managerial role in the operation of a business firm.

Galbraith, with extraordinary foresight and a provocative style, acknowledges the benefits of marketing as propounded by the previous articles. But he focuses on the difficulties engendered by marketing successes. Bauer and Greyser point out that many of the differences in viewpoint between marketing's supporters and its critics are basically semantic differences. There is need, they argue, for marketing students to dialogue with their critics.

This last point is particularly important to note as Kotler and Levy show that the concepts and techniques of marketing are applicable not only to products but also to people, organizations, and ideas—including Galbraith's thesis that resources should be shifted from the private to the public sector. In the last article in Part I, Sturdivant underscores the need for a broader perspective for marketing activities as he graphically chronicles the problems faced by disadvantaged consumers in modern society.

1

Marketing Myopia

Theodore Levitt

Every major industry was once a growth industry. But some that are now riding a wave of growth enthusiasm are very much in the shadow of decline. Others which are thought of as seasoned growth industries have actually stopped growing. In every case the reason growth is threatened, slowed, or stopped is *not* because the market is saturated. It is because there has been a failure of management.

FATEFUL PURPOSES

The failure is at the top. The executives responsible for it, in the last analysis, are those who deal with broad aims and policies. Thus:

> The railroads did not stop growing because the need for passenger and freight transportation declined. That grew. The railroads are in trouble today not because the need was filled by others (cars, trucks, airplanes, even telephones), but because it was *not* filled by the railroads themselves. They let others take customers away from them because they assumed themselves to be in the railroad business rather than in the transportation business. The reason they defined their industry wrong was because they were railroad-oriented instead of

Reprinted by permission of the publishers from Edward C. Bursk & John F. Chapman, editors, *Modern Marketing Strategy*, Cambridge, Mass.: Harvard University Press, ©1964, by the President and Fellows of Harvard College, originally published in the *Harvard Business Review*, Vol. 38 (July–August, 1960), pp. 24–47. This article won the 1960 McKinsey Award as best article of the year. The retrospective commentary was published in the *Harvard Business Review*, Vol. 53 (September–October, 1975), copyright © by the President and Fellows of Harvard College; all rights reserved. At the time of publication, 265,000 reprints of the article were distributed.

Theodore Levitt, a professor in the Harvard Business School, is the author of many widely-read publications, including *Innovation in Marketing* and numerous articles. He received his B.A. from Antioch College and the Ph.D. in economics from Ohio State University. His latest book is *Marketing for Business Growth.*

transportation-oriented; they were product-oriented instead of customer-oriented.

Hollywood barely escaped being totally ravished by television. Actually, all the established film companies went through drastic reorganizations. Some simply disappeared. All of them got into trouble not because of TV's inroads but because of their own myopia. As with the railroads, Hollywood defined its business incorrectly. It thought it was in the movie business when it was actually in the entertainment business. "Movies" implied a specific, limited product. This produced a fatuous contentment which from the beginning led producers to view TV as a threat. Hollywood scorned and rejected TV when it should have welcomed it as an opportunity—an opportunity to expand the entertainment business.

Today TV is a bigger business than the old narrowly defined movie business ever was. Had Hollywood been customer-oriented (providing entertainment), rather than product-oriented (making movies), would it have gone through the fiscal purgatory that it did? I doubt it. What ultimately saved Hollywood and accounted for its recent resurgence was the wave of new young writers, producers, and directors whose previous successes in television had decimated the old movie companies and toppled the big movie moguls.

There are other less obvious examples of industries that have been and are now endangering their futures by improperly defining their purposes. I shall discuss some in detail later and analyze the kind of policies that lead to trouble. Right now it may help to show what a thoroughly customer-oriented management *can* do to keep a growth industry growing, even after the obvious opportunities have been exhausted; and here there are two examples that have been around for a long time. They are nylon and glass—specifically, E. I. duPont de Nemours & Company and Corning Glass Works:

Both companies have great technical competence. Their product orientation is unquestioned. But this alone does not explain their success. After all, who was more pridefully product-oriented and product-conscious than the erstwhile New England Textile companies that have been so thoroughly massacred? The duPonts and the Cornings have succeeded not primarily because of their product or research orientation but because they have been thoroughly customer-oriented also. It is constant watchfulness for opportunities to apply their technical know-how to the creation of customer-satisfying uses which accounts for their prodigious output of successful new products. Without a very sophisticated eye on the customer, most of their new products might have been wrong, their sales methods useless.

Aluminum has also continued to be a growth industry, thanks to the efforts of two wartime-created companies which deliberately set about creating new customer-satisfying uses. Without Kaiser Aluminum & Chemical Corporation and Reynolds Metals Company, the total demand for aluminum today would be vastly less than it is.

Some may argue that it is foolish to set the railroads off against aluminum or the movies off against glass. Are not aluminum and glass naturally so versatile that the industries are bound to have more growth opportunities than the railroads and movies? This view commits precisely the error I have been talking about. It defines an industry, or a product, or a cluster of know-how so narrowly as to guarantee its premature senescence. When we mention "railroads," we should make sure we mean "transportation." As transporters, the railroads still have a good chance for very considerable growth. They are not limited to the railroad business as such (though in my opinion rail transportation is potentially a much stronger transportation medium than is generally believed).

What the railroads lack is not opportunity, but some of the same managerial imaginativeness and audacity that made them great. Even an amateur like Jacques Barzun can see what is lacking when he says:

> I grieve to see the most advanced physical and social organization of the last century go down in shabby disgrace for lack of the same comprehensive imagination that built it up. [What is lacking is] the will of the companies to survive and to satisfy the public by inventiveness and skill.[1]

SHADOW OF OBSOLESCENCE

It is impossible to mention a single major industry that did not at one time qualify for the magic appellation of "growth industry." In each case its assumed strength lay in the apparently unchallenged superiority of its product. There appeared to be no effective substitute for it. It was itself a runaway substitute for the product it so triumphantly replaced. Yet one after another of these celebrated industries has come under a shadow. Let us look briefly at a few more of them, this time taking examples that have so far received a little less attention:

Dry cleaning. This was once a growth industry with lavish prospects. In an age of wool garments, imagine being finally able to get them safely and easily clean. The boom was on.

Yet here we are 30 years after the boom started and the industry is in trouble. Where has the competition come from? From a better way of cleaning? No. It has come from synthetic fibers and chemical additives that have cut the need for dry cleaning. But this is only the beginning. Lurking in the wings and ready to make chemical dry cleaning totally obsolescent is that powerful magician, ultrasonics.

---

[1] Jacques Barzun, "Trains and the Mind of Man," *Holiday* February 1960, p. 21.

Electric utilities. This is another one of those supposedly "no-substitute" products that has been enthroned on a pedestal of invincible growth. When the incandescent lamp came along, kerosene lights were finished. Later the water wheel and the steam engine were cut to ribbons by the flexibility, reliability, simplicity, and just plain easy availability of electric motors. The prosperity of electric utilities continues to wax extravagant as the home is converted into a museum of electric gadgetry. How can anybody miss by investing in utilities, with no competition, nothing but growth ahead?

But a second look is not quite so comforting. A score of nonutility companies are well advanced toward developing a powerful chemical fuel cell which could sit in some hidden closet of every home silently ticking off electric power. The electric lines that vulgarize so many neighborhoods will be eliminated. So will the endless demolition of streets and service interruptions during storms. Also on the horizon is solar energy, again pioneered by nonutility companies.

Who says that the utilities have no competition? They may be natural monopolies now, but tomorrow they may be natural deaths. To avoid this prospect, they too will have to develop fuel cells, solar energy, and other power sources. To survive, they themselves will have to plot the obsolescence of what now produces their livelihood.

Grocery stores. Many people find it hard to realize that there ever was a thriving establishment known as the "corner grocery store." The supermarket has taken over with a powerful effectiveness. Yet the big food chains of the 1930's narrowly escaped being completely wiped out by the aggressive expansion of independent supermarkets. The first genuine supermarket was opened in 1930, in Jamaica, Long Island. By 1933 supermarkets were thriving in California, Ohio, Pennsylvania, and elsewhere. Yet the established chains pompously ignored them. When they chose to notice them, it was with such derisive descriptions as "cheapy," "horse-and-buggy," "cracker-barrel store-keeping," and "unethical opportunities."

The executive of one big chain announced at the time that he found it "hard to believe that people will drive for miles to shop for foods and sacrifice the personal service chains have perfected and to which Mrs. Consumer is accustomed."[2] As late as 1936, the National Wholesale Grocers convention and the New Jersey Retail Grocers Association said there was nothing to fear. They said that the supers' narrow appeal to the price buyer limited the size of their market. They had to draw from miles around. When imitators came, there

[2] For more details see M. M. Zimmerman, *The Super Market: A Revolution in Distribution* (New York, McGraw-Hill Book Company, Inc. 1955), p. 48.

would be wholesale liquidations as volume fell. The current high sales of the supers was said to be partly due to their novelty. Basically people wanted convenient neighborhood grocers. If the neighborhood stores "cooperate with their suppliers, pay attention to their costs, and improve their services," they would be able to weather the competition until it blew over.[3]

It never blew over. The chains discovered that survival required going into the supermarket business. This meant the wholesale destruction of their huge investments in corner store sites and in established distribution and merchandising methods. The companies with "the courage of their convictions" resolutely stuck to the corner store philosophy. They kept their pride but lost their shirts.

Self-deceiving Cycle

But memories are short. For example, it is hard for people who today confidently hail the twin messiahs of electronics and chemicals to see how things could possibly go wrong with these galloping industries. They probably also cannot see how a reasonably sensible businessman could have been as myopic as the famous Boston millionaire who 50 years ago unintentionally sentenced his heirs to poverty by stipulating that his entire estate be forever invested exclusively in electric street-car securities. His posthumous declaration, "There will always be a big demand for efficient urban transportation," is no consolation to his heirs who sustain life by pumping gasoline at automobile filling stations.

Yet, in a casual survey I recently took among a group of intelligent business executives, nearly half agreed that it would be hard to hurt their heirs by tying their estates forever to the electronics industry. When I then confronted them with the Boston street car example, they chorused unanimously, "That's different!" But is it? Is not the basic situation identical?

In truth, *there is no such thing* as a growth industry, I believe. There are only companies organized and operated to create and capitalize on growth opportunities. Industries that assume themselves to be riding some automatic growth escalator invariably descent into stagnation. The history of every dead and dying "growth" industry shows a self-deceiving cycle of bountiful expansion and undetected decay. There are four conditions which usually guarantee this cycle:

1. The belief that growth is assured by an expanding and more affluent population.

[3] Ibid., pp. 45–47.

2. The belief that there is no competitive substitute for the industry's major product.
3. Too much faith in mass production and in the advantages of rapidly declining unit costs as output rises.
4. Preoccupation with a product that lends itself to carefully controlled scientific experimentation, improvement, and manufacturing cost reduction.

I should like now to begin examining each of these conditions in some detail. To build my case as boldly as possible, I shall illustrate the points with reference to three industries—petroleum, automobiles, and electronics—particularly petroleum, because it spans more years and more vicissitudes. Not only do these three have excellent reputations with the general public and also enjoy the confidence of sophisticated investors, but their managements have become known for progressive thinking in areas like financial control, product research, and management training. If obsolescence can cripple even these industries, it can happen anywhere.

POPULATION MYTH

The belief that profits are assured by an expanding and more affluent population is dear to the heart of every industry. It takes the edge off the apprehensions everybody understandably feels about the future. If consumers are multiplying and also buying more of your product or service, you can face the future with considerably more comfort than if the market is shrinking. An expanding market keeps the manufacturer from having to think very hard or imaginatively. If thinking is an intellectual response to a problem, then the absence of a problem leads to the absence of thinking. If your product has an automatically expanding market, then you will not give much thought to how to expand it.

One of the most interesting examples of this is provided by the petroleum industry. Probably our oldest growth industry, it has an enviable record. While there are some current apprehensions about its growth rate, the industry itself tends to be optimistic. But I believe it can be demonstrated that it is undergoing a fundamental yet typical change. It is not only ceasing to be a growth industry, but may actually be a declining one, relative to other business. Although there is widespread unawareness of it, I believe that within 25 years the oil industry may find itself in much the same position of retrospective glory that the railroads are now in. Despite its pioneering work in developing and applying the present-value method of investment evaluation, in employee relations, and in working with backward countries, the petroleum business is a distressing example of how complacency and wrongheadedness can stubbornly convert opportunity into near disaster.

One of the characteristics of this and other industries that have believed very strongly in the beneficial consequences of an expanding population, while at the same time being industries with a generic product for which there has appeared to be no competitive substitute, is that the individual companies have sought to outdo their competitors by improving on what they are already doing. This makes sense, of course, if one assumes that sales are tied to the country's population strings, because the customer can compare products only on a feature-by-feature basis. I believe it is significant, for example, that not since John D. Rockefeller sent free kerosene lamps to China has the oil industry done anything really outstanding to create a demand for its product. Not even in product improvement has it showered itself with eminence. The greatest single improvement, namely, the development of tetraethyl lead, came from outside the industry, specifically from General Motors and duPont. The big contributions made by the industry itself are confined to the technology of oil exploration, production, and refining.

Asking for Trouble

In other words, the industry's efforts have focused on improving the *efficiency* of getting and making its product, not really on improving the generic product or its marketing. Moreover, its chief product has continuously been defined in the narrowest possible terms, namely, gasoline, not energy, fuel, or transportation. This attitude has helped assure that:

> Major improvements in gasoline quality tend not to originate in the oil industry. Also, the development of superior alternative fuels comes from outside the oil industry, as will be shown later.
>
> Major innovations in automobile fuel marketing are originated by small new oil companies that are not primarily preoccupied with production or refining. These are the companies that have been responsible for the rapidly expanding multipump gasoline stations, with their successful emphasis on large and clean layouts, rapid and efficient driveway service, and quality gasoline at low prices.

Thus, the oil industry is asking for trouble from outsiders. Sooner or later, in this land of hungry inventors and entrepreneurs, a threat is sure to come. The possibilities of this will become more apparent when we turn to the next dangerous belief of many managements. For the sake of continuity, because this second belief is tied closely to the first, I shall continue with the same example.

Idea of Indispensability

The petroleum industry is pretty much persuaded that there is no competitive substitute for its major product, gasoline—or if there is, that it will continue to be a derivative of crude oil, such as diesel fuel or kerosene jet fuel.

There is a lot of automatic wishful thinking in this assumption. The trouble is that most refining companies own huge amounts of crude oil reserves. These have value only if there is a market for products into which oil can be converted—hence the tenacious belief in the continuing competitive superiority of automobile fuels made from crude oil.

This idea persists despite all historic evidence against it. The evidence not only shows that oil has never been a superior product for any purpose for very long, but it also shows that the oil industry has never really been a growth industry. It has been a succession of different businesses that have gone through the usual historic cycles of growth, maturity, and decay. Its over-all survival is owed to a series of miraculous escapes from total obsolescence, of last minute and unexpected reprieves from total disaster reminiscent of the Perils of Pauline.

Perils of Petroleum

I shall sketch in only the main episodes:

First, crude oil was largely a patent medicine. But even before that fad ran out, demand was greatly expanded by the use of oil in kerosene lamps. The prospect of lighting the world's lamps gave rise to an extravagant promise of growth. The prospects were similar to those the industry now holds for gasoline in other parts of the world. It can hardly wait for the underdeveloped nations to get a car in every garage.

In the days of the kerosene lamp, the oil companies competed with each other and against gaslight by trying to improve the illuminating characteristics of kerosene. Then suddenly the impossible happened. Edison invented a light which was totally nondependent on crude oil. Had it not been for the growing use of kerosene in space heaters, the incandescent lamp would have completely finished oil as a growth industry at that time. Oil would have been good for little else than axle grease.

Then disaster and reprieve struck again. Two great innovations occurred, neither originating in the oil industry. The successful development of coal-burning domestic central-heating systems made the space heater obsolescent. While the industry reeled, along came its most magnificent boost yet—the internal combustion engine, also invented by outsiders. Then when the prodigious expansion for gasoline finally began to level off in the 1920's, along came the miraculous escape of a central oil heater. Once again, the escape was provided by an outsider's invention and development. And when that market weakened, wartime demand for aviation fuel came to the rescue. After the war the expansion of civilian aviation, the dieselization of railroads, and the explosive demand for cars and trucks kept the industry's growth in high gear.

Meanwhile centralized oil heating—whose boom potential had only recently been proclaimed—ran into severe competition from natural gas. While the oil companies themselves owned the gas that now competed with their oil, the industry did not originate the natural gas revolution, nor has it to this day greatly profited from its gas ownership. The gas revolution was made by newly formed transmission companies that marketed the product with an aggressive ardor. They started a magnificent new industry, first against the advice and then against the resistance of the oil companies.

By all the logic of the situation, the oil companies themselves should have made the gas revolution. They not only owned the gas; they also were the only people experienced in handling, scrubbing, and using it, the only people experienced in pipeline technology and transmission, and they understood heating problems. But, partly because they knew that natural gas would compete with their own sale of heating oil, the oil companies pooh-poohed the potentials of gas.

The revolution was finally started by oil pipeline executives who, unable to persuade their own companies to go into gas, quit and organized the spectacularly successful gas transmission companies. Even after their success became painfully evident to the oil companies, the latter did not go into gas transmission. The multibillion dollar business which should have been theirs went to others. As in the past, the industry was blinded by its narrow preoccupation with a specific product and the value of its reserves. It paid little or no attention to its customers' basic needs and preferences.

The postwar years have not witnessed any change. Immediately after World War II the oil industry was greatly encouraged about its future by the rapid expansion of demand for its traditional line of products. In 1950 most companies projected annual rates of domestic expansion of around 6% through at least 1975. Though the ratio of crude oil reserves to demand in the Free World was about 20 to 1, with 10 to 1 being usually considered a reasonable working ratio in the United States, booming demand sent oil men searching for more without sufficient regard to what the future really promised. In 1952 they "hit" in the Middle East; the ratio skyrocketed to 42 to 1. If gross additions to reserves continue at the average rate of the past five years (37 billion barrels annually), then by 1970 the reserve ratio will be up to 45 to 1. This abundance of oil has weakened crude and product prices all over the world.

Management cannot find much consolation today in the rapidly expanding petrochemical industry, another oil-using idea that did not originate in the leading firms. The total United States production of petrochemicals is equivalent to about 2% (by volume) of the demand for all petroleum products. Although the petrochemical industry is now expected to grow by about 10% per year, this will not offset other drains on the growth of crude oil consumption. Furthermore, while petrochemical products are many and growing, it is well to remember that there are nonpetroleum sources of the basic raw material, such as coal. Besides, a lot of plastics can be produced with relatively little oil. A 50,000-barrel-per-day oil refinery is now considered the absolute minimum size for efficiency. But a 50,000–barrel-per-day chemical plant is a giant operation.

Oil has never been a continuously strong growth industry. It has grown by fits and starts, always miraculously saved by innovations and developments not of its own making. The reason it has not grown in a smooth progression is that each time it thought it had a superior product safe from the possibility of competitive substitutes, the product turned out to be inferior and notoriously subject to obsolescence. Until now, gasoline (for motor fuel, anyhow) has escaped this fate. But, as we shall see later, it too may be on its last legs.

The point of all this is that there is no guarantee against product obsolescence. If a company's own research does not make it obsolete, another's will. Unless an industry is especially lucky, as oil has been until now, it can easily go down in a sea of red figures—just as the railroads have, as the buggy whip manufacturers have, as the corner grocery chains have, as most of the big movie companies have, and indeed as many other industries have.

The best way for a firm to be lucky is to make its own luck. That requires knowing what makes a business successful. One of the greatest enemies of this knowledge is mass production.

PRODUCTION PRESSURES

Mass-production industries are impelled by a great drive to produce all they can. The prospect of steeply declining unit costs as output rises is more than most companies can usually resist. The profit possibilities look spectacular. All effort focuses on production. The result is that marketing gets neglected.

John Kenneth Galbraith contends that just the opposite occurs.[4] Output is so prodigious that all effort concentrates on trying to get rid of it. He says this accounts for singing commercials, desecration of the countryside with advertising signs, and other wasteful and vulgar practices. Galbraith has a finger on something real, but he misses the strategic point. Mass production does indeed generate great pressure to "move" the product. But what usually gets emphasized is selling, not marketing. Marketing, being a more sophisticated and complex process, gets ignored.

The difference between marketing and selling is more than semantic. Selling focuses on the needs of the seller, marketing on the needs of the buyer. Selling is preoccupied with the seller's need to convert his product into cash; marketing with the idea of satisfying the needs of the customer by means of the product and the whole cluster of things associated with creating, delivering, and finally consuming it.

In some industries the enticements of full mass production have been so powerful that for many years top management in effect has told the sales departments, "You get rid of it; we'll worry about profits." By contrast, a truly marketing-minded firm tries to create value-satisfying goods and services that consumers will want to buy. What it offers for sale includes not only the generic product or service, but also how it is made available to the customer, in what form, when, under what conditions, and at what terms of trade. Most important, what it offers for sale is determined not by the seller but by the buyer. The seller takes his cues from the buyer in such a way that the product becomes a consequence of the marketing effort, not vice versa.

Lag in Detroit

This may sound like an elementary rule of business, but that does not keep it from being violated wholesale. It is certainly more violated than honored. Take the automobile industry:

> Here mass production is most famous, most honored, and has the greatest impact on the entire society. The industry has hitched its fortune to the relentless requirements of the annual model change, a policy that makes customer orientation an especially urgent necessity. Consequently the auto companies annually spend millions of dollars on consumer research. But the fact that the new compact cars are selling so well in their first year indicates that Detroit's vast researches have for a long time failed to reveal what the customer really wanted. Detroit was not persuaded that he wanted anything different from what he had been getting until it lost millions of customers to other small car manufacturers.

[4] *The Affluent Society* (Boston, Houghton-Mifflin Company, 1958), pp. 152–160.

How could this unbelievable lag behind consumer wants have been per-petuated so long? Why did not research reveal consumer preferences before consumers' buying decisions themselves revealed the facts? Is that not what consumer research is for—to find out before the fact what is going to happen? The answer is that Detroit never really researched the customer's wants. It only researched his preferences between the kinds of things which it had already decided to offer him. For Detroit is mainly product-oriented, not customer-oriented. To the extent that the customer is recognized as having needs that the manufacturer should try to satisfy, Detroit usually acts as if the job can be done entirely by product changes. Occasionally attention gets paid to financing, too, but that is done more in order to sell than to enable the customer to buy.

As for taking care of other customer needs, there is not enough being done to write about. The areas of the greatest unsatisfied needs are ignored, or at best get stepchild attention. These are at the point of sale and on the matter of automotive repair and maintenance. Detroit views these problem areas as being of secondary importance. That is underscored by the fact that the retailing and servicing ends of this industry are neither owned and operated nor controlled by the manufacturers. Once the car is produced, things are pretty much in the dealer's inadequate hands. Illustrative of De-troit's arm's-length attitude is the fact that, while servicing holds enormous sales-stimulating, profit-building opportunities, only 57 of Chevrolet's 7,000 dealers provide night maintenance service.

Motorists repeatedly express their dissatisfaction with servicing and their apprehensions about buying cars under the present selling setup. The anxieties and problems they encounter during the auto buying and maintenance processes are probably more intense and widespread today than 30 years ago. Yet the automobile companies do not *seem* to listen to or take their cues from the anguished consumer. If they do listen, it must be through the filter of their own preoccupation with production. The marketing effort is still viewed as a necessary consequence of the product, not vice versa, as it should be. That is the legacy of mass production, with its parochial view that profit resides essentially in low-cost full production.

What Ford Put First

The profit lure of mass production obviously has a place in the plans and strategy of business management, but it must always follow hard thinking about the customer. This is one of the most important lessons that we can learn from the contradictory behavior of Henry Ford. In a sense Ford was both the most brilliant and the most senseless marketer in American history. He was senseless because he refused to give the customer anything but a black car. He was brilliant because he fashioned a production system designed to fit market needs. We habitually celebrate him for the wrong reason, his production genius. His real genius was marketing. We think he was able to cut his selling price and therefore sell millions of $500 cars because his invention of the assembly line had reduced the costs. Actually he invented the assembly line because he had concluded that at $500 he could sell millions of cars. Mass production was the *result* not the cause of his low prices.

Ford repeatedly emphasized this point, but a nation of production-oriented business managers refuses to hear the great lesson he taught. Here is his operating philosophy as he expressed it succinctly:

> Our policy is to reduce the price, extend the operations, and improve the article. You will notice that the reduction of price comes first. We have never considered any costs as fixed. Therefore we first reduce the price to the point where we believe more sales will result. Then we go ahead and try to make the prices. We do not bother about the costs. The new price forces the costs down. The more usual way is to take the costs and then determine the price, and although that method may be scientific in the narrow sense; it is not scientific in the broad sense, because what earthly use is it to know the cost if it tells you that you cannot manufacture at a price at which the article can be sold? But more to the point is the fact that, although one may calculate what a cost is, and of course all of our costs are carefully calculated, no one knows what a cost ought to be. One of the ways of discovering . . . is to name a price so low as to force everybody in the place to the highest point of efficiency. The low price makes everybody dig for profits. We make more discoveries concerning manufacturing and selling under this forced method than by any method of leisurely investigation.[5]

Product Provincialism

The tantalizing profit possibilities of low unit production costs may be the most seriously self-deceiving attitude that can afflict a company, particularly a "growth" company where an apparently assured expansion of demand already tends to undermine a proper concern for the importance of marketing and the customer.

The usual result of this narrow preoccupation with so-called concrete matters is that instead of growing, the industry declines. It usually means that the product fails to adapt to the constantly changing patterns of consumer needs and tastes, to new and modified marketing institutions and practices, or to product developments in competing or complementary industries. The industry has its eyes so firmly on its own specific product that it does not see how it is being made obsolete.

The classical example of this is the buggy whip industry. No amount of product improvement could stave off its death sentence. But had the industry defined itself as being in the transportation business rather than the buggy whip business, it might have survived.

---

[5] Henry Ford, *My Life and Work* (New York, Doubleday, Page & Company, 1923), pp. 146–147.

It would have done what survival always entails, that is, changing. Even if it had only defined its business as providing a stimulant or catalyst to an energy source, it might have survived by becoming a manufacturer of, say, fanbelts or air cleaners.

What may some day be a still more classical example is again, the oil industry. Having let others steal marvelous opportunities from it (e.g., natural gas, as already mentioned, missile fuels, and jet engine lubricants), one would expect it to have taken steps never to let that happen again. But this is not the case. We are now getting extraordinary new developments in fuel systems specifically designed to power automobiles. Not only are these developments concentrated in firms outside the petroleum industry, but petroleum is almost systematically ignoring them, securely content in its wedded bliss to oil. It is the story of the kerosene lamp versus the incandescent lamp all over again. Oil is trying to improve hydrocarbon fuels rather than to develop *any* fuels best suited to the needs of their users, whether or not made in different ways and with different raw materials from oil.

Here are some of the things which nonpetroleum companies are working on:

Over a dozen such firms now have advanced working models of energy systems which, when perfected, will replace the internal combustion engine and eliminate the demand for gasoline. The superior merit of each of these systems is their elimination of frequent, time-consuming, and irritating refueling stops. Most of these systems are fuel cells designed to create electrical energy directly from chemicals without combustion. Most of them use chemicals that are not derived from oil, generally hydrogen and oxygen.

Several other companies have advanced models of electric storage batteries designed to power automobiles. One of these is an aircraft producer that is working jointly with several electric utility companies. The latter hope to use off-peak generating capacity to supply overnight plug-in battery regeneration. Another company, also using the battery approach, is a medium-size electronics firm with extensive small-battery experience that it developed in connection with its work on hearing aids. It is collaborating with an automobile manufacturer. Recent improvements arising from the need for high-powered miniature power storage plants in rockets have put us within reach of a relatively small battery capable of withstanding great overloads or surges of power. Germanium diode applications and batteries using sintered-plate and nickel-cadmium techniques promise to make a revolution in our energy sources.

Solar energy conversion systems are also getting increasing attention. One usually cautious Detroit auto executive recently ventured that solar-powered cars might be common by 1980.

As for the oil companies, they are more or less "watching developments," as one research director put it to me. A few are doing a bit of research on fuel cells, but almost always confined to developing cells powered by hydrocarbon chemicals. None of them are enthusiastically researching fuel cells, batteries, or solar power plants. None of them are spending a fraction as much on research in these profoundly important areas as they are on the usual run-of-the-mill things like reducing combustion chamber deposit in gasoline engines. One major integrated petroleum company recently took a tentative look at the fuel cell and concluded that although "the companies actively working on it indicate a belief in ultimate success . . . the timing and magnitude of its impact are too remote to warrant recognition in our forecasts."

One might, of course, ask: Why should the oil companies do anything different? Would not chemical fuel cells, batteries, or solar energy kill the present product lines? The answer is that they would indeed, and that is precisely the reason for the oil firms having to develop these power units before their competitors, so they will not be companies without an industry.

Management might be more likely to do what is needed for its own preservation if it thought of itself as being in the energy business. But even that would not be enough if it persists in imprisoning itself in the narrow grip of its tight product orientation. It has to think of itself as taking care of customer needs, not finding, refinings, or even selling oil. Once it genuinely thinks of its business as taking care of people's transportation needs, nothing can stop it from creating its own extravagantly profitable growth.

Creative Destruction

Since words are cheap and deeds are dear, it may be appropriate to indicate what this kind of thinking involves and leads to. Let us start at the beginning—the customer. It can be shown that motorists strongly dislike the bother, delay, and experience of buying gasoline. People actually do not buy gasoline. They cannot see it, taste it, feel it, appreciate it, or really test it. What they buy is the right to continue driving their cars. The gas station is like a tax collector to whom people are compelled to pay a periodic toll as the price of using their cars. This makes the gas station a basically unpopular institution. It can never be made popular or pleasant, only less unpopular, less unpleasant.

To reduce its unpopularity completely means eliminating it. Nobody likes a tax collector, not even a pleasantly cheerful one. Nobody likes to interrupt a trip to buy a phantom product, not even from a handsome Adonis or a seductive Venus. Hence, companies that are working on exotic fuel substitutes which will eliminate the need for frequent refueling are heading directly into the outstretched arms of the irritated motorists. They are riding a wave of inevitability, not because they are creating something which is technologically superior or more sophisticated, but because they are satisfying a powerful customer need. They are also eliminating noxious odors and air pollution.

Once the petroleum companies recognize the customer-satisfying logic of what another power system can do, they will see that they have no more choice about working on an efficient, long-lasting fuel (or some way of delivering present fuels without bothering the motorist) than the big food chains had a choice about going into the supermarket business, or the vacuum tube companies had a choice about making semiconductors. For their own good the oil firms will have to destroy their own highly profitable assets. No amount of wishful thinking can save them from the necessity of engaging in this form of "creative destruction."

I phrase the need as strongly as this because I think management must make quite an effort to break itself loose from conventional ways. It is all too easy in this day and age for a company or industry to let its sense of purpose become dominated by the economies of full production and to develop a dangerously lopsided product orientation. In short, if management lets itself drift, it invariably drifts in the direction of thinking of itself as producing goods and services, not customer satisfactions. While it probably will not descend to the depths of telling its salesmen, "You get rid of it; we'll worry about profits," it can, without knowing it, be practicing precisely that formula for withering decay. The historic fate of one growth industry after another has been its suicidal product provincialism.

DANGERS OF R & D

Another big danger to a firm's continued growth arises when top management is wholly transfixed by the profit possibilities of technical research and development. To illustrate I shall turn first to a new industry--electronics--and then return once more to the oil companies. By comparing a fresh example with a familiar one, I hope to emphasize the prevalence and insidiousness of a hazardous way of thinking.

Marketing Shortchanged

In the case of electronics, the greatest danger which faces the glamorous new companies in this field is not that they do not pay enough attention to research and development, but that they pay *too much* attention to it. And the fact that the fastest growing electronics firms owe their eminence to their heavy emphasis on technical research is completely beside the point. They have vaulted to affluence on a sudden crest of unusually strong general receptiveness to new technical ideas. Also, their success has been shaped in the virtually guaranteed market of military subsidies and by military orders that in many cases actually preceded the existence of facilities to make the products. Their expansion has, in other words, been almost totally devoid of marketing effort.

Thus, they are growing up under conditions that come dangerously close to creating the illusion that a superior product will sell itself. Having created a successful company by making a superior product, it is not surprising that management continues to be oriented toward the product rather than the people who consume it. It develops the philosophy that continued growth is a matter of continued product innovation and improvement.

A number of other factors tend to strengthen and sustain this belief:

1. Because electronic products are highly complex and sophisticated, managements become top-heavy with engineers and scientists. This creates a selective bias in favor of research and production at the expense of marketing. The organization tends to view itself as making things rather than satisfying customer needs. Marketing gets treated as a residual activity, "something else" that must be done once the vital job of product creation and production is completed.
2. To this bias in favor of product research, development, and production is added the bias in favor of dealing with controllable variables. Engineers and scientists are at home in the world of concrete things like machines, test tubes, production lines, and even balance sheets. The abstractions to which they feel kindly are those which are testable or manipulatable in the laboratory, or, if not testable, then functional, such as Euclid's axioms. In short, the managements of the new glamour-growth companies tend to favor those business activities which lend themselves to careful study, experimentation, and control—the hard, practical, realities of the lab, the shop, the books.

What gets shortchanged are the realities of the *market*. Consumers are unpredictable, varied, fickle, stupid, shortsighted, stubborn, and generally bothersome. This is not what the engineer-managers say, but deep down in their consciousness it is what they believe. And this accounts for their concentrating on what they know and what they can control, namely, product research, engineering, and production. The emphasis on production becomes particularly attractive when the product can be made at declining unit costs. There is no more inviting way of making money than by running the plant full blast.

Today the top-heavy science-engineering-production orientation of so many electronics companies works reasonably well because they are pushing into new frontiers in which the armed services have pioneered virtually assured markets. The companies are in the felicitous position of having to fill, not find markets; of not having to discover what the customer needs and wants, but of having the customer voluntarily come forward with specific new product demands. If a team of consultants had been assigned specifically to design a business situation calculated to prevent the emergence and development of a customer-oriented marketing viewpoint, it could not have produced anything better than the conditions just described.

Stepchild Treatment

The oil industry is a stunning example of how science, technology, and mass production can divert an entire group of companies from their main task. To the extent the consumer is studied at all (which is not much), the focus is forever on getting information which is designed to help the oil companies improve what they are now doing. They try to discover more convincing advertising themes, more effective sales promotional drives, what the market shares of the various companies are, what people like or dislike about service station dealers and oil companies, and so forth. Nobody seems as interested in probing deeply into the basic human needs that the industry might be trying to satisfy as in probing into the basic properties of the raw material that the companies work with in trying to deliver customer satisfactions.

Basic questions about customers and markets seldom get asked. The latter occupy a stepchild status. They are recognized as existing, as having to be taken care of, but not worth very much real thought or dedicated attention. Nobody gets as excited about the customers in his own backyard as about the oil in the Sahara Desert. Nothing illustrates better the neglect of marketing than its treatment in the industry press:

> The centennial issue of the *American Petroleum Institute Quarterly*, published in 1959 to celebrate the discovery of oil in Titusville, Pennsylvania, contained 21 feature articles proclaiming the industry's greatness. Only one of these talked about its achievements in marketing, and that was only a pictorial record of how service station architecture has changed. The issue also contained a special section on "New Horizons," which was devoted to

showing the magnificent role oil would play in America's future. Every reference was ebulliently optimistic, never implying once that oil might have some hard competition. Even the reference to atomic energy was a cheerful catalogue of how oil would help make atomic energy a success. There was not a single apprehension that the oil industry's affluence might be threatened or a suggestion that one "new horizon" might include new and better ways of serving oil's present customers.

But the most revealing example of the stepchild treatment that marketing gets was still another special series of short articles on "The Revolutionary Potential of Electronics." Under that heading this list of articles appeared in the table of contents:

"In the Search for Oil"

"In Production Operations"

"In Refinery Processes"

"In Pipeline Operations"

Significantly, every one of the industry's major functional areas is listed, *except* marketing. Why? Either it is believed that electronics holds no revolutionary potential for petroleum marketing (which is palpably wrong), or the editors forgot to discuss marketing (which is more likely, and illustrates its stepchild status).

The order in which the four functional areas are listed also betrays the alienation of the oil industry from the consumer. The industry is implicitly defined as beginning with the search for oil and ending with its distribution from the refinery. But the truth is, it seems to me, that the industry begins with the needs of the customer for its products. From that primal position its definition moves steadily backstream to areas of progressively lesser importance, until it finally comes to rest at the "search for oil."

Beginning & End

The view that an industry is a customer-satisfying process, not a goods-producing process, is vital for all businessmen to understand. An industry begins with the customer and his needs, not with a patent, a raw material, or a selling skill. Given the customer's needs, the industry develops backwards, first concerning itself with the physical *delivery* of customer satisfactions. Then it moves back further to *creating* the things by which these satisfactions are in part achieved. How these materials are created is a matter of indifference to the customer, hence the particular form of manufacturing, processing, or what-have-you cannot be considered as a vital aspect of the industry. Finally, the industry moves back still further to *finding* the raw materials necessary for making its products.

The irony of some industries oriented toward technical research and development is that the scientists who occupy the high executive positions are totally unscientific when it comes to defining their companies' over-all needs and purposes. They violate the first two rules of the scientific method—being aware of and defining their companies' problems, and then developing testable hypotheses about solving them. They are scientific only about the convenient things, such as laboratory and product experiments. The reason that the customer (and the satisfaction of his deepest needs) is not considered as being "the problem" is not because there is any certain belief that no such problem exists, but because an organizational lifetime has conditioned management to look in the opposite direction. Marketing is a stepchild.

I do not mean that selling is ignored. Far from it. But selling, again, is not marketing. As already pointed out, selling concerns itself with the tricks and techniques of getting people to exchange their cash for your product. It is not concerned with the values that the exchange is all about. And it does not, as marketing invariably does, view the entire business process as consisting of a tightly integrated effort to discover, create, arouse, and satisfy customer needs. The customer is somebody "out there" who, with proper cunning, can be separated from his loose change.

Actually, not even selling gets much attention in some technologically minded firms. Because there is a virtually guaranteed market for the abundant flow of their new products, they do not actually know what a real market is. It is as if they lived in a planned economy, moving their products routinely from factory to retail outlet. Their successful concentration on products tends to convince them of the soundness of what they have been doing, and they fail to see the gathering clouds over the market.

CONCLUSION

Less than 75 years ago American railroads enjoyed a firece loyalty among astute Wall Streeters. European monarchs invested in them heavily. Eternal wealth was thought to be the benediction for anybody who could scrape a few thousand dollars together to put into rail stocks. No other form of transportation could compete with the railroads in speed, flexibility, durability, economy, and growth potentials. As Jacques Barzun put it, "By the turn of the century it was an institution, an image of man, a tradition, a code of honor, a source of poetry, a nursery of boyhood desires, a sublimest of toys, and the most solemn machine—next to the funeral hearse—that marks the epochs in man's life."[6]

---

[6] Op. cit., p. 20.

Even after the advent of automobiles, trucks, and airplanes, the railroad tycoons remained imperturbably self-confident. If you had told them 60 years ago that in 30 years they would be flat on their backs, broke, and pleading for government subsidies, they would have thought you totally demented. Such a future was simply not considered possible. It was not even a discussable subject, or an askable question, or a matter which any sane person would consider worth speculating about. The very thought was insane. Yet a lot of insane notions now have matter-of-fact acceptance—for example, the idea of 100-ton tubes of metal moving smoothly through the air 20,000 feet above the earth, loaded with 100 sane and solid citizens casually drinking martinis—and they have dealt cruel blows to the railroads.

What specifically must other companies do to avoid this fate? What does customer orientation involve? These questions have in part been answered by the preceding examples and analysis. It would take another article to show in detail what is required for specific industries. In any case, it should be obvious that building an effective customer-oriented company involves far more than good intentions or promotional tricks; it involves profound matters of human organization and leadership. For the present, let me merely suggest what appear to be some general requirements.

Visceral Feel of Greatness

Obviously the company has to do what survival demands. It has to adapt to the requirements of the market, and it has to do it sooner rather than later. But mere survival is a so-so aspiration. Anybody can survive in some way or other, even the skid-row bum. The trick is to survive gallantly, to feel the surging impulse of commercial mastery; not just to experience the sweet smell of success, but to have the visceral feel of enterpreneurial greatness.

No organization can achieve greatness without a vigorous leader who is driven onward by his own pulsating *will to succeed*. He has to have a vision of grandeur, a vision that can produce eager followers in vast numbers. In business, the followers are the customers. To produce these customers, the entire corporation must be viewed as a customer-creating and customer-satisfying organism. Management must think of itself not as producing products but as providing customer-creating value satisfactions. It must push this idea (and everything it means and requires) into every nook and cranny of the organization. It has to do this continuously and with the kind of flair that excites and stimulates the people in it. Otherwise, the company will be merely a series of pigeonholed parts, with no consolidating sense of purpose or direction.

In short, the organization must learn to think of itself not as producing goods or services but as *buying customers,* as doing the things that will make people *want* to do business with it. And the chief executive himself has the inescapable responsibility for creating this environment, this viewpoint, this attitude, this aspiration. He himself must set the company's style, its direction, and its goals. This means he has to know precisely where he himself wants to go, and to make sure the whole organization is enthusiastically aware of where that is. This is a first requisite of leadership, for *unless he knows where he is going, any road will take him there.*

If any road is okay, the chief executive might as well pack his attaché case and go fishing. If an organization does not know or care where it is going, it does not need to advertise that fact with a ceremonial figurehead. Everybody will notice it soon enough.

1975: RETROSPECTIVE COMMENTARY

Amazed, finally, by his literary success, Isaac Bashevis Singer reconciled an attendant problem: "I think the moment you have published a book, it's not any more your private property . . . . If it has value, everybody can find in it what he finds, and I cannot tell the man I did not intend it to be so." Over the past 15 years, "Marketing Myopia" has become a case in point. Remarkably, the article spawned a legion of loyal partisans—not to mention a host of unlikely bedfellows.

Its most common and, I believe, most influential consequence is the way certain companies for the first time gave serious thought to the question of what businesses they are really in.

The strategic consequences of this have in many cases been dramatic. The best-known case, of course, is the shift in thinking of oneself as being in the "oil business" to being in the "energy business." In some instances the payoff has been spectacular (getting into coal, for example) and in others dreadful (in terms of the time and money spent so far on fuel cell research). Another successful example is a company with a large chain of retail shoe stores that redefined itself as a retailer of moderately priced, frequently purchased, widely assorted consumer specialty products. The result was a dramatic growth in volume, earnings, and return on assets.

Some companies, again for the first time, asked themselves whether they wished to be masters of certain technologies for which they would seek markets, or be masters of markets for which they would seek customer-satisfying products and services.

Choosing the former, one company has declared, in effect, "We are experts in glass technology. We intend to improve and expand that expertise with the object of creating products that will attract customers." This decision has forced the company into a much more systematic and customer-sensitive look at possible markets and users, even though its stated strategic object has been to capitalize on glass technology.

Deciding to concentrate on markets, another company has determined that "we want to help people (primarily women) enhance their beauty and sense of youthfulness." This company has expanded its line of cosmetic products, but has also entered the fields of proprietary drugs and vitamin supplements.

All these examples illustrate the "policy" results of "Marketing Myopia." On the operating level, there has been, I think, an extraordinary heightening of sensitivity to customers and consumers. R&D departments have cultivated a greater "external" orientation toward uses, users, and markets—balancing thereby the previously one–sided "internal" focus on materials and methods; upper management has realized that marketing and sales departments should be somewhat more willingly accommodated than before; finance departments have become more receptive to the legitimacy of budgets for market research and experimentation in marketing; and salesmen have been better trained to listen to and understand customer needs and problems, rather than merely to "push" the product.

A Mirror, Not a Window

My impression is that the article has had more impact in industrial-products companies than in consumer-products companies—perhaps because the former had lagged most in customer orientation. There are at least two reasons for this lag: (1) industrial-products companies tend to be more capital intensive, and (2) in the past, at least, they have had to rely heavily on communicating face-to-face the technical character of what they made and sold. These points are worth explaining.

Capital-intensive businesses are understandably preoccupied with magnitudes, especially where the capital, once invested, cannot be easily moved, manipulated, or modified for the production of a variety of products—e.g., chemical plants, steel mills, airlines, and railroads. Understandably, they seek big volumes and operating efficiencies to pay off the equipment and meet the carrying costs.

At least one problem results: corporate power becomes disproportionately lodged with operating or financial executives. If you read the charter of one of the nation's largest companies, you will see that the chairman of the finance committee, not the chief executive officer, is the "chief." Executives with such backgrounds have an almost trained incapacity to see that getting "volume" may require understanding and serving many discrete and sometimes small market segments, rather than going after a perhaps mythical batch of big or homogeneous customers.

These executives also often fail to appreciate the competitive changes going on around them. They observe the changes, all right, but devalue their significance or underestimate their ability to nibble away at the company's markets.

Once dramatically alerted to the concept of segments, sectors, and customers, though, managers of capital-intensive businesses have become more responsive to the necessity of balancing their inescapable preoccupation with "paying the bills" or breaking even with the fact that the best way to accomplish this may be to pay more attention to segments, sectors, and customers.

The second reason industrial-products companies have probably been more influenced by the article is that, in the case of the more technical industrial products or services, the necessity of clearly communicating product and service characteristics to prospects results in a lot of face-to-face "selling" effort. But precisely because the product is so complex, the situation produces salesmen who know the product more than they know the customer, who are more adept at explaining what they have and what it can do than learning what the customer's needs and problems are. The result has been a narrow product orientation rather than a liberating customer orientation, and "service" often suffered. To be sure, sellers said, "We have to provide service," but they tended to define service by looking into the mirror rather than out the window. They *thought* they were looking out the window at the customer, but it was actually a mirror—a reflection of their own product-oriented biases rather than a reflection of their customers' situations.

A Manifesto, Not a Prescription

Not everything has been rosy. A lot of bizarre things have happened as a result of the article:

• Some companies have developed what I call "marketing mania"— they've become obsessively responsive to every fleeting whim of the customer. Mass production operations have been converted to approximations of job shops, with cost and price consequences far exceeding the willingness of customers to buy the product.

- Management has expanded product lines and added new lines of business without first establishing adequate control systems to run more complex operations.
- Marketing staffs have suddenly and rapidly expanded themselves and their research budgets without either getting sufficient prior organizational support or, thereafter, producing sufficient results.
- Companies that are functionally organized have converted to product, brand, or market-based organizations with the expectation of instant and miraculous results. The outcome has been ambiguity, frustration, confusion, corporate infighting, losses, and finally a reversion to functional arrangements that only worsened the situation.
- Companies have attempted to "serve" customers by creating complex and beautifully efficient products or services that buyers are either too risk-averse to adopt or incapable of learning how to employ—in effect, there are now steam shovels for people who haven't yet learned to use spades. This problem has happened repeatedly in the so-called service industries (financial services, insurance, computer-based services) and with American companies selling in less-developed economies.

"Marketing Myopia" was not intended as analysis or even prescription; it was intended as manifesto. It did not pretend to take a balanced position. Nor was it a new idea—Peter F. Drucker, J. B. McKitterick, Wroe Alderson, John Howard, and Neil Borden had each done more original and balanced work on "the marketing concept." My scheme, however, tied marketing more closely to the inner orbit of business policy. Drucker—especially in *The Concept of the Corporation* and *The Practice of Management*—originally provided me with a great deal of insight.

My contribution, therefore, appears merely to have been a simple, brief, and useful way of communicating an existing way of thinking. I tried to do it in a very direct, but responsible, fashion, knowing that few readers (customers), especially managers and leaders, could stand much equivocation or hesitation. I also knew that the colorful and lightly documented affirmation works better than the tortuously reasoned explanation.

But why the enormous popularity of what was actually such a simple pre-existing idea? Why its appeal throughout the world to resolutely restrained scholars, implacably temperate managers, and high government officials, all accustomed to balanced and thoughtful calculation? Is it that concrete examples, joined to illustrate a simple idea and presented with some attention to literacy, communicate better than massive analytical reasoning that reads as though it were translated from the German? Is it that provocative assertions are more memorable and persuasive than restrained and balanced explanations, no matter who the audience? Is it that the character of the message is as much the message as its content? Or was mine not simply a different tune, but a new symphony? I don't know.

Of course, I'd do it again and in the same way, given my purposes, even with what more I now know—the good and the bad, the power of facts and the limits of rhetoric. If your mission is the moon, you don't use a car. Don Marquis's cockroach, Archy, provides some final consolation: "an idea is not responsible for who believes in it."

2

The Analytical Framework
For Marketing

Wroe Alderson

My assignment is to discuss the analytical framework for marketing. Since our general purpose here is to consider the improvement of the marketing curriculum, I assume that the paper I have been asked to present might serve two functions. The first is to present a perspective of marketing which might be the basis of a marketing course at either elementary or advanced levels. The other is to provide some clue as to the foundations in the social sciences upon which an analytical framework for marketing may be built.

Economics has some legitimate claim to being the original science of markets. Received economic theory provides a framework for the analysis of marketing functions which certainly merits the attention of marketing teachers and practitioners. It is of little importance whether the point of view I am about to present is a version of economics, a hybrid of economics and sociology, or the application of a new emergent general science of human behavior to marketing problems. The analytical framework which I find congenial at least reflects some general knowledge of the social sciences as well as long experience in marketing analysis. In the time available I can do no more than present this view in outline or skeleton form and leave you to determine how to classify it or whether you can use it.

An advantageous place to start for the analytical treatment of

Reprinted from Delbert Duncan (ed.), *Proceedings: Conference of Marketing Teachers from Far Western States* (Berkeley: University of California, 1958), pp. 15-28.

Wroe Alderson was, until his death, professor at the Wharton School of Finance and Commerce at the University of Pennsylvania and director of that school's Management Science Center. He also founded a management consulting firm and served as president of the American Marketing Association. He studied at the George Washington University, the University of Pennsylvania, and the Massachusetts Institute of Technology and was author or editor of several books on marketing. His *Marketing Behavior and Executive Action* is hailed as a landmark in marketing thought.

marketing is with the radical heterogeneity of markets. Heterogeneity is inherent on both the demand and the supply sides. The homogeneity which the economist assumes for certain purposes is not an antecedent condition for marketing. Insofar as it is ever realized, it emerges out of the marketing process itself.

The materials which are useful to man occur in nature in heterogeneous mixtures which might be called conglomerations since these mixtures have only a random relationship to human needs and activities. The collection of goods in the possession of a household or an individual also constitutes a heterogeneous supply, but it might be called an assortment since it is related to anticipated patterns of future behavior. The whole economic process may be described as a series of transformations from meaningless to meaningful heterogeneity. Marketing produces as much homogeneity as may be needed to facilitate some of the intermediate economic processes but homogeneity has limited significance or utility for consumer behavior or expectations.

The marketing process matches materials found in nature or goods fabricated from these materials against the needs of households or individuals. Since the consuming unit has a complex pattern of needs, the matching of these needs creates an assortment of goods in the hands of the ultimate consumer. Actually the marketing process builds up assortments at many stages along the way, each appropriate to the activities taking place at that point. Materials or goods are associated in one way for manufacturing, in another way for wholesale distribution, and in still another for retail display and selling. In between the various types of heterogeneous collections relatively homogeneous supplies are accumulated through the process of grading, refining, chemical reduction and fabrication.

Marketing brings about the necessary transformations in heterogeneous supplies through a multiphase process of sorting. Matching of every individual need would be impossible if the consumer had to search out each item required or the producer had to find the users of a product one by one. It is only the ingenious use of intermediate sorts which make it possible for a vast array of diversified products to enter into the ultimate consumer assortments as needed. Marketing makes mass production possible first by providing the assortment of supplies needed in manufacturing and then taking over the successive transformations which ultimately produce the assortment in the hands of consuming units.

To some who have heard this doctrine expounded, the concept of sorting seems empty, lacking in specific behavioral content, and hence unsatisfactory as a root idea for marketing. One answer is that sorting is a more general and embracing concept than allocation, which many economists regard as the root idea of their science. Allocation is only one of the four basic types of sorting, all of which are involved in marketing. Among these four, allocation is certainly no more significant than assorting, one being the breaking down of a homogeneous supply and the other the building up of a heterogeneous supply. Assorting, in fact, gives more direct expression to the final aim of marketing but allocation performs a major function along the way.

There are several basic advantages in taking sorting as a central concept. It leads directly to a fundamental explanation of the contribution of marketing to the overall economy of human effort in producing and distributing goods. It provides a key to the unending search for efficiency in the marketing function itself. Finally, sorting as the root idea of marketing is consistent with the assumption that heterogeneity is radically and inherently present on both sides of the market and that the aim of marketing is to cope with the heterogeneity of both needs and resources.

At this stage of the discussion it is the relative emphasis on assorting as contrasted with allocation which distinguishes marketing theory from at least some versions of economic theory. This emphasis arises naturally from the preoccupation of the market analyst with consumer behavior. One of the most fruitful approaches to understanding what the consumer is doing is the idea that she is engaged in building an assortment, in replenishing or extending an inventory of goods for use by herself and her family. As evidence that this paper is not an attempt to set up a theory in opposition to economics it is acknowledged that the germ of this conception of consumer behavior was first presented some eighty years ago by the Austrian economist Böhm-Bawerk.

The present view is distinguished from that of Böhm-Bawerk in its greater emphasis on the probabilistic approach to the study of market behavior. In considering items for inclusion in her assortment the consumer must make judgments concerning the relative probabilities of future occasions for use. A product in the assortment is intended to provide for some aspect of future behavior. Each such occasion for use carries a rating which is a product of two factors, one a judgment as to the probability of its incidence and the other a measure of the urgency of the need in case it should arise. Consumer goods vary with respect to both measures. One extreme might be illustrated by cigarettes with a probability of use approaching certainty but with relatively small urgency or penalty for deprivation on the particular occasion for use. At the other end of the scale would be a home fire extinguisher with low probability but high urgency attaching to the expected occasion of use.

All of this means that the consumer buyer enters the market as a problem-solver. Solving a problem, either on behalf of a household or on behalf of a marketing organization means reaching a decision in the face of uncertainty. The consumer buyer and the marketing executive are opposite numbers in the double search which pervades marketing; one looking for the goods required to complete an assortment, the other looking for the buyers who are uniquely qualified to use his goods. This is not to say that the behavior of either consumers or executives can be completely characterized as rational problem-solvers. The intention rather is to assert that problem-solving on either side of the market involves a probabilistic approach to heterogeneity on the other side. In order to solve his own problems arising from the heterogeneous demand, the marketing executive should understand the processes of consumer decisions in coping with heterogeneous supplies.

The viewpoint adopted here with respect to the competition among sellers is essentially that which is associated in economics with such names as Schumpeter, Chamberlin and J. M. Clark and with the emphasis on innovative competition, product differentiation and differential advantage. The basic assumption is that every firm occupies a position which is in some respects unique, being differentiated from all others by characteristics of its products, its services, its geographic location or its specific combination of these features. The survival of a firm requires that for some group of buyers it should enjoy a differential advantage over all other suppliers. The sales of any active marketing organization come from a core market made up of buyers with a preference for this source and a fringe market which finds the source acceptable, at least for occasional purchases.

In the case of the supplier of relatively undifferentiated products or services such as the wheat farmer, differential advantage may pertain more to the producing region than to the individual producer. This more diffused type of differential advantage often becomes effective in the market through such agencies as the marketing cooperative. Even the individual producer of raw materials, however, occupies a position in the sense that one market or buyer provides the customary outlet for his product rather than another. The essential point for the present argument is that buyer and seller are not paired at random even in the marketing of relatively homogeneous products but are related to some scale of preference or priority.

Competition for differential advantage implies goals of survival and growth for the marketing organization. The firm is perenially seeking a favorable place to stand and not merely immediate profits from its operations. Differential advantage is subject to change and neutralization by competitors. In dynamic markets differential advantage can only be preserved through continuous innovation. Thus competition presents an analogy to a succession of military campaigns rather than to the pressures and attrition of a single battle. A competitor may gain ground through a successful campaign based on new product features or merchandising ideas. It may lose ground or be forced to fall back on its core position because of the successful campaigns of others. The existence of the core position helps to explain the paradox of survival in the face of the destructive onslaughts of innovative competition.

Buyers and sellers meet in market transactions, each side having tentatively identified the other as an answer to its problem. The market transaction consumes much of the time and effort of all buyers and sellers. The market which operates through a network of costless transactions is only a convenient fiction which economists adopt for certain analytical purposes. Potentially the cost of transactions is so high that controlling or reducing this cost is a major objective in market analysis and executive action. Among economists John R. Commons has given the greatest attention to the transaction as the unit of collective action. He drew a basic distinction between strategic and routine transactions which for present purposes may best be paraphrased as fully negotiated and routine transactions.

The fully negotiated transaction is the prototype of all exchange transactions. It represents a matching of supply and demand after canvassing all of the factors which might affect the decision on either side. The routine transaction proceeds under a set of rules and assumptions established by previous negotiation or as a result of techniques of pre-selling which take the place of negotiation. Transactions on commodity and stock exchanges are carried out at high speed and low cost but only because of carefully established rules governing all aspects of trading. The economical routines of self-service in a super market are possible because the individual items on display have been pre-sold. The routine transaction is the end-result of previous marketing effort and ingenious organization of institutions and processes. Negotiation is implicit in all routine transactions. Good routines induce both parties to save time and cost by foregoing explicit negotiation.

The negotiated transaction is the indicated point of departure for the study of exchange values in heterogeneous markets. Many considerations enter into the decision to trade or not to trade on either side of the market. Price is the final balancing or integrating factor which permits the deal to be made. The seller may accept a lower price if relieved from onerous requirements. The buyer may pay a higher price if provided with specified services. The integrating price is one that assures an orderly flow of goods so long as the balance of other considerations remains essentially unchanged. Some economists are uneasy about the role of the negotiated transaction in value determination since bargaining power may be controlling within wide bargaining limits. These limits as analyzed by Commons are set by reference to the best alternatives available to either partner rather than by the automatic control of atomistic competition. This analysis overlooks a major constraint on bargaining in modern markets. Each side has a major stake in a deal that the other side can live with. Only in this way can a stable supply relationship be established so as to achieve the economics of transactional routines. Negotiation is not a zero sum game since the effort to get the best of the other party transaction by transaction may result in a loss to both sides in terms of mounting transactional cost.

In heterogeneous markets price plays an important role in matching a segment of supply with the appropriate segment of demand. The seller frequently has the option of producing a stream-lined product at a low price, a deluxe product at a high price or selecting a price-quality combination somewhere in between. There are considerations which exert a strong influence on the seller toward choosing the price line or lines which will yield the greatest dollar volume of sales. Assuming that various classes of consumers have conflicting claims on the productive capacity of the supplier, it might be argued that the price-quality combination which maximized gross revenue represented the most constructive compromise among these claims. There are parallel considerations with respect to the claims of various participants in the firm's activities on its operating revenue. These claimants include labor, management, suppliers of raw materials and stockholders. Assuming a perfectly fluid situation with respect to bargaining among these claimants, the best chance for a satisfactory solution is at the level of maximum gross revenue. The argument becomes more complicated when the claims of stockholders are given priority, but the goal would still be maximum gross revenue as suggested in a recent paper by William J. Baumol. My own intuition and experience lead me to believe that the maximization of gross revenue is a valid goal of marketing management in heterogeneous markets and adherence to this norm appears to be widely prevalent in actual practice.

What has been said so far is doubtless within the scope of economics or perhaps constitutes a sketch of how some aspects of economic theory might be reconstructed on the assumption of heterogeneity rather than homogeneity as the normal and prevailing condition of the market. But there are issues raised by such notions as enterprise survival, expectations, and consumer behavior, which in my opinion cannot be resolved within the present boundaries of economic science. Here marketing must not hesitate to draw upon the concepts and techniques of the social sciences for the enrichment of its perspective and for the advancement of marketing as an empirical science.

The general economist has his own justifications for regarding the exchange process as a smoothly functioning mechanism which operates in actual markets or which should be taken as the norm and standard to be enforced by government regulation. For the marketing man, whether teacher or practitioner, this Olympian view is untenable. Marketing is concerned with those who are obliged to enter the market to solve their problems, imperfect as the market may be. The persistent and rational action of these participants is the main hope for eliminating or moderating some of these imperfections so that the operation of the market mechanism may approximate that of the theoretical model.

To understand market behavior the marketing man takes a closer look at the nature of the participants. Thus he is obliged, in my opinion, to come to grips with the organized behavior system. Market behavior is primarily group behavior. Individual action in the market is most characteristically action on behalf of some group in which the individual holds membership. The organized behavior system is related to the going concern of John R. Commons but with a deeper interest in what keeps it going. The organized behavior system is also a much broader concept including the more tightly organized groups acting in the market such as business firms and households and loosely connected systems such as the trade center and the marketing channel.

The marketing man needs some rationale for group behavior, some general explanation for the formation and persistence of organized behavior systems. He finds this explanation in the concept of expectations. Insofar as conscious choice is involved, individuals operate in groups because of their expectations of incremental satisfactions as compared to what they could obtain operating alone. The expected satisfactions are of many kinds, direct and indirect. In a group that is productive activity is held together because of an expected surplus over individual output. Other groups such as households and purely social organizations expect direct satisfactions from group association and activities. They also expect satisfactions from future activities facilitated by the assortment of goods held in common. Whatever the character of the system, its vitality arises from the expectations of the individual members and the vigor of their efforts to achieve them through group action. While the existence of the group is entirely derivative, it is capable of operating as if it had a life of its own and was pursuing goals of survival and growth.

Every organized behavior system exhibits a structure related to the functions it performs. Even in the simplest behavior system there must be some mechanism for decision and coordination of effort if the system is to provide incremental satisfaction. Leadership emerges at an early stage to perform such functions as directing the defense of the group. Also quite early is the recognition of the rationing function by which the leader allocates the available goods or satisfactions among the members of the group.

As groups grow in size and their functions become more complex functional specialization increases. The collection of individuals forming a group with their diversified skills and capabilities is a meaningful heterogeneous ensemble vaguely analogous to the assortment of goods which facilitates the activities of the group. The group, however, is held together directly by the generalized expectations of its members. The assortment is held together by a relatively weak or derivative bond. An item "belongs" to the assortment only so long as it has some probability of satisfying the expectations of those who possess it.

This outline began with an attempt to live within the framework of economics or at least within an economic framework amplified to give fuller recognition to heterogeneity on both sides of the market. We have now plunged into sociology in order to deal more effectively with the organized behavior system. Meanwhile we attempt to preserve the line of communication to our origins by basing the explanations of group behavior on the quasi-economic concept of expectations.

The initial plunge into sociology is only the beginning since the marketing man must go considerably further in examining the functions and structure of organized behavior systems. An operating group has a power structure, a communication structure and an operating structure. At each stage an effort should be made to employ the intellectual strategy which has already been suggested. That is, to relate sociological notions to the groundwork of marketing economics through the medium of such concepts as expectations and the processes of matching and sorting.

All members of an organized behavior system occupy some position or status within its power structure. There is a valid analogy between the status of an individual or operating unit within the system and the market position of the firm as an entity. The individual struggles for status within the system having first attained the goal of membership. For most individuals in an industrial society, status in some operating system is a prerequisite for satisfying his expectations. Given the minimal share in the power of the organization inherent in membership, vigorous individuals may aspire to the more ample share of power enjoyed by leadership. Power in the generalized sense referred to here is an underlying objective on which the attainment of all other objectives depends. This aspect of organized behavior has been formulated as the power principle, namely, "The rational individual will act in such a way to promote the power to act." The word "promote" deliberately glosses over an ambivalent attitude toward power, some individuals striving for enhancement and others being content to preserve the power they have.

Any discussion which embraces power as a fundamental concept creates uneasiness for some students on both analytical and ethical ground. My own answer to the analytical problem is to define it as control over expectations. In these terms it is theoretically possible to measure and evaluate power, perhaps even to set a price on it. Certainly it enters into the network of imputations in a business enterprise. Management allocates or rations status and recognition as well as or in lieu of material rewards. As for the ethical problem, it does not arise unless the power principle is substituted for ethics as with Machiavelli. Admitting that the power principle is the essence of expediency, the ethical choice of values and objectives is a different issue. Whatever his specific objectives, the rational individual will wish to serve them expediently.

If any of this discussion of power seems remote from marketing let it be remembered that the major preoccupation of the marketing executive, as pointed out by Oswald Knauth, is with the creation or the activation of organized behavior systems such as marketing channels and sales organizations. No one can be effective in building or using such systems if he ignores the fundamental nature of the power structure.

The communication structure serves the group in various ways. It promotes the survival of the system by reinforcing the individual's sense of belonging. It transmits instructions and operating commands or signals to facilitate coordinated effort. It is related to expectations through the communication of explicit or implied commitments. Negotiations between suppliers and customers and much that goes on in the internal management of a marketing organization can best be understood as a two-way exchange of commitments. A division sales manager, for example, may commit himself to produce a specified volume of sales. His superior in turn may commit certain company resources to support his efforts and make further commitments as to added rewards as an incentive to outstanding performance.

For some purposes it is useful to regard marketing processes as a flow of goods and a parallel flow of informative and persuasive messages. In these terms the design of communication facilities and channels becomes a major aspect of the creation of marketing systems.

Marketing has yet to digest and apply the insights of the rapidly developing field of communication theory which in turn has drawn freely from both engineering and biological and social sciences. One stimulating idea expounded by Norbert Wiener and others is that of the feedback of information in a control system. Marketing and advertising research are only well started on the task of installing adequate feedback circuits for controlling the deployment of marketing effort.

Social psychology is concerned with some problems of communication which are often encountered in marketing systems. For example, there are the characteristic difficulties of vertical communication which might be compared to the transmission of telephone messages along a power line. Subordinates often hesitate to report bad news to their superiors fearing to take the brunt of emotional reactions. Superiors learn to be cautious in any discussion of the subordinate's status for fear that a casual comment will be interpreted as a commitment. There is often a question as to when a subordinate should act and report and when he should refer a matter for decision upstream. Progress in efficiency, which is a major goal in marketing, depends in substantial part on technological improvement in communication facilities and organizational skill in using them.

The third aspect of structure involved in the study of marketing systems is operating structure. Effective specialization within an organization requires that activities which are functionally similar be placed together but properly coordinated with other activities. Billing by wholesaler grocers, for example, has long been routinized in a separate billing department. In more recent years the advances in mechanical equipment have made it possible to coordinate inventory control with billing, using the same set of punch cards for both functions. Designing an operating structure is a special application of sorting. As in the sorting of goods to facilitate handling, there are generally several alternative schemes for classifying activities presenting problems of choice to the market planner.

Functional specialization and the design of appropriate operating structures is a constant problem in the effective use of marketing channels. Some functions can be performed at either of two or more stages. One stage may be the best choice in terms of economy or effectiveness. Decisions on the placement of a function may have to be reviewed periodically since channels do not remain static. Similar considerations arise in the choice of channels. Some types of distributors or dealers may be equipped to perform a desired service while others may not. Often two or more channels with somewhat specialized roles are required to move a product to the consumer. The product's sponsor can maintain perspective in balancing out these various facilities by thinking in terms of a total operating system including his own sales organization and the marketing channels employed.

The dynamics of market organization pose basic problems for the marketing student and the marketing executive in a free enterprise economy. Reference has already been made to the competitive pursuit of differential advantage. One way in which a firm can gain differential advantage is by organizing the market in a way that is favorable to its own operations. This is something else than the attainment of a monopolistic position in relation to current or potential competitors. It means creating a pattern for dealing with customers or suppliers which persists because there are advantages on both sides. Offering guarantees against price declines on floor stocks is one example of market organization by the seller. Attempts to systematize the flow of orders may range from various services offered to cutomers or suppliers all the way to complete vertical integration. Another dynamic factor affecting the structure of markets may be generalized under the term "closure." It frequently happens that some marketing system is incomplete or out of balance in some direction. The act of supplying the missing element constitutes closure, enabling the system to handle a greater output or to operate at a new level of efficiency. The incomplete system in effect cries out for closure. To observe this need is to recognize a form of market opportunity. This is one of the primary ways in which new enterprises develop, since there may be good reasons why the missing service cannot be performed by the existing organizations which need the service. A food broker, for example, can cover a market for several accounts of moderate size in a way that the individual manufacturer would not be able to cover it for himself.

There is a certain compensating effect between closure as performed by new or supplementary marketing enterprises and changes in market organization brought about by the initiative of existing firms in the pursuit of differential advantage. The pursuit of a given form of advantage, in fact, may carry the total marketing economy out of balance in a given direction creating the need and opportunity for closure. Such an economy could never be expected to reach a state of equilibrium, although the tendency toward structural balance is one of the factors in its dynamics. Trade regulation may be embraced within this dynamic pattern as an attempt of certain groups to organize the market to their own advantage through political means. Entering into this political struggle to determine the structure of markets are some political leaders and some administrative officials who regard themselves as representing the consumer's interests. It seems reasonable to believe that the increasing sophistication and buying skill of consumers is one of the primary forces offsetting the tendency of the free market economy to turn into something else through the working out of its inherent dynamic forces. This was the destiny foreseen for the capitalistic system by Schumpeter, even though he was one of its staunchest advocates.

The household as an organized behavior system must be given special attention in creating an analytical framework for marketing. The household is an operating entity with an assortment of goods and assets and with economic functions to perform. Once a primary production unit, the household has lost a large part of these activities to manufacturing and service enterprises. Today its economic operations are chiefly expressed through earning and spending. In the typical household there is some specialization between the husband as primary earner and the wife as chief purchasing agent for the household. It may be assumed that she becomes increasingly competent in buying as she surrenders her production activities such as canning, baking and dressmaking, and devotes more of her time and attention to shopping. She is a rational problem solver as she samples what the market has to offer in her effort to maintain a balanced inventory or assortment of goods to meet expected occasions of use. This is not an attempt to substitute Economic Woman for the discredited fiction of Economic Man. It is only intended to assert that the decision structure of consumer buying is similar to that for industrial buying. Both business executive and housewife enter the market as rational problem solvers, even though there are other aspects of personality in either case.

An adequate perspective on the household for marketing purposes must recognize several facets of its activities. It is an organized behavior system with its aspects of power, communication, and operating structure. It is the locus of forms of behavior other than instrumental or goal-seeking activities. A convenient three-way division, derived from the social sciences, recognizes instrumental, congenial, and symptomatic behavior. Congenial behavior is that kind of activity engaged in for its own sake and presumably yielding direct satisfactions. It is exemplified by the act of consumption as compared to all of the instrumental activities which prepare the way for consumption. Symptomatic behavior reflects maladjustment and is neither pleasure-giving in itself nor an efficient pursuit of goals. Symptomatic behavior is functional only to the extent that it serves as a signal to others that the individual needs help.

Some studies of consumer motivation have given increasing attention to symptomatic behavior or to the projection of symptoms of personality adjustment which might affect consumer buying. The present view is that the effort to classify individuals by personality types is less urgent for marketing than the classification of families. Four family types with characteristically different buying behavior have been suggested growing out of the distinction between the instrumental and congenial aspects of normal behavior. Even individuals who are fairly well adjusted in themselves will form a less than perfect family if not fully adapted to each other.

On the instrumental side of household behavior it would seem to be desirable that the members be well coordinated as in any other operating system. If not, they will not deliver the maximum impact in pursuit of family goals. On the congenial side it would appear desirable for the members of a household to be compatible. That means enjoying the same things, cherishing the same goals, preferring joint activities to solitary pursuits or the company of others. These two distinctions yield an obvious four-way classification. The ideal is the family that is coordinated in its instrumental activities and compatible in its congenial activities. A rather joyless household which might nevertheless be well managed and prosperous in material terms is the coordinated but incompatible household. The compatible but unco-ordinated family would tend to be happy-go-lucky and irresponsible with obvious consequences for buying behavior. The household which was both uncoordinated and incompatible would usually be tottering on the brink of dissolution. It might be held together formally by scruples against divorce, by concern for children, or by the dominant power of one member over the others. This symptomology of families does not exclude an interest in the readjustment of individuals exhibiting symptomatic behavior. Such remedial action lies in the sphere of the psychiatrist and the social worker, whereas the marketer is chiefly engaged in supplying goods to families which are still functioning as operating units.

All of the discussion of consumers so far limits itself to the activities of the household purchasing agent. Actually the term consumption as it appears in marketing and economic literature nearly always means consumer buying. Some day marketing may need to look beyond the act of purchasing to a study of consumption proper. The occasion for such studies will arise out of the problems of inducing consumers to accept innovations or the further proliferation of products to be included in the household assortment. Marketing studies at this depth will not only borrow from the social sciences but move into the realm of esthetic and ethical values. What is the use of a plethora of goods unless the buyer derives genuine satisfaction from them? What is the justification of surfeit if the acquisition of goods serves as a distraction from activities which are essential to the preservation of our culture and of the integrity of our personalities?

It has been suggested that a study of consumption might begin with the problem of choice in the presence of abundance. The scarce element then is the time or capacity for enjoyment. The bookworm confronted with the thousands of volumes available in a great library must choose in the face of this type of limitation.

The name hedonomics would appear to be appropriate for this field of study suggesting the management of the capacity to enjoy. Among the problems for hedonomics is the pleasure derived from the repetition of a familiar experience as compared with the enjoyment of a novel experience or an old experience with some novel element. Another is the problem of direct experience versus symbolic experience, with the advantages of intensity on the one hand and on the other the possibility of embracing a greater range of possible ideas and sensations by relying on symbolic representations. Extensive basic research will probably be necessary before hedonomics can be put to work in marketing or for the enrichment of human life through other channels.

This paper barely suffices to sketch the analytical framework for marketing. It leaves out much of the area of executive decision-making in marketing on such matters as the weighing of uncertainties and the acceptance of risk in the commitment of resources. It leaves out market planning which is rapidly becoming a systematic discipline centering in the possibilities for economizing time and space as well as resources. It leaves out all but the most casual references to advertising and demand formation. Advertising is certainly one of the most difficult of marketing functions to embrace within a single analytical framework. It largely ignores the developing technology of physical distribution. Hopefully what it does accomplish is to show how the essentially economic problems of marketing may yield to a more comprehensive approach drawing on the basic social sciences for techniques and enriched perspective.

3

Marketing and Economic Development

Peter F. Drucker

MARKETING AS A BUSINESS DISCIPLINE

The distinguished pioneer of marketing, whose memory we honor today, was largely instrumental in developing marketing as a systematic business discipline—in teaching us how to go about, in an orderly, purposeful and planned way to find and create customers; to identify and define markets; to create new ones and promote them; to integrate customers' needs, wants, and preferences, and the intellectual and creative capacity and skills of an industrial society, toward the design of new and better products and of new distributive concepts and processes.

On this contribution and similar ones of other Founding Fathers of marketing during the last half century rests the rapid emergence of marketing as perhaps the most advanced, certainly the most "scientific" of all functional business disciplines.

But Charles Coolidge Parlin also contributed as a Founding Father toward the development of marketing as a *social discipline.* He helped give us the awareness, the concepts, and the tools that make us understand marketing as a dynamic process of society through which business enterprise is integrated productively with society's purposes and human values. It is in marketing, as we now understand

Reprinted from the *Journal of Marketing,* published by the American Marketing Association (January, 1958), pp. 252–259. This article is based on the Charles Coolidge Parlin Memorial Lecture sponsored by the Philadelphia Chapter of the American Marketing Association in 1957.

Peter F. Drucker, an internationally recognized management consultant and professor at Claremont Graduate School, is perhaps best known for his widely-read management books, including *Managing for Results* and *Management: Tasks, Responsibilities, Practices.* A native of Vienna, he holds an LL.D. degree from the University of Frankfort and honorary degrees from two American universities and from one in Japan.

it, that we satisfy individual and social values, needs, and wants—be it through producing goods, supplying services, fostering innovation, or creating satisfaction. Marketing, as we have come to understand it, has its focus on the customer, that is, on the individual making decisions within a social structure and within a personal and social value system. Marketing is thus the process through which economy is integrated into society to serve human needs.

I am not competent to speak about marketing in the first sense, marketing as a functional discipline of business. I am indeed greatly concerned with marketing in this meaning. One could not be concerned, as I am, with the basic institutions of industrial society in general and with the management of business enterprise in particular, without a deep and direct concern with marketing. But in this field I am a consumer of marketing alone—albeit a heavy one. I am not capable of making a contribution. I would indeed be able to talk about the wants and needs I have which I, as a consumer of marketing, hope that you, the men of marketing, will soon supply:—a theory of pricing, for instance, that can serve, as true theories should, as the foundation for actual pricing decisions and for an understanding of price behavior; or a consumer-focused concept and theory of competition. But I could not produce any of these "new products" of marketing which we want. I cannot contribute myself. To use marketing language, I am not even "effective demand," in these fields as yet.

THE ROLE OF MARKETING

I shall today in my remarks confine myself to the second meaning in which marketing has become a discipline: The role of marketing in economy and society. And I shall single out as my focus the role of marketing in the economic development, especially of underdeveloped "growth" countries.

My thesis is very briefly as follows. Marketing occupies a critical role in respect to the development of such "growth" areas. Indeed marketing is the most important "multiplier" of such development. It is in itself in every one of these areas the least developed, the most backward part of the economic system. Its development, above all others, makes possible economic integration and the fullest utilization of whatever assets and productive capacity an economy already possesses. It mobilizes latent economic energy. It contributes to the greatest needs: that for the rapid development of entrepreneurs and managers, and at the same time it may be the easiest area of managerial work to get going. The reason is that, thanks to men like Charles Coolidge Parlin, it is the most systematized and, therefore, the most learnable and the most teachable of all areas of business management and entrepreneurship.

INTERNATIONAL AND INTERRACIAL
INEQUALITY

Looking at this world of ours, we see some essentially new facts.

For the first time in man's history the whole world is united and unified. This may seem a strange statement in view of the conflicts and threats of suicidal wars that scream at us from every headline. But conflict has always been with us. What is new is that today all of mankind shares the same vision, the same objective, the same goal, the same hope, and believes in the same tools. This vision might, in gross over-simplification, be called "industrialization."

It is the belief that it is possible for man to improve his economic lot through systematic, purposeful, and directed effort—individually as well as for an entire society. It is the belief that we have the tools at our disposal—the technological, the conceptual, and the social tools —to enable man to raise himself, through his own efforts, at least to a level that we in this country would consider poverty, but which for most of our world would be almost unbelievable luxury.

And this is an irreversible new fact. It has been made so by these true agents of revolution in our times: the new tools of communication—the dirt road, the truck, and the radio, which have penetrated even the furthest, most isolated and most primitive community.

This is new, and cannot be emphasized too much and too often. It is both a tremendous vision and a tremendous danger in that catastrophe must result if it cannot be satisfied, at least to a modest degree.

But at the same time we have a new, unprecedented danger, that of international and interracial inequality. We on the North American continent are a mere tenth of the world population, including our Canadian friends and neighbors. But we have at least 75 per cent of the world income. And the 75 per cent of the world population whose income is below $100 per capita a year receive together perhaps no more than 10 per cent of the world's income. This is inequality of income, as great as anything the world has ever seen. It is accompanied by very high equality of income in the developed countries, especially in ours where we are in the process of proving that an industrial society does not have to live in extreme tension between the few very rich and the many very poor as lived all earlier societies of man. But what used to be national inequality and economic tension is now rapidly becoming international (and unfortunately also interracial) inequality and tension.

This is also brand new. In the past there were tremendous differences between societies and cultures: in their beliefs, their concepts, their ways of life, and their knowledge. The Frankish knight who went on Crusade was an ignorant and illiterate boor, according to the standards of the polished courtiers of Constantinople or of his Moslem enemies. But economically his society and theirs were exactly alike. They had the same sources of income, the same productivity of labor, the same forms and channels of investment, the same economic institutions, and the same distribution of income and wealth. Economically the Frankish knight, however much a barbarian he appeared, was at home in the societies of the East; and so was his serf. Both fitted in immediately and without any difficulty.

And this has been the case of all societies that went above the level of purely primitive tribe.

The inequality in our world today, however, between nations and races, is therefore a new—and a tremendously dangerous—phenomenon.

What we are engaged in today is essentially a race between the promise of economic development and the threat of international worldwide class war. The economic development is the opportunity of this age. The class war is the danger. Both are new. Both are indeed so new that most of us do not even see them as yet. But they are the essential economic realities of this industrial age of ours. And whether we shall realize the opportunity or succumb to danger will largely decide not only the economic future of this world—it may largely decide its spiritual, its intellectual, its political, and its social future.

SIGNIFICANCE OF MARKETING

Marketing is central in this new situation. For marketing is one of our most potent levers to convert the danger into the opportunity.

To understand this we must ask: What do we mean by "underdeveloped"?

The first answer is, of course, that we mean areas of very low income. But income is, after all, a result. It is a result first of extreme agricultural over-population in which the great bulk of the people have to find a living on the land which, as a result, cannot even produce enough food to feed them, let alone produce a surplus. It is certainly a result of low productivity. And both, in a vicious circle, mean that there is not enough capital for investment and very low productivity of what is being invested—owing largely to misdirection of investment into unessential and unproductive channels.

All this we know today and understand. Indeed we have learned during the last few years a very great deal both about the structure of an under-developed economy and about the theory and dynamics of economic development.

What we tend to forget, however, is that the essential aspect of an "under-developed" economy and the factor of absence which keeps it "under-developed," is the inability to organize economic efforts and energies, to bring together resources, wants, and capacities, and so to convert a self-limiting static system into creative, self-generating organic growth.

And this is where marketing comes in.

Lack of Development in "Under-developed" Countries

First, in every "under-developed" country I know of, marketing is the most under-developed—or the least developed—part of the economy, if only because of the strong, pervasive prejudice against the middleman.

As a result, these countries are stunted by inability to make effective use of the little they have. Marketing might by itself go far toward changing the entire economic tone of the existing system—without any change in methods of production, distribution of population, or of income.

It would make the producers capable of producing marketable products by providing them with standards, with quality demands, and with specifications for their product. It would make the product capable of being brought to markets instead of perishing on the way. And it would make the consumer capable of discrimination, that is, of obtaining the greatest value for his very limited purchasing power.

In every one of these countries, marketing profits are characteristically low. Indeed the people engaged in marketing barely eke out a subsistence living. And "mark-ups" are minute by our standards. But marketing costs are outrageously high. The waste in distribution and marketing, if only from spoilage or from the accumulation of unsalable inventories that clog the shelves for years, has to be seen to be believed. And marketing service is by and large all but non-existent.

What is needed in any "growth" country to make economic

development realistic, and at the same time produce a vivid demonstration of what economic development can produce, is a marketing system:—a system of physical distribution, a financial system to make possible the distribution of goods, and finally actual marketing, that is, an actual system of integrating wants, needs, and purchasing power of the consumer with capacity and resources of production.

This need is largely masked today because marketing is so often confused with the traditional "trader and merchant" of which every one of these countries has more than enough. It would be one of our most important contributions to the development of "underdeveloped" countries to get across the fact that marketing is something quite different.

It would be basic to get across the triple function of marketing—the function of crystallizing and directing demand for maximum productive effectiveness and efficiency; the function of guiding production purposefully toward maximum consumer satisfaction and consumer value; the function of creating discrimination that then gives rewards to those who really contribute excellence, and that then also penalizes the monopolist, the slothful, or those who only want to take but do not want to contribute or to risk.

Utilization by the Entrepreneur

Marketing is also the most easily accessible "multiplier" of managers and entrepreneurs in an "under-developed" growth area. And managers and entrepreneurs are the foremost need of these countries. In the first place, "economic development" is not a force of nature. It is the result of the action, the purposeful, responsible, risk-taking action, of men as entrepreneurs and managers.

Certainly it is the entrepreneur and manager who alone can convey to the people of these countries an understanding of what economic development means and how it can be achieved.

Marketing can convert latent demand into effective demand. It cannot, by itself, create purchasing power. But it can uncover and channel all purchasing power that exists. It can, therefore, create rapidly the conditions for a much higher level of economic activity than existed before, can create the opportunities for the entrepreneur.

It then can create the stimulus for the development of modern, responsible, professional management by creating opportunity for the producer who knows how to plan, how to organize, how to lead people, how to innovate.

In most of these countries markets are of necessity very small.

They are too small to make it possible to organize distribution for a single-product line in any effective manner. As a result, without a marketing organization, many products for which there is an adequate demand at a reasonable price cannot be distributed; or worse, they can be produced and distributed only under monopoly conditions. A marketing system is needed which serves as the joint and common channel for many producers if any of them is to be able to come into existence and to stay in existence.

This means in effect that a marketing system in the "under-developed" countries is the *creator of small business,* is the only way in which a man of vision and daring can become a businessman and an entrepreneur himself. This is thereby also the only way in which a true middle class can develop in the countries in which the habit of investment in productive enterprise has still to be created.

Developer of Standards

Marketing in an "under-developed" country is the developer of standards—of standards for product and service as well as of standards of conduct, of integrity, of reliability, of foresight, and of concern for the basic long-range impact of decisions on the customer, the supplier, the economy, and the society.

Rather than go on making theoretical statements let me point to one illustration: The impact Sears Roebuck has had on several countries of Latin America. To be sure, the countries of Latin America in which Sears operates—Mexico, Brazil, Cuba, Venezuela, Colombia, and Peru—are not "under-developed" in the same sense in which Indonesia or the Congo are "under-developed." Their average income, although very low by our standards, is at least two times, perhaps as much as four or five times, that of the truly "under-developed" countries in which the bulk of mankind still live. Still in every respect except income level these Latin American countries are at best "developing." And they have all the problems of economic development—perhaps even in more acute form than the countries of Asia and Africa, precisely because their development has been so fast during the last ten years.

It is also true that Sears in these countries is not a "low–price" merchandiser. It caters to the middle class in the richer of these countries, and to the upper middle class in the poorest of these countries. Incidentally, the income level of these groups is still lower than that of the worker in the industrial sector of our economy.

Still Sears is a mass-marketer even in Colombia or Peru. What is perhaps even more important, it is applying in these "under-developed" countries exactly the same policies and principles it applies in this country, carries substantially the same merchandise (although most of it produced in the countries themselves), and applies the same concepts of marketing it uses in Indianapolis or Philadelphia. Its impact and experience are, therefore, a fair test of what marketing principles, marketing knowledge, and marketing techniques can achieve.

The impact of this one American business which does not have more than a mere handful of stores in these countries and handles no more than a small fraction of the total retail business of these countries is truly amazing. In the first place, Sears' latent purchasing power has fast become actual purchasing power. Or, to put it less theoretically, people have begun to organize their buying and to go out for value in what they do buy.

Secondly, by the very fact that it builds one store in one city, Sears forces a revolution in retailing throughout the whole surrounding area. It forces store modernization. It forces consumer credit. It forces a different attitude toward the customer, toward the store clerk, toward the supplier, and toward the merchandise itself. It forces other retailers to adopt modern methods of pricing, of inventory control, of training, of window display, and what have you.

The greatest impact Sears has had, however, is the multiplication of new industrial business for which Sears creates a marketing channel. Because it has had to sell goods manufactured in these countries rather than import them (if only because of foreign exchange restrictions), Sears has been instrumental in getting established literally hundreds of new manufacturers making goods which, a few years ago, could not be made in the country, let alone be sold in adequate quantity. Simply to satisfy its own marketing needs, Sears has had to insist on standards of workmanship, quality, and delivery—that is, on standards of production management, of technical management, and above all of the management of people—which, in a few short years, have advanced the art and science of management in these countries by at least a generation.

I hardly need to add that Sears is not in Latin America for reasons of philanthropy, but because it is good and profitable business with extraordinary growth potential. In other words, Sears is in Latin America because marketing is the major opportunity in a "growth economy"—precisely because its absence is a major economic gap and the greatest need.

The Discipline of Marketing

Finally, marketing is critical in economic development because marketing has become so largely systematized, so largely both learnable and teachable. It is the discipline among all our business disciplines that has advanced the furthest.

I do not forget for a moment how much we still have to learn in marketing. But we should also not forget that most of what we have learned so far we have learned in a form in which we can express it in general concepts, in valid principles and, to a substantial degree, in quantifiable measurements. This, above all others, was the achievement of that generation to whom Charles Coolidge Parlin was leader and inspiration.

A critical factor in this world of ours is the learnability and teachability of what it means to be an entrepreneur and manager. For it is the entrepreneur and the manager who alone can cause economic development to happen. The world needs them, therefore, in very large numbers; and it needs them fast.

Obviously this need cannot be supplied by our supplying entrepreneurs and managers, quite apart from the fact that we hardly have the surplus. Money we can supply. Technical assistance we can supply, and should supply more. But the supply of men we can offer to the people in the "under-developed" countries is of necessity a very small one.

The demand is also much too urgent for it to be supplied by slow evolution through experience, or through dependence on the emergence of "naturals." The danger that lies in the inequality today between the few countries that have and the great many countries that have not is much too great to permit a wait of centuries. Yet it takes centuries if we depend on experience and slow evolution for the supply of entrepreneurs and managers adequate to the needs of a modern society.

There is only one way in which man has ever been able to short-cut experience, to telescope development, in other words, to *learn something.* That way is to have available the distillate of experience and skill in the form of knowledge, of concepts, of generalization, of measurement—in the form of *discipline,* in other words.

THE DISCIPLINE OF ENTREPRENEURSHIP

Many of us today are working on the fashioning of such a discipline of entrepreneurship and management. Maybe we are further along than most of us realize.

Certainly in what has come to be called "Operation Research and Synthesis" we have the first beginnings of a systematic approach to the entrepreneurial task of purposeful risk-taking and innovation—

so far only an approach, but a most promising one, unless indeed we become so enamored with the gadgets and techniques as to forget purpose and aim.

We are at the beginning perhaps also of an understanding of the basic problems of organizing people of diversified and highly advanced skill and judgment together in one effective organization, although again no one so far would, I am convinced, claim more for us than that we have begun at last to ask intelligent questions.

But marketing, although it only covers one functional area in the field, has something that can be called a discipline. It has developed general concepts, that is, theories that explain a multitude of phenomena in simple statements. It even has measurements that record "facts" rather than opinions. In marketing, therefore, we already possess a learnable and teachable approach to this basic and central problem not only of the "under-developed" countries but of all countries. All of us have today the same survival stake in economic development. The risk and danger of international and interracial inequality are simply too great.

Marketing is obviously not a cure-all, not a panacea. It is only one thing we need. But it answers a critical need. At the same time marketing is most highly developed.

Indeed without marketing as the hinge on which to turn, economic development will almost have to take the totalitarian form. A totalitarian system can be defined economically as one in which economic development is being attempted without marketing, indeed as one in which marketing is suppressed. Precisely because it first looks at the values and wants of the individual, and because it then develops people to act purposefully and responsibly—that is, because of its effectiveness in developing a free economy—marketing is suppressed in a totalitarian system. If we want economic development in freedom and responsibility, we have to build it on the development of marketing.

In the new and unprecedented world we live in, a world which knows both a new unity of vision and growth and a new and most dangerous cleavage, marketing has a special and central role to play. This role goes beyond "getting the stuff out the back door," beyond "getting the most sales with the least cost," beyond "the optimal integration of our values and wants as customers, citizens, and persons, with our productive resources and intellectual achievements"—the role marketing plays in a developed society.

In a developing economy, marketing is, of course, all of this. But in addition, in an economy that is striving to break the age-old bondage of man to misery, want, and destitution, marketing is also the catalyst for the transmutation of latent resources into actual resources, of desires into accomplishments, and the development of responsible economic leaders and informed economic citizens.

4

The Marketing Revolution

Robert J. Keith

The consumer, not the company, is in the middle.

In today's economy the consumer, the man or woman who buys the product, is at the absolute dead center of the business universe. Companies revolve around the customer, not the other way around.

Growing acceptance of this consumer concept has had, and will have, far-reaching implications for business, achieving a virtual revolution in economic thinking. As the concept gains ever greater acceptance, marketing is emerging as the most important single function in business.

A REVOLUTION IN SCIENCE

A very apt analogy can be drawn with another revolution, one that goes back to the sixteenth century. At that time astronomers had great difficulty predicting the movements of the heavenly bodies. Their charts and computations and celestial calendars enabled them to estimate the approximate positions of the planets on any given date. But their calculations were never exact—there was always a variance.

Then a Polish scientist named Nicolaus Copernicus proposed a very simple answer to the problem. If, he proposed, we assume that the sun, and not the earth, is at the center of our system, and that the earth moves around the sun instead of the sun moving around the earth, all our calculations will prove correct.

Reprinted from the *Journal of Marketing,* published by the American Marketing Association (January, 1960), pp. 35–38.

Robert J. Keith is president of The Pillsbury Company and is a director of Pillsbury and other national companies. During his 25 years with Pillsbury, his responsibility has centered around the grocery products division and the refrigerated-products division.

The Pole's idea raised a storm of controversy. The earth, everyone knew, was at the center of the universe. But another scientist named Galileo put the theory to test—and it worked. The result was a complete upheaval in scientific and philosophic thought. The effects of Copernicus' revolutionary idea are still being felt today.

A REVOLUTION IN MARKETING

In much the same way American business in general—and Pillsbury in particular—is undergoing a revolution of its own today: a marketing revolution.

This revolution stems from the same idea stated in the opening sentence of this article. No longer is the company at the center of the business universe. Today the customer is at the center.

Our attention has shifted from problems of production to problems of marketing, from the product we *can* make to the product the consumer *wants* us to make, from the company itself to the market place.

The marketing revolution has only begun. It is reasonable to expect that its implications will grow in the years to come, and that lingering effects will be felt a century, or more than one century, from today.

So far the theory has only been advanced, tested, and generally proved correct. As more and more businessmen grasp the concept, and put it to work, our economy will become more truly marketing oriented.

PILLSBURY'S PATTERN: FOUR ERAS

Here is the way the marketing revolution came about at Pillsbury. The experience of this company has followed a typical pattern. There has been nothing unique, and each step in the evolution of the marketing concept has been taken in a way that is more meaningful because the steps are, in fact, typical.

Today in our company the marketing concept finds expression in the simple statement, "Nothing happens at Pillsbury until a sale is made." This statement represents basic reorientation on the part of our management. For, not too many years ago, the ordering of functions in our business placed finance first, production second, and sales last.

How did we arrive at our present point of view? Pillsbury's progress in the marketing revolution divides neatly into four separate eras—eras which parallel rather closely the classic pattern of development in the marketing revolution.

1st ERA—PRODUCTION ORIENTED

First came the era of manufacturing. It began with the formation of the company in 1869 and continued into the 1930s. It is significant that the *idea* for the formation of our company came from the *availability* of high-quality wheat and the *proximity* of water power—and not from the availability and proximity of growing major market areas, or the demand for better, less expensive, more convenient flour products.

Of course, these elements were potentially present. But the two major elements which fused in the mind of Charles A. Pillsbury and prompted him to invest his modest capital in a flour mill were, on the one hand, wheat, and, on the other hand, water power. His principal concern was with production, not marketing.

His thought and judgment were typical of the business thinking of his day. And such thinking was adequate and proper for the times.

Our company philosophy in this era might have been stated this way: "We are professional flour millers. Blessed with a supply of the finest North American wheat, plenty of water power, and excellent milling machinery, we produce flour of the highest quality. Our basic function is to mill high-quality flour, and of course (and almost incidentally) we must hire salesmen to sell it, just as we hire accountants to keep our books."

The young company's first new product reveals an interesting example of the thinking of this era. The product was middlings, the bran left over after milling. Millfeed, as the product came to be known, proved a valuable product because it was an excellent nutrient for cattle. But the impetus to launch the new product came not from a consideration of the nutritional needs of cattle or a marketing analysis. It came primarily from the desire to dispose of a by-product! The new product decision was production oriented, not marketing oriented.

2nd ERA—SALES ORIENTED

In the 1930s Pillsbury moved into its second era of development as a marketing company. This was the era of sales For the first time we began to be highly conscious of the consumer, her wants, and her prejudices, as a key factor in the business equation. We established a commercial research department to provide us with facts about the market.

We also became more aware of the importance of our dealers, the wholesale and retail grocers who provided a vital link in our chain of distribution from the mill to the home. Knowing that consumers and dealers as well were vital to the company's success, we could no longer simply mark them down as unknowns in our figuring. With this realization, we took the first step along the road to becoming a marketing company.

Pillsbury's thinking in this second era could be summed up like this: "We are a flour-milling company, manufacturing a number of products for the consumer market. We must have a first-rate sales organization which can dispose of all the products we can make at a favorable price. We must back up this sales force with consumer advertising and market intelligence. We want our salesmen and our dealers to have all the tools they need for moving the output of our plants to the consumer."

Still not a marketing philosophy, but we were getting closer.

3rd ERA—MARKETING ORIENTED

It was at the start of the present decade that Pillsbury entered the marketing era. The amazing growth of our consumer business as the result of introducing baking mixes provided the immediate impetus. But the groundwork had been laid by key men who developed our sales concepts in the middle forties.

With the new cake mixes, products of our research program, ringing up sales on the cash register, and with the realization that research and production could produce literally hundreds of new and different products, we faced for the first time the necessity for selecting the best new products. We needed a set of criteria for selecting the kind of products we would manufacture. We needed an organization to establish and maintain these criteria, and for attaining maximum sale of the products we did select.

We needed, in fact, to build into our company a new management function which would direct and control all the other corporate functions from procurement to production to advertising to sales. This function was marketing. Our solution was to establish the present marketing department.

This department developed the criteria which we would use in determining which products to market. *And these criteria were, and are, nothing more nor less than those of the consumer herself.* We moved the mountain out to find out what Mahomet, and Mrs. Mahomet, wanted. The company's purpose was no longer to mill flour, nor to manufacture a wide variety of products, but to satisfy the needs and desires, both actual and potential, of our customers.

If we were to restate our philosophy during the past decade as simply as possible, it would read: "We make and sell products for consumers."

The business universe, we realized, did not have room at the center for Pillsbury or any other company or groups of companies. It was already occupied by the customers.

This is the concept at the core of the marketing revolution. How did we put it to work for Pillsbury?

The Brand-manager Concept

The first move was to transform our small advertising department into a marketing department. The move involved far more than changing the name on organizational charts. It required the introduction of a new, and vitally important, organizational concept—the brand-manager concept.

The brand-manager idea is the very backbone of marketing at Pillsbury. The man who bears the title, brand manager, has total accountability for results. He directs the marketing of his product as if it were his own business. Production does its job, and finance keeps the profit figures. Otherwise, the brand manager has total responsibility for marketing his product. This responsibility encompasses pricing, commercial research, competitive activity, home service and publicity coordination, legal details, budgets, advertising plans, sales promotion, and execution of plans. The brand manager must think first, last, and always of his sales target, the consumer.

Marketing permeates the entire organization. Marketing plans and executes the sale—all the way from the inception of the product idea, through its development and distribution, to the customer purchase. Marketing begins and ends with the consumer. New product ideas are conceived after careful study of her wants and needs, her likes and dislikes. Then marketing takes the idea and marshals all the forces of the corporation to translate the idea into product and the product into sales.

In the early days of the company, consumer orientation did not seem so important. The company made flour, and flour was a staple—no one would question the availability of a market. Today we must determine whether the American housewife will buy lemon pudding cake in preference to orange angel food. The variables in the equation have multiplied just as the number of products on the grocers' shelves have multiplied from a hundred or so into many thousands.

When we first began operating under this new marketing concept, we encountered the problems which always accompany any major reorientation. Our people were young and frankly immature in some areas of business; but they were men possessed of an idea and they fought for it. The idea was almost too powerful. The marketing concept proved its worth in sales, but it upset many of the internal balances of the corporation. Marketing-oriented decisions resulted in peaks and valleys in production, schedules, labor, and inventories. But the system worked. It worked better and better as maverick marketing men became motivated toward tonnage and profit.

4th ERA—MARKETING CONTROL

Today marketing is coming into its own. Pillsbury stands on the brink of its fourth major era in the marketing revolution.

Basically, the philosophy of this fourth era can be summarized this way: "We are moving from a company which has the marketing concept to a marketing company."

Marketing today sets company operating policy short-term. It will come to influence long-range policy more and more. Where today consumer research, technical research, procurement, production, advertising, and sales swing into action under the broad canopy established by marketing, tomorrow capital and financial planning, ten-year volume and profit goals will also come under the aegis of marketing. More than any other function, marketing must be tied to top management.

Today our marketing people know more about inventories than anyone in top management. Tomorrow's marketing man must know capital financing and the implications of marketing planning on long-range profit forecasting.

Today technical research receives almost all of its guidance and direction from marketing. Tomorrow marketing will assume a more creative function in the advertising area, both in terms of ideas and media selection.

The marketing revolution has only begun. There are still those who resist its basic idea, just as there are always those who will resist change in business, government, or any other form of human institution.

As the marketing revolution gains momentum, there will be more changes. The concept of the customer at the center will remain valid; but business must adjust to the shifting tastes and likes and desires and needs which have always characterized the American consumer.

For many years the geographical center of the United States lay in a small Kansas town. Then a new state, Alaska, came along, and the center shifted to the north and west. Hawaii was admitted to the Union and the geographical mid-point took another jump to the west. In very much the same way, modern business must anticipate the restless shifting of buying attitudes, as customer preferences move north, south, east, or west from a liquid center. There is nothing static about the marketing revolution, and that is part of its fascination. The old order has changed, yielding place to the new—but the new order will have its quota of changes, too.

At Pillsbury, as our fourth era progresses, marketing will become the basic motivating force for the entire corporation. Soon it will be true that every activity of the corporation—from finance to sales to production—is aimed at satisfying the needs and desires of the consumer. When that stage of development is reached, the marketing revolution will be complete.

5

The Affluent Society

John Kenneth Galbraith

INTRODUCTION

Wealth is not without its advantages and the case to the contrary, although it has often been made, has never proved widely persuasive. But, beyond doubt, wealth is the relentless enemy of understanding. The poor man has always a precise view of his problem and its remedy: he hasn't enough and he needs more. The rich man can assume or imagine a much greater variety of ills and he will be correspondingly less certain of their remedy. Also, until he learns to live with his wealth, he will have a well-observed tendency to put it to the wrong purposes or otherwise to make himself foolish.

As with individuals so with nations. And the experience of nations with well-being is exceedingly brief. Nearly all throughout all history have been very poor. The exception, almost insignificant in the whole span of human existence, has been the last few generations in the comparatively small corner of the world populated by Europeans. Here, and especially in the United States, there has been great and quite unprecedented affluence.

The ideas by which the people of this favored part of the world interpret their existence, and in measure guide their behavior, were not forged in a world of wealth. These ideas were the product of a world in which poverty had always been man's normal lot, and any

From *The Affluent Society*. Copyright © 1958 by John Kenneth Galbraith. Reprinted by permission of the publisher, Houghton Mifflin Company. There is now available a Revised 1969 Edition of *The Affluent Society*. From *The Affluent Society* by J. K. Galbraith, copyright © 1969 by J. K. Galbraith (Hamish Hamilton, London).

John Kenneth Galbraith a noted economist and social critic, recently retired as professor of economics at Harvard University. He received M.S. and Ph.D. degrees from the University of California (Berkeley); was deputy administrator, Office of Price Administration during World War II, and Ambassador to India during 1961–63. In addition to *The Affluent Society*, his best known works are *American Capitalism: The Theory of Countervailing Power, The New Industrial State*, and *Economics and the Public Purpose*.

other state was in degree unimaginable. This poverty was not the elegant torture of the spirit which comes from contemplating another man's more spacious possessions. It was the unedifying mortification of the flesh—from hunger, sickness, and cold. Those who might be freed temporarily from such burden could not know when it would strike again, for at best hunger yielded only perilously to privation. It is improbable that the poverty of the masses of the people was made greatly more bearable by the fact that a very few—those upon whose movements nearly all recorded history centers—were very rich.

No one would wish to argue that the ideas which interpreted this world of grim scarcity would serve equally well for the contemporary United States. Poverty was the all-pervasive fact of that world. Obviously it is not of ours. One would not expect that the preoccupations of a poverty-ridden world would be relevant in one where the ordinary individual has access to amenities—foods, entertainment, personal transportation, and plumbing—in which not even the rich rejoiced a century ago. So great has been the change that many of the desires of the individual are no longer even evident to him. They become so only as they are synthesized, elaborated, and nurtured by advertising and salesmanship, and these, in turn, have become among our most important and talented professions. Few people at the beginning of the nineteenth century needed an adman to tell them what they wanted.

It would be wrong to suggest that the economic ideas which once interpreted the world of mass poverty have made no adjustment to the world of affluence. There have been many adjustments, including some that have gone unrecognized or have been poorly understood. But there has also been a remarkable resistance. And the total alteration in underlying circumstances has not been squarely faced. As a result we are guided, in part, by ideas that are relevant to another world; and as a further result we do many things that are unnecessary, some that are unwise, and a few that are insane. We enhance substantially the risk of depression and thereby the threat to our affluence itself.

. . . .

No student of social matters in these days can escape feeling how precarious is the existence of that with which he deals. Western man has escaped for the moment the poverty which was for so long his all-embracing fate. The unearthly light of a handful of nuclear explosions would signal his return to utter deprivation if, indeed, he survived at all. I venture to think that the ideas here offered bear on our chances for escape from this fate. Illusion is a comprehensive ill. The rich man who deludes himself into behaving like a mendicant may conserve his fortune although he will not be very happy. The affluent country which conducts its affairs in accordance with rules of another and poorer age also foregoes opportunities. And in misunderstanding itself it will, in any time of difficulty, implacably prescribe for itself the wrong remedies. This the reader will discover is, to a disturbing degree, our present tendency.

Yet it would be a mistake to be too gravely depressed. The problems of an affluent world, which does not understand itself, may be serious, and they can needlessly threaten the affluence itself. But they are not likely to be as serious as those of a poor world where the simple exigencies of poverty preclude the luxury of misunderstanding but where, also and alas, no solutions are to be had.

. . . .

As Tawney observed, we are rarely conscious of the quality of the air we breathe. But in Los Angeles, where it is barely sufficient for its freight, we take it seriously. Similarly those who reside on a recently reclaimed desert see in the water in the canals the evidence of their unnatural triumph over nature. And the Chicagoan in Sarasota sees in his tanned belly the proof of his intelligence in escaping his dark and frozen habitat. But where sun and rain are abundant, though they are no less important, they are taken for granted. In the world of Ricardo goods were scarce. They were also closely related, if not to the survival, at least to the elemental comforts of man. They fed him, covered him when he was out of doors, and kept him warm when he was within. It is not surprising that the production by which these goods were obtained was central to men's thoughts.

Now goods are abundant. More die in the United States of too much food than of too little. Where the population was once thought to press on the food supply, now the food supply presses relentlessly on the population. No one can seriously suggest that the steel which comprises the extra four or five feet of purely decorative distance on our automobiles is of prime urgency. For many women and some men clothing has ceased to be related to protection from exposure and has become, like plumage, almost exclusively erotic. Yet production remains central to our thoughts. There is no tendency to take it, like sun and water, for granted; on the contrary, it continues to measure the quality and progress of our civilization.

Our preoccupation with production is, in fact, the culminating consequence of powerful historical and psychological forces—forces which only by an act of will we can hope to escape. Productivity, as we have seen, has enabled us to avoid or finesse the tensions anciently associated with inequality and its inconvenient remedies. It has become central to our strivings to reduce insecurity. And as we shall observe . . . its importance is buttressed by a highly dubious but widely accepted psychology of want; by an equally dubious but equally accepted interpretation of national interest; and by powerful vested interest. So all embracing, indeed, is our sense of the importance of production as a goal that the first reaction to any questioning of this attitude will be, "What else is there?"

THE PARAMOUNT POSITION OF PRODUCTION

As with the bear and her cubs we must expect the reaction to be increasingly sharp as the danger becomes more threatening. In part it will take the form of a purely assertive posture. "There is still an economic problem"; "We still have poverty"; "It is human nature to want more"; "Without increasing production there will be stagnation"; "We must show the Russians." But the ultimate refuge will remain in the theory of consumer demand. This is a formidable structure; it has already demonstrated its effectiveness in defending the urgency of production. In a world where affluence is rendering the old ideas obsolete, it will continue to be the bastion against the misery of new ones.

The theory of consumer demand, as it is now widely accepted, is based on two broad propositions, neither of them quite explicit but both extremely important for the present value system of economists. The first is that the urgency of wants does not diminish appreciably as more of them are satisfied or, to put the matter more precisely, to the extent that this happens it is not demonstrable and not a matter of any interest to economists or for economic policy. When man has satisfied his physical needs, then psychologically grounded desires take over. These can never be satisfied or, in any case, no progress can be proved. The concept of satiation has very little standing in economics. It is neither useful nor scientific to speculate on the comparative cravings of the stomach and the mind.

The second proposition is that wants originate in the personality of the consumer or, in any case, that they are given data for the economist. The latter's task is merely to seek their satisfaction. He has no need to inquire how these wants are formed. His function is sufficiently fulfilled by maximizing the goods that supply the wants.

The examination of these two conclusions must now be pressed. The explanation of consumer behavior has its ancestry in a much older problem, indeed the oldest problem of economics, that of price determination. Nothing originally proved more troublesome in the explanation of prices, i.e., exchange values, than the indigestible fact that some of the most useful things had the least value in exchange and some of the least useful has the most. As Adam Smith observed: "Nothing is more useful than water; but it will purchase scarce anything; scarce anything can be had in exchange for it. A diamond, on the contrary, has scarce any value in use: but a very great quantity of other goods may frequently be had in exchange for it."

In explaining value, Smith thought it well to distinguish between "value in exchange" and "value in use" and sought thus to reconcile the paradox of high utility and low exchangeability. This distinction begged questions rather than solved them and for another hundred years economists sought for a satisfactory formulation. Finally, toward the end of the last century—though it is now recognized that their work had been extensively anticipated—the three economists of marginal utility (Karl Menger, an Austrian; William Stanley Jevons, an Englishman; and John Bates Clark, an American) produced more or less simultaneously the explanation which in broad substance still serves. The urgency of desire is a function of the quantity of goods which the individual has available to satisfy that desire. The larger the stock the less the satisfactions from an increment. And the less, also, the willingness to pay. Since diamonds for most people are in comparatively meager supply, the satisfaction from an additional one is great, and the potential willingness to pay is likewise high. The case of water is just the reverse. It also follows that where the supply of a good can be readily increased at low cost, its value in exchange will reflect that ease of reproduction and the low urgency of the marginal desires it thus comes to satisfy. This will be so no matter how difficult it may be (as with water) to dispense entirely with the item in question.

The doctrine of diminishing marginal utility, as it was enshrined in the economics textbooks, seemed to put economic ideas squarely on the side of the diminishing importance of production under conditions of increasing affluence. With increasing per capita real income, men are able to satisfy additional wants. These are of a lower order of urgency. This being so, the production that provides the goods that satisfy these less urgent wants must also be of smaller (and declining) importance. In Ricardo's England the supply of bread for many was meager. The satisfaction resulting from an increment in the bread supply—from a higher money income, bread prices being the same, or the same money income, bread prices being lower—was great. Hunger was lessened; life itself might be extended. Certainly any measure to increase the bread supply merited the deep and serious interest of the public-spirited citizen.

In the contemporary United States the supply of bread is plentiful and the supply of bread grains even redundant. The yield of satisfactions from a marginal increment in the wheat supply is small. To a Secretary of Agriculture it is indubitably negative. Measures to increase the wheat supply are not, therefore, a socially urgent preoccupation of publicly concerned citizens. These are more likely to be found spending their time devising schemes for the effective control of wheat production. And having extended their bread consumption to the point where its marginal utility is very low, people have gone on to spend their income on other things. Since these other goods entered their consumption pattern after bread, there is a presumption that they are not very urgent either—that *their* consumption has been carried, as with wheat, to the point where marginal utility is small or even negligible. So it must be assumed that the importance of marginal increments of all production is low and declining. The effect of increasing affluence is to minimize the importance of economic goals. Production and productivity become less and less important.

The concept of diminishing marginal utility was, and remains, one of the indispensable ideas of economics. Since it conceded so much to the notion of diminishing urgency of wants, and hence of production, it was remarkable indeed that the situation was retrieved. This was done—and brilliantly. The diminishing urgency of wants was not admitted.

THE DEPENDENCE EFFECT

The notion that wants do not become less urgent the more amply the individual is supplied is broadly repugnant to common sense. It is something to be believed only by those who wish to believe. Yet the conventional wisdom must be tackled on its own terrain. Intertemporal comparisons of an individual's state of mind do rest on doubtful grounds. Who can say for sure that the deprivation which afflicts him with hunger is more painful than the deprivation which afflicts him with envy of his neighbor's new car? In the time that has passed since he was poor his soul may have become subject to a new and deeper searing. And where a society is concerned, comparisons between marginal satisfactions when it is poor and those when it is affluent will involve not only the same individual at different times but different individuals at different times. The scholar who wishes to believe that with increasing affluence there is no reduction in the urgency of desires and goods is not without points for debate. However plausible the case against him, it cannot be proven. In the defense of the conventional wisdom this amounts almost to invulnerability.

However, there is a flaw in the case. If the individual's wants are to be urgent they must be original with himself. They cannot be urgent if they must be contrived for him. And above all they must not be contrived by the process of production by which they are satisfied. For this means that the whole case for the urgency of production, based on the urgency of wants, falls to the ground. One cannot defend production as satisfying wants if that production creates the wants.

Were it so that a man on arising each morning was assailed by demons which instilled in him a passion sometimes for silk shirts, sometimes for kitchenware, sometimes for chamber pots, and sometimes for orange squash, there would be every reason to applaud the effort to find the goods, however odd, that quenched this flame. But should it be that his passion was the result of his first having cultivated the demons, and should it also be that his effort to allay it stirred the demons to ever greater and greater effort, there would be question as to how rational was his solution. Unless restrained by conventional attitudes, he might wonder if the solution lay with more goods or fewer demons.

So it is that if production creates the wants it seeks to satisfy, or if the wants emerge *pari passu* with the production, then the urgency of the wants can no longer be used to defend the urgency of the production. Production only fills a void that it has itself created.

The point is so central that it must be pressed. Consumer wants can have bizarre, frivolous, or even immoral origins, and an admirable case can still be made for a society that seeks to satisfy them. But the case cannot stand if it is the process of satisfying wants that creates the wants. For then the individual who urges the importance of production to satisfy these wants is precisely in the position of the onlooker who applauds the efforts of the squirrel to keep abreast of the wheel that is propelled by his own efforts.

That wants are, in fact, the fruit of production will now be denied by few serious scholars. And a considerable number of economists, though not always in full knowledge of the implications, have conceded the point. In the observation cited at the end of the preceding chapter Keynes noted that needs of "the second class," i.e., those that are the result of efforts to keep abreast or ahead of one's fellow being "may indeed by insatiable; for the higher the general level the higher still are they." And emulation has always played a considerable role in the views of other economists of want creation. One man's consumption becomes his neighbor's wish. This already means that the process by which wants are satisfied is also the process by which wants are created. The more wants that are satisfied the more new ones are born.

However, the argument has been carried farther. A leading modern theorist of consumer behavior, Professor Duesenberry, has stated explicitly that "ours is a society in which one of the principal social goals is a higher standard of living. . . . [This] has great significance for the theory of consumption . . . the desire to get superior goods takes on a life of its own. It provides a drive to higher expenditure which may even be stronger than that arising out of the needs which are supposed to be satisfied by that expenditure." The implications of this view are impressive. The notion of independently established need now sinks into the background. Because the society sets great store by ability to produce a high living standard, it evaluates people by the products they possess. The urge to consume is fathered by the value system which emphasizes the ability of the society to produce. The more that is produced the more that must be owned in order to maintain the appropriate prestige. The latter is an important point, for, without going as far as Duesenberry in reducing goods to the role of symbols of prestige in the affluent society, it is plain that his argument fully implies that the production of goods creates the want that the goods are presumed to satisfy.

The even more direct link between production and wants is provided by the institutions of modern advertising and salesmanship. These cannot be reconciled with the notion of independently determined desires, for their central function is to create desires—to bring into being wants that previously did not exist.* This is accomplished by the producer of the goods or at his behest. A broad empirical relationship exists between what is spent on production of consumers' goods and what is spent in synthesizing the desires for that production. A new consumer product must be introduced with a suitable advertising campaign to arouse an interest in it. The path for an expansion

---

*Advertising is not a simple phenomenon. It is also important in competitive strategy and want creation is, ordinarily, a complementary result of efforts to shift the demand curve of the individual firm at the expense of others or (less importantly, I think) to change its shape by increasing the degree of product differentiation. Some of the failure of economists to identify advertising with want creation may be attributed to the undue attention that its use in purely competitive strategy has attracted. It should be noted, however, that the competitive manipulation of consumer desire is only possible, at least on any appreciable scale, when such need is not strongly felt.

of output must be paved by a suitable expansion in the advertising budget. Outlays for the manufacturing of a product are not more important in the strategy of modern business enterprise than outlays for the manufacturing of demand for the product. None of this is novel. All would be regarded as elementary by the most retarded student in the nation's most primitive school of business administration. The cost of this want formation is formidable. In 1956 total advertising expenditure—though, as noted, not all of it may be assigned to the synthesis of wants—amounted to about ten billion dollars. For some years it had been increasing at a rate in excess of a billion dollars a year. Obviously, such outlays must be integrated with the theory of consumer demand. They are too big to be ignored.

But such integration means recognizing that wants are dependent on production. It accords to the producer the function both of making the goods and of making the desires for them. It recognizes that production, not only passively through emulation, but actively through advertising and related activities, creates the wants it seeks to satisfy.

The businessman and the lay reader will be puzzled over the emphasis which I give to a seemingly obvious point. The point is indeed obvious. But it is one which, to a singular degree, economists have resisted. They have sensed, as the layman does not, the damage to established ideas which lurks in these relationships. As a result, incredibly, they have closed their eyes (and ears) to the most obtrusive of all economic phenomena, namely modern want creation.

This is not to say that the evidence affirming the dependence of wants on advertising has been entirely ignored. It is one reason why advertising has so long been regarded with such uneasiness by economists. Here is something which cannot be accommodated easily to existing theory. More pervious scholars have speculated on the urgency of desires which are so obviously the fruit of such expensively contrived campaigns for popular attention. Is a new breakfast cereal or detergent so much wanted if so much must be spent to compel in the consumer demand the sense of want? But there has been little tendency to go on to examine the implications of this for the theory of consumer demand and even less for the importance of production and productive efficiency. These have remained sacrosanct. More often the uneasiness has been manifested in a general disapproval of advertising and advertising men, leading to the occasional suggestion that they shouldn't exist. Such suggestions have usually been ill received.

And so the notion of independently determined wants still survives. In the face of all the forces of modern salesmanship it still rules, almost undefiled, in the textbooks. And it still remains the economist's mission— and on few matters is the pedagogy so firm—to seek unquestioningly the means for filling these wants. This being so, production remains of prime urgency. We have here, perhaps, the ultimate triumph of the conventional wisdom in its resistance to the evidence of the eyes. To equal it one must imagine a humanitarian who was long ago persuaded of the grievous shortage of hospital facilities in the town. He continues to importune the passers-by for money for more beds and refuses to notice that the town doctor is deftly knocking over pedestrians with his car to keep up the occupancy.

And in unraveling the complex we should always be careful not to overlook the obvious. The fact that wants can be synthesized by advertising, catalyzed by salesmanship, and shaped by the discreet manipulations of the persuaders shows that they are not very urgent. A man who is hungry need never be told of his need for food. If he is inspired by his appetite, he is immune to the influence of Messrs. Batten, Barton, Durstine & Osborn. The latter are effective only with those who are so far removed from physical want that they do not already know what they want. In this state alone men are open to persuasion.

The general conclusion of these pages is of such importance for this essay that it had perhaps best be put with some formality. As a society becomes increasingly affluent, wants are increasingly created by the process by which they are satisfied. This may operate passively. Increases in consumption, the counterpart of increases in production, act by suggestion or emulation to create wants. Or producers may proceed actively to create wants through advertising and salesmanship. Wants thus come to depend on output. In technical terms it can no longer be assumed that welfare is greater at an all-round higher level of production than at a lower one. It may be the same. The higher level of production has, merely, a higher level of want creation necessitating a higher level of want satisfaction. There will be frequent occasion to refer to the way wants depend on the process by which they are satisfied. It will be convenient to call it the Dependence Effect.

We may now contemplate briefly the conclusions to which this analysis has brought us.

Plainly the theory of consumer demand is a peculiarly treacherous friend of the present goals of economics. At first glance it seems to defend the continuing urgency of production and our preoccupation with it as a goal. The economist does not enter into the dubious moral arguments about the importance or virtue of the wants to be satisfied. He doesn't pretend to compare mental states of the same or different people at different times and to suggest that one is less urgent than another. The desire is there. That for him is sufficient. He sets about in a workmanlike way to satisfy desire, and accordingly he sets the proper store by the production that does. Like woman's his work is never done.

But this rationalization, handsomely though it seems to serve, turns destructively on those who advance it once it is conceded that wants are themselves both passively and deliberately the fruits of the process by which they are satisfied. Then the production of goods satisfies the wants that the consumption of these goods creates or that the producers of goods synthesize. Production induces more wants and the need for more production. So far, in a major *tour de force*, the implications have been ignored. But this obviously is a perilous solution. It cannot long survive discussion.

Among the many models of the good society no one has urged the squirrel wheel. Moreover, as we shall see presently, the wheel is not one that revolves with perfect smoothness. Aside from its dubious cultural charm, there are serious structural weaknesses which may one day embarrass us.

THE BILL COLLECTOR COMETH

The situation is this. Production for the sake of the goods produced is no longer very urgent. The significance of marginal increments (or decrements) in the supply of goods is slight. We sustain a sense of urgency only because of attitudes that trace to the world not of today but into which economics was born. These are reinforced by an untenable theory of consumer demand, an obsolete, erroneous, and even somewhat dangerous identification of production with military power, and by a system of vested interests which marries both liberals and conservatives to the importance of production.

At the same time production does remain important and urgent for its effect on economic security. When men are unemployed, society does not miss the goods they do not produce. The loss here is marginal. But the men who are without work *do* miss the income they no longer earn. Here the effect is not marginal. It involves all or a large share of the men's earnings and hence all or a large share of what they are able to buy. And, we note, high and stable production is the broad foundation of the economic security of virtually every other group—of farmers, white collar workers, and both large businessmen and small. The depression also remains the major uncovered risk of the modern large corporation. It is for reasons of economic security that we must produce at capacity.

The simple conclusions will not be well regarded by the conventional wisdom. To urge the importance of production because of its bearing on economic security, and to suggest that the product is in any way incidental, is disturbing. It brings the economic society to the brink of the dubious world of make-work and boondoggling. One of the escapes from this world is to make all wants urgent, and no doubt we have here another reason for the obscurantist rationalization of consumer demand. It still seems more satisfactory to say that we need the goods than to stress the real point which is that social well-being and contentment require that we have enough production to provide income to the willing labor force. But if anyone has surviving doubts as to where the real priorities lie, let him apply a simple test. Let him assume that a President, or other candidate for re-election to major public office, has the opportunity of defending a large increase in man-hour productivity which has been divided equally between greatly increased total output and greatly increased unemployment. And let it be assumed that as an alternative he might choose unchanged productivity which has left everyone employed. That full employment is more desirable than increased production combined with unemployment would be clear alike to the most sophisticated and the most primitive politician.

The foregoing provides the basic rule of procedure for the remainder of this essay. It shows that we need not be much concerned with the supply of goods for their own sake. The urgencies here are founded not on substance but on myth. And, indeed, our ultimate purpose is to see the opportunities that emerge as this myth is dispelled. But in all this we must be exceedingly conscious of the importance of production for its bearing on the economic security of individuals. As a source of income for people its importance remains undiminished. This function of production must be carefully safeguarded.

But myth is rarely benign. And the system of illusions which causes us to attach such importance to production for its own sake is itself damaging or dangerous. One danger arises in the devices by which we fabricate wants and this, indeed nurtures a threat to the security of employment and income which production provides. Our failure to solve the problem of inflation is also the result of present attitudes toward the production of goods. And the way that present attitudes cause us to emphasize the supply of some as distinct from all goods and services is the source of deeper social dangers. To these problems, beginning with the dangers inherent in the present methods of manufacturing wants, the essay now turns.

. . . .

In a society in which the production and sale of goods seems sacrosanct there will be extreme hesitation over measures which will seem to restrain the financing of consumers' goods and hence their sale. Measures to prevent the competitive liberalization of consumer credit terms will encounter the heaviest resistance. When regarded in relation to the underlying interest in stability and economic security, such precautionary measures have a much stronger claim for attention. They promise to help keep the process of synthesizing demand and the purchasing power to make it effective from damaging the continuity of production and employment. The regulation of the terms and conditions of consumer credit, while it has been undertaken in the past in wartime, is not a power presently possessed by the United States government. It is, however, a commonplace in the United Kingdom.

However, the more substantial remedy lies deeper. Not all goods and services are subject to sale on the installment plan and to the attentions of the bill collector. Automobiles and radios and wall-to-wall carpeting are; the services of the schools, hospitals, and public libraries are not. To the extent that an economy concentrates its efforts on the first it will be subject to the vagaries of want-*cum*-debt creation. As it devotes it energies to serving itself with health, education, and other like services, it will reduce its danger. We have already seen that the preoccupation with production is a selective one. In particular it is heavily centered on those goods which by their character or by tradition are in the domain of private production. It concentrates energies, in other words, on producing the products which are subject to the greatest instability. It carries this indeed to the point where the manufacture of wants may itself be a tenuous process. A different arrangement for satisfying our needs—one, for example, that allotted a larger proportion of resources to those needs that are in the public domain—would thus be an important step toward stability. In one of the paradoxes with which economics is replete it might even, by contributing to the reliability of production, insure a greater total private product.

THE THEORY OF SOCIAL BALANCE

It is not till it is discovered that high individual incomes will not purchase the mass of mankind immunity from cholera, typhus, and ignorance, still less secure them the positive advantages of educational opportunity and economic security, that slowly and reluctantly, amid prophecies of moral degeneration and economic disaster, society begins to make collective provision for needs which no ordinary individual, even if he works overtime all his life, can provide himself.

—R. H. Tawney
Equality (4th revised ed.), pp. 134–35.

The final problem of the productive society is what it produces. This manifests itself in an implacable tendency to provide an opulent supply of some things and a niggardly yield of others. This disparity carries to the point where it is a cause of social discomfort and social unhealth. The line which divides our area of wealth from our area of poverty is roughly that which divides privately produced and marketed goods and services from publicly rendered services. Our wealth in the first is not only in startling contrast with the meagerness of the latter, but our wealth in privately produced goods is, to a marked degree, the cause of crisis in the supply of public services. For we have failed to see the importance, indeed the urgent need, of maintaining a balance between the two.

This disparity between our flow of private and public goods and services is no matter of subjective judgment. On the contrary, it is a source of the most extensive comment which only stops short of the direct contrast being made here. In the years following World War II, the papers of any major city—those of New York were an excellent example—told daily of the shortages and shortcomings in the elementary municipal and metropolitan services. The schools were old and overcrowded. The police force was under strength and underpaid. The parks and playgrounds were insufficient. Streets and empty lots were filthy, and the sanitation staff was underequipped and in need of men. Access to the city by those who work there was uncertain and painful and becoming more so. Internal transportation was overcrowded, unhealthful, and dirty. So was the air. Parking on the streets had to be prohibited, and there was no space elsewhere. These deficiencies were not in new and novel services but in old and established ones. Cities have long swept their streets, helped their people move around, educated them, kept order, and provided horse rails for vehicles which sought to pause. That their residents should have a nontoxic supply of air suggests no revolutionary dalliance with socialism.

The discussion of this public poverty competed, on the whole successfully, with the stories of ever-increasing opulence in privately produced goods. The Gross National Product was rising. So were retail sales. So was personal income. Labor productivity had also advanced. The automobiles that could not be parked were being produced at an expanded rate. The children, though without schools, subject in the playgrounds to the affectionate interest of adults with odd tastes, and disposed to increasingly imaginative forms of delinquency, were admirably equipped with television sets. We had difficulty finding storage space for the great surpluses of food despite a national disposition to obesity. Food was grown and packaged under private auspices. The care and refreshment of the mind, in contrast with the stomach, was principally in the public domain. Our colleges and universities were severely overcrowded and underprovided, and the same was true of the mental hospitals.

The contrast was and remains evident not alone to those who read. The family which takes its mauve and cerise air-conditioned, power-steered, and power-braked automobile out for a tour passes through cities that are badly paved, made hideous by litter, blighted buildings, billboards, and posts for wires that should long since have been put underground. They pass on into a countryside that has been rendered largely invisible by commercial art. (The goods which the latter advertise have an absolute priority in our value system. Such aesthetic considerations as a view of the countryside accordingly come second. On such matters we are consistent.) They picnic on exquisitely packaged food from a portable icebox by a polluted stream and go on to spend the night at a park which is a menace to public health and morals. Just before dozing off on an air mattress, beneath a nylon tent, amid the stench of decaying refuse, they may reflect vaguely on the curious unevenness of their blessings. Is this, indeed, the American genius?

ON SECURITY AND SURVIVAL

In our society the increased production of goods—privately produced goods—is, as we have seen, a basic measure of social achievement. This is partly the result of the great continuity of ideas which links the present with a world in which production indeed meant life. Partly it is a matter of vested interest. Partly it is a product of the elaborate obscurantism of the modern theory of consumer need. Partly it reflects an erroneous view of the problem of national security. And partly, we have seen, the preoccupation with production is forced quite genuinely upon us by tight nexus between production and economic security. However, it is a reasonable assumption that most people pressed to explain our concern for production—a pressure that is not often exerted—would be content to suggest that it serves the happiness of most men and women. That is sufficient.

The pursuit of happiness is admirable as a social goal. But the notion of happiness lacks philosophical exactitude; there is agreement neither on its substance nor its source. . . . A society has one higher task than to consider its goals, to reflect on its pursuit of happiness and harmony and its success in expelling pain, tension, sorrow, and the ubiquitous curse of ignorance. It must also, so far as this may be possible, insure its own survival.

The ideas with which this essay is concerned bear heavily on this considerable goal. The survival of a society rests on the same factors which make its survival worth while, for the simple but compelling reason that illusion is the enemy of both.

The nature of the deployment of the resources that would best serve our survival is beyond the scope of this essay. For myself I have little faith in the safety or security which derives from a never-ending arms race—from a competition to elaborate ever more agonizing weapons and to counter those of the enemy. If the possibility exists, the risks of negotiation and settlement, however great these may be, would still seem to provide a better prospect for survival than reliance on weapons which we can only hope are too terrible to use.

But whatever the paths to survival, the problem is the same. Were the Russians to disappear from the world, or become overnight as tractable as church mice, there would remain vast millions of hungry and discontented people in the world. Without the promise of relief from that hunger and privation, disorder would still be inevitable. The promise of such relief requires that we have available or usable resources. The requirement is, of course, much more urgent in a world in which differing economic and political systems are in competition.

Even when the arms race ends, as it must, the scientific and technological frontier will remain. Either as an aspect of international competition, or in pursuit of the esteem and satisfaction which go with discovery, we shall want to seek to cross it and be in on the crossing. In the field of consumer satisfaction, as we should by now agree, there is little on which one can fault the American performance. But this is not all and, as we should now, hopefully, also agree, an economy that is preoccupied however brilliantly with the production of private consumer products is supremely ill fitted for many of these frontier tasks. Under the best of circumstances its research will be related to these products rather than to knowledge. The conventional wisdom will provide impressive arguments to the contrary. No one should be fooled.

And not only does a great part of modern scientific work lie outside the scope of the market and private enterprise but so does a large area of application and development. Private enterprise did not get us atomic energy. It has shown relatively slight interest in its development for power for the reason that it could not clearly be fitted into commercial patterns of cost and profit. Though no one doubts the vigor with which it addresses itself to travel within the United States, General Motors has little interest in travel through space.

As matters now stand, we have almost no institutions that are by central design and purpose directed to participation in modern scientific and technological progress and its large-scale application. We have no organization capable, for example, of taking on the large-scale development of atomic power generators or radically new departures in passenger-carrying aircraft in advance of knowledge that these will be commercially feasible. Much has been accomplished by research and development, not immediately subject to commercial criteria, under the inspiration of military need. This has done more to save us from the partial technological stagnation that is inherent in a consumers' goods economy than we imagine. But it is also a narrow and perilous prop, and it has the further effect of associating great and exciting scientific advances with an atmosphere of fear and even terror.

Nor is this all. The day will not soon come when the problems of either the world or our own polity are solved. Since we do not know the shape of the problems we do not know the requirements for solution. But one thing is tolerably certain. Whether the problem be that of a burgeoning population and of space in which to live with peace and grace, or whether it be the depletion of the materials which nature has stocked in the earth's crust and which have been drawn upon more heavily in this century than in all previous time together, or whether it be that of occupying minds no longer committed to the stockpiling of consumer goods, the basic demand on America will be on its resources of ability, intelligence, and education. The test will be less the effectiveness of our material investment than the effectiveness of our investment in men. We live in a day of grandiose generalization. This one can be made with confidence.

Education, no less than national defense or foreign assistance, is in the public domain. It is subject to the impediments to resource allocation between private and public use. So, once again, our hope for survival, security, and contentment returns us to the problem of guiding resources to the most urgent ends.

To furnish a barren room is one thing. To continue to crowd in furniture until the foundation buckles is quite another. To have failed to solve the problem of producing goods would have been to continue man in his oldest and most grievous misfortune. But to fail to see that we have solved it and to fail to proceed thence to the next task, would be fully as tragic.

6

The Dialogue That
Never Happens

Raymond A. Bauer
Stephen A. Greyser

In recent years government and business spokesmen alike have advocated
a "dialogue" between their two groups for the reduction of friction and
the advancement of the general good. Yet, all too often, this is a dialogue
that never happens. Rather, what passes for dialogue *in form* is often a
sequence of monologues *in fact*, wherein each spokesman merely grants
"equal time" to the other and pretends to listen while preparing his
own next set of comments. Obviously, this is not always the case; and,
if taken literally, it tends to minimize some real progress being made.

Our aim here is to try to facilitate and stimulate that progress
by exploring what lies behind the dialogue that never happens and by
suggesting what can be done—on both sides—to develop more meaningful and effective business-government interactions.

In this context, we link "government spokesmen" with "critics."
Naturally, not all in government are critics of business, and vice versa.
However, almost all critics seek redress of their grievances via government action and seek government spokesmen to present their views
"in behalf of the public."

Reprinted by permission from *Harvard Business Review*, Vol. 45 (November–December 1967),
pp. 2-4, 6, 8, 10, 12, 186, 188, and 190. Copyright © 1967 by the President and Fellows of
Harvard College; all rights reserved.

Raymond A. Bauer is professor of business administration at the Harvard Business School.
He received a B.S. degree from Northwestern University, and his M.A. and Ph.D. from Harvard,
with social anthropology as his area of specialization. He has written texts on American business and public policies and on advertising from the consumer point of view, including *Advertising in America*. Dr. Bauer is past president of the Association for Public Opinion Research.

Stephen A. Greyser is also professor of business administration at the Harvard Business School,
where he teaches advertising and is executive director of the Marketing Science Institute. His
M.B.A. and D.B.A. are from Harvard. He co-authored *Advertising in America* with R. A. Bauer
and is a frequent contributor to scholarly journals on issues of marketing, advertising, and
public policy.

Our primary focus will be in the field of marketing—particularly selling and advertising—which is perhaps the most controversial and most frequently criticized single zone of business. Marketing seems to be the area where achieving true dialogue is most difficult and where business and government spokesmen most seem to talk past each other.

Before examining why this takes place, let us look at two comments on advertising that illustrate the lack of dialogue. The first comment is that of Donald F. Turner, Assistant Attorney General in charge of the Antitrust Division of the Justice Department:

> There are three steps to informed choice: (1) the consumer must know the product exists; (2) the consumer must know how the product performs; and (3) he must know how it performs compared to other products. If advertising only performs step one and appeals on other than a performance basis, informed choice cannot be made.[1]

The other comment is that of Charles L. Gould, Publisher, the San Francisco *Examiner:*

> No government agency, no do-gooders in private life can possibly have as much interest in pleasing the consuming public as do . . . successful companies. For, in our economy, their lives literally depend on keeping their customers happy.[2]

DOUBLE-ENTENDRES

Why do business and government spokesmen talk past each other in discussing ostensibly the same marketplace? We think it is because each has a basically different model of the consumer world in which marketing operates. This misunderstanding grows from different perceptions about a number of key words.

The first word is *competition*. The critics of business think of competition tacitly as strictly price differentiation. Modern businessmen, however, as marketing experts frequently point out, think of competition primarily in terms of product differentiation, sometimes via physical product developments and sometimes via promotional themes. The important thing is that price competition plays a relatively minor role in today's marketplace.

Some of the perplexity between these two views of competition has to do with confusion over a second word, *product*. In the critic's

---

[1] Statement made at the Ninth Annual American Federation of Advertising Conference on Government Relations held in Washington, D.C., February 1967.
[2] *Ibid.*

view, a product is the notion of some entity which has a primary identifiable function only. For example, an automobile is a device for transporting bodies, animate or inanimate; it ordinarily has four wheels and a driver, and is powered by gasoline. There are variants on this formula (three-wheeled automobiles) which are legitimate, provided the variants serve the same function. Intuitively the businessman knows there is something wrong with this notion of the product because the product's secondary function may be his major means of providing differentiation (an auto's looks, horsepower, and so on).

Then there is the term *consumer needs,* which the business critic sees as corresponding to a product's primary function—for example, needs for transportation, nutrition, recreation (presumably for health purposes), and other things. The businessman, on the other hand, sees needs as virtually *any* consumer lever he can use to differentiate his product.

Next, there is the notion of *rationality.* The critic, with a fixed notion of "needs" and "product," sees any decision that results in an efficient matching of product to needs as rational. The businessman, taking no set position on what a person's needs should be, contends that any decision the customer makes to serve his own perceived self-interest is rational.

The last addition to our pro tem vocabulary is *information.* The critic fits information neatly into his view that a rational decision is one which matches product function and consumer needs, rather circularly defined as the individual's requirement for the function the product serves. Any information that serves that need is "good" information. To the businessman, information is basically any data or argument that will (truthfully) put forth the attractiveness of a product in the context of the consumer's own buying criteria.

Exhibit 1 summarizes our views of these two different models of the consumer world. We realize that we may have presented a somewhat exaggerated dichotomy. But we think the models are best demonstrated by this delineation of the pure views of contrasting positions, recognizing that both sides modify them to some extent.

VIEWS OF HUMAN NATURE

A review of our "vocabulary with a double meaning" and the two models of the consumer world shows that the critic's view is based on a conviction that he knows what "should be." In contrast, the businessman's view is based on militant agnosticism with regard to "good" or "bad" value judgments which might be made (by anyone) about individual marketplace transactions.

The businessman's view of human nature may be the more flattering, perhaps excessively so. Certainly, the marketer's notion of "consumer sovereignty" compliments the consumer in attributing to him the capacity to decide what he needs and to make his choice competently even under exceedingly complex circumstances. It also sometimes challenges him to do so. This perhaps undeserved flattery glosses over some obvious flaws in the market mechanism. It is rooted in the belief that this mechanism, even though imperfect in specific instances, is better than administrative procedures for regulating the market.

The critic takes a far less optimistic view of human nature—both the consumer's and the seller's. He thinks that the seller often (sometimes intentionally) confuses consumers with a welter of one-sided argumentation. Such information, in the critic's eye, not only lacks impartiality, but usually focuses on secondary product functions and is not geared to consumer needs.

Both sets of assumptions are, we think, at least partially justified. Customers do have limited information and limited capacity to process it. This is the way of the world. Furthermore, there is no reason to believe that every seller has every customer's interest as his own primary concern in every transaction, even though in the long run it probably is in the seller's own best interest to serve every customer well.

EXHIBIT 1. *Two Different Models of the Consumer World*

Key words	Critic's view	Businessman's view
Competition	Price competition	Product differentiation
Product	Primary function only	Differentiation through secondary function
Consumer needs	Correspond point-for-point to primary functions	Any customer desire on which the product can be differentiated
Rationality	Efficient matching of product to customer needs	Any customer decision that serves the customer's own perceived self-interest
Information	Any data that facilitate the fit of a product's proper function with the customer's needs.	Any data that will (truthfully) put forth the attractiveness of the product in the eyes of the customer

All of this disagreement comes to focus on a point where both business and government are in agreement; namely, modern products are sufficiently complex that the individual consumer is in a rather poor position to judge their merits quickly and easily. The businessman says that the customer should be, and often is, guided in his judgment by knowledge of brand reputation and manufacturer integrity, both of which are enhanced by advertising. The critic argues that the customer should be, but too seldom is, aided by impartial information sources primarily evaluating product attributes.

These conflicting views of vocabulary and human nature are reflected in several specific topic areas.

BRANDS AND RATING SERVICES

One of these areas is the relationship of national branding to consumer rating services, the latter being a traditional source of "impartial information" for consumers. Somehow the crux of this relationship seems to have escaped most people's attention: Consumer rating services are possible *only because* of the existence of a limited number of brands for a given product. In order for a rating to be meaningful, two conditions are necessary:

1. *Identifiability*—the consumer must be able to recognize the products and brands rated.
2. *Uniformity*—manufacturers must habitually produce products of sufficiently uniform quality that consumer and rating service alike can learn enough from a sample of the product to say or think something meaningful about another sample of the same product which may be bought in some other part of the country at some later time. This is a seldom realized aspect of national branding.

It is generally assumed by both groups that the "consumer movement" is basically opposed to heavily advertised branded goods. The stereotype of *Consumer Reports* is that it regularly aims at shunting trade away from national brands to Sears, to Montgomery Ward, or to minor brands. Yet the one study made of this issue showed that, contrary to the stereotype, *Consumer Reports* had consistently given higher ratings to the heavily advertised national brands than to their competitors.[3]

---

[3] Eugene R. Beem and John S. Ewing, "Business Appraises Consumer Testing Agencies," *Harvard Business Review*, Vol. 32 (March–April 1954), pp. 113–126, especially p. 121.

What we have here is an instance of the consumer movement and brand-name manufacturers being ideologically blinded by different models of the market world. The consumer movement concentrates on the notion of a product having a definable primary function that should take precedence over virtually all other attributes of the product. True, some concessions have recently been made to aesthetics. But, on the whole, the consumer movement is suspicious of the marketing world that strives to sell products on the basis of secondary attributes which the consumer movement itself regards with a jaundiced eye.

The evidence available to the consumer movement is that, in general, national advertising is *not* accompanied by poorer performance on primary criteria. But the consumer movement fails to realize that it *takes for granted* the central claim for advertised branded products—namely, that by being identifiable and uniform in quality, they offer the customer an opportunity to make his choice on the basis of his confidence in a particular manufacturer.

But the manufacturers of nationally branded products and their spokesmen have been equally blind. First of all, we know of none who has pointed out the extent to which any form of consumer rating must be based on the identifiability and uniformity of branded products. The only situation where this does not apply is when the rating service can instruct the consumer in how to evaluate the product—for example, looking for marbleizing in beef. However, this is limited to products of such a nature that the customer can, with but little help, evaluate them for himself, it cannot apply to products for which he has to rely on the technical services of an independent evaluator or on the reputation of the manufacturer.

Moreover, except for such big-ticket items as automobiles, consumer rating services usually test products only once in several years. In other words, they rate not only a *sample* of a manufacturer's products but also a sample of his performance *over time*. Thus, if one "follows the ratings" and buys an air conditioner or a toaster this year, he may buy it on the rating of a product made one, two, or three years ago. Similarly, if one buys a new automobile, he depends in part on the repair record (reported by at least one rating service) for previous models of that brand.

In large part, then, consumer rating services are devices for rating *manufacturers!* This is not to say they do not rate specific products. Sometimes they even draw fine distinctions between different models from the same company. But in the course of rating products, they also rate manufacturers. What more could the manufacturer ask for? Is this not what he claims he strives for?

Basic Dichotomy

More to the point, what is it that has kept the consumer movement and brand-name manufacturers from paying attention to this area of shared overlapping interests? Neither will quarrel with the exposure either of factual deception or of product weaknesses on dimensions that both agree are essential to the product. This is not where the problem is. The problem is that the manufacturer *sells* one thing and the rating service *rates* another.

The concept of a "product" that dominates the thinking of rating services and the thought processes of those who suggest more "impartial evaluation information" for consumers (e.g., Donald Turner of the Department of Justice and Congressman Benjamin Rosenthal of New York) is that a product is an entity with a single, primary, specifiable function—or, in the case of some products, such as food, perhaps a limited number of functions, e.g., being nutritious, tasty, and visually appealing. The specific goal of many proposed ratings—with their emphasis on the physical and technical characteristics of products—is to free the customer from the influence of many needs to which the marketer addresses himself, mostly particularly the desire for ego enhancement, social acceptance, and status.

The marketer, oddly enough, tends to accept a little of the critics' view of what a product is. Marketing texts, too, speak of primary and secondary functions of a product as though it were self-evident that the aesthetic ego-gratifying, and status-enhancing aspects of the product were hung on as an afterthought. If this is true, why are Grecian vases preserved to be admired for their beauty? And why did nations of yore pass sumptuary laws to prevent people from wearing clothes inappropriate to their status?

We shall shortly explore what may lie behind this confusion about the nature of products. First, however, let us examine another topical area in which similar confusion exists.

"MATERIALIST SOCIETY"

The selling function in business is regularly evaluated by social commentators in relationship to the circumstance that ours is a "materialist society." We could say we do not understand what people are talking about when they refer to a materialist society, beyond the fact that our society does possess a lot of material goods. But, in point of fact, we think *they* do not understand what they are talking about. Let us elucidate.

At first hearing, one might conclude that criticism of a materialist society is a criticism of the extent to which people spend their resources of time, energy, and wealth on the acquisition of material things. One of the notions that gets expressed is that people should be more interested in pursuing nonmaterial goals.

The perplexing matter is, however, that the criticism becomes strongest on the circumstance that people *do* pursue nonmaterial goals—such as ego enhancement, psychic security, social status, and so on—but use material goods as a means of achieving them. Perhaps the distinctive feature of our society is the extent to which *material* goods are used to attain *nonmaterial* goals.

Now there are many ways in which societies satisfy such needs. For example, there are ways of attaining status that do not involve material goods of any substance. Most societies grant status to warriors and other heroes, to wise men who have served the society, and so on. Often the external manifestation of this status is rigidly prescribed and involves signs whose material worth is insignificant: A hero wears a medal, a ribbon in his lapel, or a certain type of headdress, or he may be addressed by an honorific title.

However, in societies that value economic performance, it is not uncommon for material goods to be used as status symbols. Indians of the Southwest, for example, favor sheep as a symbol even to the extent of overtaxing the grazing lands and lowering the economic status of the tribe. As a practical matter, this might be more damaging to the welfare of the Navaho than is the damage that many low-income Negroes do to their own individual welfares when, as research shows, they insist on serving a premium-priced brand of scotch.

Many of the things about which there is complaint are not self-evidently bad. Art collecting is generally considered a "good thing." But take the worst instance of a person who neurotically seeks self-assurance by buying art objects. Clinically, one might argue that he would do himself a lot more long-run good with psychotherapy even though, when one considers the resale value of the art objects, he may have taken the more economical course of action. Similarly, it is not self-evident that the promotion of toiletries to the youth as a symbol of transition to manhood is inherently cruel—unless the commercials are especially bad! It is clear, however, that there is no societal consensus that the transition to manhood should be symbolized by the use of toiletries.

What seems to be the nub of the criticism of our society as a materialist one is that simultaneously a great number of nonmaterial goals are served by material goods, and there is no consensus that this should be so. Behind this is our old friend (or enemy): the concept of a product as serving solely a primary function. In the perspective of history and of other societies, this is a rather peculiar notion. Who in a primitive society would contend that a canoe paddle should not be carved artistically, or that a chief should not have a more elaborate paddle than a commoner?

Much of the confusion over the words on our list seems to be a residue of the early age of mass production. The production engineer, faced with the task of devising ways to turn out standardized products at low cost, had to ask himself, "What are the irreducible elements of this product?" This was probably best epitomized in Henry Ford's concept of the automobile, and his comment that people could have any color they wanted so long as it was black. Clearly, Ford thought it was immoral even to nourish the thought that a product ought to look good, let alone that it should serve various psychic and social functions.

But all this was closely related to the mass producer's effort to find the irreducible essence of what he manufactured. This effort broke up the natural organic integrity of products, which, at almost all times in all societies, have served multiple functions.

Many writers have called attention to the fact that in recent times our society has passed from the period of simple-minded mass production to that of product differentiation on attributes beyond the irreducible primary function. As yet, however, we do not think there is adequate appreciation of the impact of the residue of the early period of mass production on thinking about what a product is. In that period even very complex products were converted into commodities. Since each performed essentially the same primary function, the chief means of competition was pricing.

PRODUCTS AS COMMODITIES

At this point, we shall argue that the thinking of those who criticize the selling function is based on a model for the marketing of commodities. This factor does not exhaust the criticism, but we believe it is at the core of present misunderstandings over the concepts on which we have focused our discussion.

On the one hand, to the extent that products are commodities, it is possible to specify the function or functions which all products in that category should serve. It follows that a person who buys and uses such a commodity for some purpose other than for what it was intended has indeed done something odd, although perhaps useful to him (for example, baseball catchers who use foam-rubber "falsies" to pad their mitts). In any event, it is possible both to specify the basis on which the commodity should be evaluated and the information a person is entitled to have in order to judge that product. A person searching for a commodity ought first to find out whether it serves this function and then to ask its price.

On the other hand, to the extent that products are *not* commodities, it is impossible to expect that price competition will necessarily be the main basis of competition. Likewise, it is impossible to specify what information is needed or what constitutes rational behavior. Is it rational for a person to buy toothpaste because its advertiser claims it has "sex appeal"? Presumably people would rather look at clean than dingy teeth, and presumably people also like to have sex appeal—at least up to the point where it gets to be a hazard or a nuisance.

But it does not follow, insofar as we can see, that ratings—or grade labeling—should discourage product differentiation or the promotion of products on a noncommodity basis. If the consumer were assured that all products in a given rating category performed their primary functions about equally well, could it not be argued that those attributes which differentiate the products on other functions would then become increasingly interesting and important? Or, to be more specific, what makes it possible for "instant-on" TV tuning to be promoted—other than a presumed agreement, by both manufacturer and consumers, that the TV set performs its primary function little better or worse than its competition?

This is a facet of competition not appreciated by the opponents of grade-labeling, who have argued that it would reduce competition. Perhaps it would be more helpful if the opponents of grade labeling first gathered some evidence on what has actually happened to competition in countries where grade labeling has been introduced. (The head of one major relevant trade association recently told one of us that he knew of no such research.)

TOWARD MORE INFORMATION

Readers will note that we have indulged in considerable speculation in this article. But most of the issues on which we have speculated are researchable. Relatively little, for example, is really known about how businesses actually see themselves carrying out "the practice of competition," or even about the actual competitive mechanisms of setting prices. Furthermore, in all of this, there is no mention of the *consumer's* view of these various concepts or of his model of the marketing process. To be sure, we can be reasonably certain of some things. For example, we know that consumers do regard products as serving needs beyond the bare essentials. Yet it would be helpful to know far more about their views of the overall marketing process.

What we propose as a worthwhile endeavor is an independent assessment of the consumer's view of the marketing process, focusing on information needs from his point of view. Thus, rather than businessmen lamenting the critics' proposals for product-rating systems and the critics bemoaning what seem to be obvious abuses of marketing tools, both sides ought to move toward proposing an information system for the consumer that takes into account *his* needs and *his* information-handling capacities while still adhering to the realities of the marketing process.

For those who have the reading habit, it will be obvious that this proposal is but an extension of the conclusions reached by members of the American Marketing Association's Task Force on "Basic Problems in Marketing" for the improvement of relations between marketing and government.[4] In brief, along with suggested studies on the influence of government policies and programs on corporate marketing decisions, a special study was recommended in the area of consumer-buyer decision-making and behavior:

> It is of the highest importance to investigate the impacts of the host of governmental regulations, facilities, aids, and interventions upon the quality and efficiency of consumer-buyer decision-making.[5]

The report went on to state that, particularly in light of the generally recognized drift from *caveat emptor* toward *caveat venditor*, "abundant basic research opportunities and needs exist" in the area of government impact and consumer-buyer behavior.

WHAT CAN BUSINESSMEN DO?

Certainly there is a crying need for more information and, as we have tried to illustrate, for fresh analytic thinking on almost all of the issues

---

[4] See E. T. Grether and Robert J. Holloway, "Impact of Government upon the Market System," *Journal of Marketing,* Vol. 31 (April 1967), pp. 1-5; and Seymour Banks, "Commentary on Impact of Government upon the Market System," ibid., pp. 5-7.

[5] Grether and Holloway, *Ibid.,* p. 5.

on which government and business are butting heads. We have elaborated on the different models of how the marketplace does, and should, work because we think their existence explains the largest part of why marketers and their critics often talk past each other, even when they have the best intentions of engaging in a dialogue. The other part is explained by the relative absence of facts. As we have noted, the consumer's view of the market-advertising process and his informational needs represent an important (and relatively unprobed) research area.

Returning to the "dialogue," we should add a further problem beyond that of business and government spokesmen talking past one another. Inasmuch as many on both sides see themselves as representing their colleagues' views, partisanship becomes mixed with the aforementioned misunderstanding. Since such partisanship is likely to address itself to stereotyped views of "the other side," the comments become irrelevant. That many well-qualified firsthand commentators are regarded as self-serving by their critics is a point aptly made by Denis Thomas. Equally apt is his corollary observation that those "who view business . . . from a suitably hygenic distance lose no marks for partiality even if their facts are wrong."[6]

How then can effective interactions take place? Obviously, the key parts will be played by:

1. Thoughtful business and government leaders.
2. Marketers and their critics who take the time to consider and to understand (even if they do not agree with) each others' premises and assumptions.
3. Those who engage in meaningful dialogue oriented to fact finding rather than fault finding.
4. Those on both sides who address themselves to solving the problems of the real, rather than the presumed, public.

Beyond the parts played by thoughtful business and government people, we see a distinctive role for schools of business in bringing about meaningful interaction. Business schools are a unique resource both in their understanding of the business system and in their capability to conduct relevant research. Other faculties, at least equally competent and objective in research, generally do not have the depth of understanding of why things are the way they are—a necessary precursor to relevant study. We hasten to add that grasping how something *does* operate implies no consent that this is how it *should* operate, now or in the future.

Both in research and as participants (or moderators) in dialogue, business school faculties can play a significant role.

Business and government should sponsor the necessary research.

---

[6] *The Visible Persuaders* (London: Hutchinson, 1967), p. 11.

The particular need for business is to recognize that the era of exclusively partisan pleading must end. . . . Academic "insurance" of the objective conduct of the research and presentation of findings should bring about a degree of governmental acceptance and set the standard for any subsequent research.

We can use more of this, and more of it is beginning to take place. A dialogue is always most profitable when the parties have something to talk about.

7

Broadening the Concept of Marketing

Philip Kotler
Sidney J. Levy

The term "marketing" connotes to most people a function peculiar to business firms. Marketing is seen as the task of finding and stimulating buyers for the firm's output. It involves product development, pricing, distribution, and communication; and in the more progressive firms, continuous attention to the changing needs of customers and the development of new products, with product modifications and services to meet these needs. But whether marketing is viewed in the old sense of "pushing" products or in the new sense of "customer satisfaction engineering," it is almost always viewed and discussed as a business activity.

It is the authors' contention that marketing is a pervasive societal activity that goes considerably beyond the selling of toothpaste, soap, and steel. Political contests remind us that candidates are marketed as well as soap; student recruitment by colleges reminds us that higher education is marketed; and fund raising reminds us that "causes" are marketed. Yet these areas of marketing are typically ignored by the student of marketing. Or they are treated cursorily as public relations or publicity activities. No attempt is made to incorporate these phenomena

"Broadening the Concept of Marketing," by Philip Kotler and Sidney J. Levy. Reprinted from the *Journal of Marketing* (January 1969), pp. 10-15, published by the American Marketing Association. This article received the 1969 Alpha Kappa Psi award as outstanding article of the year.

Philip Kotler, Harold T. Martin professor of marketing at Northwestern University, received his Ph.D. in economics from Massachusetts Institute of Technology. He did post doctoral work in mathematics and behavioral sciences at Harvard and the University of Chicago respectively. His articles have appeared in numerous scholarly journals; several have won best article awards. His *Marketing Management: Analysis, Planning and Control* is widely used.

Sidney J. Levy is professor of marketing at Northwestern University and vice president of Social Research, Inc. He earned his Ph.D. in psychology at the University of Chicago. He is the author of *Promotion: A Behavioral View* and many articles.

in the body proper of marketing thought and theory. No attempt is made to redefine the meaning of product development, pricing, distribution, and communication in these newer contexts to see if they have a useful meaning. No attempt is made to examine whether the principles of "good" marketing in traditional product areas are transferable to the marketing of services, persons, and ideas.

The authors see a great opportunity for marketing people to expand their thinking and to apply their skills to an increasingly interesting range of social activity. The challenge depends on the attention given to it; marketing will either take on a broader social meaning or remain a narrowly defined business activity.

THE RISE OF ORGANIZATIONAL MARKETING

One of the most striking trends in the United States is the increasing amount of society's work being performed by organizations other than business firms. As a society moves beyond the stage where shortages of food, clothing, and shelter are the major problems, it begins to organize to meet other social needs that formerly had been put aside. Business enterprises remain a dominant type of organization, but other types of organizations gain in conspicuousness and in influence. Many of these organizations become enormous and require the same rarefied management skills as traditional business organizations. Managing the United Auto Workers, Defense Department, Ford Foundation, World Bank, Catholic Church, and University of California has become every bit as challenging as managing Procter and Gamble, General Motors, and General Electric. These nonbusiness organizations have an increasing range of influence, affect as many livelihoods, and occupy as much media prominence as major business firms.

All of these organizations perform the classic business functions. Every organization must perform a financial function insofar as money must be raised, managed, and budgeted according to sound business principles. Every organization must perform a production function in that it must conceive of the best way of arranging inputs to produce the outputs of the organization. Every organization must perform a personnel function in that people must be hired, trained, assigned, and promoted in the course of the organization's work. Every organization must perform a purchasing function in that it must acquire materials in an efficient way through comparing and selecting sources of supply.

When we come to the marketing function, it is also clear that every organization performs marketing-like activities whether or not they are recognized as such. Several examples can be given.

The police department of a major U.S. city, concerned with the poor image it has among an important segment of its population, developed a campaign to "win friends and influence people." One highlight of this campaign is a "visit your police station" day in which tours are conducted to show citizens the daily operations of the police department, including the crime laboratories, police lineups, and cells. The police department also sends officers to speak at public schools and carries out a number of other activities to improve its community relations.

Most museum directors interpret their primary responsibility as "the proper preservation of an artistic heritage for posterity."[1] As a result, for many people museums are cold marble mausoleums that house miles of relics that soon give way to yawns and tired feet. Although museum attendance in the United States advances each year, a large number of citizens are uninterested in museums. Is this indifference due to failure in the manner of presenting what museums have to offer? This nagging question led the new director of the Metropolitan Museum of Art to broaden the museum's appeal through sponsoring contemporary art shows and "happenings." His marketing philosophy of museum management led to substantial increases in the Met's attendance.

The public school system in Oklahoma City sorely needed more public support and funds to prevent a deterioration of facilities and exodus of teachers. It recently resorted to television programming to dramatize the work the public schools were doing to fight the high school dropout problem, to develop new teaching techniques, and to enrich the children. Although an expensive medium, television quickly reached large numbers of parents whose response and interest were tremendous.

Nations also resort to international marketing campaigns to get across important points about themselves to the citizens of other countries. The junta of Greek colonels who seized power in Greece in 1967 found the international publicity surrounding their cause to be extremely unfavorable and potentially disruptive of international recognition. They hired a major New York public relations firm and soon full-page newspaper ads appeared carrying the headline "Greece Was Saved From Communism," detailing in small print why the takeover was necessary for the stability of Greece and the world.[2]

---

[1] This is the view of Sherman Lee, Director of the Cleveland Museum, quoted in *Newsweek*, Vol. 71 (April 1, 1968), p. 55.

[2] "PR for Colonels," *Newsweek*, Vol. 71 (March 18, 1968), p. 70.

An anti-cigarette group in Canada is trying to press the Canadian legislature to ban cigarettes on the grounds that they are harmful to health. There is widespread support for this cause but the organization's funds are limited, particularly measured against the huge advertising resources of the cigarette industry. The group's problem is to find effective ways to make a little money go a long way in persuading influential legislators of the need for discouraging cigarette consumption. This group has come up with several ideas for marketing antismoking to Canadians, including television spots, a paperback book featuring pictures of cancer and heart disease patients, and legal research on company liability for the smoker's loss of health.

What concepts are common to these and many other possible illustrations of organizational marketing? All of these organizations are concerned about their "product" in the eyes of certain "consumers" and are seeking to find "tools" for furthering their acceptance. Let us consider each of these concepts in general organizational terms.

Products

Every organization produces a "product" of at least one of the following types:

Physical products. "Product" first brings to mind everyday items like soap, clothes, and food, and extends to cover millions of *tangible* items that have a market value and are available for purchase.

Services. Services are *intangible* goods that are subject to market transaction such as tours, insurance, consultation, hairdos, and banking.

Persons. Personal marketing is an endemic *human* activity, from the employee trying to impress his boss to the statesman trying to win the support of the public. With the advent of mass communications, the marketing of persons has been turned over to professionals. Hollywood stars have their press agents, political candidates their advertising agencies, and so on.

Organizations. Many organizations spend a great deal of time marketing themselves. The Republican Party has invested considerable thought and resources in trying to develop a modern look. The American Medical Association decided recently that it needed to launch a campaign to improve the image of the American doctor.[3] Many charitable

---

[3] "Doctors Try an Image Transplant," *Business Week*, No. 2025 (June 22, 1968), p. 64.

organizations and universities see selling their *organization* as their primary responsibility.

Ideas. Many organizations are mainly in the business of selling *ideas* to the larger society. Population organizations are trying to sell the idea of birth control, and the Women's Christian Temperance Union is still trying to sell the idea of prohibition.

Thus the "product" can take many forms, and this is the first crucial point in the case for broadening the concept of marketing.

Consumers

The second crucial point is that organizations must deal with many groups that are interested in their products and can make a difference in its success. It is vitally important to the organization's success that it be sensitive to, serve, and satisfy these groups. One set of groups can be called the *suppliers. Suppliers* are those who provide the management group with the inputs necessary to perform its work and develop its product effectively. Suppliers include employees, vendors of the materials, banks, advertising agencies, and consultants.

The other set of groups are the *consumers* of the organization's product, of which four sub-groups can be distinguished. The *clients* are those who are the immediate consumers of the organization's product. The clients of a business firm are its buyers and potential buyers; of a service organization those receiving the services, such as the needy (from the Salvation Army) or the sick (from County Hospital); and of a protective or a primary organization, the members themselves. The second group is the *trustees* or *directors,* those who are vested with the legal authority and responsibility for the organization, oversee the management, and enjoy a variety of benefits from the "product." The third group is the active *publics* that take a specific interest in the organization. For a business firm, the active publics include consumer rating groups, governmental agencies, and pressure groups of various kinds. For a university, the active publics include alumni and friends of the university, foundations, and city fathers. Finally, the fourth consumer group is the *general public.* These are all the people who might develop attitudes toward the organization that might affect its conduct in some way. Organizational marketing concerns the programs designed by management to create satisfactions and favorable attitudes in the organization's four consuming groups: clients, trustees, active publics, and general public.

Students of business firms spend much time studying the various tools under the firm's control that affect product acceptance: product improvement, pricing, distribution, and communication. All of these tools have counterpart applications to nonbusiness organizational activity.

Nonbusiness organizations to various degrees engage in product improvement, especially when they recognize the competition they face from other organizations. Thus, over the years churches have added a host of nonreligious activities to their basic religious activities to satisfy members seeking other bases of human fellowship. Universities keep updating their curricula and adding new student services in an attempt to make the educational experience relevant to the students. Where they have failed to do this, students have sometimes organized their own courses and publications, or have expressed their dissatisfaction in organized protest. Government agencies such as license bureaus, police forces, and taxing bodies are often not responsive to the public because of monopoly status; but even here citizens have shown an increasing readiness to protest mediocre services, and more alert bureaucracies have shown a growing interest in reading the user's needs and developing the required product services.

All organizations face the problem of pricing their products and services so that they cover costs. Churches charge dues, universities charge tuition, governmental agencies charge fees, fund-raising organizations send out bills. Very often specific product charges are not sufficient to meet the organization's budget, and it must rely on gifts and surcharges to make up the difference. Opinions vary as to how much the users should be charged for the individual services and how much should be made up through general collection. If the university increases its tuition, it will have to face losing some students and putting more students on scholarship. If the hospital raises its charges to cover rising costs and additional services, it may provoke a reaction from the community. All organizations face complex pricing issues although not all of them understand good pricing practice.

Distribution is a central concern to the manufacturer seeking to make his goods conveniently accessible to buyers. Distribution also can be an important marketing decision area for nonbusiness organizations. A city's public library has to consider the best means of making its books available to the public. Should it establish one large library with an extensive collection of books, or several neighborhood branch libraries with duplication of books? Should it use bookmobiles that bring the books to the customers instead of relying exclusively on the customers coming to the books? Should it distribute through school libraries? Similarly the police department of a city must think through the problem of distributing its protective services efficiently through the community. It has to determine how much protective service to allocate to different neighborhoods; the respective merits of squad cars, motorcycles, and foot patrolmen; and the positioning of emergency phones.

Customer communication is an essential activity of all organizations although many nonmarketing organizations often fail to accord it the importance it deserves. Managements of many organizations think they have fully met their communication responsibilities by setting up advertising and/or public relations departments. They fail to realize that *everything about an organization talks.* Customers form impressions of an organization from its physical facilities, employees, officers, stationery, and a hundred other company surrogates. Only when this is appreciated do the members of the organization recognize that they all are in marketing, whatever else they do. With this understanding they can assess realistically the impact of their activities on the consumers.

CONCEPTS FOR EFFECTIVE MARKETING MANAGEMENT IN NONBUSINESS ORGANIZATIONS

Although all organizations have products, markets, and marketing tools, the art and science of effective marketing management have reached their highest state of development in the business type of organization. Business organizations depend on customer goodwill for survival and have generally learned how to sense and cater to their needs effectively. As other types of organizations recognize their marketing roles, they will turn increasingly to the body of marketing principles worked out by business organizations and adapt them to their own situations.

What are the main principles of effective marketing management as they appear in most forward-looking business organizations? Nine concepts stand out as crucial in guiding the marketing effort of a business organization.

Generic Product Definition

Business organizations have increasingly recognized the value of placing a broad definition on their products, one that emphasizes the basic customer need(s) being served. A modern soap company recognizes that its basic product is cleaning, not soap; a cosmetics company sees its basic product as beauty or hope, not lipsticks and makeup; a publishing company sees its basic product as information, not books.

The same need for a broader definition of its business is incumbent upon nonbusiness organizations if they are to survive and grow. Churches at one time tended to define their product narrowly as that of producing religious services for members. Recently, most churchmen have decided that their basic product is human fellowship. There was a time when educators said that their product was the three R's. Now most of them define their product as education for the whole man. They try to serve the social, emotional, and political needs of young people in addition to intellectual needs.

Target Groups Definition

A generic product definition usually results in defining a very wide market, and it is then necessary for the organization, because of limited resources, to limit its product offering to certain clearly defined groups within the market. Although the generic product of an automobile company is transportation, the company typically sticks to cars, trucks, and buses, and stays away from bicycles, airplanes, and steamships. Furthermore, the manufacturer does not produce every size and shape of car but concentrates on producing a few major types to satisfy certain substantial and specific parts of the market.

In the same way, nonbusiness organizations have to define their target groups carefully. For example, in Chicago the YMCA defines its target groups as men, women and children who want recreational opportunities and are willing to pay $20 or more a year for them. The Chicago Boys Club, on the other hand, defines its target group as poorer boys within the city boundaries who are in want of recreational facilities and can pay $1 a year.

Differentiated Marketing

When a business organization sets out to serve more than one target group, it will be maximally effective by differentiating its product offerings and communications. This is also true for nonbusiness organizations. Fund-raising organizations have recognized the advantage of treating clients, trustees, and various publics in different ways. These groups require differentiated appeals and frequency of solicitation.

Labor unions find that they must address different messages to different parties rather than one message to all parties. To the company they may seem unyielding, to the conciliator they may appear willing to compromise, and to the public they seek to appear economically exploited.

Customer Behavior Analysis

Business organizations are increasingly recognizing that customer needs and behavior are not obvious without formal research and analysis; they cannot rely on impressionistic evidence. Soap companies spend hundreds of thousands of dollars each year researching how Mrs. Housewife feels about her laundry, how, when, and where she does her laundry, and what she desires of a detergent.

Fund raising illustrates how an industry has benefited by replacing stereotypes of donors with studies of why people contribute to causes. Fund raisers have learned that people give because they are getting something. Many give to community chests to relieve a sense of guilt because of their elevated state compared to the needy. Many give to medical charities to relieve a sense of fear that they may be struck by a disease whose cure has not yet been found. Some give to feel pride. Fund raisers have stressed the importance of identifying the motives operating in the marketplace of givers as a basis for planning drives.

Differential Advantages

In considering different ways of reaching target groups, an organization is advised to think in terms of seeking a differential advantage. It should consider what elements in its reputation or resources can be exploited to create a special value in the minds of its potential customers. In the same way Zenith has built a reputation for quality and International Harvester a reputation for service, a nonbusiness organization should base its case on some dramatic value that competitive organizations lack. The small island of Nassau can compete against Miami for the tourist trade by advertising the greater dependability of its weather; the Heart Association can compete for funds against the Cancer Society by advertising the amazing strides made in heart research.

Multiple Marketing Tools

The modern business firm relies on a multitude of tools to sell its product, including product improvement, consumer and dealer advertising, salesman incentive programs, sales promotions, contests, multiple-size offerings, and so forth. Likewise nonbusiness organizations also can reach their audiences in a variety of ways. A church can sustain the interest of its members through discussion groups, newsletters, news releases, campaign drives, annual reports, and retreats. Its "salesmen" include the religious head, the board members, and the present members in terms of attracting potential members. Its advertising includes announcements of weddings, births and deaths, religious pronouncements, and newsworthy developments.

Integrated Marketing Planning

The multiplicity of available marketing tools suggests the desirability of overall coordination so that these tools do not work at cross purposes. Over time, the business firms have placed under a marketing vice-president activities that were previously managed in a semi-autonomous fashion, such as sales, advertising, and marketing research. Nonbusiness organizations typically have not integrated their marketing activities. Thus, no single officer in the typical university is given total responsibility for studying the needs and attitudes of clients, trustees, and publics, and undertaking the necessary product development and communication programs to serve these groups. The university administration instead includes a variety of "marketing" positions such as dean of students, director of alumni affairs, director of public relations, and director of development; coordination is often poor.

Continuous Marketing Feedback

Business organizations gather continuous information about changes in the environment and about their own performance. They use their salesmen, research department, specialized research services, and other means to check on the movement of goods, actions of competitors, and feelings of customers to make sure they are progressing along satisfactory lines. Nonbusiness organizations typically are more casual about collecting vital information on how they are doing and what is happening in the marketplace. Universities have been caught off guard by underestimating the magnitude of student grievance and unrest, and so have major cities underestimated the degree to which they were failing to meet the needs of important minority constituencies.

Marketing Audit

Change is a fact of life, although it may proceed almost invisibly on a day-to-day basis. Over a long stretch of time, it might be so fundamental as to threaten organizations that have not provided for periodic reexaminations of their purposes. Organizations can grow set in their ways and unresponsive to new opportunities or problems. Some great American companies are no longer with us because they did not change definitions of their businesses, and their products lost relevance in a changing world. Political parties become unresponsive after they enjoy power for a while and every so often experience a major upset. Many union leaders grow insensitive to new needs and problems until one day they find themselves out of office. For an organization to remain viable, its management must provide for periodic audits of its objectives, resources, and opportunities. It must reexamine its basic business, target groups, differential advantage, communication channels, and messages in the light of current trends and needs. It might recognize when change is needed and make it before it is too late.

IS ORGANIZATIONAL MARKETING A
SOCIALLY USEFUL ACTIVITY?

Modern marketing has two different meanings in the minds of people who use the term. One meaning of marketing conjures up the terms selling, influencing, persuading. Marketing is seen as a huge and increasingly dangerous technology, making it possible to sell persons on buying things, propositions, and causes they either do not want or which are bad for them. This was the indictment in Vance Packard's *Hidden Persuaders* and numerous other social criticisms, with the net effect that a large number of persons think of marketing as immoral or entirely self-seeking in its fundamental premises. They can be counted on to resist the idea of organizational marketing as so much "Madison Avenue."

The other meaning of marketing unfortunately is weaker in the public mind; it is the concept of sensitively *serving and satisfying human needs*. This was the great contribution of the marketing concept that was promulgated in the 1950s, and that concept now counts many business firms as its practitioners. The marketing concept holds that the problem of all business firms in an age of abundance is to develop customer loyalties and satisfaction, and the key to this problem is to focus on the customer's needs.[4] Perhaps the short-run problem of business firms is to sell people on buying the existing products, but the long-run problem is clearly to create the products that people need. By this recognition that effective marketing requires a consumer orientation instead of a product orientation, marketing has taken a new lease on life and tied its economic activity to a higher social purpose.

It is this second side of marketing that provides a useful concept for all organizations. All organizations are formed to serve the interest of particular groups: hospitals serve the sick, schools serve the students, governments serve the citizens, and labor unions serve the members. In the course of evolving, many organizations lose sight of their original mandate, grow hard, and become self-serving. The bureaucratic mentality begins to dominate the original service mentality. Hospitals may become perfunctory in their handling of patients, schools treat their students as nuisances, city bureaucrats behave like petty tyrants toward the citizens, and labor unions try to run instead of serve their members. All of these actions tend to build frustration in the consuming groups. As a result some withdraw meekly from these organizations, accept frustration as part of their condition, and find their satisfactions elsewhere. This used to be the common reaction of ghetto Negroes and college students in the face of indifferent city and university bureaucracies. But new possibilities have arisen, and now the same consumers refuse to withdraw so readily. Organized dissent and protest are seen to be an answer, and many organizations thinking of themselves as responsible have been stunned into recognizing that they have lost touch with their constituencies. They had grown unresponsive.

Where does marketing fit into this picture? Marketing is that function of the organization that can keep in constant touch with the organization's consumers, read their needs, develop "products" that meet these needs, and build a program of communications to express the organization's purposes. Certainly selling and influencing will be large parts of organizational marketing; but, properly seen, selling follows rather than precedes the organization's drive to create products to satisfy its consumers.

CONCLUSION

It has been argued here that the modern marketing concept serves very naturally to describe an important facet of all organizational activity.

---

[4] Theodore Levitt, "Marketing Myopia, " *Harvard Business Review,* Vo. 38 (July–August, 1960), pp. 45–56.

All organizations must develop appropriate products to serve their sundry consuming groups and must use modern tools of communication to reach their consuming publics. The business heritage of marketing provides a useful set of concepts for guiding all organizations.

The choice facing those who manage nonbusiness organizations is not whether to market or not to market, for no organization can avoid marketing. The choice is whether to do it well or poorly, and on this necessity the case for organizational marketing is basically founded.

8

Better Deal for Ghetto Shoppers

Frederick D. Sturdivant

However remote and unreal the newspaper photos of large numbers of looters carrying furniture, groceries, appliances, and other merchandise through the streets of many of this nation's major cities may seem, their message for U.S. business is profound. "Such poverty as we have today in all our great cities degrades the poor," warned George Bernard Shaw in 1928, "and infects with its degradation the whole neighborhood in which they live. And whatever can degrade a neighborhood can degrade a country and a continent and finally the whole civilized world. . . ."[1]

Over the past two years an epidemic of this contagious disease has struck with great violence in Los Angeles, New York, Rochester, Chicago, San Francisco, Newark, Detroit, and other large U.S. cities. There is the threat of more riots to come. A major share of the responsibility for halting the epidemic and preventing further assaults on the structure of society rests with the business community.

No informed citizen questions the presence of large numbers of people living in poverty in the United States. Indeed, most Americans have tired of the debate which attempts to quantify and measure a state of existence that is too qualitative and miserable to be measured precisely. Many companies have participated in private and governmental

Reprinted by permission from *Harvard Business Review*, Vol. 46 (March–April 1968), pp. 130–132, 135–139. Copyright © 1968 by the President and Fellows of Harvard College; all rights reserved.

Frederick D. Sturdivant is Meshulam Riklis Professor of Business and its Environment at The Ohio State University. He is an authority on the problems of disadvantaged consumers. He has written many articles and edited a definitive anthology, *The Ghetto Marketplace*. His Ph.D. is from Northwestern University; he has served on the faculties of the University of Southern California, University of Texas, and Harvard Business School.

[1] *The Intelligent Woman's Guide to Socialism and Capitalism* (Garden City, N.Y.: Doubleday, 1928), p. 42.

programs by hiring and training individuals from disadvantaged areas.[2] In fact, efforts to deal with the dilemma of the underskilled and unemployed have represented the major thrust of the business community's commitment to the War on Poverty. In some areas of high unemployment such programs have led to significant improvements in local conditions.

While few would question the importance of training and employing the disadvantaged, a fundamental point is generally ignored. *The most direct contact between the poor and the business community is at the retail level.* The greatest opportunity to assist and to revolutionize the daily lives of the poor rests in the retailing communities serving poverty areas.

While it is a great step forward to create jobs for the unemployed or to train men for better-paying jobs, such improvements can be nullified when the worker and members of his family enter the marketplace as consumers. Very little may be gained if they are confronted with a shopping situation that generally offers them higher prices, inferior merchandise, high-pressure selling, hidden and inflated interest charges, and a degrading shopping environment. Such conditions are closely related to the frustrations that have produced the spectacle of looted and burned stores throughout the nation.

A TALE OF TWO GHETTOS

The first of the terribly destructive and bloody Negro riots took place in the south central section of Los Angeles in August 1965. In the aftermath of the nearly week-long Watts riots, which seemed to set the pattern for subsequent revolts around the country, it was apparent that retail establishments had been the primary target of the rioters. Of the more than 600 buildings damaged by looting and fire, over 95 percent were retail stores. According to the report of the Governor's Commission on the Los Angeles Riots, "The rioters concentrated primarily on food markets, liquor stores, furniture stores, department stores, and pawnshops."[3]

Manufacturing firms and other kinds of business facilities in the area, which in many cases contained valuable merchandise and fixtures, were virtually untouched, as were public buildings such as schools,

---

[2] See Alfonso J. Cervantes, "To Prevent a Chain of Super-Watts," *Harvard Business Review*, Vol. 45 (September–October 1967), p. 55.

[3] The Governor's Commission on the Los Angeles Riots, *Violence in the City—An End or a Beginning?* (Los Angeles, December 1965), pp. 23–24.

libraries, and churches. Not one of the twenty-six Operation Head Start facilities in the Watts area was touched.

Even a cursory survey of the damage would indicate that a "vengeance pattern" might have been followed. The various news media covering the riots reported many interviews which revealed a deep-seated resentment toward retailers because of alleged exploitation. The possibility that the rioters were striking back at unethical merchants was reinforced by the fact that one store would be looted and burned while a competing unit across the street survived without so much as a cracked window.

In the fall of 1965, facts and questions like these prompted a two-year study of consumer-business relations in two disadvantaged sections of Los Angeles:

1. As the center of the Los Angeles riots, Watts was an excellent place to begin the study. Consumers and merchants were very willing to discuss their experiences and to explore the causes of the riots. Civil rights groups and merchants' organizations were eager to cooperate with an "objective" research effort which would vindicate their respective points of view. In effect, there were a number of advantages in studying the conditions in Watts while the rubble still littered the streets and participants in the destruction were seeking to be heard.

2. But Watts by itself was not sufficient for an objective investigation. The basic retail structure of the area had been virtually destroyed, and it was impossible to contact many of the merchants who had been burned out by the rioters. In addition, feelings were so intense on both sides that the danger of distortion was greatly magnified. Since the population of the area was heavily black, the investigation might have become a study of exploitation of this minority rather than an analysis of the relations between business and the poor in general. Therefore, a second study area was selected—a disadvantaged section of the Mexican-American community in east Los Angeles.

In each area, more than 25 percent of the population fell below the government's $3000 poverty line. In addition, each area had high unemployment (7.7 percent for Mexican-Americans and 10.1 percent for Negroes), a high incidence of broken homes (17.2 percent for Mexican-Americans and 25.5 percent for Negroes, and the many other household and community characteristics which are associated with ghettos.[4]

Over a period of two years, more than 2000 interviews were held with consumers and merchants in these two poverty areas, numerous

---

[4]California Department of Industrial Relations, *Negroes and Mexican-Americans in South and East Los Angeles* (San Francisco, July 1966); these data understate both the income and unemployment problems since they cover the entire area and not just the poorest sections analyzed in this study.

shopping forays were conducted, and price-quality comparisons were made with stores serving the more prosperous sections of Los Angeles and surrounding communities. Although there were a number of interesting differences between the findings in the two areas (the differences were based for the most part on cultural factors), the evidence points to two basic flaws in local retailing which were present in each of the areas:

1. The prevalence of small, inefficient, uneconomical units
2. A tendency on the part of many stores to prey on an undereducated and relatively immobile population with high-pressure, unethical methods

These findings, I believe, apply rather generally to the retail segments serving disadvantaged areas in U.S. cities.

A WORKABLE SOLUTION

Most critics of business-consumer relations in disadvantaged areas have called for legislation designed to protect consumers and for consumer-education programs. Indeed, laws designed to protect consumers from hidden and inflated interest charges and other forms of unethical merchandising should be passed and vigorously enforced. Consumer economics should be a part of elementary and secondary school curricula, and adult education programs should be available in disadvantaged areas. However, these approaches are hardly revolutionary, and they hold little promise of producing dramatic changes in the economic condition of the disadvantaged.

A crucial point seems to have been largely ignored by the critics and in the various bills introduced in the state legislatures and in Congress. This is the difficulty of improvement so long as the retailing segments of depressed areas are dominated by uneconomically small stores—by what I call an "atomistic" structure. Indeed, many legislators seem eager to perpetuate the system by calling for expanded activities by the Small Business Administration in offering assistance to more small firms that do business in the ghettos. Another common suggestion is for the federal government to offer low-cost insurance protection to these firms. This proposal, too, may do more to aggravate than relieve. If the plight of the ghetto consumer is to be dramatically relieved, this will not come about through measures designed to multiply the number of inefficient retailers serving these people.

Real progress will come only if we can find some way to extend into the ghettos the highly advanced, competitive retailing system that has so successfully served other sectors of the economy. To make this advance possible, we must remove the economic barriers that restrict entry by progressive retailers, for stores are managed by businessmen, not social workers.

How can these barriers be removed?

Investment Guarantee Plan

Since shortly after the close of World War II, the federal government has had a program designed to eliminate certain barriers to investment by U.S. corporations in underdeveloped countries. In effect, the government has said that it is in the best interest of the United States if our business assists in the economic development of certain foreign countries. In a number of Latin American countries, for instance, the program has protected U.S. capital against loss through riots or expropriation. The investment guarantee program does not assure U.S. firms of a profit; that challenge rests with management. But companies are protected against the abnormal risks associated with building facilities in underdeveloped countries. If a guarantee program can stimulate investment in Colombia, why not in Watts or Harlem?

I propose a program, to be administered by the Department of Commerce, under which potential retail investors would be offered investment guarantees for building (or buying) a store in areas designated as "disadvantaged." A contract between the retail firm and the Commerce Department would guarantee the company full reimbursement for physical losses resulting from looting, burning, or other damages caused by civil disorders as well as from the usual hazards of natural disasters. In addition, the contract would call for compensation for operating losses sustained during periods of civil unrest in the area. To illustrate:

- A Montgomery Ward store established in the heart of Watts would, under this program, be insured for the book value of the establishment against damages caused by natural or human events. If the firm emerged from a period of rioting without suffering any physical damages, but was forced to cease operations during the period of the riots, Montgomery Ward would be compensated for operating losses resulting from the forced closure.

Costs and Restrictions. The costs to a company for an investment guarantee would be minimal in terms of both financial outlay and loss of managerial autonomy. An annual fee of 0.5 percent of the amount of insured assets would be charged. There is no actuarial basis for this rate; rather, the fees are charged to cover the costs of administering the program and building a reserve against possible claims.

There would be no restriction on either the size of the investment or the term of the guarantee contract. The contract would be terminated by the government only if the firm violated the terms of the agreement or if the economic character of the area improved to the point that it was no longer classified as disadvantaged.

In addition to paying annual premiums, the participating companies would be required to conform to state and local laws designed to protect consumers (or minimum federal standards where local legislation is not in effect). A participating retailer found guilty of violating state law regarding, let us say, installment charges would have his contract terminated.

In effect, the ethical merchandiser would find no restrictions on his usual managerial freedom. So long as he abided by the law, his investment would be protected, and he would have complete freedom in selecting his merchandise, setting prices, advertising, and the other areas of managerial strategy.

Enlarged Investment Credit

The guarantee program would offer the manager maximum discretion, but it would not assure him of a profit. The guarantee phase of the program merely attempts to place the ghetto on a par with nonghetto areas with respect to investment risk. The final barrier, the high costs associated with doing business in such areas, would have to be offset by offering businesses enlarged investment credits. Credits of perhaps 10 percent (as compared to the usual 7 percent under other programs) could be offered as an inducement to outside retailers. Firms participating in the guarantee program would be eligible for such investment credits on all facilities constructed in disadvantaged areas.

The more generous investment credits would serve as a source of encouragement not only for building new facilities, but also for expanding and modernizing older stores that had been allowed to decline. For example, the Sears Roebuck and J. C. Penney stores located (as earlier mentioned) in transitional and declining areas would be likely targets for physical improvements.

Key to Transformation

Perhaps the most important characteristic of the investment guarantee and credit program is the nature of the relationship that would exist between the government and the business community. The government is cast in the role of the stimulator or enabler without becoming involved in the management of the private company. The program is also flexible in that incentives could be increased or lowered as conditions warrant. If the investment credits should fail to provide a sufficient stimulus, additional incentives in the form of lower corporate income-tax rates could be added. On the other hand, as an area becomes increasingly attractive as a retail location, the incentives could be reduced or eliminated.

If implemented with vigor and imagination, this program could lead to a dramatic transformation of the retail segment serving ghetto areas. While size restrictions would not be imposed, the provisions of the program would be most attractive to larger retail organizations. Thus, the "atomistic" structure of the retail community would undergo major change as the marginal retailers face competition with efficient mass distributors. The parasitic merchants would also face a bleak future. The study in Los Angeles revealed no instance in which a major retail firm was guilty of discriminatory pricing or inflated credit charges. In addition, the agency administering the investment program could make periodic studies of the practices of participating firms, and use these investigations to prod companies, if necessary, to assure their customers of equitable treatment.

CONCLUSION

No one program will solve a problem as basic and complex as that of the big-city ghetto. A variety of projects and measures is needed. While the program I propose has great potential, its promise is more likely to be realized if it is supported by other kinds of action to strengthen local businesses. For instance:

- Various "activist" groups have been bringing pressure on unethical retailers. In Watts, some limited efforts have been made to boycott retailers who do not conform to a code of conduct that has been promulgated. In Washington, D.C., a militant civil rights organization, ACT, has launched a national campaign to encourage bankruptcy filings by poor merchants; it has devised an ingenious scheme that could deal a severe blow to parasitic retailers.
- In Roxbury, Massachusetts (a part of Boston), Negroes are organizing buying cooperatives. Such cooperatives have limited potential, but many people believe they can compensate for at least some of the problems of smallness and inefficiency which plague "mom and pop" stores in the area.

Some corporate executives are trying to help Negro businessmen develop managerial know-how. Business-school students have recently got into this act too. A group of second-year students at the Harvard Business School, with the financial backing of the Ford Foundation, is providing free advice and instruction to Negroes running retail stores and other firms in Boston. The instruction covers such basic matters as purchasing, bookkeeping, credit policy, tax reporting, and pricing.

· Some large stores are reportedly considering giving franchises to retailers in ghetto areas. Assuming the franchises are accompanied by management assistance, financial help, and other advantages of a tie-in with a large company, this step could help to strengthen a number of local retailers.

· Some of the large-scale renewal projects undertaken by business have, as a secondary benefit, introduced residents of run-down areas to progressive retailing. In the 1950s, a 100-acre slum section of south Chicago was razed and turned into a 2009-apartment community with a shopping center. In the shopping center were branches of various well-known organizations—Goldblatt's Department Store, Jewel Tea Supermarket, Walgreen Drug Stores, and others. Similarly, if a group of Tampa business leaders succeed in current plans to rebuild part of Tampa's downtown business district, such leading stores as Macy's, Jordan Marsh, Bon Marche, and Sears Roebuck plan to open branches in the new buildings. In both cases, residents of the poor areas adjoining the shopping sections would be able to take advantage of progressive retailing.

Projects like the foregoing would be welcome allies of the program proposed in this article. For this program, despite its many great advantages, will not be easy to carry out. The major retailers attracted to disadvantaged areas will face many challenges. Studies will have to be undertaken to help them adapt successfully to local conditions. Creative and imaginative managers will be needed at the store level.

The new program should be good for retailers from the standpoint of profits. In addition, retail leaders should derive a great deal of satisfaction from demonstrating that U.S. enterprise is capable of contributing significantly to the solution of the major domestic crisis of the twentieth century. An efficient and competitive retail community in a ghetto would certainly discourage ineffective and unethical store managers in the area. And while the new program would not solve all of the problems of the nation's cities, it could do a great deal to reduce the injustices suffered by the poor and to eliminate the bitterness that feeds the spreading civil disorders.

PART
II

CONSUMER
ANALYSIS

The marketing objectives of any firm are to identify potential customers and to convince them that the firm's products will satisfy their needs. These objectives imply an understanding of human behavior, especially of the behavioral role of "consumer." The articles in Part II are some of marketing's most significant attempts to analyze consumer behavior.

The normative framework for analyzing the consumer is provided by economic theory. Katona has led the movement to integrate economic theory and the behavioral sciences in order to arrive at a sound theory of rational economic behavior. Bayton's work is an excellent overview of how certain psychological concepts are useful in understanding consumer behavior. Similarly, Kotler offer insights from five different social sciences into the processes of human behavior. Then Howard and Sheth combine insights from the various disciplines into one model of consumer behavior.

Conceptual articles such as these have inspired considerable empirical research. Two of the best articles are included here. Haire's work with projective techniques pioneers in applying scientific research methodology to consumer analysis. Similarly, Pessemier's experiment has inspired considerable investigation of this technique for estimating demand relationships.

The last two articles in Part II examine the influence of interpersonal relationships on consumer behavior. The general theory of group influence is given in the first paper by the Foundation for Research on Human Behavior. The second FRHB paper applies this general framework to a classification scheme for distinguishing among consumers on the basis of adoption rates of new products.

9

Rational Behavior and Economic Behavior

George Katona

While attempts to penetrate the boundary lines between psychology and sociology have been rather frequent during the last few decades, psychologists have paid little attention to the problems with which another sister discipline, economics, is concerned. One purpose of this paper is to arouse interest among psychologists in studies of economic behavior. For that purpose it will be shown that psychological principles may be of great value in clarifying basic questions of economics and that the psychology of habit formation, of motivation, and of group belonging may profit from studies of economic behavior.

A variety of significant problems, such as those of the business cycle or inflation, of consumer saving or business investment, could be chosen for the purpose of such demonstration. This paper, however, will be concerned with the most fundamental assumption of economics, the principle of rationality. In order to clarify the problems involved in this principle, which have been neglected by contemporary psychologists, it will be necessary to contrast the most common forms of methodology used in economics with those employed in psychology and to discuss the role of empirical research in the social sciences.

THEORY AND HYPOTHESES

Economic theory represents one of the oldest and most elaborate theoretical structures in the social sciences. However, dissatisfaction

Reprinted from *Psychological Review* (September, 1953), pp. 307-318. Copyright 1953 by the American Psychological Association. Reprinted by permission.

George Katona, a native of Hungary, received a Ph.D. in psychology from Gottingen University and has pioneered in combining psychology and economics. He is program director of the Survey Research Center and professor of economics and psychology at the University of Michigan. His two best-known books are *The Powerful Consumer* and *Mass Consumption Society*.

with the achievements and uses of economic theory has grown considerably during the past few decades on the part of economists who are interested in what actually goes on in economic life. And yet leading sociologists and psychologists have recently declared, "Economics is today, in a theoretical sense, probably the most highly elaborated sophisticated, and refined of the disciplines dealing with action."[1]

To understand the scientific approach of economic theorists, we may divide them into two groups. Some develop an a priori system from which they deduce propositions about how people *should* act under certain assumptions. Assuming that the sole aim of businessmen is profit maximization, these theorists deduce propositions about marginal revenues and marginal costs, for example, that are not meant to be suited for testing. In developing formal logics of economic action, one of the main considerations is elegance of the deductive system, based on the law of parsimony. A wide gap separates these theorists from economic research of an empirical-statistical type which registers what they call aberrations or deviations, due to human frailty, from the norm set by theory.

A second group of economic theorists adheres to the proposition that it is the main purpose of theory to provide hypotheses that can be tested. This group acknowledges that prediction of future events represents the most stringent test of theory. They argue, however, that reality is so complex that it is necessary to begin with simplified propositions and models which are known to be unreal and not testable.[2] Basic among these propositions are the following three which traditionally have served to characterize the economic man or the rational man:

1. The principle of complete information and foresight. Economic conditions—demand, supply, prices, etc.—are not only given but also known to the rational man. This applies as well to future conditions about which there exists no uncertainty, so that rational choice can always be made. (In place of the assumption of certainty of future developments, we find nowadays more frequently the assumption that risks prevail but the probability of occurrence of different alternatives is known; this does not constitute a basic difference.)

---

[1] T. Parsons and E. A. Shils, (Editors), *Toward a General Theory of Action* (Cambridge, Mass.: Harvard University Press, 1951).

[2] A variety of methods used in economic research differ, of course, from those employed by the two groups of economic theorists. Some research is motivated by dissatisfaction with the traditional economic theory; some is grounded in a systematization greatly different from traditional theory (the most important example of such systematization is national income accounting); some research is not clearly based on any theory; finally, some research has great affinity with psychological and sociological studies.

2. The principle of complete mobility. There are no institutional or psychological factors which make it impossible, or expensive, or slow, to translate the rational choice into action.

3. The principle of pure competition. Individual action has no great influence on prices because each man's choice is independent from any other person's choice and because there are no "large" sellers or buyers. Action is the result of individual choice and is not group-determined.

Economic theory is developed first under these assumptions. The theorists then introduce changes in the assumptions so that the theory may approach reality. One such step consists, for instance, of introducing large-scale producers, monopolists, and oligopolists, another of introducing time lags, and still another of introducing uncertainty about the probability distribution of future events. The question raised in each case is this: Which of the original propositions needs to be changed, and in what way, in view of the new assumptions?

The fact that up to now the procedure of gradual approximation to reality has not been completely successful does not invalidate the method. It must also be acknowledged that propositions were frequently derived from unrealistic economic models which were susceptible to testing and stimulated empirical research. In this paper, we shall point to a great drawback of this method of starting out with a simplified a priori system and making it gradually more complex and more real—by proceeding in this way one tends to lose sight of important problems and to disregard them.

The methods most commonly used in psychology may appear at first sight to be quite similar to the methods of economics which have just been described. Psychologists often start with casual observations, derive from them hypotheses, test those through more systematic observations, reformulate and revise their hypotheses accordingly, and test them again. The process of hypotheses-observations-hypotheses-observations often goes on with no end in sight. Differences from the approach of economic theory may be found in the absence in psychological research of detailed systematic elaboration prior to any observation. Also, in psychological research, findings and generalizations in one field of behavior are often considered as hypotheses in another field of behavior. Accordingly, in analyzing economic behavior[3] and trying to understand rationality, psychologists can draw on (a) the theory of learning and thinking, (b) the theory of group belonging,

---

[3] The expression "economic behavior" is used in this paper to mean behavior concerning economic matters (spending, saving, investing, pricing, etc.) Some economic theorists use the expression to mean the behavior of the "economic man," that is, the behavior postulated in their theory of rationality.

and (c) the theory of motivation. This will be done in this paper.

HABITUAL BEHAVIOR AND GENUINE DECISION MAKING

In trying to give noneconomic examples of "rational calculus," economic theorists have often referred to gambling. From some textbooks one might conclude that the most rational place in the world is the Casino in Monte Carlo where odds and probabilities can be calculated exactly. In contrast, some mathematicians and psychologists have considered scientific discovery and the thought processes of scientists as the best examples of rational or intelligent behavior.[4] An inquiry about the possible contributions of psychology to the analysis of rationality may then begin with a formulation of the differences between (a) associative learning and habit formation and (b) problem solving and thinking.

The basic principle of the first form of behavior is repetition. Here the argument of Guthrie holds: "The most certain and dependable information concerning what a man will do in any situation is information concerning what he did in that situation on its last occurrence."[5] This form of behavior depends upon the frequency of repetition as well as on its recency and on the success of past performances. The origins of habit formation have been demonstrated by experiments about learning nonsense syllables, lists of words, mazes, and conditioned responses. Habits thus formed are to some extent automatic and inflexible.

In contrast, problem-solving behavior has been characterized by the arousal of a problem or question, by deliberation that involves reorganization and "direction," by understanding of the requirements of the situation, by weighing of alternatives and taking their consequences into consideration and, finally, by choosing among alternative courses of action.[6] Scientific discovery is not the only example of

---

[4] Reference should be made first of all to Max Wertheimer who in his book *Productive Thinking* uses the terms "sensible" and "intelligent" rather than "rational." Since we are mainly interested here in deriving conclusions from the psychology of thinking, the discussion of psychological principles will be kept extremely brief. See M. Wertheimer, *Productive Thinking* (New York: Harper, 1945); G. Katona, *Organizing and Memorizing* (New York: Columbia University Press, 1940); and G. Katona, *Psychological Analysis of Economic Behavior* (New York: McGraw-Hill, 1951), especially Chapters 3 and 4.

[5] E. R. Guthrie, *Psychology of Learning* (New York: Harper, 1935), p. 228.

[6] Cf. the following statement by a leading psychoanalyst: "Rational behavior is behavior that is effectively guided by an understanding of the situation to which one is reacting." French adds two steps that follow the choice between alternative goals, namely, commitment to a goal and commitment to a plan to reach a goal. See T. M. French. *The Integration of Behavior* (Chicago: University of Chicago Press, 1952).

such procedures; they have been demonstrated in the psychological laboratory as well as in a variety of real-life situations. Problem solving results in action which is new rather than repetitive; the actor may have never behaved in the same way before and may not have learned of any others having behaved in the same way.

Some of the above terms, defined and analyzed by psychologists, are also being used by economists in their discussion of rational behavior. In discussing, for example, a manufacturer's choice between erecting or not erecting a new factory, or raising or not raising his prices or output, reference is usually made to deliberation and to taking the consequences of alternative choices into consideration. Nevertheless, it is not justified to identify problem-solving behavior with rational behavior. From the point of view of an outside observer, habitual behavior may prove to be fully rational or the most appropriate way of action under certain circumstances. All that is claimed here is that the analysis of two forms of behavior—habitual versus genuine decision making—may serve to clarify problems of rationality. We shall proceed therefore by deriving six propositions from the psychological principles. To some extent, or in certain fields of behavior, these are findings or empirical generalizations; to some extent, or in other fields of behavior, they are hypotheses.

1. Problem-solving behavior is a relatively rare occurrence. It would be incorrect to assume that everyday behavior consistently manifests such features as arousal of a problem, deliberation, or taking consequences of the action into consideration. Behavior which does not manifest these characteristics predominates in everyday life and in economic activities as well.

2. The main alternative to problem-solving behavior is not whimsical or impulsive behavior (which was considered the major example of "irrational" behavior by nineteenth-century philosophers). When genuine decision making does not take place, habitual behavior is the most usual occurrence: people act as they have acted before under similar circumstances, without deliberating and choosing.

3. Problem-solving behavior is recognized most commonly as a deviation from habitual behavior. Observance of the established routine is abandoned when in driving home from my office, for example, I learn that there is a parade in town and choose a different route, instead of automatically taking the usual one. Or, to mention an example of economic behavior: Many businessmen have rules of thumb concerning the timing for reorders of merchandise; yet sometimes they decide to place new orders even though their inventories have not reached the usual level of depletion (for instance, because they anticipate price increases), or not to order merchandise even though that level has been reached (because they expect a slump in sales).

4. Strong motivational forces—stronger than those which elicit habitual behavior—must be present to call forth problem-solving behavior. Being in a "crossroad situation," facing "choice points," or perceiving that something new has occurred are typical instances in which we are motivated to deliberate and choose. Pearl Harbor and the Korean aggression are extreme examples of "new" events; economic behavior of the problem-solving type was found to have prevailed widely after these events.

5. Group belonging and group reinforcement play a substantial role in changes of behavior due to problem solving. Many people become aware of the same events at the same time; our mass media provide the same information and often the same interpretation of events to groups of people (to businessmen, trade union members, sometimes to all Americans). Changes in behavior resulting from new events may therefore occur among very many people at the same time. Some economists[7] argued that consumer optimism and pessimism are unimportant because usually they will cancel out; in the light of sociopsychological principles, however, it is probable, and has been confirmed by recent surveys, that a change from optimistic to pessimistic attitudes, or vice versa, sometimes occurs among millions of people at the same time.

6. Changes in behavior due to genuine decision making will tend to be substantial and abrupt, rather than small and gradual. Typical examples of action that results from genuine decisions are cessation of purchases or buying waves, the shutting down of plants or the building of new plants, rather than an increase or decrease of production by 5 or 10 per cent.[8]

Because of the preponderance of individual psychological assumptions in classical economics and the emphasis placed on group behavior in this discussion, the change in underlying conditions which has occurred during the last century may be illustrated by a further example. It is related—the author does not know whether the story is true or fictitious—that the banking house of the Rothschilds, still in its infancy at that time, was one of the suppliers of the armies of Lord Wellington in 1815. Nathan Mayer Rothschild accompanied the armies and was present at the Battle of Waterloo. When he became convinced that Napoleon was decisively defeated, he released carrier pigeons so as to transmit the news to his associates in London and reverse the commodity position of his bank. The carrier pigeons arrived in London before the news of the victory became public knowledge.

---

[7] J. M. Keynes, *The General Theory of Employment, Interest and Money* (New York: Harcourt, Brace, 1936), p. 95.

[8] Some empirical evidence supporting these six propositions in the area of economic behavior has been assembled by the Survey Research Center of the University of Michigan. See G. Katona, "Psychological Analysis of Business Decisions and Expectations," *American Economic Review* (1946), pp. 44–63.

The profits thus reaped laid, according to the story, the foundation to the outstanding position of the House of Rothschild in the following decades.

The decision to embark on a new course of action because of new events was then made by one individual for his own profit. At present, news of a battle, or of change of government, or of rearmament programs, is transmitted in short order by press and radio to the public at large. Businessmen—the manufacturers or retailers of steel or clothing, for instance—usually receive the same news about changes in the price of raw materials or in demand, and often consult with each other. Belonging to the same group means being subject to similar stimuli and reinforcing one another in making decisions. Acting in the same way as other members of one's group or of a reference group have acted under similar circumstances may also occur without deliberation and choice. New action by a few manufacturers will, then, frequently or even usually not be compensated by reverse action on the part of others. Rather the direction in which the economy of an entire country moves—and often the world economy as well—will tend to be subject to the same influences.

After having indicated some of the contributions which the application of certain psychological principles to economic behavior may make, we turn to contrasting that approach with the traditional theory of rationality. Instead of referring to the formulations of nineteenth-century economists, we shall quote from a modern version of the classical trend of thought. The title of a section in a recent article by Kenneth J. Arrow is "The Principle of Rationality." He describes one of the criteria of rationality as follows: "We can imagine the individual as listing, once and for all, all conceivable consequences of his actions in order of his preference for them."[9] We are first concerned with the expression "all conceivable consequences." This expression seems to contradict the principle of selectivity of human behavior. Yet habitual behavior is highly selective since it is based on (repeated) past experience, and problem-solving behavior likewise is highly selective since reorganization is subject to a certain direction instead of consisting of trial (and error) regarding all possible avenues of action.

Secondly, Arrow appears to identify rationality with consistency in the sense of repetition of the same choice. It is part and parcel of rational behavior, according to Arrow, that an individual "makes the same choice each time he is confronted with the same set of alternatives."[10]

---

[9] K. J. Arrow, "Mathematical Models in the Social Sciences," in D. Lerner and H. D. Lasswell (Editors), *The Policy Sciences* (Stanford: Stanford University Press, 1951), p. 135.

[10] In his recent book Arrow adds after stating that the economic man "will make the same decision each time he is faced with the same range of alternatives": "The ability to make consistent decisions is one of the symptoms of an integrated personality." See K. J. Arrow, *Social Choice and Individual Values* (New York: Wiley, 1951), p. 2.

Proceeding in the same way on successive occasions appears, however, a characteristic of habitual behavior. Problem-solving behavior, on the other hand, is flexible. Rationality may be said to reflect adaptability and ability to act in a new way when circumstances demand it, rather than to consist of rigid or repetitive behavior.

Thirdly, it is important to realize the differences between the concepts, action, decision, and choice. It is an essential feature of the approach derived from considering problem-solving behavior that there is action without deliberate decision and choice. It then becomes one of the most important problems of research to determine under what conditions genuine decision and choice occur prior to an action. The three concepts are, however, used without differentiation in the classical theory of rationality and also, most recently, by Parsons and Shils. According to the theory of these authors, there are "five discrete choices (explicit or implicit) which every actor makes before he can act;" before there is action "a decision must always be made (explicitly or implicitly, consciously or unconsciously)."[11]

There exists, no doubt, a difference in terminology, which may be clarified by mentioning a simple case: Suppose my telephone rings: I lift the receiver with my left hand and say, "Hello." Should we then argue that I made several choices, for instance, that I decided not to lift the receiver with my right hand and not to say, "Mr. Katona speaking"? According to our use of the terms decision and choice, my action was habitual and did not involve "taking consequences into consideration."[12] Parsons and Shils use the terms decision and choice in a different sense, and Arrow may use the terms "all conceivable consequences" and "same set of alternatives" in a different sense from the one employed in this paper. But the difference between the two approaches appears to be more far-reaching. By using the terminology of the authors quoted, and by constructing a theory of rational action on the basis of this terminology, fundamental problems are disregarded. If every action by definition presupposes decision making, and if the malleability of human behavior is not taken into consideration, a one-sided theory of rationality is developed and empirical research is confined to testing a theory which covers only some of the aspects of rationality.

This was the case recently in experiments devised by Mosteller

---

[11] T. Parsons and E. A. Shils, *op. cit.*

[12] If I have reason not to make known that I am at home, I may react to the ringing of the telephone by fright, indecision, and deliberation (should I lift the receiver or let the telephone ring?) instead of reacting in the habitual way. This is an example of problem-solving behavior characterized as deviating from habitual behavior. The only example of action mentioned by Parsons and Shils, "a man driving his automobile to a lake to go fishing," may be habitual or may be an instance of genuine decision making.

and Nogee. These authors attempt to test basic assumptions of economic theory, such as the rational choice among alternatives, by placing their subjects in a gambling situation (a variation of poker dice) and compelling them to make a decision, namely, to play or not to play against the experimenter. Through their experiments the authors prove that "it is feasible to measure utility experimentally,"[13] but they do not shed light on the conditions under which rational behavior occurs or on the inherent features of rational behavior. Experiments in which making a choice among known alternatives is prescribed do not test the realism of economic theory.

MAXIMIZATION

Up to now we have discussed only one central aspect of rationality—means rather than ends. The end of rational behavior, according to economic theory, is maximization of profits in the case of business firms and maximization of utility in the case of people in general.

A few words, first, on maximizing profits. This is usually considered the simpler case because it is widely held (a) that business firms are in business to make profits and (b) that profits, more so than utility, are a quantitative, measurable concept.

When empirical research, most commonly in the form of case studies, showed that businessmen frequently strove for many things in addition to profits or in place of profits, most theorists were content with small changes in their systems. They redefined profits so as to include long-range profits and what has been called nonpecuniary or psychic profits. Striving for security or for power was identified with striving for profits in the more distant future; purchasing goods from a high bidder who was a member of the same fraternity as the purchaser, rather than from the lowest bidder—to cite an example often used in textbooks—was thought to be maximizing of nonpecuniary profits. Dissatisfaction with this type of theory construction is rather widespread. For example, a leading theorist wrote recently:

> If *whatever* a business man does is explained by the principle of profit maximization—because he does what he likes to do, and he likes to do what maximizes the sum of his pecuniary and non-pecuniary profits—the analysis acquires the character of a system of definitions and tautologies, and loses much of its value as an explanation of reality.[14]

---

[13] F. Mosteller and P. Nogee, "An Experimental Measurement of Utility," *Journal of Political Economy* (1951), pp. 371–405.
[14] F. Machlup, "Marginal Analysis and Empirical Research," *American Economic Review* (1946), p. 526.

The same problem is encountered regarding maximization of utility. Arrow defines rational behavior as follows: ". . . among all the combinations of commodities an individual can afford, he chooses that combination which maximizes his utility or satisfaction"[15] and speaks of the "traditional identification of rationality with maximization of some sort."[16] An economic theorist has recently characterized this type of definition as follows:

> The statement that a person seeks to maximize utility is (in many versions) a tautology: it is impossible to conceive of an observational phenomenon that contradicts it. . . . What if the theorem is contradicted by observation: Samuelson says it would not matter much in the case of utility theory; I would say that it would not make the slightest difference. For there is a free variable in his system: the tastes of consumers. . . . Any contradiction of a theorem derived from utility theory can always be attributed to a change of tastes, rather than to an error in the postulates or logic of the theory.[17]

What is the way out of this difficulty? Can psychology, and specifically the psychology of motivation, help? We may begin by characterizing the prevailing economic theory as a single-motive theory and contrast it with a theory of multiple motives. Even in case of a single decision of one individual, multiplicity of motives (or of vectors or forces in the field), some reinforcing one another and some conflicting with one another, is the rule rather than the exception. The motivational patterns prevailing among different individuals making the same decision need not be the same; the motives of the same individual who is in the same external situation at different times may likewise differ. This approach opens the way (a) for a study of the relation of different motives to different forms of behavior and (b) for an investigation of changes in motives. Both problems are disregarded by postulating a single-motive theory and by restricting empirical studies to attempts to confirm or contradict that theory.

The fruitfulness of the psychological approach may be illustrated first by a brief reference to business motivation. We may rank the diverse motivational patterns of businessmen by placing the striving for high immediate profits (maximization of short-run profits, to use economic terminology; charging whatever the market can bear, to use a popular expression) at one extreme of the scale. At the other extreme we place the striving for prestige or power. In between we discern

---

[15] K. J. Arrow, *op cit.*

[16] K. J. Arrow, *Social Choice and Individual Values* (New York: Wiley, 1951). The quotation refers specifically to Samuelson's definition but also applies to that of Arrow.

[17] G. J. Stigler, "Review of P. A. Samuelson's Foundations of Economic Analysis," *Journal of American Statistical Association* (1948), p. 603.

striving for security, for larger business volume, or for profits in the more distant future. Under what kinds of business conditions will motivational patterns tend to conform with the one or the other end of the scale? Preliminary studies would seem to indicate that the worse the business situation is, the more frequent is striving for high immediate profits, and the better the business situation is, the more frequent is striving for nonpecuniary goals.[18]

Next we shall refer to one of the most important problems of consumer economics as well as of business-cycle studies, the deliberate choice between saving and spending. Suppose a college professor receives a raise in his salary or makes a few hundred extra dollars through a publication. Suppose, furthermore, that he suggest thereupon to his wife that they should buy a television set while the wife argues that the money should be put in the bank as a reserve against a "rainy day." Whatever the final decision may be, traditional economic theory would hold that the action which gives the greater satisfaction was chosen. This way of theorizing is of little value. Under what conditions will one type of behavior (spending) and under what conditions will another type of behavior (saving) be more frequent? Psychological hypotheses according to which the strength of vectors is related to the immediacy of needs have been put to a test through nationwide surveys over the past six years.[19] On the basis of survey findings the following tentative generalization was established: Pessimism, insecurity, expectation of income declines or bad times in the near future promote saving (putting the extra money in the bank), while optimism, feeling of security, expectation of income increases, or good times promote spending (buying the television set, for instance).

Psychological hypotheses, based on a theory of motivational patterns which change with circumstances and influence behavior, thus stimulated empirical studies. These studies, in turn, yielded a better understanding of past developments and also, we may add, better predictions of forthcoming trends than did studies based on the classical theory. On the other hand, when conclusions about utility or rationality were made on an a priori basis, researchers lost sight of important problems.[20]

[18] G. Katona, *Psychological Analysis of Economic Behavior* (New York: McGraw-Hill, 1951), pp. 193–213.

[19] In the Surveys of Consumer Finances, conducted annually since 1946 by the Survey Research Center of the University of Michigan for the Federal Reserve Board and reported in the *Federal Reserve Bulletin*. See a forthcoming publication of the Survey Research Center on consumer buying and inflation during 1950–52.

[20] It should not be implied that the concepts of utility and maximization are of no value for empirical research. Comparison between maximum utility as determined from the vantage point of an observer with the pattern of goals actually chosen (the "subjective maximum"), which is based on insufficient information, may be useful. Similar considerations apply to such newer concepts as "minimizing regrets" and the "minimax."

DIMINISHING UTILITY, SATURATION, AND ASPIRATION

Among the problems to which the identification of maximizing utility with rationality gave rise, the measurability of utility has been prominent. At present the position of most economists appears to be that while interpersonal comparison of several consumers' utilities is not possible, and while cardinal measures cannot be attached to the utilities of one particular consumer, ordinal ranking of the utilities of each individual can be made. It is asserted that I can always say either that I prefer A to B, or that I am indifferent to having A or B, or that I prefer B to A. The theory of indifference curves is based on this assumption.

In elaborating the theory further, it is asserted that rational behavior consists not only of preferring more of the same goods to less ($2 real wages to $1, or two packages of cigarettes to one package, for the same service performed) but also of deriving diminishing increments of satisfaction from successive units of a commodity.[21] In terms of an old textbook example, one drink of water has tremendous value to a thirsty traveler in a desert; a second, third, or fourth drink may still have some value but less and less so; an nth drink (which he is unable to carry along) has no value at all. A generalization derived from this principle is that the more of a commodity or the more money a person has, the smaller are his needs for that commodity or for money, and the smaller his incentives to add to what he has.

In addition to using this principle of saturation to describe the behavior of the rational man, modern economists applied it to one of the most pressing problems of contemporary American economy. Prior to World War II the American people (not counting business firms) owned about 45 billion dollars in liquid assets (currency, bank deposits, government bonds) and these funds were highly concentrated among relatively few families; most individual families held no liquid assets at all (except for small amounts of currency). By the end of the year 1945, however, the personal liquid-asset holdings had risen to about 140 billion dollars and four out of every five families owned some bank deposits or war bonds. What is the effect of this great change on spending and saving? This question has been answered by several leading economists in terms of the saturation principle presented above. "The rate of saving is . . . a diminishing function of the wealth the individual holds"[22] because "the availability of liquid assets raises consumption generally by reducing the impulse to save."[23] More

---

[21] This principle of diminishing utility was called a "fundamental tendency of human nature" by the great nineteenth century economist, Alfred Marshall.

[22] G. Haberler, *Prosperity and Depression*, 3rd ed. (Geneva: League of Nations, 1941), p. 199.

[23] The last quotation is from the publication of the U.S. Department of Commerce, *Survey of Current Business*, May 1950, p. 10.

specifically: a person who owns nothing or very little will exert himself greatly to acquire some reserve funds, while a person who owns much will have much smaller incentives to save. Similarly, incentives to increase one's income are said to weaken with the amount of income. In other words, the strength of motivation is inversely correlated with the level of achievement.

In view of the lack of contact between economists and psychologists, it is hardly surprising that economists failed to see the relevance for their postulates of the extensive experimental work performed by psychologists on the problem of levels of aspiration. It is not necessary in this paper to describe these studies in detail. It may suffice to formulate three generalizations as established in numerous studies of goal-striving behavior:[24]

1. Aspirations are not static, they are not established once for all time.
2. Aspirations tend to grow with achievement and decline with failure.
3. Aspirations are influenced by the performance of other members of the group to which one belongs and by that of reference groups.

From these generalizations hypotheses were derived about the influence of assets on saving which differed from the postulates of the saturation theory. This is not the place to describe the extensive empirical work undertaken to test the hypotheses. But it may be reported that the saturation theory was not confirmed; the level-of-aspiration theory likewise did not suffice to explain the findings. In addition to the variable "size of liquid-asset holdings," the studies had to consider such variables as income level, income change, and saving habits. (Holders of large liquid assets are primarily people who have saved a high proportion of their income in the past!)[25]

The necessity of studying the interaction of a great number of variables and the change of choices over time leads to doubts regarding the universal validity of a one-dimensional ordering of all alternatives. The theory of measurement of utilities remains an empty frame unless people's established preferences of A over B and of B over C provide indications about their probable future behavior. Under what conditions do people's preferences give us such clues, and under what conditions do they not? If at different times A and B are seen in different contexts—because of changed external conditions or the acquisition of new experiences—we may have to distinguish among several dimensions.

The problem may be illustrated by an analogy. Classic economic theory postulates a one-dimensional ordering of all alternatives; Gallup asserts that answers to questions of choice can always be ordered

---

[24] K. Lewin, et al., "Level of Aspiration," in J. Hunt (Editor), *Personality and the Behavior Disorders* (New York: Ronald, 1944).

[25] The empirical work was part of the economic behavior program of the Survey Research Center under the direction of the author.

on a yes-uncertain (don't know)-no continuum; are both arguments subject to the same reservations? Specifically, if two persons give the same answer to a poll question (e.g., both say "Yes, I am for sending American troops to Europe" or "Yes, I am for the Taft-Hartley Act") may they mean different things so that their identical answers do not permit any conclusions about the similarity of their other attitudes and their behavior? Methodologically it follows from the last argument that yes-no questions need to be supplemented by open-ended questions to discern differences in people's level of information and motivation. It also follows that attitudes and preferences should be ascertained through a multi-question approach (or scaling) which serves to determine whether one or several dimensions prevail.

ON THEORY CONSTRUCTION

In attempting to summarize our conclusions about the respective merits of different scientific approaches, we might quote the conclusions of Arrow which he formulated for social science in general rather than for economics:

> To the extent that formal theoretical structures in the social sciences have not been based on the hypothesis of rational behavior, their postulates have been developed in a manner which we may term *ad hoc*. Such propositions. . . depend, of course, on the investigator's intuition and common sense.[26]

The last sentence seems strange indeed. One may argue the other way around and point out that such propositions as "the purpose of business is to make profits" or "the best businessman is the one who maximizes profits" are based on intuition or supposed common sense, rather than on controlled observation. The main problem raised by the quotation concerns the function of empirical research. There exists an alternative to developing an axiomatic system into a full-fledged theoretical model in advance of testing the theory through observations. Controlled observations should be based on hypotheses, and the formulation of an integrated theory need not be delayed until all observations are completed. Yet theory construction is part of the process of hypothesis-observation-revised hypothesis and prediction-observation, and systematization should rely on some empirical research. The proximate aim of scientific research is a body of empirically validated generalizations and not a theory that is valid under any and all circumstances.

---

[26] K. J. Arrow, "Mathematical Models in the Social Sciences," in D. Lerner and H. D. Lasswell (Editors), *The Policy Sciences* (Stanford: Stanford University Press, 1951), p. 137.

The dictum that "theoretical structures in the social sciences must be based on the hypothesis of rational behavior" presupposes that it is established what rational behavior is. Yet, instead of establishing the characteristics of rational behavior a priori, we must first determine the conditions a_1, b_1, c_1 under which behavior of the type x_1, y_1, z_1 and the conditions a_2, b_2, c_2 under which behavior of the type x_2, y_2, z_2 is likely to occur. Then, if we wish, we may designate one of the forms of behavior as rational. The contributions of psychology to this process are not solely methodological; findings and principles about noneconomic behavior provide hypotheses for the study of economic behavior. Likewise, psychology can profit from the study of economic behavior because many aspects of behavior, and among them the problems of rationality, may be studied most fruitfully in the economic field.

This paper was meant to indicate some promising leads for a study of rationality, not to carry such study to its completion. Among the problems that were not considered adequately were the philosophical ones (rationality viewed as a value concept), the psychoanalytic ones (the relationships between rational and conscious, and between irrational and unconscious), and those relating to personality theory and the roots of rationality. The emphasis was placed here on the possibility and fruitfulness of studying forms of rational behavior, rather than the characteristics of *the* rational man. Motives and goals that change with and are adapted to circumstances, and the relatively rare but highly significant cases of our becoming aware of problems and attempting to solve them, were found to be related to behavior that may be called truly rational.

10

Motivation, Cognition, Learning - Basic Factors in Consumer Behavior

James A. Bayton

MOTIVATION, COGNITION, LEARNING

The analysis of consumer behavior presented here is derived from diverse concepts of several schools of psychology—from psychoanalysis to reinforcement theory.

Human behavior can be grouped into three categories—motivation, cognition, and learning. Motivation refers to the drives, urges, wishes, or desires which initiate the sequence of events known as "behavior." Cognition is the area in which all of the mental phenomena (perception, memory, judging, thinking, etc.) are grouped. Learning refers to those changes in behavior which occur through time relative to external stimulus conditions.

Each broad area is pertinent to particular problems of consumer behavior. All three together are pertinent to a comprehensive understanding of consumer behavior.

MOTIVATION

Human Needs

Behavior is initiated through needs. Some psychologists claim that words such as "motives," "needs," "wishes," and "drives" should not

Reprinted from the *Journal of Marketing,* published by the American Marketing Association (January, 1958), pp. 282-289. This article won the 1958 Alpha Kappa Psi Award as best article of the year.

James A. Bayton is vice president of a public opinion research firm. He received his B.S. from Howard University and his M.S. and Ph.D. in psychology from the University of Pennsylvania. He has taught at several colleges, currently teaches at Howard, and has published work on motivation and consumer behavior.

be used as synonyms; others are content to use them interchangeably. There is one virtue in the term "drive" in that it carries the connotation of a force pushing the individual into action.

Motivation arises out of tension-systems which create a state of disequilibrium for the individual. This triggers a sequence of psychological events directed toward the selection of a goal which the individual *anticipates* will bring about release from the tensions and the selection of patterns of action which he *anticipates* will bring him to the goal.

One problem in motivation theory is deriving a basic list of the human needs. Psychologists agree that needs fall into two general categories—those arising from tension-systems physiological in nature (biogenic needs such as hunger, thirst, and sex), and those based upon tension-systems existing in the individual's subjective psychological state and in his relations with others (psychogenic needs).

Although there is not much disagreement as to the list of specific biogenic needs, there is considerable difference of opinion as to the list of specific psychogenic needs. However, the various lists of psychogenic needs can be grouped into three broad categories:

1. *Affectional needs*—the needs to form and maintain warm, harmonious, and emotionally satisfying relations with others.
2. *Ego-bolstering needs*—the needs to enhance or promote the personality; to achieve; to gain prestige and recognition; to satisfy the ego through domination of others.
3. *Ego-defensive needs*—the needs to protect the personality; to avoid physical and psychological harm; to avoid ridicule and "loss of face"; to prevent loss of prestige; to avoid or to obtain relief from anxiety.

One pitfall in the analysis of motivation is the assumption that a particular situation involves just one specific need. In most instances the individual is driven by a combination of needs. It seems likely that "love" brings into play a combination of affectional, ego-bolstering, and ego-defensive needs as well as biogenic needs. Within the combination some needs will be relatively strong, others relatively weak. The strongest need within the combination can be called the "prepotent" need. A given consumer product can be defined in terms of the specific need-combination involved and the relative strengths of these needs.

Another pitfall is the assumption that identical behaviors have identical motivational backgrounds. This pitfall is present whether we are thinking of two different individuals or the same individual at two different points in time. John and Harry can be different in the motivational patterns leading to the purchase of their suits. Each could have one motivational pattern influencing such a purchase at age twenty and another at age forty.

Ego-Involvement

One important dimension of motivation is the degree of ego-involvement. The various specific need-patterns are not equal in significance to the individual. Some are superficial in meaning; others represent (for the individual) tremendous challenges to the very essence of existence. There is some evidence that one of the positive correlates of degree of ego-involvement is the amount of cognitive activity (judging, thinking, etc.) involved. This means that consumer goods which tap low degrees of ego-involvement will be purchased with a relatively lower degree of conscious decision-making activity than goods which tap higher degrees of ego-involvement. Such a factor must be considered when decisions are made on advertising and marketing tactics.

At times the ego-involvement factor is a source of conflict between client and researcher. This can occur when research reveals that the product taps a low degree of ego-involvement within consumers. The result is difficult for a client to accept; because *he* is ego-involved and, therefore, cognitively active about his product, consumers must certainly be also. It is hard for such a client to believe that consumers simply do not engage in a great deal of cognitive activity when they make purchases within his product class. One way to ease this particular client-researcher conflict would be for the researcher to point out this implication of the ego-involvement dimension.

"True" and Rationalized Motives

A particular difficulty in the study of motivation is the possibility that there can be a difference between "true" motives and rationalized motives. Individuals sometimes are unaware of the exact nature of drives initiating their behavior patterns. When this occurs, they attempt to account for their behavior through "rationalization" by assigning motivations to their behavior which are acceptable to their personality structures. They may do this with no awareness that they are rationalizing. There can be other instances, however, in which individuals are keenly aware of their motivations, but feel it would be harmful or socially unacceptable to reveal them. When this is the case, they deliberately conceal their motivations.

These possibilities create a problem for the researcher. Must he assume that every behavior pattern is based upon unconscious motivation? If not, what criteria are to be used in deciding whether to be alert to unconscious motivation for this behavior pattern and not that one? What is the relative importance of unconscious motives, if present, and rationalized motives? Should rationalized motives be ignored? After all, rationalized motives have a certain validity for the individual—they are the "real" motives insofar as he is aware of the situation.

The situation is even more complicated than this—what about the dissembler? When the individual actually is dissembling, the researcher must attempt to determine the true motives. But, how shall we determine whether we are faced with a situation where the respondent is rationalizing or dissembling? In a given case, did a projective technique reveal an unconscious motive or the true motive of a dissembler? Conceptually, rationalized motives and dissembled motives are not equal in psychological implication; but it is rare, if ever, that one finds attempts to segregate the two in consumer research directed toward the analysis of motivation. This failure is understandable, to some extent, because of the lack of valid criteria upon which to base the distinction.

COGNITION

Need arousal

Motivation, thus, refers to a state of need-arousal—a condition exerting "push" on the individual to engage in those activities which he anticipates will have the highest probability of bringing him gratification of a particular need-pattern. Whether gratification actually will be attained or not is a matter of future events. Central to the psychological activities which now must be considered in the sequence are the complex of "mental" operations and forces known as the cognitive process. We can view these cognitive processes as being *purposive* in that they serve the individual in his attempts to achieve satisfaction of his needs. These cognitive processes are *regulatory* in that they determine in large measure the direction and particular steps taken in his attempt to attain satisfaction of the initiating needs.

The Ego-superego Concept

The ego-superego concept is pertinent to a discussion of cognitive activities which have been triggered by needs. Discussions of the ego-superego concept usually come under the heading of motivation as an aspect of personality. It is our feeling that motivation and the consequences of motivation should be kept systematically "clean." In the broadest sense, ego and superego are mental entities in that they involve memory, perceiving, judging, and thinking.

The Ego. The ego is the "executive," determining how the individual shall seek satisfaction of his needs. Through perception, memory, judging, and thinking the ego attempts to integrate the needs, on the one hand, and the conditions of the external world, on the other, in such manner that needs can be satisfied without danger or harm to the individual. Often this means that gratification must be postponed until a situation has developed, or has been encountered, which does not contain harm or danger. The turnpike driver who does not exceed the speed limit because he sees signs saying there are radar checks is under the influence of the ego. So is the driver who sees no cars on a straight stretch and takes the opportunity to drive at excessive speed.

The Superego. The superego involves the ego-ideal and conscience. The ego-ideal represents the positive standards of ethical and moral conduct the individual has developed for himself. Conscience is, in a sense, the "judge," evaluating the ethics and morality of behavior and, through guilt-feelings, administering punishment when these are violated. If a driver obeys the speed limit because he would feel guilty in doing otherwise, he is under the influence of the superego. (The first driver above is under the influence of the ego because he is avoiding a fine, not guilt feelings.)

Specific Examples

Credit is a form of economic behavior based to some extent upon ego-superego considerations. It is generally felt that one cause of consumer-credit expansion has been a shift away from the superego's role in attitudes toward credit. The past ego-ideal was to build savings; debt was immoral—something to feel guilty about, to avoid, to hide. These two superego influences restrained the use of credit. For some cultural reason, credit and debt have shifted away from the superego dominance and are now more under the control of the ego—the primary concern now seems to be how much of it can be used without risking financial danger.

The purchasing of specific consumer goods can be considered from the point of view of these two influences. Certain goods (necessities, perhaps) carry little superego influence, and the individual is psychologically free to try to maximize the probability of obtaining satisfaction of his needs while minimizing the probability of encountering harm in so doing. Other goods, however, tap the superego. When a product represents an aspect of the ego-ideal there is a strong positive force to possess it. Conversely, when a product involves violation of the conscience, a strong negative force is generated against its purchase.

Let us assume that, when the need-push asserts itself, a variety of goal-objects come into awareness as potential sources of gratification. In consumer behavior these goal-objects may be different brand names. The fact that a particular set of goal-objects come into awareness indicates the generic character of this stage in the cognitive process— a class of goal-objects is seen as containing the possible satisfier. What the class of goal-objects and the specific goal-objects within the class "promise" in terms of gratification are known as "expectations."

There are, then, two orders of expectation: generic expectancies, and object-expectancies. Suppose the needs were such that the individual "thought" of brands of frozen orange juice. Some of the generic expectations for frozen orange juice are a certain taste, quality, source of vitamin C, protection against colds, and ease of preparation. The particular brands carry expectations specifically associated with one brand as against another. The expectation might be that brand A has a more refreshing taste than brand B.

In many instances, cognitive competition occurs between two or more generic categories before it does between goal-objects within a generic category. Much consumer-behavior research is directed toward the investigation of generic categories—tires, automobiles, appliances, etc. But perhaps not enough attention has been given to the psychological analysis of cognitive competition between generic categories. An example of a problem being studied is the competition between television viewing, movie going, and magazine reading. For a particular producer, cognitive competition within the pertinent generic category is usually of more concern than cognitive competition between his generic category and others. The producer usually wants only an intensive analysis of consumer psychology with respect to the particular generic category of which his product is a member.

Let us now assume that under need-push four alternative goal-objects (brands A, B, C, and D) came into awareness. Why these particular brands and not others? Why are brands E and F absent? An obvious reason for brand E's absence might be that the individual had never been exposed to the fact that brand E exists. He had been exposed to brand F, however. Why is it absent? The problem here is one of memory—a key cognitive process. The producers of brands E and F obviously are faced with different problems.

Two sets of circumstances contain the independent variables

that determine whether a given item will be remembered. One is the nature of the experience resulting from actual consumption or utilization of the goal-object. This will be discussed later when we come to the reinforcement theory of learning. The other is the circumstances present on what might be called vicarious exposures to the goal-object—vicarious in that at the time of exposure actual consumption or utilization of the goal-object does not occur. The most obvious example would be an advertisement of the goal-object. Of course, the essential purpose of an advertisement is to expose the individual to the goal-object in such a manner that at some subsequent time it will be remembered readily. The search for the most effective methods of doing this by manipulation of the physical aspects of the advertisement and the appeals used in it is a continuing effort in consumer-behavior research. Finally, for many consumers these two sets of circumstances will be jointly operative. Experiences with the goal-object and subsequent vicarious exposures can coalesce to heighten the memory potential for them.

Making a Choice

With, say, four brands in awareness, the individual must now make a choice. What psychological factors underlie this choice? The four brands could be in awareness due to the memory factor because they are immediately present in the environment; or some because they are in the environment, and the others because of memory.

The first problem is the extent to which the items are differentiated. The various goal objects have attributes which permit the individual to differentiate between them. The brand name is one attribute; package another; design still another. These differentiating attributes (from the point of view of the consumer's perceptions) can be called signs or cues. All such signs are not equally important in consumer decisions. Certain of them are depended upon much more than others. For example, in a study of how housewives select fresh oranges, the critical or key signs were thickness of skin, color of skin, firmness of the orange, and presence or absence of "spots" on the skin.

The signs have expectancies associated with them. Package (a sign) can carry the expectancy of quality. Thinskin oranges carry the expectancy of juice; spots carry the expectancy of poor taste quality and insufficient amount of juice. Often sign-expectancies determined through consumer research are irrelevant or invalid. Signs are irrelevant when they do not represent a critical differentiating attribute of a goal-object. Certain discolorations on oranges have nothing to do with their intrinsic quality. Expectancies are invalid when they refer to qualities that do not in fact exist in association with a particular sign.

The different goal-objects in awareness can be assessed in terms of the extent to which they arouse similar expectancies. This phenomenon of similarity of expectations within a set of different goal-objects is known as generalization. One goal-object (brand A, perhaps) because of its associated expectancies, can be assumed to have maximum appeal within the set of alternative goal-objects. The alternates then can be ordered in terms of how their associated expectancies approximate those of brand A. Is this ordering and the psychological distances between the items of the nature of:

Brand A		Brand A
Brand B		
	or	Brand B
Brand C		Brand C

These differences in ordering and psychological distance are referred to as generalization gradients. In the first case, the expectancies associated with brand B are quite similar to those of brand A, but are not quite as powerful in appeal. Brand C has relatively little of this. In the second case, the generalization gradient is of a different form, showing that brand B offers relatively little psychological competition to brand A. (There will also be generalization gradients with respect to cognitive competition between generic categories.) In addition to the individual producer being concerned about the memory potential of his particular brand, he needs to determine the nature of the generalization gradient for his product and the products of his competitors. Mere ordering is not enough—the "psychological distances" between positions must be determined, also, and the factor determining these distances is similarity and expectancy.

The discussion above was concerned with cognitive processes as they relate to mental representation of goal-objects under the instigation of need-arousal. The items brought into awareness, the differentiating sign-expectancies, and the generalization gradient are the central factors in the particular cognitive field aroused under a given "need-push." One important dimension has not yet been mentioned—instrumental acts. These are acts necessary in obtaining the goal-object and the acts involved in consuming or utilizing it. Examples are: "going downtown" to get to a department store, squeezing the orange to get its juice, ease of entry into service stations, and the operations involved in do-it-yourself house painting.

Instrumental acts can have positive or negative value for the individual. One who makes fewer shopping trips to downtown stores because of traffic and parking conditions displays an instrumental act with negative value. Frozen foods are products for which much of the appeal lies in the area of instrumental acts. The development of automatic transmissions and of power-steering automobiles are examples of product changes concerned with instrumental acts. The point is that concentration upon cognitive reactions to the goal-object, *per se*, could be masking critical aspects of the situation based upon cognitive reactions to the instrumental acts involved in obtaining or utilizing the goal-object.

LEARNING

Goal-object

Starting with need-arousal, continuing under the influence of cognitive processes, and engaging in the necessary action, the individual arrives at consumption or utilization of a goal-object. Using our consumer-behavior illustration, let us say that the consumer bought brand A and is now in the process of consuming or utilizing it. We have now arrived at one of the most critical aspects of the entire psychological sequence. It is with use of the goal-object that degree of gratification of the initial needs will occur.

Reinforcement

When consumption or utilization of the goal-object leads to gratification of the initiating needs there is "reinforcement." If at some later date the same needs are aroused, the individual will tend to repeat the process of selecting and getting to the same goal-object. If brand A yields a high degree of gratification, then at some subsequent time, when the same needs arise, the consumer will have an increased tendency to select brand A once again. Each succeeding time that brand A brings gratification, further reinforcement occurs, thus further increasing the likelihood that in the future, with the given needs, brand A will be selected.

This type of behavioral change—increasing likelihood that an act will be repeated—is learning; and reinforcement is necessary for learning to take place. Continued reinforcement will influence the cognitive processes. Memory of the goal-object will be increasingly enhanced; particular sign-expectancies will be more and more firmly established; and the generalization gradient will be changed in that the psychological distance on this gradient between brand A and the competing brands will be increased.

Habit

One of the most important consequences of continued reinforcement is the influence this has on the extent to which cognitive processes enter the picture at the times of subsequent need-arousal. With continued reinforcement, the amount of cognitive activity decreases; the individual engages less and less in decision-making mental activities. This can continue until, upon need-arousal, the goal-obtaining activities are practically automatic. At this stage there is a habit.

Note this use of the term "habit." One frequently hears that a person does certain things by "*force* of habit," that habit is an initiator of behavioral sequences. Actually habits are not initiating forces in themselves; habits are repeated response patterns accompanied by a minimum of cognitive activity. There must be some condition of need-arousal before the habit-type response occurs. This has serious implications in the field of consumer behavior. The promotional and marketing problems faced by a competitor of brand A will be of one type if purchase behavior for brand A is habitual, of another if this is not true. If the purchase is largely a habit, there is little cognitive activity available for the competitor to "work on."

Frequency of repeating a response is not a valid criterion for determining whether or not a habit exists. An act repeated once a week can be just as much a habit as one repeated several times a day. The frequency of a response is but an index of the frequency with which the particular need-patterns are aroused. Frequency of response also is often used as a measure of the *strength* of a habit. The test of the strength of a habit is the extent to which an individual will persist in an act after it has ceased providing need gratification. The greater this persistence, the stronger was the habit in the first place.

PROBLEM—CONCEPT—RESEARCH

The above views integrate concepts in contemporary psychology which seem necessary for a comprehensive explanation of human behavior, and apply these concepts to the analysis of consumer behavior. Each psychological process touched upon contains areas for further analysis and and specification.

Some type of comprehensive theory of human behavior is necessary as a *working tool* to avoid a lack of discipline in attacking problems in consumer behavior. Too frequently a client with a practical problem approaches a researcher with an indication that all that is needed is a certain methodology—depth interviewing, scaling, or projective devices, for example.

The first step should be to take the practical problem and translate it into its pertinent conceptual entities. This phase of the problem raises the question of motivations. Here is a question involving relevance and validity of sign-expectancies. There is a question dealing with a generalization gradient, etc. Once the pertinent conceptual entities have been identified, and only then, we arrive at the stage of hypothesis formulation. Within each conceptual entity, a relationship between independent and dependent variables is established as a hypothesis to be tested.

Often the relation between conceptual entities must be investigated. For example, what is the effect of continuing reinforcement on a specific generalization gradient? Within the same research project, one psychological entity can be a dependent variable at one phase of the research and an independent variable at another. At one time we might be concerned with establishing the factors associated with differential memory of sign-expectancies. At another time we could be concerned with the influence of remembered sign-expectancies upon subsequent purchase-behavior.

Discipline requires that one turn to methodology only when the pertinent conceptual entities have been identified and the relationships between independent and dependent variables have been expressed in the form of hypotheses. Fundamentally this sequence in the analysis of a problem serves to delimit the methodological possibilities. In any event, the methodologies demanded are those which will produce unambiguous tests of each particular hypothesis put forth. Finally, the results must be translated into the terms of the original practical problem.

We have used the term "discipline" in this phase of our discussion. The researcher must discipline himself to follow the above steps. Some find this a difficult thing to do and inevitably their data become ambiguous. They must resort to improvisation in order to make sense of the results *after* the project is completed. A research project is truly a work of art when the conceptual analysis, the determination of the hypotheses, and the methodologies have been developed in such an "air-tight sequence that practially all that is necessary is to let the facts speak for themselves.

11

Behavioral Models for Analyzing Buyers

Philip Kotler

In times past, management could arrive at a fair understanding of its buyers through the daily experience of selling to them. But the growth in the size of firms and markets has removed many decision-makers from direct contact with buyers. Increasingly, decision-makers have had to turn to summary statistics and to behavioral theory, and are spending more money today than ever before to try to understand their buyers.

Who buys? How do they buy? And why? The first two questions relate to relatively overt aspects of buyer behavior, and can be learned about through direct observation and interviewing.

But uncovering *why* people buy is an extremely difficult task. The answer will tend to vary with the investigator's behavioral frame of reference.

The buyer is subject to many influences which trace a complex course through his psyche and lead eventually to overt purchasing responses. This conception of the buying process is illustrated in Figure 1. Various influences and their modes of transmission are shown at the left. At the right are the buyer's responses in choice of product, brand, dealer, quantities, and frequency. In the center stands the buyer and his mysterious psychological processes. The buyer's psyche is a "black box" whose workings can be only partially deduced. The marketing strategist's challenge to the behavioral scientist is to construct a more specific model of the mechanism in the black box. Unfortunately no generally accepted model of the mechanism

Reprinted from the *Journal of Marketing*, published by the American Marketing Association, Vol. 29, No. 4, October 1965, pp. 37–45.

Philip Kotler, Harold T. Martin professor of marketing at Northwestern University, received his Ph.D. in economics from the Massachusetts Institute of Technology. He did post-doctoral work in mathematics and in the behavioral sciences at Harvard University and the University of Chicago respectively. His articles have appeared in numerous scholarly journals; several have won best article awards. His textbook, *Marketing Management: Analysis, Planning, and Control,* is widely used.

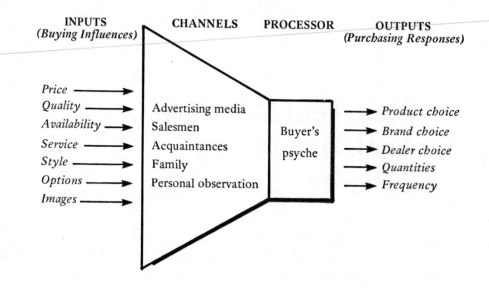

| INPUTS (Buying Influences) | CHANNELS | PROCESSOR | OUTPUTS (Purchasing Responses) |

Price ⟶
Quality ⟶
Availability ⟶
Service ⟶
Style ⟶
Options ⟶
Images ⟶

Advertising media
Salesmen
Acquaintances
Family
Personal observation

Buyer's psyche

⟶ *Product choice*
⟶ *Brand choice*
⟶ *Dealer choice*
⟶ *Quantities*
⟶ *Frequency*

FIGURE 1. *The buying process conceived as a system of inputs and outputs.*

exists. The human mind, the only entity in nature with deep powers of understanding, still remains the least understood. Scientists can explain planetary motion, genetic determination, and molecular behavior. Yet they have only partial, and often partisan, models of *human* behavior.

Nevertheless, the marketing strategist should recognize the potential interpretative contributions of different partial models for explaining buyer behavior. Depending upon the product, different variables and behavioral mechanisms may assume particular importance. A psychoanalytic behavioral model might throw much light on the factors operating in cigarette demand, while an economic behavioral model might be useful in explaining machine-tool purchasing. Sometimes alternative models may shed light on different demand aspects of the same product.

What are the most useful behavioral models for interpreting the transformation of buying influences into purchasing responses? Five different models of the buyer's "black box" are presented in the present article, along with their respective marketing applications: (1) the Marshallian model, stressing economic motivations; (2) the Pavlovian model, learning; (3) the Freudian model, psychoanalytic motivations; (4) the Veblenian model, social-psychological factors; and (5) the

Hobbesian model, organizational factors. These models represent radically different conceptions of the mainsprings of human behavior.

THE MARSHALLIAN ECONOMIC MODEL

Economists were the first professional group to construct a specific theory of buyer behavior. The theory holds that purchasing decisions are the result of largely "rational" and conscious economic calculations. The individual buyer seeks to spend his income on those goods that will deliver the most utility (satisfaction) according to his tastes and relative prices.

The antecedents for this view trace back to the writings of Adam Smith and Jeremy Bentham. Smith set the tone by developing a doctrine of economic growth based on the principle that man is motivated by self-interest in all his actions.[1] Bentham refined this view and saw man as finely calculating and weighing the expected pleasures and pains of every contemplated action.[2]

Bentham's "felicific calculus" was not applied to consumer behavior (as opposed to entrepreneurial behavior) until the late 19th century. Then, the "marginal-utility" theory of value was formulated independently and almost simultaneously by Jevons[3] and Marshall[4] in England, Menger[5] in Austria, and Walras[6] in Switzerland.

Alfred Marshall was the great consolidator of the classical and neoclassical tradition in economics; and his synthesis in the form of demand-supply analysis constitutes the main source of modern microeconomic thought in the English-speaking world. His theoretical work aimed at realism, but his method was to start with simplifying assumptions and to examine the effect of a change in the single variable (say, price) when all other variables were held constant.

He would "reason out" the consequences of the provisional assumptions and in subsequent steps modify his assumptions in the direction of more realism. He employed the "measuring rod of money" as an indicator of the intensity of human psychological desires. Over the years his methods and assumptions have been refined into what is

---

[1] Adam Smith, *An Inquiry into the Nature and Causes of the Wealth of Nations*, 1776 (New York: The Modern Library, 1937).

[2] Jeremy Bentham, *An Introduction to the Principles of Morals and Legislation*, 1780 (Oxford, England: Clarendon Press, 1907).

[3] William S. Jevons, *The Theory of Political Economy* (New York: The Macmillan Company, 1871).

[4] Alfred Marshall, *Principles of Economics* 1890 (London: The Macmillan Company, 1927).

[5] Karl Menger, *Principles of Economics*, 1871 (Glencoe, Illinois: Free Press, 1950).

[6] Leon Walras, *Elements of Pure Economics*, 1874 (Homewood, Illinois: Richard D. Irwin, Inc., 1954).

now known as *modern utility theory:* economic man is bent on maximizing his utility, and does this by carefully calculating the "felicific" consequences of any purchase.

As an example, suppose on a particular evening that John is considering whether to prepare his own dinner or dine out. He estimates that a restaurant meal would cost $2.00 and a home-cooked meal 50 cents. According to the Marshallian model, if John expects less than four times as much satisfaction from the restaurant meal as the home-cooked meal, he will eat at home. The economist typically is not concerned with how these relative preferences are formed by John, or how they may be psychologically modified by new stimuli.

Yet John will not always cook at home. The principle of diminishing marginal utility operates. Within a given time interval—say, a week—the utility of each additional home-cooked meal diminishes. John gets tired of home meals and other products become relatively more attractive.

John's *efficiency* in maximizing his utility depends on the adequacy of his information and his freedom of choice. If he is not perfectly aware of costs, if he misestimates the relative delectability of the two meals, or if he is barred from entering the restaurant, he will not maximize his potential utility. His choice processes are rational, but the results are inefficient.

Marketing Applications of Marshallian Model

Marketers usually have dismissed the Marshallian model as an absurd figment of ivory-tower imagination. Certainly the behavioral essence of the situation is omitted, in viewing man as calculating the marginal utility of a restaurant meal over a home-cooked meal.

Eva Mueller has reported a study where only one-fourth of the consumers in her sample bought with any substantial degree of deliberation.[7] Yet there are a number of ways to view the model.

From one point of view the Marshallian model is tautological and therefore neither true nor false. The model holds that the buyer acts in the light of his best "interest." But this is not very informative.

A second view is that this is a *normative* rather than a *descriptive* model of behavior. The model provides logical norms for buyers who want to be "rational." Although the consumer is not likely to employ economic analysis to decide between a box of Kleenex and Scotties, he may apply economic analysis in deciding whether to buy a new car.

[7]Eva Mueller, "A Study of Purchase Decisions," Part 2, *Consumer Behavior, The Dynamics of Consumer Reaction*, edited by Lincoln H. Clark (New York: New York University Press, 1954), pp. 36-87.

Industrial buyers even more clearly would want an economic calculus for making good decisions.

A third view is that economic factors operate to a greater or lesser extent in all markets, and, therefore, must be included in any comprehensive description of buyer behavior.

Furthermore, the model suggests useful behavioral hypotheses such as: (a) The lower the price of the product, the higher the sales. (b) The lower the price of substitute products, the lower the sales of this product; and the lower the price of complementary products, the higher the sales of this product. (c) The higher the real income, the higher the sales of this product, provided that it is not an "inferior" good. (d) The higher the promotional expenditures, the higher the sales.

The validity of these hypotheses does not rest on whether *all* individuals act as economic calculating machines in making their purchasing decisions. For example, some individuals may buy *less* of a product when its price is reduced. They may think that the quality has gone down, or that ownership has less status value. If a majority of buyers view price reductions negatively, then sales may fall, contrary to the first hypothesis.

But for most goods a price reduction increases the relative value of the goods in many buyers' minds and leads to increased sales. This and the other hypotheses are intended to describe average effects.

The impact of economic factors in actual buying situations is studied through experimental design or statistical analyses of past data. Demand equations have been fitted to a wide variety of prod-ucts—including beer, refrigerators, and chemical fertilizers.[8] More recently, the impact of economic variables on the fortunes of different brands has been pursued with significant results, particularly in the case of coffee, frozen orange juice, and margarine.[9]

But economic factors alone cannot explain all the variations in sales. The Marshallian model ignores the fundamental question of how product and brand preferences are formed. It represents a useful frame of reference for analyzing only one small corner of the "black box."

THE PAVLOVIAN LEARNING MODEL

The designation of a Pavlovian learning model has its origin in the experiments of the Russian psychologist Pavlov, who rang a bell each

---

[8]See Erwin E. Nemmers, *Managerial Economics* (New York: John Wiley & Sons, Inc., 1962), Part II.

[9]See Lester G. Telser, "The Demand for Branded Goods as Estimated from Consumer Panel Data," *Review of Economics and Statistics*, Vol. 44 (August, 1962), pp. 300-324; and William F. Massey and Ronald E. Frank, "Short Term Price and Dealing Effects in Selected Market Segments," *Journal of Marketing Research*, Vol. 2 (May, 1965), pp. 171-185.

time before feeding a dog. Soon he was able to induce the dog to salivate by ringing the bell whether or not food was supplied. Pavlov concluded that learning was largely an associative process and that a large component of behavior was conditioned in this way.

Experimental psychologists have continued this mode of research with rats and other animals, including people. Laboratory experiments have been designed to explore such phenomena as learning, forgetting, and the ability to discriminate. The results have been integrated into a stimulus-response model of human behavior, or as someone has "wise-cracked," the substitution of a rat psychology for a rational psychology.

The model has been refined over the years, and today is based on four central concepts—those of *drive, cue, response,* and *reinforcement.*[10]

Drive. Also called needs or motives, drive refers to strong stimuli internal to the individual which impel action. Psychologists draw a distinction between primary pysiological drives—such as hunger, thirst, cold, pain, and sex—and learned drives which are derived socially— such as cooperation, fear, and acquisitiveness.

Cue. A drive is very general and impels a particular response only in relation to a particular configuration of cues. Cues are weaker stimuli in the environment and/or in the individual which determine when, where, and how the subject responds. Thus, a coffee advertisement can serve as a cue which stimulates the thirst drive in a housewife. Her response will depend upon this cue and other cues, such as the time of day, the availability of other thirst-quenchers, and the cue's intensity. Often a relative change in a cue's intensity can be more impelling than its absolute level. The housewife may be more motivated by a 2-cents-off sale on a brand of coffee than the fact that this brand's price was low in the first place.

Response. The response is the organism's reaction to the configuration of cues. Yet the same configuration of cues will not necessarily produce the same response in the individual. This depends on the degree to which the experience was rewarding, that is, drive-reducing.

Reinforcement. If the experience is rewarding, a particular response is reinforced; that is, it is strengthened and there is a tendency for it to be repeated when the same configuration of cues appears again. The housewife, for example, will tend to purchase the same brand of

---

[10] See John Dollard and Neal E. Miller, *Personality and Psychotherapy* (New York: McGraw-Hill Book Company, Inc., 1950), Chapter III.

coffee each time she goes to her supermarket so long as it is rewarding and the cue configuration does not change. But if a learned response or habit is not reinforced, the strength of the habit diminishes and may be extinguished eventually. Thus, a housewife's preference for a certain coffee may become extinct if she finds the brand out of stock for a number of weeks.

Forgetting, in contrast to extinction, is the tendency for learned associations to weaken, not because of the lack of reinforcement but because of nonuse.

Cue configurations are constantly changing. The housewife sees a new brand of coffee next to her habitual brand, or notes a special price deal on a rival brand. Experimental psychologists have found that the same learned response will be elicited by similar patterns of cues; that is, learned responses are *generalized.* The housewife shifts to a similar brand when her favorite brand is out of stock. This tendency toward generalization over less similar cue configurations is increased in proportion to the strength of the drive. A housewife may buy an inferior coffee if it is the only brand left and if her drive is sufficiently strong.

A counter-tendency to generalization is *discrimination.* When a housewife tries two similar brands and finds one more rewarding, her ability to discriminate between similar cue configurations improves. Discrimination increases the specificity of the cue-response connection, while generalization decreases the specificity.

Marketing Applications of Pavlovian Model

The modern version of the Pavlovian model makes no claim to provide a complete theory of behavior—indeed, such important phenomena as perception, the subconscious, and interpersonal influence are inadequately treated. Yet the model does offer a substantial number of insights about some aspects of behavior of considerable interest to marketers.[11]

An example would be in the problem of introducing a new brand into a highly competitive market. The company's goal is to extinguish existing brand habits and form new habits among consumers for its brand. But the company must first get customers to try its brand; and it has to decide between using weak and strong cues.

Light introductory advertising is a weak cue compared with

---

[11] The most consistent application of learning-theory concepts to marketing situations is found in John A. Howard, *Marketing Management: Analysis and Planning* (Homewood, Illinois: Richard D. Irwin, Inc., revised edition, 1963).

distributing free samples. Strong cues, although costing more, may be necessary in markets characterized by strong brand loyalties. For example, Folger went into the coffee market by distributing over a million pounds of free coffee.

To build a brand habit, it helps to provide for an extended period of introductory dealing. Furthermore, sufficient quality must be built into the brand so that the experience is reinforcing. Since buyers are more likely to transfer allegiance to similar brands than dissimilar brands (generalization), the company should also investigate what cues in the leading brands have been most effective. Although outright imitation would not necessarily effect the most transference, the question of providing enough similarity should be considered.

The Pavlovian model also provides guidelines in the area of advertising strategy. The American behaviorist, John B. Watson, was a great exponent of repetitive stimuli; in his writings man is viewed as a creature who can be conditioned through repetition and reinforcement to respond in particular ways.[12] The Pavlovian model emphasizes the desirability of repetition in advertising. A single exposure is likely to be a very weak cue, hardly able to penetrate the individual's consciousness sufficiently to excite his drives above the threshold level.

Repetition in advertising has two desirable effects. It "fights" forgetting, the tendency for learned responses to weaken in the absence of practice. It provides reinforcement, because after the purchase the consumer becomes selectively exposed to advertisements of the products.

The model also provides guidelines for copy strategy. To be effective as a cue, an advertisement must arouse strong drives in the person. The strongest product-related drives must be identified. For candy bars, it may be hunger; for safety belts, fear; for hair tonics, sex; for automobiles, status. The advertising practitioner must dip into his cue box—words, colors, pictures—and select that configuration of cues that provides the strongest stimulus to these drives.

THE FREUDIAN PSYCHOANALYTIC MODEL

The Freudian model of man is well known, so profound has been its impact on 20th century thought. It is the latest of a series of philosophical "blows" to which man has been exposed in the last 500 years. Copernicus destroyed the idea that man stood at the center of the universe; Darwin tried to refute the idea that man was a special

---

[12] John B. Watson, *Behaviorism* (New York: The People's Institute Publishing Company, 1925).

creation; and Freud attacked the idea that man even reigned over his own psyche.

According to Freud, the child enters the world driven by instinctual needs which he cannot gratify by himself. Very quickly and painfully he realizes his separateness from the rest of the world and yet his dependence on it.

He tries to get others to gratify his needs through a variety of blatant means, including intimidation and supplication. Continual frustration leads him to perfect more subtle mechanisms for gratifying his instincts.

As he grows, his psyche becomes increasingly complex. A part of his psyche—the id—remains the reservoir of his strong drives and urges. Another part—the ego—becomes his conscious planning center for finding outlets for his drives. And a third part—his super-ego—channels his instinctive drives into socially approved outlets to avoid the pain of guilt or shame.

The guilt or shame which man feels toward some of his urges—especially his sexual urges—causes him to repress them from his consciousness. Through such defense mechanisms as rationalization and sublimation, these urges are denied or become transmuted into socially approved expressions. Yet these urges are never eliminated or under perfect control; and they emerge, sometimes with a vengeance, in dreams, in slips-of-the-tongue, in neurotic and obsessional behavior, or ultimately in mental breakdown where the ego can no longer maintain the delicate balance between the impulsive power of the id and the oppressive power of the super-ego.

The individual's behavior, therefore, is never simple. His motivational well-springs are not obvious to a casual observer nor deeply understood by the individual himself. If he is asked why he purchased an expensive foreign sports car, he may reply that he likes its maneuverability and its looks. At a deeper level he may have purchased the car to impress others or to feel young again. At a still deeper level, he may be purchasing the sports car to achieve substitute gratification for unsatisfied sexual strivings.

Many refinements and changes in emphasis have occurred in this model since the time of Freud. The instinct concept has been replaced by a more careful delineation of basic drives; the three parts of the psyche are regarded now as theoretical concepts rather than actual entities; and the behavioral perspective has been extended to include cultural as well as biological mechanisms.

Instead of the role of the sexual urge in psychic development—Freud's discussion of oral, anal, and genital stages and possible fixations and traumas—Adler[13] emphasized the urge for power and how its

[13] Alfred Adler, *The Science of Living* (New York: Greenberg, 1929).

thwarting manifests itself in superiority and inferiority complexes; Horney[14] emphasized cultural mechanisms; and Fromm[15] and Erikson[16] emphasized the role of existential crises in personality development. These philosophical divergencies, rather than debilitating the model, have enriched and extended its interpretative value to a wider range of behavioral phenomena.

Marketing Applications of Freudian Model

Perhaps the most important marketing implication of this model is that buyers are motivated by *symbolic* as well as *economic-functional* product concerns. The change of a bar of soap from a square to a round shape may be more important in its sexual than its functional connotations. A cake mix that is advertised as involving practically no labor may alienate housewives because the easy life may evoke a sense of guilt.

Motivational research has produced some interesting and occasionally some bizarre hypotheses about what may be in the buyer's mind regarding certain purchases. Thus, it has been suggested at one time or another that

- Many a businessman doesn't fly because of a fear of posthumous guilt—if he crashed, his wife would think of him as stupid for not taking a train.
- Men want their cigars to be odoriferous, in order to prove that they (the men) are masculine.
- A woman is very serious when she bakes a cake because unconsciously she is going through the symbolic act of giving birth.
- A man buys a convertible as a substitute mistress.
- Consumers prefer vegetable shortening because animal fats stimulate a sense of sin.
- Men who wear suspenders are reacting to an unresolved castration complex.

There are admitted difficulties of proving these assertions. Two prominent motivational researchers, Ernest Dichter and James Vicary, were employed independently by two separate groups in the prune industry to determine why so many people dislike prunes. Dichter found, among other things, that the prune aroused feelings of old age and insecurity in people, whereas Vicary's main finding was that

---

[14] Karen Horney, *The Neurotic Personality of Our Time* (New York: W. W. Norton & Co., 1937).

[15] Erich Fromm, *Man For Himself* (New York: Holt, Rinehart & Winston, Inc., 1947).

[16] Erik Erikson, *Childhood and Society* (New York: W. W. Norton & Co., 1949).

Americans had an emotional block about prunes' laxative qualities.[17] Which is the more valid interpretation? Or if they are both operative, which motive is found with greater statistical frequency in the population?

Unfortunately the usual survey techniques—direct observation and interviewing—can be used to establish the representativeness of more superficial characteristics—age and family size, for example—but are not feasible for establishing the frequency of mental states which are presumed to be deeply buried within each individual.

Motivational researchers have to employ time-consuming projective techniques in the hope of throwing individual egos off guard. When carefully administered and interpreted, techniques such as word association, sentence completion, picture interpretation, and role-playing can provide some insights into the minds of the small group of examined individuals; but a "leap of faith" is sometimes necessary to generalize these findings to the population.

Nevertheless, motivation research can lead to useful insights and provide inspiration to creative men in the advertising and packaging world. Appeals aimed at the buyer's private world of hopes, dreams, and fears can often be as effective in stimulating purchase as more rationally directed appeals.

THE VEBLENIAN SOCIAL-PSYCHOLOGICAL MODEL

While most economists have been content to interpret buyer behavior in Marshallian terms, Thorstein Veblen struck out in different directions.

Veblen was trained as an orthodox economist but evolved into a social thinker greatly influenced by the new science of social anthropology. He saw man as primarily a *social animal*—conforming to the general forms and norms of his larger culture and to the more specific standards of the subcultures and face-to-face groupings to which his life is bound. His wants and behavior are largely molded by his present group memberships and his aspired group memberships.

Veblen's best-known example of this is in his description of the leisure class.[18] His hypothesis is that much of economic consumption is motivated not by intrinsic needs or satisfaction so much as by prestige

---

[17]L. Edward Scriven, "Rationality and Irrationality in Motivation Research," in Robert Ferber and Hugh G. Wales, editors, *Motivation and Marketing Behavior* (Homewood, Illinois: Richard D. Irwin, Inc., 1958), pp. 69-70.

[18]Thorstein Veblen, *The Theory of the Leisure Class* (New York: Macmillan Publishing Co., Inc., 1899).

seeking. He emphasized the strong emulative factors operating in the choice of conspicuous goods like clothes, cars, and houses.

Some of his points, however, seem overstated by today's perspective. The leisure class does not serve as everyone's reference group; many persons aspire to the social patterns of the class immediately above them. And important segments of the affluent class practice conspicuous underconsumption rather than overconsumption. There are many people in all classes who are more anxious to "fit in" than to "stand out." As an example, William H. Whyte found that many families avoided buying air conditioners and other appliances before their neighbors did.[19]

Veblen was not the first nor the only investigator to comment on social influences in behavior; but the incisive quality of his observations did much to stimulate further investigations. Another stimulus came from Karl Marx, who held that each man's world-view was determined largely by his relationship to the "means of production."[20] The early field work in primitive societies by social anthropologists like Boas[21] and Malinowski[22] and the later field work in urban societies by men like Park[23] and Thomas[24] contributed much to understanding the influence of society and culture. The research of early Gestalt psychologists—men like Wertheimer,[25] Köhler,[26] and Koffka[27]—into the mechanisms of perception led eventually to investigations of small-group influence on perception.

MARKETING APPLICATIONS OF VEBLENIAN MODEL

The various streams of thought crystallized into the modern social sciences of sociology, cultural anthropology, and social psychology. Basic to them is the view that man's attitudes and behavior are influenced by several levels of society—culture, subcultures, social classes, reference groups, and face-to-face groups. The challenge to the marketer is to determine which of these social levels are the most important in influencing the demand for his product.

[19] William H. Whyte, Jr., "The Web of Word of Mouth," *Fortune,* Vol. 50 (November, 1954), pp. 140 ff.

[20] Karl Marx, *The Communist Manifesto,* 1848 (London: Martin Lawrence, Ltd., 1934).

[21] Franz Boas, *The Mind of Primitive Man* (New York: Macmillan Publishing Co., Inc., 1922).

[22] Bronislaw Malinowski, *Sex and Repression in Savage Society* (New York: Meridian Books, 1955).

[23] Robert E. Park, *Human Communities* (Glencoe, Illinois: Free Press, 1952).

[24] William I. Thomas, *The Unadjusted Girl* (Boston: Little, Brown and Company, 1928).

[25] Max Wertheimer, *Productive Thinking* (New York: Harper & Brothers, 1945).

[26] Wolfgang Köhler, *Gestalt Psychology* (New York: Liveright Publishing Co., 1947).

[27] Kurt Koffka, *Principles of Gestalt Psychology* (New York: Harcourt, Brace and Co., 1935)

Culture

The most enduring influences are from culture. Man tends to assimilate his culture's mores and folkways and to believe in their absolute rightness until deviants appear within his culture or until he confronts members of another culture.

Subcultures

A culture tends to lose it homogeneity as its population increases. When people no longer are able to maintain face-to-face relationships with more than a small proportion of other members of a culture, smaller units or subcultures develop, which help to satisfy the individual's needs for more specific identity.

The subcultures are often regional entities, because the people of a region, as a result of more frequent interactions, tend to think and act alike. But subcultures also take the form of religions, nationalities, fraternal orders, and other institutional complexes which provide a broad identification for people who may otherwise be strangers. The subcultures of a person play a large role in his attitude formation and become another important predictor of certain values he is likely to hold.

Social Class

People become differentiated not only horizontally but also vertically through a division of labor. The society becomes stratified socially on the basis of wealth, skill, and power. Sometimes castes develop in which the members are reared for certain roles, or social classes develop in which the members feel empathy with others sharing similar values and economic circumstances.

Because social class involves different attitudinal configurations, it becomes a useful independent variable for segmenting markets and predicting reactions. Significant differences have been found among different social classes with respect to magazine readership, leisure activities, food imagery, fashion interests, and acceptance of innovations. A sampling of attitudinal differences in class is the following:

Members of the *upper-middle* class place an emphasis on professional competence; indulge in expensive status symbols; and more often than not show a taste, real or otherwise, for theater and the arts. They want their children to show high achievement and precocity and develop into physicists, vice-presidents, and judges. This class likes to deal in ideas and symbols.

Members of the *lower-middle* class cherish respectability, savings, a college education, and good housekeeping. They want their children to show self-control and prepare for *careers* as accountants, lawyers, and engineers.

Members of the *upper-lower* class try to keep up with the times, if not with the Joneses. They stay in older neighborhoods but buy new kitchen appliances. They spend proportionately less than the middle class on major clothing articles, buying a new suit mainly for an important ceremonial occasion. They also spend proportionately less on services, preferring to do their own plumbing and other work around the house. They tend to raise large families and their children generally enter manual occupations. This class also supplies many local businessmen, politicians, sports stars, and labor-union leaders.

Reference Groups

There are groups in which the individual has no membership but with which he identifies and may aspire to—reference groups. Many young boys identify with big-league baseball players or astronauts, and many young girls identify with Hollywood stars. The activities of these popular heroes are carefully watched and frequently imitated. These reference figures become important transmitters of influence, although more along lines of taste and hobby than basic attitudes.

Face-to-face Groups

Groups that have the most immediate influence on a person's tastes and opinions are face-to-face groups. This includes all the small "societies" with which he comes into frequent contact: his family, close friends, neighbors, fellow workers, fraternal associates, and so forth. His informal group memberships are influenced largely by his occupation, residence, and stage in the life cycle.

The powerful influence of small groups on individual attitudes has been demonstrated in a number of social psychological experiments.[28] There is also evidence that this influence may be growing.

---

[28] See, for example, Solomon E. Asch, "Effects of Group Pressure Upon the Modification & Distortion of Judgments," in Dorwin Cartwright and Alvin Zander, *Group Dynamics* (Evanston, Illinois: Row, Peterson & Co., 1953), pp. 151-162; and Kurt Lewin, "Group Decision and Social Change," in Theodore M. Newcomb and Eugene L. Hartley, editors, *Readings in Social Psychology* (New York: Henry Holt Co., 1952).

David Riesman and his coauthors have pointed to signs which indicate a growing amount of *other-direction,* that is, a tendency for individuals to be increasingly influenced by their peers in the definition of their values rather than by their parents and elders.[29]

For the marketer, this means that brand choice may increasingly be influenced by one's peers. For such products as cigarettes and automobiles, the influence of peers is unmistakable.

The role of face-to-face groups has been recognized in recent industry campaigns attempting to change basic product attitudes. For years the milk industry has been trying to overcome the image of milk as a "sissified" drink by portraying its use in social and active situations. The men's wear industry is trying to increase male interest in clothes by advertisements indicating that business associates judge a man by how well he dresses.

Of all face-to-face groups, the person's family undoubtedly plays the largest and most enduring role in basic attitude formation. From them he acquires a mental set not only toward religion and politics, but also toward thrift, chastity, food, human relations, and so forth. Although he often rebels against parental values in his teens, he often accepts these values eventually. Their formative influence on his eventual attitudes is undeniably great.

Family members differ in the types of product messages they carry to other family members. Most of what parents know about cereals, candy, and toys comes from their children. The wife stimulates family consideration of household appliances, furniture, and vacations. The husband tends to stimulate the fewest purchase ideas, with the exception of the automobile and perhaps the home.

The marketer must be alert to what attitudinal configurations dominate in different types of families, and also to how these change over time. For example, the parent's conception of the child's rights and privileges has undergone a radical shift in the last 30 years. The child has become the center of attention and orientation in a great number of households, leading some writers to label the modern family a "filiarchy." This has important implications not only for how to market to today's family, but also on how to market to tomorrow's family when the indulged child of today becomes the parent.

The Person

Social influences determine much but not all of the behavioral variations in people. Two individuals subject to the same influences are

[29] David Riesman, Reuel Denney, and Nathan Glazer, *The Lonely Crowd* (New Haven, Connecticut: Yale University Press, 1950).

not likely to have identical attitudes, although these attitudes will probably converge at more points than those of two strangers selected at random. Attitudes are really the product of social forces interacting with the individual's unique temperament and abilities.

Furthermore, attitudes do not automatically guarantee certain types of behavior. Attitudes are predispositions felt by buyers before they enter the buying process. The buying process itself is a learning experience and can lead to a change in attitudes.

Alfred Politz noted at one time that women stated a clear preference for G.E. refrigerators over Frigidaire, but that Frigidaire continued to outsell G.E.[30] The answer to this paradox was that preference was only one factor entering into behavior. When the consumer preferring G.E. actually undertook to purchase a new refrigerator, her curiosity led her to examine the other brands. Her perception was sensitized to refrigerator advertisements, sales arguments, and different product features. This led to learning and a change in attitudes.

THE HOBBESIAN ORGANIZATIONAL-FACTORS MODEL

The foregoing models throw light mainly on the behavior of family buyers.

But what of the large number of people who are organizational buyers? They are engaged in the purchase of goods not for the sake of consumption, but for further production or distribution. Their common denominator is the fact that they (1) are paid to make purchases for others and (2) operate within an organizational environment.

How do organizational buyers make their decisions? There seem to be two competing views. Many marketing writers have emphasized the predominance of rational motives in organizational buying.[31] Organizational buyers are represented as being most impressed by cost, quality, dependability, and service factors. They are portrayed as dedicated servants of the organization, seeking to secure the best terms. This view has led to an emphasis on performance and use characteristics in much industrial advertising.

Other writers have emphasized personal motives in organizational buyer behavior. The purchasing agent's interest to do the best for his company is tempered by his interest to do the best for himself. He may be tempted to choose among salesmen according to the extent

---

[30] Alfred Politz, "Motivation Research—Opportunity or Dilemma?" in Ferber and Wales, same reference as footnote 17, at pp. 57–58.

[31] See Melvin T. Copeland, *Principles of Merchandising* (New York: McGraw-Hill Book Co., Inc., 1924).

they entertain or offer gifts. He may choose a particular vendor because this will ingratiate him with certain company officers. He may shortcut his study of alternative suppliers to make his work day easier.

In truth, the buyer is guided by both personal and group goals; and this is the essential point. The political model of Thomas Hobbes comes closest of any model to suggesting the relationship between the two goals.[32] Hobbes held that man is "instinctively" oriented toward preserving and enhancing his own well-being. But this would produce a "war of every man against every man." This fear leads men to unite with others in a corporate body. The corporate man tries to steer a careful course between satisfying his own needs and those of the organization.

Marketing Applications of Hobbesian Model

The import of the Hobbesian model is that organizational buyers can be appealed to on both personal and organizational grounds. The buyer has his private aims, and yet he tries to do a satisfactory job for his corporation. He will respond to persuasive salesmen and he will respond to rational product arguments. However, the best "mix" of the two is not a fixed quantity; it varies with the nature of the product, the type of organization, and the relative strength of the two drives in the particular buyer.

Where there is substantial similarity in what suppliers offer in the way of products, price, and service, the purchasing agent has less basis for rational choice. Since he can satisfy his organizational obligations with any one of a number of suppliers, he can be swayed by personal motives. On the other hand, where there are pronounced differences among the competing vendors' products, the purchasing agent is held more accountable for his choice and probably pays more attention to rational factors. Short-run personal gain becomes less motivating than the long-run gain which comes from serving the organization with distinction.

The marketing strategist must appreciate these goal conflicts of the organizational buyer. Behind all the ferment of purchasing agents to develop standards and employ value analysis lies their desire to avoid being thought of as order clerks, and to develop better skills in reconciling personal and organizational objectives.[33]

---

[32] Thomas Hobbes, *Leviathan*, 1651 (London: G. Routledge and Sons, 1887).

[33] For an insightful account, see George Strauss, "Tactics of Lateral Relationship: The Purchasing Agent," *Administrative Science Quarterly*, Vol. 7 (September, 1962), pp. 161-186.

SUMMARY

Think back over the five different behavioral models of how the buyer translates buying influences into purchasing responses.

- Marshallian man is concerned chiefly with economic cues—prices and income—and makes a fresh utility calculation before each purchase.
- Pavlovian man behaves in a largely habitual rather than thoughtful way; certain configurations of cues will set off the same behavior because of rewarded learning in the past.
- Freudian man's choices are influenced strongly by motives and fantasies which take place deep within his private world.
- Veblenian man acts in a way which is shaped largely by past and present social groups.
- And finally, Hobbesian man seeks to reconcile individual gain with organizational gain.

Thus, it turns out that the "black box" of the buyer is not so black after all. Light is thrown in various corners by these models. Yet no one has succeeded in putting all these pieces of truth together into one coherent instrument for behavioral analysis. This, of course, is the goal of behavioral science.

12

A Theory of Buyer Behavior

John A. Howard
Jagdish N. Sheth

In the last fifteen years, considerable research on consumer behavior both at the conceptual and empirical levels has accumulated. This can be gauged by reviews of the research.[1] As a consequence we believe that sufficient research exists in both the behavioral sciences and consumer behavior to attempt a comprehensive theory of buyer behavior. Furthermore, broadly speaking, there are two major reasons at the basic research level which seem to have created the need to take advantage of this opportunity. The first reason is that a great variety exists in today's effort to understand the consumer, and unfortunately there is no integration of this variety. The situation resembles the seven blind men touching different parts of the elephant and making inferences about the animal which differ, and occasionally contradict one another. A comprehensive theory of buyer behavior would hopefully not only provide a framework for integrating the existing variety but also would prepare the researcher to adopt appropriate research designs which would control sources of influences other than those he is immediately interested in. The difficulty of replicating a study and the possibility of getting contradictory findings will be minimized accordingly.

Reprinted from Reed Moyer, (ed.) *Changing Marketing Systems . . . Consumer, Corporate and Government Interfaces: Proceedings of the 1967 Winter Conference of the American Marketing Association,* 1967, published by the American Marketing Association.

John A. Howard is professor in the Graduate School of Business, Columbia University. He is a distinguished marketing scholar who has directed studies of consumer behavior for both company and public policy purposes. In addition to *The Theory of Consumer Behavior,* his books include *Marketing Management: Analysis and Control* and *Marketing Theory.*

Jagdish N. Sheth is research professor of business administration at the University of Illinois. He received his Ph.D. from Columbia University and has served on the faculties of Columbia University and the Sloan School of Management, M.I.T. He is a prolific author in areas of consumer psychology, multivariate methods, and international marketing.

[1] Jagdish N. Sheth, "A Review of Buyer Behavior," *Management Science,* Vol. 13 (August, 1967), pp. B718–B756; John A. Howard, *Marketing Theory* (Boston, Mass.: Allyn and Bacon, 1965).

The second major basic research reason for a comprehensive theory is the potential application of research in buying behavior to human behavior in general. In asserting the need to validate psychological propositions in a real world context Sherif has repeatedly and eloquently argued for applied research.[2] Also, McGuire argues that social psychology is moving toward theory-oriented research in *natural settings* because a number of forces are encouraging the movement away from laboratory research, and he cites the current work in buyer behavior as one of these forces.[3]

Again, one way that we can contribute to "pure" areas of behavioral science is by attempting a comprehensive theory which would help to identify and to iron out our own inconsistencies and contradictions. Such an attempt looks ambitious on the surface, but after several years of work and drawing upon earlier work,[4] we are confident that it can be achieved.

A BRIEF SUMMARY OF THE THEORY

Before we describe each component of the theory in detail, it will be helpful to discuss briefly the essentials of our view of the consumer choice process.

Much of buying behavior is more or less repetitive brand choice decisions. During his life cycle, the buyer establishes purchase cycles for various products which determine how often he will buy a given product. For some products, this cycle is very lengthy, as for example in buying durable appliances, and, therefore, he buys the product quite infrequently. For many other products, however, the purchase cycle is short and he buys the product frequently as is the case for many grocery and personal care items. Since there is usually the element of repeat buying, we must present a theory which incorporates the dynamics of purchase behavior over a period of time if we wish to capture the central elements of the empirical process.

In the face of repetitive brand choice decisions, the consumer simplifies his decision process by storing relevant information and routinizing his decision process. What is crucial, therefore, is to identify the elements of decision making, to observe the structural or substantive changes that occur in them over time due to the repetitive

[2] Musafer Sherif and Carolyn Sherif, "Interdisciplinary Coordination as a Validity Check: Retrospect and Prospects," in M. Sherif (ed.), *Problems of Interdisciplinary Relationships in the Social Sciences* (Chicago: Aldine Publishing Company, 1968).

[3] William J. McGuire, "Some Impending Reorientations in Social Psychology," *Journal of Experimental Social Psychology*, Vol. 3 (1967), pp. 124–139.

[4] Patrick Suppes, *Information Processing and Choice Behavior* (Technical Paper No. 9: Institute for Mathematical Studies in the Social Sciences, Stanford University, January 31, 1966), p. 27; John A. Howard, *op. cit.*

nature, and show how a combination of the decision elements affect search processes and the incorporation of information from the buyer's commercial and social environment.

The buyer, having been motivated to buy a product class, is faced with a brand choice decision. The elements of his decision are: (1) a set of motives, (2) several courses of action, and (3) decision mediators by which the motives are matched with the alternatives. Motives are specific to a product class, and they reflect the underlying needs of the buyer. The alternative courses of actions are the purchase of one of the various brands with their potential to satisfy the buyer's motives. There are two important notions involved in the definition of alternatives as brands. First, the brands which are alternatives of the buyer's choice decision at any given time are generally a small number, collectively called his "evoked set." The size of the evoked set is only two or three, a fraction of the brands he is aware of and still smaller fraction of the total number of brands actually available in the market. Second, any two consumers may have quite different alternatives in their evoked sets.

The decision mediators are a set of rules that the buyer employs to match his motives and his means of satisfying those motives. They serve the function of ordering and structuring the buyer's motives and then ordering and structuring the various brands based on their potential to satisfy these ordered motives. The decision mediators develop by the process of learning about the buying situation. They are, therefore, influenced by information from the buyer's environment and even more importantly by the actual experience of purchasing and consuming the brand.

When the buyer is just beginning to purchase a product class such as when a purchase is precipitated by a change in his life cycle, he lacks experience. In order, therefore, to develop the decision mediators, he *actively seeks information* from his commercial and social environments. The information that he either actively seeks or accidentally receives is subject to perceptual processes which not only limits the intake of information (magnitude of information is affected) but modifies it to suit his own frame of reference (quality of information is affected). These modifications are significant since they distort the neat "marketing stimulus–consumer response" relation.

Along with active search for information, the buyer may, to some extent, generalize from past similar experiences. Such generalization can be due to physical similarity of the new product class to the old product class. For example, in the initial purchases of Scotch whisky, the buyer may generalize his experiences in buying of gin. Generalization can also occur even when the two product classes are physically dissimilar but have a common meaning such as deriving from a company-wide brand name. For example, the buyer could generalize his experiences in buying a refrigerator or range to his first purchase of a dishwasher of the same brand.

Whatever the source, the buyer develops sufficient decision mediators to enable him to choose a brand which seems to have the best potential for satisfying his motives. If the brand proves satisfactory, the potential of that brand to satisfy his motives is increased. The result is that the probability of buying that brand is likewise increased. With repeated satisfactory purchases of one or more brands, the buyer is likely to manifest a routinized decision process whereby the sequential steps in buying are well structured so that some event which triggers the process may actually complete the choice decision. Routinized purchasing implies that his decision mediators are well established and that the buyer has strong brand preferences.

The phase of repetitive decision making, in which the buyer reduces the complexity of a buying situation with the help of information and experience, is called the *psychology of simplification.* Decision making can be divided into three stages and used to illustrate the psychology of simplification: Extensive Problem Solving, Limited Problem Solving and Routinized Response Behavior. The further he is along in simplifying his environment, the less is the tendency toward active search behavior. The environmental stimuli related to the purchase situation become more meaningful and less ambiguous. Furthermore, the buyer establishes more cognitive consistency among the brands as he moves toward routinization and the incoming information is then screened both with regard to its magnitude and quality. He becomes less attentive to stimuli which do not fit his cognitive structure and he distorts those stimuli which are forced upon him.

A surprising phenomenon, we believe, occurs in many instances of frequently purchased products such as in grocery and personal care items. The buyer, after attaining routinization of his decision process, may find himself in too simple a situation. He is likely to feel the monotony or boredom associated with such repetitive decision making. It is also very likely that he is dissatisfied with even the most preferred brand. In both cases, he may feel that all existing alternatives including the preferred brand are unacceptable. He therefore feels a need to *complicate* his buying situation by considering new brands, and this process can be called the *psychology of complication.* The new situation causes him to identify a new brand, and so he begins again to simplify in the manner described earlier. Thus with a frequently-purchased item buying is a continuing process with its ups and downs in terms of information seeking analogous to the familiar cyclical fluctuations in economic activity.

Any theory of human behavior needs some means for explaining individual differences. The marketing manager also is interested in differentiated masses of buyers. He wants to understand and separate individual differences so that he can classify or segment the total market based upon individual differences. By understanding the psychology of the individual buyer we may achieve this classification. Depending on the internal state of the buyer, a given stimulus may result in a given response. For example, one buyer who urgently needs a product may respond to the ad of a brand in that product class by buying it whereas another buyer who does not need the product may simply notice the ad and store the information or ignore the ad. A construct such as "level of motivation" will then explain the divergent reactions to the same stimulus. Alternatively, two buyers may both urgently need a product, but they buy two different brands. This can be explained by another construct: predisposition toward a brand.

Figure 1 represents the theory of buyer behavior. The central rectangular box isolates the various internal state variables and processes which combined together show the state of the buyer. The inputs to the rectangular box are the stimuli from the marketing and social environments. The outputs are a variety of responses that the buyer is likely to manifest based on the interaction between the stimuli and his internal state. Besides the inputs and outputs, there are a set of seven influences which affect the variables in the rectangular box.[5] These variables appear at the top of the diagram and are labelled "exogenous variables." Their function is to provide a means of adjusting for the interpersonal differences discussed above. The variables within the rectangular box serve the role of endogenous variables in the sense that changes in them are explained but they are something less than endogenous variables. They are not well defined and hence are not measurable. They are hypothetical constructs. Their values are inferred from relations among the output intervening variables. Several of the exogenous variables such as personality, social class and culture have traditionally been treated as part of the endogenous variables. We believe that they affect more specific variables, and by conceptualizing their effect as via the hypothetical constructs, we can better understand their role.

---

[5] Terminology in a problem area that cuts across both economics and psychology is different because each discipline has often defined its terms differently from the other. We find the economist's definitions of exogenous versus endogenous, and theory versus model more useful than those of the psychologist. The psychologists' distinction of hypothetical constructs and intervening variables, however, provides a helpful breakdown of endogenous variables. Finally, for the sake of exposition we have often here not clearly distinguished between the theory and its empirical counterparts. Although this practice encourages certain ambiguities, and we lay ourselves open to the charge of reifying our theory, we believe that for most readers it will simplify the task of comprehending the material.

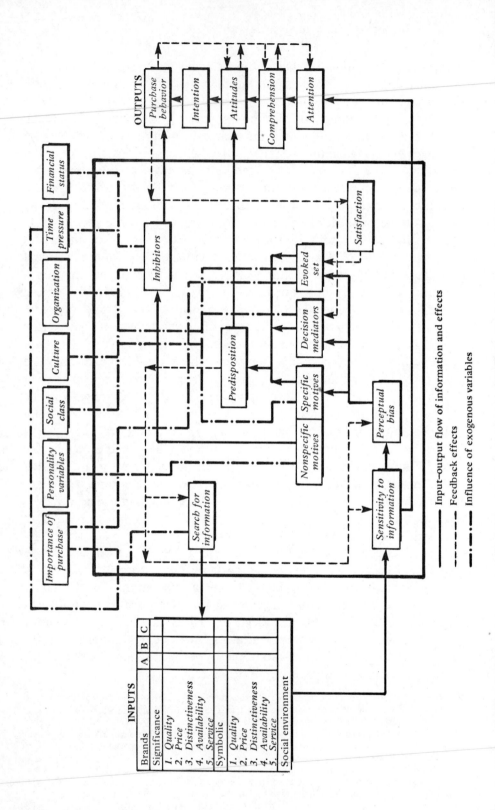

FIGURE 1. A theory of buyer behavior

Thus it will be seen that the theory of buyer behavior has four major components: the stimulus variables, the response variable, the hypothetical constructs and the exogenous variables. We will elaborate on each of the components below both in terms of their substance and their interrelationships.

Stimulus Variables

At any point in time, the hypothetical constructs which reflect the buyer's internal state are affected by numerous stimuli from the environment. The environment is classified as Commercial or Social. The commercial environment is the marketing activities of various firms by which they attempt to communicate to the buyer. From the buyer's point of view, these communications basically come either via the physical brands themselves or some linguistic or pictorial representations of the attributes of the brands. If the elements of the brands such as price, quality, service, distinctiveness or availability are communicated through the physical brands (significates) then the stimuli are defined and classified as significative stimuli. If, on the other hand, the attributes are communicated in linguistic or pictorial symbols such as in mass media, billboards, catalogs, salesmen, etc., then the stimuli from commercial sources are classified as symbolic stimuli. We view the marketing mix as the optimum allocation of funds between the two major channels of communication—significative or symbolic—to the buyer.

Each commercial input variable is hypothesized to be multivariate. Probably the five major dimensions of a brand—price, quality, distinctiveness, availability and service—summarize the various attributes. The same dimensions are present in both significative or symbolic communication which become the input stimuli for the buyer. However, certain dimensions may be more appropriately conveyed by significative rather than symbolic communication and vice versa. For example, price is easily communicated by both channels; shape may best be communicated by two-dimensional pictures rather than verbal communication. Finally, size may not be easily communicated by any symbolic representation: the physical product (significate) may be necessary.

The third stimulus input variable is socal stimuli. It refers to the information that the buyer's social environment provides regarding a purchase decision. The most obvious is word of mouth communication.

The inputs to the buyer's mental state from the three major sources are then processed and stored by their interaction with a series of hypothetical constructs, and the buyer may react immediately or later.

Hypothetical Constructs

The hypothetical constructs and their interrelationships are the result of an integration of Hull's learning theory,[6] Osgood's cognitive theory,[7] and Berlyne's theory of exploratory behavior[8] along with other ideas.

We may classify the constructs into two classes: (i) those that have to do with perception, and (ii) those having to do with learning. Perceptual constructs serve the function of information processing while the learning constructs serve the function of concept formation. It is interesting that, after years of experience in advertising, Reeves has a very similar classification:[9] his "penetration" is analogous to perceptual variables and his "unique selling propositions" is analogous to learning variables. We will at first describe the learning constructs since they are the major components of decision making; the perceptual constructs which serve the important role of obtaining and processing information are more complex and will be described later.

Learning Constructs. The learning constructs are labeled as: (1) Motives—Specific and Nonspecific, (2) Brand Potential of Evoked Set, (3) Decision Mediators, (4) Predisposition toward the brands, (5) Inhibitors, and (6) Satisfaction with the purchase of the brand.

Motive is the impetus to action. Motives or goals may be thought of as constituting a means-end chain and hence, as being general or specific depending upon their position in the chain. Motives can refer to the buyer's specific goals in purchasing a product class. The buyer is motivated by the expectation or anticipation due to past learning of outcome from the purchase of each of the brands in his evoked set.

The specific motives—lower level motives in the means-end chain—are very closely anchored to the attributes of a product class and in this way they become purchase criteria. Examples of specific motives for buying a dietary product such as Metrecal or Sego are low calories, nutrition, taste, and value.

[6] Clark C. Hull, *Principles of Behavior* (New York: Appleton-Century-Crofts, Inc., 1943); Clark C. Hull, *A Behavior System* (New Haven: Yale University Press, 1952).

[7] Charles E. Osgood, "A Behavioristic Analysis of Perception and Meaning as Cognitive Phenomena," *Symposium on Cognition, University of Colorado, 1955* (Cambridge, Harvard University Press, 1957), pp. 75–119; Charles E. Osgood, "Motivational Dynamics of Language Behavior," in J. R. Jones (ed.), *Nebraska Symposium on Motivation, 1957* (Lincoln: University of Nebraska Press, 1957), pp. 348–423.

[8] D. E. Berlyne, "Motivational Problems Raised by Exploratory and Epistemic Behavior," in Sigmund Koch (ed.), *Psychology: A Study of a Science*, Vol. 5 (New York: McGraw-Hill Book Company, 1963).

[9] Rosser Reeves, *Reality in Advertising* (New York: Alfred A. Knopf, Inc., 1961).

Very often, several specific motives are nothing more than indicators of some underlying more general motive, that is, some motive that is higher in the means-end chain. In the above example, the specific motives of nutrition and low calories might be merely indicators of the common motive of good health.

Motives also serve the important function of raising the buyer's general motivational state or arousal and thereby tuning up the buyer, causing him to pay attention to environmental stimuli. Examples of nonspecific motives are probably anxiety, fear, many of the personality variables such as authoritarianism, exhibitionism, aggressiveness, etc., and social motives of power, status, prestige, etc. Although they are nonspecific, they are not innate, but rather learned, mostly due to acculturation. The nonspecific motives also possess a hierarchy within themselves. For example, anxiety is considered to be the source of another motive, that of the need of money.[10]

Brand Potential of Evoked Set is the second learning construct. A buyer who is familiar with a product class has an evoked set of alternatives to satisfy his motives. The elements of his evoked set are some of the brands that make up the product class. The concept is important because for this buyer the brands in his evoked set constitute competition for the seller.

A brand is, of course, a class concept like many other objects or things. The buyer attaches a *word* to this concept—a label—which is the brand name such as "Campbell's Tomato Soup." Whenever he sees a can of Campbell's Tomato Soup or hears the phrase, the image conveys to him certain satisfactions, procedures for preparation, etc. In short, it conveys certain meaning including its potential to satisfy his motives.

Various brands in the buyer's evoked set will generally satisfy the goal structure differently. One brand may possess potential to the extent that it is an ideal brand for the buyer. Another brand, on the other hand, may satisfy motives just enough to be part of his evoked set. By the process of learning the buyer obtains and stores knowledge regarding each brand's potential and then rank orders them in terms of their want-satisfying potential. The evoked set, in short, is a set of alternatives with each alternative's payoff. Predisposition mentioned below enables the buyer to choose one among them.

Decision Mediator is the third learning construct and it brings together motives and alternatives. The brand potential of each of the brands in his evoked set are the decision alternatives with their payoffs. Decision mediators are the buyer's mental rules for matching the

---

[10] J. S. Brown, *The Motivation of Behavior* (New York: McGraw-Hill Book Company, 1961).

alternatives with his motives, for rank-ordering them in terms of their want-satisfying capacity. As mental rules, they exhibit reasons wherein the cognitive elements related to the alternatives and the motives are structured. The words that he uses to describe these attributes are also the words that he thinks with and that he finds are easy to remember. The criterial attributes are important to the manufacturer because if he knows them he can deliberately build into his brand and promotion those characteristics which will differentiate his brand from competing brands.

The decision mediators thus represent enduring cognitive rules established by the process of learning, and their function is to obtain meaningful and congruent relations among brands so that the buyer can manifest goal-directed behavior. The aim of the theory of buyer behavior is not just the identification of motives and the respective brands but to show their structure as well. It is the decision mediators which provide this structure.

In view of the fact that decision mediators are learned, principles of learning become crucial in their development and change over time. There are two broad sources of learning: (1) actual experiences, and (2) information. Actual experience can be either with the *same* buying situation in the past or with a *similar* buying situation. The latter is generally labelled as generalization as discussed earlier. Similarly, information as a source of learning can be from: (1) the buyer's commercial environment, or (2) his social environment. Later, we will elaborate on each of the sources of learning.

Predisposition, the fourth construct, is the summary effect of the previous three constructs. It refers to the buyer's preference toward brands in his evoked set. It is, in fact, an aggregate index which is reflected in attitude which, in turn, is measured by attitude scales. It might be visualized as the "place" where brands in Evoked Set are compared with Mediator's choice criteria to yield a judgment on the relative contribution of the brands to the buyer's motives. This judgment includes not only an estimate of the value of the brand to him but also an estimate of the confidence with which he holds that position. This uncertainty aspect of Predisposition can be called "brand ambiguity," in that, the more confident he holds it, the less ambiguous is the connotative meaning of the brand to the buyer and the more likely he is to buy it.[11]

Inhibitors, the fifth learning construct, are forces in the environment which create important disruptive influences in the actual purchase of a brand even when the buyer has reasoned out that that brand will best satisfy his motives. In other words, when the buyer is both

---

[11] George S. Day, "Buyer Attitudes and Brand Choice Behavior," Unpublished Ph.D. Dissertation, Graduate School of Business, Columbia University, 1967.

predisposed to buy a brand and has the motivation to buy some brand in the product class, he may not buy it because several environmental forces inhibit its purchase and prevent him from satisfying his preferences.

We postulate at least four types of inhibitors. They are: (1) high price of the brand, (2) lack of availability of the brand, (3) time pressure on the buyer, and (4) the buyer's financial status. The first two are part of the environmental stimuli, and therefore, they are part of the input system. The last two come from the two exogenous variables of the same name. It should be pointed out that social constraints emanating from other exogenous variables may also create temporary barriers to the purchase of a brand.

An essential feature of all inhibitors is that they are *not internalized* by the buyer because their occurrence is random and strictly situational. However, some of the inhibitors may persist systematically over time as they concern a given buyer. If they persist long enough, the buyer is likely to incorporate them as part of his decision mediators and thus to internalize them. The consequence is that they may affect even the structure of alternatives and motives.

Satisfaction, the last of the learning constructs, refers to the degree of congruence between the actual consequences from purchase and consumption of a brand and what was expected from it by the buyer at the time of purchase. If the actual outcome is adjudged by the buyer as *at least* equal to the expected, the buyer will feel satisfied. If, on the other hand, the actual outcome is adjudged as less than what he expected, the buyer will feel dissatisfied and his attitude will be less favorable. Satisfaction or dissatisfaction with a brand can exist with respect to any one of the different attributes. If the brand proves more satisfactory than he expected, the buyer has a tendency to enhance the attractiveness of the brand. Satisfaction will, therefore, affect the reordering of the brands in the evoked set for the next buying decision.

Relations Among Learning Constructs. Underlying Predisposition toward the brands and related variables, several important notions are present. The simplest way to describe them is to state that we may classify a decision process as either Extensive Problem Solving, Limited Problem Solving or Routinized Response Behavior depending on the strength of Predisposition toward the brands. In the early phases of buying, the buyer has not yet developed decision mediators well enough; specifically his product class concept is not well formed and predisposition is low. As he acquires information and gains experience in buying and consuming the brand, Decision Mediators become firm and Predisposition toward a brand is generally high.

In Extensive Problem Solving, Predisposition toward the brands is low. None of the brands is discriminated enough based on their criterial attributes for the buyer to show greater brand preference toward any one brand. At this state of decision making, brand ambiguity is high with the result that the buyer actively seeks information from his environment. Due to greater search for information, there exists a greater *latency of response*—the time interval from the initiation of a decision to its completion. Similarly, deliberation or reasoning will be high since he lacks a well-defined product class concept which is the denotative aspect of mediator. He is also likely to consider many brands as part of Evoked Set, and stimuli coming from the commercial environment are less likely to trigger any immediate purchase reaction.

When Predisposition toward the brands is moderate, the buyer's decision process can be called Limited Problem Solving. There still exists brand ambiguity since the buyer is not able to discriminate and compare brands so that he may prefer one brand over others. He is likely to seek information but not to the extent that he seeks it in Extensive Problem Solving. More importantly, he seeks information more on a relative basis to compare and discriminate various brands rather than to compare them absolutely on each of the brands. His deliberation or thinking is much less since Decision Mediators are tentatively well defined Evoked Set will consist of a small number of brands, each having about the same degree of preference.

In Routinized Response Behavior, the buyer will have a high level of Predisposition toward brands in his evoked set. Furthermore, he has now accumulated sufficient experience and information to have little brand ambiguity. He will in fact discriminate among brands enough to show a strong preference toward one or two brands in the evoked set. He is unlikely to actively seek any information from his environment since such information is not needed. Also, whatever information he passively or accidentlly receives, he will subject it to selective perceptual processes so that only congruent information is allowed. Very often, the congruent information will act as "triggering cues" to motivate him to manifest purchase behavior. Much of impulse purchase, we believe, is really the outcome of a strong predisposition and such a facilitating commercial stimulus as store display. The buyer's evoked set will consist of a few brands toward which he is highly predisposed. However, he will have greater preference toward one or two brands in his evoked set and less toward others.

As mentioned earlier, Predisposition is an aggregate index of decision components. Thus, any changes in the components due to learning from experience or information imply some change in Predisposition. The greater the learning, the more the predisposition toward the brands in the evoked set. The exact nature of learning will be described later when we discuss the dynamics of buying behavior.

Perceptual Constructs. Another set of constructs serves the function of information procurement and processing relevant to a purchase decision. As mentioned earlier, information can come from any one of the three stimulus inputs—significative commercial stimuli, symbolic commercial stimuli, and social stimuli. Once again we will here only describe the constructs; their utilization by the buyer will be explained when we discuss the dynamics of buying behavior. The perceptual constructs in Figure 1 are: (1) Sensitivity to Information, (b) Perceptual Bias, and (c) Search for Information.

A perceptual phenomenon implies either ignoring a physical event which could be a stimulus, seeing it attentively or sometimes imagining what is not present in reality. All perceptual phenomena essentially create some change in quantity or quality of objective information.

Sensitivity to Information refers to the opening and closing of sensory receptors which control the intake of information. The manifestation of this phenomenon is generally called perceptual vigilance (paying attention) or perceptual defense (ignoring the information). Sensitivity to Information, therefore, primarily serves as a gatekeeper to information entering into the buyer's mental state. It thus controls the quantity of information input.

Sensitivity to Information, according to Berlyne,[12] is a function of the degree of ambiguity of the stimuli to which the buyer is exposed. If the stimulus is very familiar or too simple, the ambiguity is low and the buyer will not pay attention unless he is predisposed to such information from past learning. Furthermore, if ambiguity of the stimulus continues to be low, the buyer feels a sense of monotony and actually seeks other information, and this act can be said to *complicate* his environment. If the stimulus is very complex and ambiguous, the buyer finds it hard to comprehend and, therefore, he ignores it by resorting to perceptual defense. Only if the stimulus is in the moderate range of ambiguity is the buyer motivated to pay attention and to freely absorb the objective information.

In a single communication, the buyer may at first find the communication complex and ambiguous and so he will resort to perceptual

---

[12]Berlyne, *op. cit.*

defense and tend to ignore it. As some information enters, however, he finds that it is really at the medium level of ambiguity and so pays attention. On the other hand, it might be that the more he pays attention to it, the more he finds the communication too simple and, therefore, ignores it as the process of communication progresses.

A second variable which governs Sensitivity to Information is the buyer's predisposition toward the brand about which the information is concerned. The more interesting the information, the more likely the buyer is to open up his receptors and therefore to pay attention to the information. Hess has recently measured this by obtaining the strength of pupil dilation.

Perceptual Bias is the second perceptual construct. The buyer not only selectively attends to information, but he may actually distort it once it enters his mental state. In other words, quality of information can be altered by the buyer. This aspect of the perceptual process is summarized in Perceptual Bias. The buyer may distort the cognitive elements contained in information to make them congruent with his own frame of reference as determined by the amount of information he already has stored. A series of cognitive consistency theories have been recently developed to explain how this congruency is established and what the consequences are in terms of the distortion of information that we might expect.[13] Most of the qualitative change in information arises because of feedback from various decision components such as Motives, Evoked Set and Decision Mediators. These relations are too complex, however, to describe in the summary.

The perceptual phenomena described above are likely to be less operative if the information is received from the buyer's social environment. This is because: (i) the source of social information, such as a friend, is likely to be favorably regarded by the buyer and therefore proper, undistorted reception of information will occur, and (ii) the information itself is modified by the social environment (the friend) so that it conforms to the needs of the buyer and, therefore, further modification is less essential.

Search for Information is the third perceptual construct. During the total buying phase which extends over time and involves several repeat purchases of a product class, there are stages when the buyer *actively* seeks information. It is very important to distinguish the times when he passively receives information from the situations where he actively seeks it. We believe that perceptual distortion is less operative

---

[13]S. Feldman (ed.), *Cognitive Consistency: Motivational Antecedents and Behavioral Consequents* (Academic Press, 1966); Martin Fishbein (ed.), *Readings in Attitude Theory and Measurement* (New York: John Wiley & Sons, 1967).

in the latter instances and that a commercial communication, therefore, at that stage has a high probability of influencing the buyer.

The active seeking of information occurs when the buyer senses ambiguity of the brands in his evoked set. As we saw earlier, this happens in the Extensive Problem Solving and Limited Problem Solving phases of the decision process. The ambiguity of brand exists because the buyer is not certain of the outcomes from each brand. In other words, he has not yet learned enough about the alternatives to establish an expectancy of potential of the brands to satisfy his motives. This type of brand ambiguity is essentially confined to initial buyer behavior which we have called Extensive Problem Solving. However, ambiguity may still exist despite knowledge of the potential of alternative brands. This ambiguity is with respect to his inability to discriminate because his motives are not well structured: he does not know how to order them. He may then seek information which will resolve the conflict among goals, a resolution that is implied in his learning of the appropriate product class aspect of decision mediators that we discussed earlier.

There is yet another stage of total buying behavior in which the buyer is likely to seek information. It is when the buyer has not only routinized his decision process but he is so familiar and satiated with repeat buying that he feels bored. Then, all the existing alternatives in his evoked set including the most preferred brand become unacceptable to him. He seeks change or variety in that buying situation. In order to obtain this change, he actively searches for information on other alternatives (brands) that he never considered before. At this stage, he is particularly receptive to any information about new brands. Incidentally, here is an explanation for advertising in a highly stable industry. This phenomenon has long baffled both the critics and defenders of the institution of advertising. Newcomers to the market and forgetting do not provide a plausible explanation.

We have so far described the stimulus input variables and the hypothetical constructs. Now we proceed to describe the output of the system—the responses of the buyer.

Response Variables

The complexity of buyer behavior does not stop with the hypothetical constructs. Just as there is a variety of inputs, there exists a variety of buyer responses which becomes relevant for different areas of marketing strategy. This variety of consumer responses can be easily appreciated from the diversity of measures to evaluate advertising effectiveness. We have attempted to classify and order this diversity of buyer responses in the output variables. Most of the output variables are directly related to some and not other constructs. Each output variable serves different purposes both in marketing practice and fundamental research. Let us at first describe each variable and then provide a rationale for their interrelationships.

Attention.　Attention is related to Sensitivity to Information. It is a response of the buyer which indicates the magnitude of his information intake. Attention is measured continuously during the time interval when the buyer receives information. There are several psychophysical methods of quantifying the degree of attention that the buyer pays to a message. The pupil dilation is one.

Comprehension. Comprehension refers to the store of knowledge about the brand that the buyer possesses at any point in time. This knowledge could vary from his simply being aware of a single brand's existence to a complete description of the attributes of the product class of which the brand is an element. It reflects the denotative meaning of the brand and in that sense it is strictly in the cognitive realm. It lacks the motivational aspects of behavior. Some of the standard measures of advertising effectiveness such as awareness, aided or unaided recall, and recognition may capture different aspects of the buyer's comprehension of the brand.

Attitude toward a Brand.　Attitude toward a brand is the buyer's evaluation of the brand's potential to satisfy his motives. It, therefore, includes the connotative aspects of the brand concept: it contains those aspects of the brand which are relevant to the buyer's goals. Attitude is directly related to Predisposition and so it consists of both the evaluation of a brand in terms of the criteria of choice from Mediator and the confidence with which that evaluation is held.

Intention to Buy.　Intention to buy is the buyer's forecast of his brand choice some time in the future. Like any forecast, it involves assumptions about future events including the likelihood of any perceived inhibitors creating barriers over the buyer's planning horizon. Intention to buy has been extensively used in the purchases of durable goods with some recent refinements in terms of the buyer's confidence in his own forecast; these studies are in terms of broadly defined product classes.[14] We may summarize this response of the buyer as something short of actual purchase behavior.

---

[14]Thomas F. Juster, *Anticipations and Purchases: An Analysis of Consumer Behavior* (Princeton University Press, 1964).

Purchase Behavior. Purchase Behavior refers to the overt act of purchasing a brand. What becomes a part of company's sales or what the consumer records in a diary as a panel member, however, is only the terminal act in the sequence of shopping and buying. Very often, it is useful to observe the complete movement of the buyer from his home to the store and his purchase in the store. Yoell, for example, shows several case histories where a time and motion study of consumer's purchase behavior have useful marketing implications.[15] We think that at times it may be helpful to go so far as to incorporate the act of consumption into the definition of Purchase Behavior. We have, for example, developed and used the technique of sequential decision making where the buyer verbally describes the sequential pattern of his purchase behavior in a given buying situation. Out of this description a "flow chart" of decision making is obtained which reveals the number and the structure of the decision rules that the buyer employs.

Purchase Behavior is the overt manifestation of the buyer's Predisposition in conjunction with any Inhibitors that may be present. It differs from Attitude to the extent that Inhibitors are taken into consideration. It differs from Intention to the extent that it is the actual manifestation of behavior which the buyer only forecasted in his intention.

Several characteristics of Purchase Behavior become useful if we observe the buyer in a repetitive buying situation. These include the incidence of buying a brand, the quantity bought, and the purchase cycle. Several stochastic models of brand loyalty, for example, have been developed in recent years.[16] Similarly, we could take the magnitude purchased and compare light buyers with heavy buyers to determine if heavy buyers are more loyal buyers.

Interrelationship of Response Variables. In Figure 1, it will be seen that we have ordered the five response variables to create a hierarchy. The hierarchy is similar to the variety of hierarchies used in practice such as AIDA (Attention, Interest, Desire and Action), to the Lavidge and Steiner hierarchy of advertising effectiveness,[17] as well as to the different mental states that a person is alleged by the anthropologists and sociologists to pass through when he adopts an innovation.[18]

---

[15] William Yoell, *A Science of Advertising through Behaviorism.* Unpublished manuscript, December, 1965.

[16] Sheth, *op. cit.*

[17] R. J. Lavidge and G. A. Steiner, "A Model for Predictive Measurements of Advertising Effectiveness," *Journal of Marketing* (October, 1961), pp. 50–68.

[18] Everett M. Rogers, *The Diffusion of Innovations* (New York: Free Press, 1962).

There are, however, some important differences which we believe will clarify certain conceptual and methodological issues raised by Palda and others.[19]

First, we have added a response variable called Attention which is crucial since it reflects whether a communication is received by the buyer. Secondly, several different aspects of the cognitive realm of behavior such as awareness, recall, recognition, etc., are lumped into one category called Comprehension to suggest that they all are varying indicators of the buyer's storage of information about a brand which can be extended to *product class,* and in this way we obtain leverage toward understanding buyer innovation. Third, we have defined Attitude to include both affective and conative aspects since anyone who wants to establish causal relations between attitude and behavior must bring the motivational aspects into attitude. Furthermore, we separate the perceptual and the preference maps of the buyer into Comprehension and Attitude respectively. Fourth, we add another variable, Intention to Buy, because there are several product classes in both durable and semi-durable goods where properly defined and measured intentions have already proved useful. To the extent that Intention incorporates the buyer's forecast of his inhibitors, it might serve the useful function of informing the firm how to remove the inhibitors before the actual purchase behavior is manifested.

Finally, and most importantly, we have incorporated several feedback effects which were described when we discussed the hypothetical constructs. We will now show the relations as direct connections among response variables but the reader should bear in mind that these "outside" relations are merely the reflection of relations among the hypothetical constructs. For example, Purchase Behavior via Satisfaction entails some consequences which affect Decision Mediators and brand potential in Evoked Set; any change in them can produce change in Predisposition. Attitude is related to Predisposition and, therefore, it can also be changed in the period from pre-purchase to post-purchase. In incorporating this feedback, we are opening the way to resolving the controversy whether Attitude causes Purchase Behavior or Purchase Behavior causes Attitude. Over a period of time, the relation is interdependent, each affecting the other. Similarly, we have a feedback from Attitude to Comprehension and Attention, the rationale for which was given when we described the perceptual constructs.

DYNAMICS OF BUYING BEHAVIOR

Let us now explain the changes in the hypothetical constructs which occur due to learning.

[19] Kristian S. Palda, "The Hypothesis of a Hierarchy of Effects: A Partial Evaluation," *Journal of Marketing Research* (February, 1966), pp. 13–24.

The learning constructs are, of course, directly involved in the change that we label "learning." Since some of the learning constructs indirectly govern the perceptual constructs by way of feedbacks, there is also an indirect effect back upon the learning constructs themselves. As mentioned earlier, learning of Decision Mediators which structure Motives and Evoked Set of Brands which contain brand potentials can occur from two broad sources: (i) past experience and (ii) information. Experience can be further classified as having been derived from buying a specified product or buying some similar product. Similarly, information can come from the buyer's commercial environment or his social environment, and if commercial, it can be significative or symbolic.

We will look at the development and change in learning constructs as due to: (i) generalization from similar buying situations, (ii) repeat buying of the same product class, and (iii) information.

Generalization from Similar Purchase Situations

Some decision mediators are common across several product classes because many motives are common to a wide variety of purchasing activity. For example, a buyer may satisfy his health motive from many product classes by looking for nutrition. Similarly, many product classes are all bought at the same place which very often leads to spatial or contiguous generalization. The capacity to generalize provides the buyer with a truly enormous range of flexibility in adapting his purchase behavior to the myriad of varying market conditions he faces.

Generalization refers to the transfer of responses and of the relevance of stimuli from past situations to new situations which are similar. It saves the buyer time and effort in seeking information in the face of uncertainty that is inevitable in a new situation. Generalization can occur at any one of the several levels of purchase activity, but we are primarily interested in generalization of those decision mediators which only involve brand choice behavior in contrast to store choice or choice of shopping time and day. In other words, we are concerned with brand generalization.

Repeat Purchase Experiences

Another source of change in the learning constructs is the repeated purchase of the same product class over a period of time.

In Figure 1 the purchase of a brand entails two types of feedbacks, one affecting the decision mediators and the other affecting the brand potential of the evoked set. First, the experience of buying with all its cognitive aspects of memory, reasoning, etc., has a learning effect on the decision mediators. This occurs irrespective of which specific brand the buyer chooses in any one purchase decision because the decision mediators like the motives are product-specific and not limited to any one brand. Hence every purchase has an incremental effect in firmly establishing the decision mediators. This is easy to visualize if we remember that buying behavior is a series of mental and motor steps while the actual choice is only its terminal act.

Purchase of a brand creates certain satisfactions for the buyer which the consumer compares with his expectations of the brand's potential and this expectation is the basis on which he made his decision in the first place. This comparison of expected and actual consequences causes him to be satisfied or dissatisfied with his purchase of the brand. Hence, the second feedback from Purchase Behavior to Satisfaction changes the attractiveness of the brand purchased. If the buyer is satisfied with his consumption, he enhances the potential of the brand and this is likely to result in greater probability of its repeat purchase. If he is dissatisfied, the potential of the brand is diminished, and its probability of repeat purchase is also similarly reduced.

If there are no inhibitory forces which influence him, the buyer will continue to buy a brand which proves satisfactory. In the initial stages of decision making he may show some tendency to oscillate between brands in order to formulate his decision mediators. In other words, he may learn by trial-and-error at first and then settle on a brand and thereafter he may buy the brand with such regularity to suggest that he is brand loyal. Unless a product is of very high risk, however, there is a limit as to how long this brand loyalty will continue: he may become bored with his preferred brand and look for something new.

Information as a Source of Learning

The third major source by which the learning constructs are changed is information from the buyer's (i) commercial environment consisting of advertising, promotion, salesmanship and retail shelf display of the competing companies, and (ii) his social environment consisting of his family, friends, reference group and social class.

We will describe the influence of information at first as if the perceptual constructs were absent. In other words, we assume that the buyer receives information with perfect fidelity as it exists in the environment. Also, we will discuss separately the information from the commercial and social environments.

Commercial Environment. The company communicates about its offerings to the buyers either by the physical brand (significates) or by symbols (pictorial or linguistic) which represent the brand. In other words, significative and symbolic communication are the two major ways of interaction between the sellers and the buyers.

In Figure 1, the influence of information is shown on Motives, Decision Mediators, Evoked Set, and Inhibitors. We believe that the influence of commercial information on motives (specific and nonspecific) is limited. The main effect is primarily to *intensify* whatever motives the buyer has rather than to create new ones. For example, physical display of the brand may intensify his motives above the threshold level which combined with strong predisposition can result in impulse (unplanned) purchase. A similar reaction is possible when an ad creates sufficient intensity of motives to provide an impetus for the buyer to go to the store. A second way to influence motives is to show the *perceived instrumentality* of the brand and thereby make it a part of the buyer's defined set of alternatives. Finally, to a very limited extent, marketing stimuli may change the *content of the motives.* The general conception both among marketing men and laymen is that marketing stimuli change the buyer's motives. However, on a closer examination it would appear that what is changed is the *intensity* of buyer's motives already provided by the social environment. Many dormant or latent motives may become stimulated. The secret of success very often lies in identifying the change in motives created by social change and intensifying them as seems to be the case in the recent projection of youthfulness in many buying situations.

Marketing stimuli are also important in determining and changing the buyer's evoked set. Commercial information tells him of the existence of the brands (awareness), their identifying characteristics (Comprehension plus brand name) and their relevance to the satisfaction of the buyer's needs (Attitude).

Marketing stimuli are also important in creating and changing the buyer's decision mediators. They become important sources for learning decision mediators when the buyer has no prior experience to rely upon. In other words, when he is in the extensive problem-solving (EPS) stage, it is marketing and social stimuli which are the important sources of learning. Similarly, when the buyer actively seeks information because all the existing alternatives are unacceptable to him, marketing stimuli become important in *changing* his decision mediators.

Finally, marketing stimuli can unwittingly create inhibitors. For example, a company feels the need to emphasize price-quality association, but it may result in high-price inhibition in the mind of the buyer. Similarly, in emphasizing the details of usage and consumption of a product, the communication may create the inhibition related to time pressure.

Social Environment. The social environment of the buyer—family, friends, reference groups—is another major source of information in his buying behavior. Most of the inputs are likely to be symbolic (linguistic) although at times the physical product may be shown to the buyer.

Information from his social environment also affects the four learning constructs: Motives, Decision Mediators, Evoked Set and Inhibitors. However, the effect on these constructs is different from that of the commercial environment. First, the information about the brands will be considerably modified by the social environment before it reaches the buyer. Most of the modifications are likely to be in the nature of adding connotative meanings to brand descriptions, and of the biasing effects of the communication's perceptual variables like Sensitivity to Information and Perceptual Bias. Second, the buyer's social environment will probably have a very strong influence on the content of his motives and their ordering to establish a goal structure. Several research studies have concentrated on such influences.[20] Third, the social environment may also affect his evoked set. This will be particularly true when the buyer lacks experience. Furthermore, if the product class is important to the buyer and he is technically incompetent or uncertain in evaluating the consequences of the brand for his needs, he may rely more on the social than on the marketing environment for information. This is well documented by several studies using the perceived risk hypothesis.[21]

Exogenous Variables

Earlier we mentioned that there are several influences operating on the buyer's decisions which we treat as exogenous, that is, we do not explain their formation and change. Many of these influences come from the buyer's social environment and we wish to separate the effects of his environment which have occurred in the past and are not related to a specific decision from those which are current and directly affect the decisions that occur during the period the buyer is being observed. The inputs during the observation period provide information to the buyer to help his current decision making. The past influences are already imbedded in the values of the perceptual and learning constructs. Strictly speaking, therefore, there is no need for some of the

---

[20] Sheth, *op. cit.*

[21] Donald F. Cox, *Risk Taking and Information Handling in Consumer Behavior* (Boston, Mass.: Graduate School of Business Administration, Harvard University, 1967).

exogenous variables which have influenced the buyer in the past. We bring them out explicitly, however, for the sake of research design where the research may control or take into account individual differences among buyers due to such past influences. Incorporating the effects of these exogenous variables will reduce the size of the unexplained variance or error in estimation which it is particularly essential to control under field conditions. Figure 1 presents a set of exogenous variables which we believe provide the control essential to obtaining satisfactory predictive relations between the inputs and the outputs of the system. Let us briefly discuss each of the exogenous variables.

Importance of Purchase refers to differential degrees of ego-involvement or commitment in different product classes. It, therefore, provides a mechanism which must be carefully examined in inter-product studies. Importance of Purchase will influence the size of the Evoked Set and the magnitude of Search for Information. The more important the product class, the larger the Evoked Set.

Time Pressure is a current exogenous variable and, therefore, specific to a decision situation. It refers to the situation when a buyer feels pressed for time due to any of several environmental influences and so must allocate his time among alternative uses. In this process a re-allocation unfavorable to the purchasing activity can occur. Time pressure will create Inhibition as mentioned earlier. It will also unfavorably affect Search for Information.

Financial Status refers to the constraint the buyer may feel because of lack of financial resources. This affects his purchase behavior to the extent that it creates a barrier to purchasing the most preferred brand. For example, a buyer may want to purchase a Mercedes-Benz but lacks sufficient financial resources and, therefore, he will settle for some low-priced American automobile such as a Ford or Chevrolet. Its effect is via Inhibitor.

Personality Traits take into consideration many of the variables such as self-confidence, self-esteem, authoritarianism and anxiety which have been researched to identify individual differences. It will be noted that these individual differences are "topic free" and, therefore, are supposed to exert their effect across product classes. We believe their effect is felt on: (i) nonspecific Motives and (ii) Evoked Set. For example, the more anxious a person, the greater the motivational arousal; dominant personalities are more likely by a small margin to buy a Ford instead of a Chevrolet; the more authoritarian a person, the narrower the category width of his evoked set.

Social and Organizational Setting (Organization) takes us to the group, to a higher level of social organization than the individual. It includes both the informal social organization such as family and reference groups which are relevant for *consumer behavior* and the formal organization which constitutes much of the environment for *industrial purchasing*. Organizational variables are those of small group interaction such as power, status and authority. We believe that the underlying process of intergroup conflicts in both industrial and consumer buying behavior are in principle very similar and that the differences are largely due to the formalization of industrial activity. Organization, both formal and social, is a crucial variable because it influences all the learning constructs.

Social Class refers to a still higher level of social organization, the social aggregate. Several indices are available to classify people into various classes. The most common perhaps is the Warner classification of people into upper-upper, lower-upper, upper-middle, lower-middle, upper-lower, and lower-lower classes. Social class mediates the relation between the input and the output by influencing: (i) specific Motives, (ii) Decision Mediators, (iii) Evoked Set, and (iv) Inhibitors. The latter influence is important particularly in the adoption of innovations.

Culture provides an even more comprehensive social framework than social class. Culture consists of patterns of behavior, symbols, ideas and their attached values. Culture will influence Motives, Decision Mediators, and Inhibitors.

CONCLUSIONS

In the preceding pages we have summarized a theory of buyer brand choice. It is complex. We strongly believe that complexity is essential to adequately describe buying behavior, from the point of view of both marketing practice and public policy.

We hope that the theory can provide new insights into past empirical data and guide future research so as to instill with coherence and unity current research which now tends to be atomistic and unrelated. We are vigorously pursuing a large research program aimed at testing the validity of the theory. The research was designed in terms of the variables specified by the theory and our most preliminary results cause us to believe that it was fruitful to use the theory in this way. Because it specifies a number of relationships, it has clearly been useful in interpreting the preliminary findings. Above all, it is an aid in communication among the researchers and with the companies involved.

Finally, a number of new ideas are set forth in the theory, but we would like to call attention to three in particular. The concept of evoked set provides a means of reducing the noise in many analyses of buying behavior. The product class concept offers a new dimension for incorporating many of the complexities of innovations and especially for integrating systematically the idea of innovation into a framework of psychological constructs. Anthropologists and sociologists have been pretty much content to deal with peripheral variables in their investigations of innovation. The habit-perception cycle in which perception and habit respond inversely offers hope for explaining a large proportion of the phenomenon that has long baffled both the critics and defenders of advertising: large advertising expenditures in a stable market where, on the surface, it would seem that people are already sated with information.

13

Projective Techniques in Marketing Research

Mason Haire

It is a well accepted maxim in merchandizing that, in many areas, we are selling the sizzle rather than the steak. Our market research techniques, however, in many of these same areas, are directed toward the steak. The sizzle is the subjective reaction of the consumer; the steak the objective characteristics of the product. The consumer's behavior will be based on the former rather than the latter set of characteristics. How can we come to know them better?

When we approach a consumer directly with questions about his reaction to a product we often get false and misleading answers to our questions. Very often this is because the question which we heard ourselves ask was not the one (or not the only one) that the respondent heard. For example: A brewery made two kinds of beer. To guide their merchandizing techniques they wanted to know what kind of people drank each kind, and particularly, what differences there were between the two groups of consumers. A survey was conducted which led up to the questions "Do you drink _____ beer?" (If *yes*) "Do you drink the *Light* or *Regular*?" (These were the two trade names under which the company marketed.) After identifying the consumers of each product is was possible to find out about the characteristics of each group so that appropriate appeals could be used, media chosen, etc.

An interesting anomaly appeared in the survey data, however. The interviewing showed (on a reliable sample) that consumers drank

Reprinted from the *Journal of Marketing,* published by the American Marketing Association (April, 1950), pp. 649-656.

Mason Haire is a professor of organizational psychology and management at the Massachusetts Institute of Technology, in the Alfred P. Sloan School of Management. A much-published writer on psychology in management and social science research applications in business, his M.A. and Ph.D. in psychology are from Harvard University. Among his many books is *Psychology in Management.*

Light over *Regular* in ratio of 3 to 1. The company had been producing and selling Regular over Light for some time in a ratio of 9 to 1. Clearly, the attempt to identify characteristics of the two kinds was a failure. What made them miss so far?

When we say "Do you drink *Light* or *Regular?*" we are at once asking which brand is used, but also, to some extent, saying "Do you drink the regular run-of-the-mill product or do you drink the one that is more refined and shows more discrimination and taste?" The preponderance of "Light" undoubtedly flows from this kind of distortion.

When we ask questions of this sort about the product we are very often asking also about the respondent. Not only do we say "What is ____ product like?" but, indirectly "What are *you* like?" Our responses are often made up of both elements inextricably interwoven. The answers to the second question will carry clichés and stereotypes, blocks, inhibitions, and distortions, whenever we approach an area that challenges the person's idea of himself.

There are many things that we need to know about a consumer's reaction to a product that he can not tell us because they are to some extent socially unacceptable. For instance, the snob appeal of a product vitally influences its sale, but it is a thing that the consumer will not like to discuss explicitly. In other cases the consumer is influenced by motives of which he is, perhaps, vaguely aware, but which he finds difficult to put into words. The interviewer-respondent relationship puts a good deal of pressure on him to reply and to make sense in his reply. Consequently, he gives us stereotypical responses that use clichés which are commonly acceptable but do not necessarily represent the true motives. Many of our motives do not, in fact, "make sense," and are not logical. The question-answer relation demands sense above all. If the response does not represent the true state of affairs the interviewer will never know it. He will go away. If it does not make sense it may represent the truth, but the respondent will feel like a fool and the interviewer will not go away. Much better produce a cliché and be rid of him.

THE NATURE OF PROJECTIVE TESTS

Still other kinds of motives exist of which the respondent may not be explicitly conscious himself. The product may be seen by him as related to things or people or values in his life, or as having a certain role in the scheme of things, and yet he may be quite unable, in response to a direct question, to describe these aspects of the object. Nevertheless, these characteristics may be of great importance as motives. How can we get at them?

Clinical psychologists have long been faced with a parallel set of problems. It is quite usual for a patient to be unable or unwilling to tell the therapist directly what kinds of things are stirring in his motivational pattern. Information about these drives is of vital importance to the process of cure, so a good deal of research has been directed towards the development of techniques to identify and define them. The development of projective techniques as diagnostic tools has provided one of the most useful means to uncover such motivations, and the market-researcher can well afford to borrow their essentials from the therapist.

Basically, a projective test involves presenting the subject with an ambiguous stimulus—one that does not quite make sense in itself—and asking him to make sense of it. The theory is that in order to make it make sense he will have to add to it—to fill out the picture—and in so doing he projects part of himself into it. Since we know what was in the original stimulus we can quite easily identify the parts that were added, and, in this way, painlessly obtain information about the person.

Examples of these tests come readily to hand. Nearly everyone is familiar with the Rorschach Test, in which a subject is shown a series of ink-blots and asked to tell what they look like. Here the stimulus is incomplete in itself, and the interpretation supplied by the patient provides useful information. This test yields fairly general answers about the personality, however, and often we would like to narrow down the area in which the patient is supplying information.

The Thematic Apperception Test offers a good example of this function. Let us suppose that with a particular patient we have reason to suppose that his relation to figures of authority is crucial to his therapeutic problem. We can give him a series of pictures where people are shown, but where the relationship of authority or the characteristics of the authoritarian figure are not complete. He is asked to tell a story about each picture. If in each story the subordinate finally kills the figure of authority we have certain kinds of knowledge; if, on the other hand, he always builds the story so the subordinate figure achieves a secure and comfortable dependence, we have quite different information. It is often quite impossible to get the subject to tell us these things directly. Either he cannot or will not do so. Indirectly, however, he will tell us how he sees authority. Can we get him, similarly, to tell us how a product looks to him in his private view of the world?

APPLICATION OF PROJECTIVE TEST IN
MARKET RESEARCH

Let us look at an example of this kind of thing in market research. For the purposes of experiment a conventional survey was made of attitudes toward Nescafé, an instant coffee. The questionnaire included the questions "Do you use instant coffee?" (If *No*) "What do you dislike about it?" The bulk of the unfavorable responses fell into the general area "I don't like the flavor." This is such an easy answer to a complex question that one may suspect it is a stereotype, which at once gives a sensible response to get rid of the interviewer and conceals other motives. How can we get behind this facade?

In this case an indirect approach was used. Two shopping lists were prepared. They were identical in all respects, except that one list specified Nescafé and one Maxwell House Coffee. They were administered to alternate subjects, with no subject knowing of the existence of the other list. The instructions were "Read the shopping list below. Try to project yourself into the situation as far as possible until you can more or less characterize the woman who bought the groceries. Then write a brief description of her personality and character. Wherever possible indicate what factors influenced your judgment."

Shopping List 1
Pound and a half of hamburger
2 loaves Wonder bread
bunch of carrots
1 can Rumford's Baking Powder
Nescafé instant coffee
2 cans Del Monte peaches
5 lbs. potatoes
Shopping List II
Pound and a half of hamburger
2 loaves Wonder bread
bunch of carrots
1 can Rumford's Baking Powder
1 lb. Maxwell House Coffee (Drip Ground)
2 cans Del Monte peaches
5 lbs. potatoes

Fifty people responded to each of the two shopping lists given above. The responses to these shopping lists provided some very interesting material. The following main characteristics of their descriptions can be given:

1. 48 per cent of the people described the woman who bought Nescafé as lazy; 4 per cent described the woman who bought Maxwell House as lazy.

2. 48 per cent of the people described the woman who bought Nescafé as failing to plan household purchases and schedules well; 12 percent described the woman who bought Maxwell House this way.

3. 4 per cent described the Nescafé woman as thrifty; 16 per cent described the Maxwell House woman as thrifty. 12 per cent described the Nescafé woman as spendrhrift; 0 per cent described the Maxwell House woman this way.

4. 16 per cent described the Nescafé woman as not a good wife; 0 per cent described the Maxwell House woman this way. 4 per cent described the Nescafé woman as a good wife; 16 per cent described the Maxwell House woman as a good wife.

A clear picture begins to form here. Instant coffee represents a departure from "home-made" coffee, and the traditions with respect to caring for one's family. Coffee-making is taken seriously, with vigorous proponents for laborious drip and filter-paper methods, firm believers in coffee boiled in a battered sauce pan, and the like. Coffee drinking is a form of intimacy and relaxation that gives it a special character.

On the one hand, coffee making is an art. It is quite common to hear a woman say, "I can't seem to make good coffee," in the same way that one might say, "I can't learn to play the violin." It is acceptable to confess this inadequacy, for making coffee well is a mysterious touch that belongs, in a shadowy tradition, to the plump, aproned figure who is a little lost outside her kitchen but who has a sure sense in it and among its tools.

On the other hand, coffee has a peculiar role in relation to the household and the home-and-family character. We may well have a picture, in the shadowy past, of a big black range that is always hot with baking and cooking, and has a big enamelled pot of coffee warming at the back. When a neighbor drops in during the morning, a cup of coffee is a medium of hospitality that does somewhat the same thing as cocktails in the late afternoon, but does it in a broader sphere.

These are real and important aspects of coffee. They are not physical characteristics of the product, but they are real values in the consumer's life, and they influence his purchasing. We need to know and assess them. The "labor-saving" aspect of instant coffee, far from being an asset, may be a liability in that it violates these traditions. How often have we heard a wife respond to "This cake is delicious!" with a pretty blush and "Thank you—I made it with such and such a prepared cake mix." This response is so invariable as to seem almost compulsive. It is almost unthinkable to anticipate a reply "Thank you, I made it with Pillsbury's flour, Fleischman's yeast, and Borden's milk." Here the specifications are unnecessary. All that is relevant is the implied "I made it"—the art and the credit are carried directly by the verb that covers the process of mixing and processing the ingredients. In ready-mixed foods there seems to be a compulsive drive to refuse credit for the product, because the accomplishment is not the housewife's but the company's.

In this experiment, as a penalty for using "synthetics" the woman who buys Nescafé pays the price of being seen as lazy, spendthrift, a poor wife, and as failing to plan well for her family. The people who rejected instant coffee in the original direct question blamed its flavor. We may well wonder if their dislike of instant coffee was not to a large extent occasioned by a fear of being seen by one's self and others in the role they projected onto the Nescafé woman in the description. When asked directly, however, it is difficult to respond with this. One can not say, "I don't use Nescafé because people will think I am lazy and not a good wife." Yet we know from these data that the feeling regarding laziness and shiftlessness was there. Later studies (reported below) showed that it determined buying habits, and that something could be done about it.

ANALYSIS OF RESPONSES

Some examples of the type of response received will show the kind of material obtained and how it may be analyzed. Three examples of each group are given below.

Descriptions of a Woman Who Bought, Among Other Things, Maxwell House Coffee

"I'd say she was a practical, frugal woman. She bought too many potatoes. She must like to cook and bake as she included baking powder. She must not care much about her figure as she does not discriminate about the food she buys."

"The woman is quite influenced by advertising as signified by the specific name brands on her shopping list. She probably is quite set in her ways and accepts no substitutes."

"I have been able to observe several hundred women shoppers who have made very similar purchases to that listed above, and the only clue that

I can detect that may have some bearing on her personality is the Del Monte peaches. This item when purchased singly along with the other more staple foods indicates that she may be anxious to please either herself or members of her family with a 'treat.' She is probably a thrifty, sensible housewife."

Descriptions of a Woman Who Bought, Among Other Things, Nescafé Instant Coffee

"This woman appears to be either single or living alone. I would guess that she had an office job. Apparently, she likes to sleep late in the morning, basing my assumption on what she bought such as Instant Coffee which can be made in a hurry. She probably also has can [sic] peaches for breakfast, cans being easy to open. Assuming that she is just average, as opposed to those dazzling natural beauties who do not need much time to make up, she must appear rather sloppy, taking little time to make up in the morning. She is also used to eating supper out, too. Perhaps alone rather than with an escort. An old maid probably."

"She seems to be lazy, because of her purchases of canned peaches and instant coffee. She doesn't seem to think, because she bought two loaves of bread, and then baking powder, unless she's thinking of making cake. She probably just got married."

"I think the woman is the type who never thinks ahead very far—the type who always sends Junior to the store to buy one item at a time. Also she is fundamentally lazy. All the items, with possible exception of the Rumford's, are easily prepared items. The girl may be an office girl who is just living from one day to the next in a sort of haphazard sort of life."

As we read these complete responses we begin to get a feeling for the picture that is created by Nescafé. It is particularly interesting to notice that the Nescafé woman is protected, to some extent, from the opprobrium of being lazy and haphazard by being seen as a single "office girl"—a role that relieves one from guilt for not being interested in the home and food preparation.

The references to peaches are significant. In one case (Maxwell House) they are singled out as a sign that the woman is thoughtfully preparing a "treat" for her family. On the other hand, when the Nescafé woman buys them it is evidence that she is lazy, since their "canned" character is seen as central.

In terms of the sort of results presented above, it may be useful to demonstrate the way these stories are coded. The following items are extracted from the six stories quoted:

Maxwell House	Nescafé

1. practical
   frugal
   likes to cook
	1. single
	   office girl
	   sloppy
	   old maid

2. influenced by advertising
   set in her ways

2. lazy
   does not plan
   newlywed

3. interested in family
   thrifty
   sensible

3. lazy
   does not plan
   office girl

Items such as these are culled from each of the stories. Little by little categories are shaped by the content of the stories themselves. In this way the respondent furnishes the dimensions of analysis as well as the scale values on these dimensions.

Second Test

It is possible to wonder whether it is true that the opprobrium that is heaped on the Nescafé woman comes from her use of a device that represents a short-cut and labor-saver in an area where she is expected to embrace painstaking time-consuming work in a ritualistic way. To test this a variation was introduced into the shopping lists. In a second experiment one hundred and fifty housewives were tested with the form given above, but a sample was added to this group which responded to a slightly different form. If we assume that the rejection in the first experiment came from the presence of a feeling about synthetic shortcuts we might assume also that the addition of one more shortcut to both lists would bring the Maxwell House woman more into line with the Nescafé woman, since the former would now have the same guilt that the Nescafé woman originally had, while the Nescafé woman, already convicted of evading her duties, would be little further injured.

In order to accomplish this a second prepared food was added to both lists. Immediately after the coffee in both lists the fictitious item, "Blueberry Fill Pie Mix" was added. The results are shown in the accompanying table.

It will be seen immediately, in the first two columns, that the group to whom the original form of the list were given showed the same kind of difference as reported above in their estimates of the two women. The group with an additional prepared food, however, brought the Maxwell Coffee woman down until she is virtually undistinguishable from the Nescafé. There seems to be little doubt but that the prepared-food-character, and the stigma of avoiding house-wifely duties is responsible for the projected personality characteristics.

TABLE 1. Personality Characteristics Ascribed to Users of Prepared Foods

If They Use	No Pre-pared Food (Maxwell House alone)		Nescafé (alone)		Maxwell House (plus Pie Mix)		Nescafé (plus Pie Mix)	
They are seen as:	Num-ber	Per Cent	Num-ber	Per Cent	Num-ber	Per Cent	Num-ber	Per Cent
Not Economical	12	17	24	32	6	30	7	35
Lazy	8	11	46	62	5	25	8	40
Poor Personality and Appearance	28	39	39	53	7	35	8	40
N =	72		74		20		20	

Relation to Purchasing

It is still relevant to ask whether the existence of these feelings in a potential consumer is related to purchasing. It is hypothesized that these personality descriptions provide an opportunity for the consumer to project hopes and fears and anxieties that are relevant to the way the product is seen, and that they represent important parts of her motivation in buying or not buying. To test this hypothesis, a small sample of fifty housewives, comparable in every way to the group just referred to, was given the original form of the shopping list (Nescafé only). In addition to obtaining the personality description, the interviewer, on a pretext, obtained permission to look at her pantry shelves and determine personally whether or not she had instant coffee of any brand. The results of this investigation are shown in the accompanying table.

The trend of these data shows conclusively that if a respondent sees the woman who buys Nescafé as having undesirable traits, she is not likely to buy instant coffee herself. The projected unacceptable characteristics go with failure to buy, and it does not seem unwarranted to assume that the association is causal.

Furthermore, these projected traits are, to some extent, additive. For instance, if a respondent describes the woman as having one bad trait only, she is about twice as likely not to have instant coffee. However, if she sees her as having two bad traits, and no good ones (e.g., lazy, cannot cook), she is about three times as likely not to have instant coffee as she is to have it. On the other hand, if she sees her as having two good traits (e.g., economical, cares for family), she is about six times as likely to have it as not.

It was pointed out earlier that some women felt it necessary to "excuse" the woman who bought Nescafé by suggesting that she

TABLE II.

The woman who buys Nescafé is seen as:	By Women Who Had Instant Coffee in the House (N = 32)		By Women Who Did Not Have Instant Coffee in the House (N = 18)	
	Number	Per Cent	Number	Per Cent
Economical**	22	70	5	28
Not economical	0	0	2	11
Cannot cook or does not like to**	5	16	10	55
Plans balanced meals*	9	29	2	11
Good housewife, plans well, cares about family**	9	29	0	0
Poor housewife, does not plan well, does not care about family*	5	16	7	39
Lazy*	6	19	7	39

*A single asterisk indicates that differences this great would be observed only 5 times out of 100 in repeated samplings of a population whose true difference is zero.

**A double asterisk indicates that the chances are 1 in 100. We are justified in rejecting the hypothesis that there is no difference between the groups.

lived alone and hence could not be expected to be interested in cooking, or that she had a job and did not have time to shop better. Women who had instant coffee in the house found excuses almost twice as often as those who did not use instant coffee (12 out of 32, or 42 per cent, against 4 out of 18, or 22 percent). These "excuses" are vitally important for merchandizing. The need for an excuse shows there is a barrier to buying in the consumer's mind. The presence of excuses shows that there is a way around the barrier. The content of the excuses themselves provides valuable clues for directing appeals toward reducing buying resistance.

CONCLUSIONS

There seems to be no question that in the experimental situation described here:

(1) Motives exist which are below the level of verbalization because they are socially unacceptable, difficult to verbalize cogently, or unrecognized.

(2) These motives are intimately related to the decision to purchase or not to purchase, and

(3) It is possible to identify and assess such motives by approaching them indirectly.

Two important general points come out of the work reported. The first is in the statement of the problem. It is necessary for us to see a product in terms of a set of characteristics and attributes which are part of the consumer's "private world," and as such may have no simple relationship to characteristics of the object in the "real" world. Each of us lives in a world which is composed of more than physical things and people. It is made up of goals, paths to goals, barriers, threats, and the like, and an individual's behavior is oriented with respect to these characteristics as much as to the "objective" ones. In the area of merchandizing, a product's character of being seen as a path to a goal is usually very much more important as a determinant of purchasing than its physical dimensions. We have taken advantage of these qualities in advertising and merchandizing for a long time by an intuitive sort of "playing-by-ear" on the subjective aspects of products. It is time for a systematic attack on the problem of the phenomenological description of objects. What kinds of dimensions are relevant to this world of goals and paths and barriers? What kind of terms will fit the phenomenological characteristics of an object in the same sense that the centimetre-gram-second system fits its physical dimensions? We need to know the answers to such questions, and the psychological definitions of valued objects.

The second general point is the methodological one that it is possible, by using appropriate techniques, to find out from the respondent what the phenomenological characteristics of various objects may be. By and large, a direct approach to this problem in terms of straightforward questions will not yield satisfactory answers. It is possible, however, by the use of indirect techniques, to get the consumer to provide, quite unselfconsciously, a description of the value-character of objects in his environment.

14

An Experimental Method for Estimating Demand

Edgar A. Pessemier

A generous increase in the available empirical data concerning demand for individual branded products would be of considerable value to economists and businessmen. For the economist these data would provide an important foundation of fact upon which the structure of microeconomic price theory could rest. For the businessman they would yield helpful indications about how buyers evaluated his brand, as well as the brands of competitors, thereby removing some of the guesswork from decisions concerning price, product design, and promotional activities. Consequently, it is interesting to find that relatively little has been done to obtain demand schedules for individual branded goods.[1] Why has this been the case? The answer can be found principally in the problem of measurement. When an attempt is made to estimate demand under market conditions, an extended period of observation is required, and the cost of gathering data is often high. Furthermore, the use of a protracted period of observation introduces a variety of uncontrolled variables whose effect cannot be accurately isolated and assessed. It appears that, so long as the market is used as the source of data, there is little hope of overcoming these difficulties.

Reprinted from *Journal of Business* (October 1960), pp. 373-383, by permission of the University of Chicago Press,© The University of Chicago Press, 1960.

Edgar A. Pessemier, Professor of Industrial Administration at Purdue University, has written extensively on mathematical models and their applications. He received his B.S. degree from the University of Notre Dame, his M.S. from New York University, and his D.B.A. from Harvard. He is the author of *New Product Decisions: An Analytical Approach*.

[1] For a summary of much of the work done in this area, see Edward R. Hawkins, "Methods of Estimating Demand," *Journal of Marketing*, April, 1957, pp. 428-38.

Hope is held, however, for obtaining simple approximations of the demand for branded goods by gathering information about the behavior of buyers in a controlled environment.[2] If the length of time between buying decisions is greatly reduced, buyers' actions can be observed without having to evaluate such disturbing factors as changes in the branded product, its promotion, its method of distribution, and its competition, or changes in the economic or psychological characteristics of the industry's buyers. By this procedure *all important influences on the buyer, except price, can be held constant* so that the independent effect of changes in price can be observed. The crucial problem that must be dealt with when research is conducted in this manner is the preservation of a sufficiently realistic situation to insure that subjects will respond in the experimental setting in approximately the same way they would in the marketplace: the state of *ceteris paribus* must include as a necessary condition an experimental environment that is not unworkably artifical.

Since this discussion is limited to an analysis of the demand for consumer goods of relatively modest unit price, the personal experience of the buyer of such goods is easy to describe. He seeks to satisfy his wants by purchasing goods from existing institutions and assortments, and he has limited time, information, and funds to use in gaining these ends. By the acts of gathering satisfactions in the market, he is expressing personal judgments about the relative value of what the market has to offer. When taken over a given period of time, the sum of the preference-motivated actions of all buyers represents demand. In other words, within the limits of the consumer's capacity to act, demand for a product depends on how consumers evaluate the product's relative worth. Since in the market it is often difficult to determine the demands or preferences for branded products over a moderate range of price variation, the question naturally arises: Can it be done in a controlled environment? An affirmative answer can be given *provided* the buyer can be placed in a position where the consequences of his actions in the experimental environment will have an impact on his well-being and conduct similar to what they would have in the market: the experimental conditions should be psychologically equivalent to the market, not necessarily physically identical. If the experimental situation

---

[2]During 1957 three reports appeared concerning important groups of game experiments: Cycil C. Herrmann and John B. Stewart, "The Experimental Game," *Journal of Marketing,* July, 1957, pp. 12–30; *Basic Research Report on Consumer Behavior* (Philadelphia: Alderson & Sessions, April 1957), pp. *1*–01–6–05; and Donald Davidson and Patrick Suppes, with Sidney Siegal, *Decision Making* (Stanford, Calif.: Stanford University Press, 1957); see also Edgar A. Pessemier, "A New Way To Determine Buying Decisions," *Journal of Marketing,* October, 1959, pp. 41–46.

is made "real" by duplicating those aspects of the market which influence buyer action, then the experimental results will closely parallel the decisions made by consumers confronted by similar conditions in everyday life.

The experiments reported here were designed to accomplish this end by having subjects go on simulated shopping trips. As it would have been on a real shopping trip, the subject's goal was to maximize the satisfaction he could obtain from prevailing market conditions and limited funds. Each participant in the experiment was told how much money he had to spend, the assortment of brands available in each class of goods from which he was to make a purchase, and the price of each item. In every case the subject made purchase decisions from assortments that contained goods which he purchased frequently for his own personal use. The participant in the experiment could maximize the satisfaction he might obtain on any one of the simulated shopping trips by selecting the brands he preferred in light of the price at which they could be purchased. Since he had a stated sum available, the act of making the selections also determined the amount of change he would receive. The experiment was administered to groups ranging in size from twenty to fifty subjects, and at the conclusion of the experiment one member of each group, selected at random, actually received the merchandise and change called for by his decisions during one of his simulated shopping trips. It seems fair to state that a reasonably close parallel to real shopping conditions was maintained during the experiment and that useful information was obtained about consumer behavior.

Although maintaining psychological equivalence was one of the principal objectives of the experiment, it should be noted that it is not essential that subjects respond precisely as they would in a real market environment. It is necessary only that any deviation which may exist be predictable. Had the study reported here been designed to do more than explore the potential value of the experimental method in deriving schedules of demand, deviations in behavior could have been examined under a number of experimental procedures. As additional experiments are undertaken, the method employed should be varied to gain sharper insights into the impact on experimental subjects of such factors as the form of presentation, the procedure followed in modifying price, the types of incentives offered, the number and complexity of the purchase decisions, and the time allowed to complete a simulated shopping trip. If a larger sample representative of the population of buyers of each class of goods is used in a future study, an examination of the behavior of various classes of buyers would also be a promising area for exploration. For example, it could be instructive to examine demand schedules for groups of subjects possessing distinct personal, social, and economic characteristics.

The experiment was administered to 228 students at Washington State University during the spring of 1959. Although convenience in handling groups was an important consideration in selecting the experimental subjects, it was possible to obtain subjects representing all social class levels and a wide range of fields of major interest. However, a higher proportion of males, upperclassmen, and business administration majors were present than would be expected in a random sample drawn from the population of approximately six thousand resident students. An extensive statistical analysis of the effect of characteristics of buyers was beyond the scope of this study, but a limited check was made which failed to uncover significant bias introduced by the particular composition of the experimental subjects.

Before the experiment began, the subjects were polled to determine whether they purchased items for their own use from four classes of goods—toothpaste, cigarettes, toilet soap, and headache remedies—and, if they did, what brands they customarily purchased. In addition to the form used to gather these facts, two sets of assortment sheets, or lists of brands, were compiled and duplicated in advance. These sheets listed seven brands of toothpaste, ten brands of cigarettes, eleven brands of toilet soap, and six brands of headache remedies and included all the brands available at the student bookstore in these classifications.[3] Because of the convenient location of the student bookstore, the particular lines of merchandise that it stocks, and the absence of effective competition, student patronage was very high. Since each assortment that was used paralleled one found in a retail store in which the subjects frequently shopped, presumably subjects were familiar with the brands and their usual prices.

On the basis of the brand preferences indicated by the subjects, it was possible to modify the prices of each subject's preferred brands on sets of assortment sheets.[4] By raising the price of the subject's preferred brands on each of a number of assortment sheets, subjects were offered their preferred brands at various increases in price while the other brands remained available at the regular price. By entering the regular price of a subject's preferred brands on a series of assortment sheets on which the prices of all brands had been reduced, it was possible to offer *all* but the subject's preferred brands at various reductions in price. Other than these changes in price, the conditions under which the subjects made their buying decisions were unaltered.

---

[3] Each classification also carried one or two additional items labeled "a new brand", this was included in the assortment to measure the tendency of consumers to buy a new brand when switching brands.

[4] To eliminate positional bias, the positions of brands in a column and the positions of sheets in a series were randomized.

As a result, subjects were given assortments from which to make selections on simulated shopping trips that *required the subject to decide whether he would buy the brand he preferred or whether he would change his usual purchasing behavior because of the difference in price.*

When the two series, containing a total of twenty simulated shopping trips, had been prepared for each individual, the experiment was administered to groups of subjects. The subjects were shown samples of the merchandise contained in the assortment sheets, and told that they had $1.75 available on each shopping trip. This sum was large enough to permit a subject to purchase the highest-priced item in each of the four classifications, if he chose to do so, and still receive change. Although the subjects were requested to assume that they had a current need for the merchandise included in the assortments, they were permitted to postpone making a purchase if they would walk a block to investigate the offerings in another store. As a result, subjects were expected to purchase a fixed number of items, but they were given an opportunity to shop.[5] In addition, the subjects were told that at the conclusion of the experiment one member of the group, chosen at random, would receive the actual merchandise and change called for by his decisions on one of his shopping trips. Finally, the subjects were asked to make the twenty simulated shopping trips, selecting those items on each trip which would give them the greatest satisfaction from a mix of merchandise and change.

Several additional precautions were taken to reduce any tendency subjects might have to try to win approval by acting "rationally." First, subjects were given no indication of what "rational" conduct might be. Second, they were asked to shop at the same speed and react in the same manner as they would on a real shopping trip. And, finally, subjects were allowed to handle the assortment sheets on which they recorded their buying decisions in a manner which would prevent the identification of a set of responses with a particular individual.

On the average, the experiment was explained and administered to a group in less than thirty minutes. If it had been practical to assemble all subjects in a single location, the nearly fifteen thousand buying decisions which were recorded could have been recorded in little more than half hour.[6] The important point is that a large amount of data about the behavior of consumers was accumulated rapidly at low cost. Even if subjects had been handled singly, at least one

[5] Because of the type of goods purchased, it was not surprising to find that only three subjects elected to investigate a second set of assortments.

[6] All 288 subjects made twenty simulated shopping trips and could have bought one item from each of four classifications on each trip. Some subjects, however, did not buy goods from all four classifications, since they did not normally either buy or use the goods included in the classifications, i.e., cigarettes for the non-smoker.

hundred buying decisions could have been recorded in an experimental environment in less than one-half hour.

In the course of the experiment it developed that five individuals were members of more than one group. As a check on consistency, they were permitted to take part in two sets of simulated shopping trips, several hours to several days apart. About 85 per cent of the decisions recorded on the second series were in direct agreement with the decisions made during the original series. And, in almost all cases where disagreement existed, the magnitudes of the differences were small.

SPECIAL USE OF "DEMAND"

As a consequence of the methods employed in the experiments, the terms "demand curves" and "demand schedules," although similar to those used in economics, are used here in a special sense. For example, with reference to Brand A toothpaste, Figure 1 shows that 81 individuals bought Brand A at its regular price of 31 cents. When the price of Brand A increased to 32 cents and all other brands remained at their regular price, 31 cents, 67 subjects continued to buy Brand A, and 14 switched to other brands of toothpaste. A like interpretation may be given to the remaining points on the upper portion of Brand A's "demand curve" as well as to the upper halves (above solid dots) of all the "demand curves" in this article.

The bottom half of the "demand curve" for Brand A was not obtained by simply lowering the price of Brand A. To do so would have required a four- to fivefold increase in the number of buying decisions made by every subject, since it would have been necessary to reduce individually the price of six brands of toothpaste, ten brands of toilet soap, and so on, through a full range of price reductions. Cutting the number of classifications included in an exploratory study or risking excessive fatigue on the part of subjects was undesirable. Therefore, the alternative of simultaneously reducing the price of all but the subject's preferred brand was adopted. The effect of this procedure was to eliminate the advantage a brand would have by being the only one available at a reduced price. In the case of Brand A, Figure 1 shows that, among those subjects who normally purchased brands other than Brand A, there were five individuals who would switch to Brand A if it and all other non-preferred brands were reduced to 30 cents. If Brand A had been the only brand offered at this one-cent reduction in price, additional switching to Brand A might have occurred. Under these

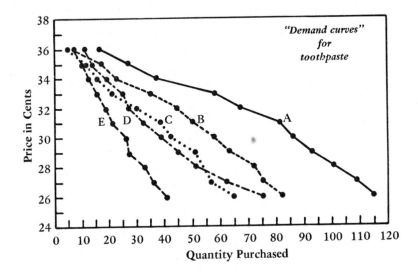

FIGURE 1. *"Demand curves" for toothpaste brands preferred by twenty or more subjects.*

circumstances switching would not have been the result of a secondary preference for Brand A so much as the result of the more direct price appeal possessed by Brand A when compared to other brands. In other words, the bottom halves of the "demand curves" understate the effect of price reductions, and the understatement should be more pronounced as the magnitude of the reduction increases.

For some purposes of comparison, "demand schedules" of the type used here may be superior to those that comply with the usual definition of demand. For example, if a seller is interested in patterns of secondary brand preference, exclusive of switching occurring principally on the basis of subjects selecting the lowest-priced item, then the procedure followed in this study would be superior. On the other hand, there will be many instances when a measure of demand in accordance with the traditional definition will be required, and a way around the difficulties associated with increasing the number of buying decisions will have to be found. If data were being gathered to aid in the solution of a specific problem, it would be practical to work with a single classification and obtain the required data without running the risk of excessive fatigue on the part of subjects.

RESULTS

The "demand curves" for the more popular brands included in the study are shown in Figures 1–4. The original price and number of

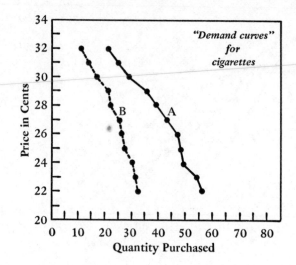

FIGURE 2. "Demand curves" for cigarette brands preferred by twenty or more subjects.

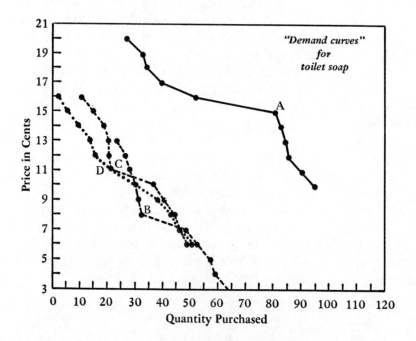

FIGURE 3. "Demand curves" for toilet soap preferred by twenty or more subjects.

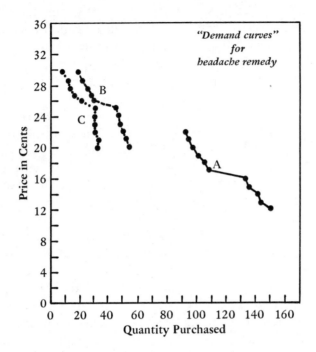

FIGURE 4. *"Demand curves" for headache-remedy brands preferred by twenty or more subjects.*

buyers who preferred the brand at that price are indicated by a solid dot adjacent to the letter designating the brand. Prices and quantities are shown through the range of a 5-cent increase and a 5-cent decrease.[7] The price elasticities for the total change to that point have been computed for increases and decreases in price of 1 cent, 2 cents, etc., through 5 cents (Table 1). The elasticities displayed for price reductions are subject to the qualifications outlined in the preceding

---

[7]An estimate of the reliability for points above the original price on a "demand curve" for the student population used in the experiment may be illustrated as follows: Let p be the probability that a person who has been chosen at random from the subpopulation of buyers of Brand A toothpaste will *not* switch to another brand if the price of Brand A is increased by three cents. A point estimate of p, call it p, is given by the fraction 37/81, the proportion of experimental subjects preferring Brand A who continued to buy it after the price of Brand A had been increased from 31 cents to 34 cents. A 90 per cent confidence interval on p is given by the formula:

$$p - 1.645 \sqrt{\frac{pq}{n}} \leqslant p \leqslant p + 1.645 \sqrt{\frac{pq}{n}}$$

For a price increase of 3 cents on Brand A toothpaste, the 90 per cent confidence interval is: $.37 < p < .55$

A similar procedure could be used for the points below the original price on a "demand curve" by letting p be the probability of choosing a person at random from the subpopulation of buyers of all brands of toothpaste other than Brand A who will switch to Brand A if all brands but the one originally preferred by the person are reduced in price by a given amount.

section and are used exclusively for purposes of comparing one brand to another. Average price elasticities for a classification have also been computed for toothpaste and cigarettes. Since these represent a weighted arithmetic average of the elasticities of all individual brands in the classification, they should not be interpreted as applying to total industry demand.

Although it is impossible to generalize about the behavior of all buyers, it is interesting to review some of the characteristics of demand displayed by those who took part in the simulated shopping trips. For simplicity, each classification will be discussed separately. To facilitate identification, the brands in each classification are lettered in alphabetical order beginning with the most popular brand and, in the text, the subscript "t" is used for toothpaste, "c" for cigarettes, "s" for toilet soap, and "b" for headache remedies; thus, for example, Brand B_t designates the second most popular brand of toothpaste.

Toothpaste. The "demand curves" in Figure 1 and the elasticities shown in Table 1 reveal that the subjects varied a good deal in the strength of their brand preferences for toothpaste. For example, Brand A_t, with its large share of the market, gains far less relatively by reducing its price than does Brand E_t, which holds a small share of the market. In addition, Brand E_t loses less relatively by increasing its price than does Brand A_t. The strategic position of a leading brand like Brand A_t will be discussed in the following section but it is worth note here that the relatively lower price elasticity of Brand E_t under price increases may be attributable in part to the specific medicinal properties of the product, not shared by the other brands in the assortment. Further, when all brands are taken together, a relatively high degree of price elasticity may be observed that remains rather stable over the range in which price was varied.

Cigarettes. The data displayed in Figure 2 and Table 1 show that, for the classification as a whole, brands of cigarettes are less price-elastic than are brands of toothpaste. On the other hand, the elasticities for cigarettes, like those for toothpaste, remain fairly uniform over the range that price varied. Both leading brands of cigarettes, Brand A_c and Brand B_c, gain a good deal less relatively from a reduction in price than do the brands that hold the remaining share of the market. The tendency of leading brands to gain less relatively from a price reduction than do minor brands shows up in both the cigarette and toothpaste classifications. As in the case of the toothpaste, the original prices of all brands of cigarettes were identical. Therefore, to gain an important share of student patronage, a brand had to utilize effectively differential non-price appeals that would prove attractive to a sizable proportion

TABLE 1 "Price Elasticity of Demand" for Selected Brands*

Product	Original Price (Cents)	+5	+4	+3	+2	+1	−1†	−2†	−3†	−4†	−5†
Toothpaste:											
Brand A....	31	5.0	5.2	5.6	4.4	5.4	1.9	2.3	2.4	2.7	2.6
Brand B....	31	5.5	5.1	5.8	6.2	3.7	5.0	4.0	4.5	4.0	4.0
Brand C....	31	5.4	5.6	6.1	7.2	7.2	3.2	4.8	3.7	3.6	4.1
Brand D....	31	5.3	5.9	4.7	3.8	4.7	5.6	5.6	5.9	5.5	5.9
Brand E....	31	4.4	3.7	5.5	3.7	3.0	7.4	4.4	5.9	5.5	5.9
All Brands‡	31	4.9	4.9	5.3	5.1	4.1	4.1	4.1	4.2	4.3	4.5
Cigarettes:											
Brand A....	27	3.4	3.6	2.9	2.2	2.5	2.5	1.6	1.3	1.7	1.6
Brand B....	27	3.0	3.0	2.9	2.2	3.2	1.1	1.1	1.8	1.6	1.5
All Brands‡	27	3.4	3.2	3.8	2.3	3.4	3.7	2.5	3.2	3.7	3.5
Toilet soap:											
Brand A....	15	2.0	2.3	2.9	3.8	5.4	0.4	0.4	0.3	0.5	0.5
Brand B....	8	0.7	0.4	0.3	0.3	0.3	4.0	2.5	2.1	1.7	1.7
Brand C....	11	2.0	2.1	2.2	2.3	3.5	4.0	4.0	3.5	3.0	2.9
Brand D....	11	1.2	0.9	0.5	0.3	0.5	7.9	5.0	4.0	3.3	2.9
Headache remedy:											
Brand A....	15	0.4	0.5	0.5	0.6	0.4	3.3	1.8	1.5	1.2	1.1
Brand B....	25	2.9	3.4	4.0	4.9	8.7	0.5	0.5	0.7	1.0	0.9
Brand C....	25	3.6	3.4	4.3	5.2	8.9	0.0	0.0	0.0	0.4	0.3

*Coefficient of elasticity = $[p/(p - p')][(q' - q)/q]$, where p = original price, p' = altered price, q = quantity demanded at original price, and q' = quantity demanded at altered price.

Basic data from which elasticities of individual brands were computed may be read directly from Figures 1–4. Brands preferred by less than twenty subjects have been excluded.

†See discussion in text of the interpretation of demand that is appropriate for price reductions.

‡A weighted arithmetic average of the elasticities of all brands in the classification.

of the buyers. To the degree that a brand was successful in doing so, it reduced the number of buyers who could be easily switched to the brand on the basis of the particular product and promotion appeals it employed. In other words, fewer buyers remain that such a brand could attract because of its past success and the particular form of differentiation it adopted. In other instances, minor brands attracted buyers by somewhat narrower appeals that particularly fill the needs of a smaller group. By concentrating on these special needs, minor brands may make it difficult for the general appeals of the more popular brands to be effective.

Toilet Soap. In contrast to the two preceding classifications, where the original prices of the brands were identical, a distinctly different condition existed in the toilet-soap classification. Here, the leading brand sold regularly at 15 cents, the second most popular brand at 8 cents, and the next two brands in order of popularity sold originally at 11 cents. The kinked demand curve for brand A_s may be attributed in large measure to the producer's early promotion of a distinct appeal to the consumer's desire for social acceptability. Besides gaining a sizable share of the market through its product and promotion policies, the producer appears to have priced the product to take advantage of the brand's marketing characteristics. If the price of Brand A_s is increased, buyers will be lost in large numbers, but relatively few buyers will be gained if price is reduced by small amounts. On the other hand, Brand B_s holds a very strong price position but a smaller market share. This brand will lose few buyers as a result of small increases in price and, if able to lower its modest price, it can attract substantial numbers of new buyers. Had the toilet-soap assortment found in a typical supermarket been used in the experiment, doubtless Brand B_s would have faced active price competition. Because such competition was absent, economy-minded subjects were not given an acceptable alternative until the price of Brand B_s increased to a marked degree. In the case of Brand C_s and D_s, both display a high degree of price elasticity when their prices are reduced, but there is a marked difference in the elasticities when their prices are increased. When Brand D_s is compared to Brand C_s, the buyers of Brand D_s show very strong brand loyalty. If the differences in original price are considered, Brand D_s also displays this characteristic when compared to Brands A_s and B_s. A partial explanation of the loyalty evidenced by the buyers of Brand D_s is found in the fact that this soap is used by a number of buyers both as a toilet soap and as a shaving soap.

Headache Remedies.   This classification, like the toilet-soap classification, contains items with different original prices. In this instance, however, the lowest-priced item, Brand A_h, has by far the largest share of the market. Like Brand B_s, the lowest-priced toilet soap, it is highly price-inelastic when its price is increased and moderately price-elastic when its price is reduced. Brands B_h and C_h, both higher-priced items, have kinked demand curves characteristic of the differentiated premium product, but in this classification these brands have been unable to attain an important market share. For the group of subjects studied here, the result of product differentiation appear to be less successful for a headache remedy than for a toilet soap. For both headache remedies and toilet soaps the atypical nature of the assortment and of the subjects limits what may be said about the over-all pricing policies of the various brands. In particular, the presence of only one brand in the lower price range creates an unusual assortment for both toilet soap and headache remedies.

CONCLUSIONS

Since the experiment reported here was exploratory, the findings cited are necessarily little more than illustrative of some kinds of facts about consumer behavior that can be obtained under simulated market conditions. Despite this limitation, it is fair to conclude that controlled experiments offer large promise as a means of attacking a variety of important problems in business and economics that have remained unsolved in the absence of basic facts concerning consumer behavior. For example, it should be practical to employ experimental methods to test the hyopthesis that for a given classification there exists a well-defined optimum market share for a single brand. It may also be possible to gain insights into the relative effectiveness of marketing several brands with strong differential appeals, in contrast to expanding the market for a single brand. Further, a better understanding might be developed concerning the degree to which a brand in a given market can expand or protect its market share by price and non-price appeals. The list of similar problems is long, too long to be included here, and the potential applications of research results range from shaping anti-trust policy to developing short-range marketing programs for brand-promoters. The essential point is that the tools of experimental research appear to offer a potentially fruitful means of attacking these problems. By imaginative design and application of experimental methods of research, it is reasonable to expect that the base of facts can be greatly broadened and important progress made toward finding solutions to a number of stubborn problems.

15

Group Influence in Marketing

Foundation for Research on Human Behavior

On the common sense level the (reference group) concept says in effect that man's behavior is influenced in different ways and in varying degrees by other people. Comparing one's own success with that of others is a frequent source of satisfaction or disappointment. Similarly, before making a decision one often considers what such and such a person or such and such a group (whose opinion one has *some* reason to follow) would do in these circumstances, or what they would think of one for making a certain decision rather than another. Put in these ways, of course, reference group influence represents an unanalyzed truism which has long been recognized. The problem to which social scientists have been addressing themselves intensively only for the last two decades, however, concerns the refinement of this common sense notion to the end that it might be applied meaningfully to concrete situations.

The real problems are to determine which kinds of groups are likely to be referred to by which kinds of individuals under which kinds of circumstances in the process of making which decisions, and to measure the extent of this reference group influence. Towards this end empirical researches have been conducted in recent years which have at least made a start in the process of refining the reference group concept.

Reference group theory as it has developed has become broad

Reprinted from *Group Influence in Marketing and Public Relations* (Ann Arbor: Foundation for Research on Human Behavior, 1956), pp. 1–12.

The Foundation for Research on Human Behavior is a nonprofit organization with headquarters at Ann Arbor, Michigan. The Foundation exists for the purpose of making grants for scientifically worthy and potentially practical research at institutions across the nation. Grants are made in consultation with a Research Advisory Committee drawn largely from contributing companies.

enough to cover a wide range of social phenomena, both with respect to the relation of the individual to the group and with respect to the type of influence exerted upon the individual by the group in question.

KINDS OF REFERENCE GROUPS

Reference groups against which an individual evaluates his own status and behavior may be of several kinds.

They may be *membership* groups to which a person actually belongs. There can be small face-to-face groups in which actual association is the rule, such as families or organizations, whether business, social, religious, or political. On the other hand, there can be groups in which actual membership is held but in which personal association is absent. (For example, membership in a political party, none of whose meetings are personally attended.)

Reference groups may be *categories* to which a person automatically belongs by virtue of age, sex, education, marital status and so on. This sort of reference group relationship involves the concept of role. For example, before taking a certain action an individual might consider whether this action would be regarded as appropriate in his role as a man or husband or educated person or older person or a combination of all of these roles. What is involved here is an individual's perception of what society, in general or that part of it with which he has any contact, expects people of his age, or sex, or education or marital status to do under given circumstances.

They may be *anticipatory* rather than actual membership groups. Thus a person who aspires to membership in a group to which he does *not* belong may be more likely to refer to it or compare himself with its standards when making a decision than he is to refer to the standards of the group in which he actually belongs but would like to leave. This involves the concept of upward mobility. When such upward mobility is sought in the social or business world it is ordinarily accompanied by a sensitivity to the attitudes of those in the groups to which one aspires, whether it involves the attitudes of country club members in the eyes of the aspiring non-member or the attitudes of management in the eyes of the ambitious wage earner or junior executive.

There are also negative, *dissociative* reference groups. These constitute the opposite side of the coin from the anticipatory membership groups. Thus an individual sometimes avoids a certain action because it is associated with a group (to which the individual may or may not in fact belong) from which he would like to dissociate himself.

INFLUENCE ON INDIVIDUAL BEHAVIOR

Reference groups influence behavior in two major ways. First, they influence *aspiration levels* and thus play a part in producing satisfaction or frustration. If the other members of one's reference group (for example, the neighbors) are wealthier, more famous, better gardeners, etc., one may be dissatisfied with one's own achievements and may strive to do as well as the other.

Second, reference groups influence *kinds* of behavior. They establish approved patterns of using one's wealth, of wearing one's fame, of designing one's garden. They set tabus too, and may have the power to apply actual sanctions (for example, exclusion from the group). They thus produce *conformity* as well as *contentment* (or discontentment).

These two kinds of influence have, however, a good deal in common. Both imply certain perceptions on the part of the individual, who attributes characteristics to the reference group which it may or may not actually have. Both involve psychological rewards and punishment.

RELATIVE DEPRIVATION—AN EXAMPLE OF
REFERENCE GROUP INFLUENCE

As already indicated, one of the chief problems in the field of reference group theory is to identify which of several groups that might serve as a frame of reference under given circumstances actually invoked by an individual.

This is sometimes difficult to get at directly, as individuals are not always *aware* of which reference groups they are evaluating their behavior against, or may not be anxious to reveal them where they are conscious of such groups.

During World War II the Research Branch of the United States Army was concerned with morale of troops under different circumstances, and the morale often seemed not to reflect objective conditions. Thus, for example, soldiers in the Military Police who had received fewer promotions than their opposite numbers in the Air Force were nevertheless more satisfied with their rank than were the average

Air Force men. Many similar phenomena were noted in which the men who were apparently suffering greater hardship on an absolute basis were more satisfied than others apparently suffering less hardship on an absolute basis. In an effort to explain these *apparent* inconsistencies the concept of "relative deprivation" was introduced. It was found that in each case there existed a reference group with which the individual soldier tended to compare his own lot. Only if he felt deprived *relative to this group* did his morale suffer. Two examples should suffice.

Army Promotions. The fact that Military Police were often more satisfied with their progress than were the more rapidly promoted Air Force Men was explained as follows: Absolute achieved status evidently was not the key to their feelings but rather the relation of the soldier's status to that of others he regarded as his standard of comparison. Thus the Private First Class in the Military Police may have been more satisfied than the Corporal in the Air Force, because in the Military Police virtually no enlisted man expected to get higher than Private First Class, while in the Air Force soldiers saw sergeants and better all around them.

Negro Troops. It was found that the morale of Northern Negroes in southern army camps was higher than that of Northern Negroes in northern camps located in the areas where presumably Negroes in general were accorded better treatment. This apparent incongruity was again explained by identifying the reference group against which the Northern Negro compared himself in each instance. The reference group which turned this apparent inconsistency into a plausible reaction in this case was the Negro civilians whom the soldiers encountered while on pass in neighboring towns. The Negro soldier's pay was the same in the North as it was in the South, but in the North he found Negro civilians making so much money in defense plants that his pay appeared small by comparison. On the other hand, relative to most Negro civilians he saw in southern towns, the Negro soldier had a position of comparative wealth and dignity. Thus the psychological values of Army life to the Negro soldier in the South relative to the Southern Negro civilian greatly exceeded the psychological values of Army life to the Negro soldier in the north relative to the Northern Negro civilian.

THE PRACTICAL VALUE OF THE REFERENCE GROUP CONCEPT IN MARKETING AND PUBLIC RELATIONS

In applying the reference group concept to practical problems in marketing and public relations three basic questions arise:

1. *Reference Group Relevance*—How do you determine whether and to what extent reference group influence is operating in a given situation? The reference group is after all just one of many influences in decision making, varying greatly in prominence from situation to situation.
2. *Reference Group Identification*—How do you identify the particular reference group or groups or individuals who are most relevant in influencing decisions under given circumstances? This is perhaps the most difficult question to answer in many cases, particularly where multiple reference groups are involved.
3. *Reference Group Identification and Effective Communication*—Once having identified the nature of the group influence operating in a given situation, how do you then make use of this knowledge in achieving the most effective *communication* with the groups or individuals?

The payoff is of course in this area, since the answers to the first two questions are of value only to the extent that they can be translated into more pertinent and effective communications, designed to influence purchasing behavior or the attitudes of various publics towards an organization.

Experimental evidence is now available which sheds light on each of these three questions. From this evidence as well as from the general advancement in the methodology of social research in recent years there have emerged some generalizations, very tentative in nature. These can be applied only with the most careful attention to the special circumstances operating in individual instances, and serve more as guides to fruitful ways of examining problems as they arise than as simple answers to problems.

Whether or not reference group influence is likely to come into play in the decisions of individuals depends on many interrelated factors. For descriptive purposes, however, it is convenient to consider some of these factors under two major headings:

1. *Influence determinants which vary primarily according to the individual making the decision,* such as the feeling of security or insecurity with respect to potential reference groups, the perception of the positions of these groups concerning kinds of behavior expected or stands on specific issues, and the extent of knowledge about the matter on which a decision must be made.
2. *Influence determinants which vary primarily according to the matter to be decided,* such as the attributes of the product, in a marketing situation, or the nature of the organization and issue at stake, in a public relations situation.

In marketing, it is rarely practical to utilize information about individual differences (the first class above), because products must be designed and advertised with large groups in mind.[1] In public relations, on the other hand, individual differences may be very important. In this area the *general* attention level with respect to a particular issue is often low. Under these circumstances the relevant public may be largely confined to a few individuals, and in such cases knowledge of the relation between these individuals and potential reference groups would certainly be to the point.

A. INDIVIDUAL DIFFERENCES AND REFERENCE GROUP INFLUENCE

1. The Relation of Security Level and Conformity to Reference Group Influence

A tentative generalization which has emerged in this area and which has been supported by some experimental evidence is this:

Individuals enjoying the greatest amount of security by virtue of their prestige and status within a group will generally conform (both publicly and privately) to the standards of that group, but are also freest to deviate from the group norms on occasions when, to their minds, particular circumstances seem to justify such deviations. On the other hand those with lowest feelings of security and least status in a group are most likely *publicly* to conform to its norms on all occasions even though harboring private opposition and resentment. The latter holds, of course, only if there are penalties associated with loss of membership in the particular group. Conformity then serves the purpose of maintaining membership in that group.

The folllowing éxperiment conducted under laboratory conditions at Yale University lent support to this hypothesis.[2]

Eighteen groups, each composed of six Yale freshmen, were formed for the experiment. They were motivated to cooperate by being told that they would meet for several sessions to work on certain problems and that the best group would win a prize. To promote group cohesion without sacrificing cooperation, each group was told that it would stop from time to time to evaluate its own members and expel any who were seriously interfering with the progress of the group. It was pointed out, however, that such expulsion was not to be taken lightly, as it would carry a considerable stigma and hence was only

---

[1] An exception to this generalization may be found in the case of personal selling, where knowledge of the individual's specific relation to and perception of certain groups would be highly relevant.

[2] J. E. Dittes and H. H. Kelley, "Effects of Different Conditions of Acceptance upon Conformity to Group Norms," *Journal of Abnormal and Social Psychology* (1956).

to be considered under very serious circumstances. The groups were given several problems on which they were asked to come to some agreement. One of these problems was in the area of juvenile delinquency. Each of the 18 groups was presented with some information about two gangs of juvenile delinquents, and asked to decide which of these gangs most deserved help from a social worker. The information was structured in such a way as to make Gang A appear to be the logical candidate for aid from the social worker. As planned by the researchers, the various units deliberated and came to the jointly-arrived-at decision that Gang A most deserved aid. After these group decisions were made, artificial images were set up in the mind of each individual as to how highly he was regarded by the group to which he belonged. This was accomplished by having the group members rate each other, in writing; however, the experiment leader did not use this information but gave each student fictitious information on how he was regarded by other members of his six-man group. One person in each group was told that he was very highly regarded, two were told that they had been given an average rating, another two that the group's regard for them was quite low, and finally one member of each group was told that he was on the verge of rejection.

After these varying images of esteem by the particular group had been established (designed to set up feelings ranging all the way from very high to very low sense of security) a new item of information about the juvenile gangs was introduced. This item introduced some counter evidence pointing rather clearly in favor of Gang B as being the logical choice for aid.

After the new evidence was introduced, private and public expressions of conformity to the originally announced judgments of the group were obtained from those of very low, average and high prestige (as artifically manipulated for experimental purposes) with the following results:

1. Men with the lowest prestige and security in relation to their group—those who believed they were on the verge of expulsion—were, when queried privately, most willing to deviate from the originally established norm of their group. However, when placed in the position of having to take a public stand these same people were most likely to conform to the originally announced norms of the groups, and least likely to deviate even though their own private inclination on the basis of the facts at hand was to do so.

2. Men with average status and security exhibited considerable conformity, even in their private opinions.

3. Men with highest status and security were found, when queried privately, to be quite willing to differ from the original group decision and felt the greatest freedom to express their non-conformity publicly.

These relationships may be expressed graphically as follows:

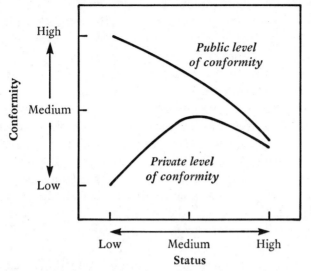

FIGURE 1. *Status determines the consistency between public and private conformity.*

Practical Implications

If a person has high status and feels very secure relative to a group, he can be appealed to directly on the merits of the case and is in the best position to take the lead in deviating should he so desire, with least risk of losing status with the group he prizes. Seeking to influence such people through reference group appeals, when the merits of the case are inconsistent with the appeals, may have little success.

On the other hand, as suggested by the data just reviewed, those with lesser status in their group and less feeling of security are most likely to be influenced in public or visible actions by appeals involving their reference group. They are more likely to observe the norms of the group than others, even if they privately disagree with its specific position, since they require acceptance from the group for their own security. However, if the reference group influence conflicts with their own judgement or works against their own best interests, they are likely to develop an underlying resistance to the idea. Such resistance may find expression in other ways.

A practical example of the operation of this principle in the field of public relations and specifically in the area of influencing legislation may be drawn from experience in Washington. Particularly on issues where mass public attention and interest is low, considerable effort is concentrated on the most crucial of all publics, Congress itself.

A Congressman of course has several reference groups, prominent among which are his constituents and the remainder of Congress. Naturally he greatly values the esteem of both of these groups. His very existence in Congress depends on the former and his self-esteem as well as the degree of cooperation he can depend upon getting for his own projects depends upon the high regard of the latter. The Congressman's status and security with regard to his constituents may be measured by such items as the size of his pluralities and the length of his service. Within Congress his status may be measured by, among other things, such items as seniority and cooperation by other members in the past.

Suppose a group was interested in changing a long standing piece of legislation which appeared to have represented the majority views of Congress for a considerable period of time. Suppose also that there was considerable merit in the proposed change, but that the public was relatively little concerned with this legislation. The Congressman's primary reference group with respect to this issue is likely, therefore, to be his colleagues in the House. A freshman Congressman with little security and status would not, even though he privately favored this new legislation, be likely to oppose publicly the prevailing reference group position, by introducing the legislation or placing his name on an initial list of sponsors, while a Congressman with security and status might be more willing to do so.

For those outside of Congress interested in seeing the measure passed, winning the support of so-called bellwethers within Congress for this would be a primary objective. Such Congressmen, by virtue of their secure position in Congress, are most free to deviate and take the lead on occasions, where the case merits it. Though they generally show considerable respect for the norms of their "club" they are also in the best position to ignore this reference group when the right occasion arises.

2. The Individual's Perception of Norms of Potential Reference Group

Perhaps one of the more obvious limitations on the relevance of a potential reference group in influencing a decision is an individual's lack of knowledge or incorrect perception of the group's actual position on an issue, even where he values the group's views or at least its acceptance of him. Thus, for example, the American Legion may be an effective reference group for a substantial number of veterans with respect to veterans' legislation. It may be much less so, however, in connection with views on international affairs. The Legion has a position on such matters, but the average veteran is much less likely to know just what that position is. Along this line, a study[3] conducted for a Church Council found issues on which the Church's national policy was not followed by a considerable portion of the Church's members. The study revealed that these differences between Church policy and the opinions of its individual members were not necessarily conscious nonconformity with group norms, but rather in many cases reflected ignorance of what those norms were.

One practical implication from these studies is that the effective influence of a reference group, even one known to command a substantial following, may be increased by giving special publicity to the position of the group on a specific issue.

3. Independent Knowledge About the Matter to Be Decided

Experimental evidence has indicated that reference group influence is particularly potent in an informational vacuum. Where the individual has little if any knowledge about the attributes of a product or the issues involved in a public relations campaign, reference group influence is maximized. On the other hand, where the individual has personal knowledge and experience, the reference group influence is likely to be *less* relevant, other things being equal. Thus, for example, in the same study of a Church and its parishioners alluded to above, it was found that uninformed parishioners tended to have the same attitudes on secular issues as did their clergymen, but among those parishioners who were politically informed and had other sources of information on these issues there was a tendency more often to ignore the positions taken by their clergymen.

B. DIFFERENT KINDS OF DECISIONS AND REFERENCE GROUP INFLUENCE

1. Marketing and Reference Group Relevance

As has already been suggested, the reference group constitutes just one of the many influences in buying decisions, and this influence varies

[3] Bureau of Applied Social Research, Columbia University.

from product to product. How then does one determine whether reference group influence is likely to be a factor in buying behavior in connection with a given product or brand? Research has been conducted on the various factors that influence buying behavior with reference to several products, and out of this have emerged some general ideas about how reference group influences may enter into purchasing.

Buying may be a completely individualistic kind of activity or it may be very much socially conditioned. Consumers are often influenced by what others buy, especially those persons with whom they compare themselves, or use as reference groups.

The conspicuousness of a product is perhaps the most general attribute bearing on its susceptibility to reference group influence. There are two aspects to conspicuousness in this particular context that help to determine reference group influence. First the article must be conspicuous in the most obvious sense that it can be seen and identified by others. Secondly it must be conspicuous in the sense of standing out and being noticed. In other words, no matter how visible a product is, if virtually everyone owns it, it is not conspicuous in the second sense of the word. This leads to a further distinction: reference groups may influence either (a) the purchase of a product, or (b) the choice of a particular brand of type, or (c) both.

The possible susceptibility of various product and brand buying to reference group influence is suggested in the following figure:

Reference group influence relatively

	weak −	strong +	
Reference group influence relatively strong +	clothing furniture magazines refrigerator (type) toilet soap	cars* cigarettes* beer (prem. vs. reg.)* drugs*	**Brand or type** +
weak −	soap canned peaches laundry soap refrigerator (brand) radios	air conditioners* instant coffee* TV (black & white)	−

− Product +

FIGURE 2. *Products and brands of consumer goods may be classified by extent to which reference groups influence their purchase.*
*The classification of all starred products is based on actual experimental evidence. Other products in this table are classified speculatively on the basis of generalizations derived from the sum of research in this area and confirmed by the judgment of seminar participants.

According to this classification a particular item might be susceptible to reference group influence in its purchase in three different ways, corresponding to three of the four cells in the above figure. Reference group influence may operate with respect to product alone (Brand + Product -) as in the upper left cell, or it may operate both with respect to brand and product (Brand + Product +) as in the upper right cell, or it may operate with respect to product but not brand (Brand - Product +) as in the lower right cell.

Only the "minus-minus" items of the kind illustrated (Brand - Product -) in the lower left cell are not likely to involve any significant reference group influence in their purchase *at the present time.*

What are some of the characteristics that place an item in a given category, and what significance do such placements have for marketing and advertising policy?

a. "Product plus, brand plus" items. Autos constitute an article where both the product and the brand are socially conspicuous. Whether or not a person buys a car, and also what particular brand he buys, is likely to be influenced by what others do. This also holds true for cigarettes, for drugs (decisions made by M.D.'s as to what to prescribe) and for beer with respect to type (premium vs. regular) as opposed to brand. Cigarettes and drugs, however, qualify as "plus-plus" items in a manner different from cars.

For example, while the car belongs to a class of products where brand differentiation is based at least substantially on real differences in attributes, the cigarette belongs to a class of product in which it is difficult to differentiate one brand from another by attributes: hence attributes are ascribed largely through reference group appeal built up by advertising. Popular images of the kinds of people who smoke various brands have been created at great cost, and in some cases additional images are being created to broaden a particular brand's market. In the case of drugs, it was found that the reference group influencing *whether* the product was used was different from that influencing the particular *brand* selected. Reference group influence was found to be prominent in determining whether or not beer was purchased at all, and also in determining whether regular or premium beer was selected. It did not appear to influence strongly choice of a particular brand.

b. "Product plus, brand minus" items. Instant coffee is one of the best examples of this class of items. Whether it is served in a household depends in considerable part on whether the housewife, in view of her own reference groups and the image she has of their attitudes towards this product, considers it appropriate to serve it. The brand itself in this instance is not conspicuous or socially important and is a matter largely for individual choice. In the case of air conditioners, it was found that little prestige attached to the particular brand used, and reference group influence related largely to the idea of purchasing the product itself. Analysis in one city revealed that the purchase of this often "visible from the outside" product was concentrated in small neighborhood areas. Clusters of conditioners were frequently located in certain rows and blocks. In many cases clusters did not even cross streets. Immediate neighbors apparently served as a powerfully influential group in the purchase of these appliances. In this general class may also be found the black and white TV set, with its antenna often visible on the outside of the house. As the saturation point in black and white TV set ownership rapidly approaches, however, the influence of reference groups may soon become minor, and the product can then be put in the "brand minus, product minus" quadrant, along with refrigerators. Color TV may remain in the "brand plus, product minus" quadrant, with type (color) rather than brand per se the element which is strongly related to reference groups.

c. "Product minus, brand plus" items. This group is made up essentially of products that all people or at least a very high proportion of people use, although differing as to type or brand.

Perhaps the leading example in this field is clothing. There could hardly be a more socially visible product than this, but the fact that everyone in our society wears clothing takes the *product* out of the area of reference group influence. The *type* of clothing purchased is, however, very heavily influenced by reference groups, with each subculture in the population (teenagers, zootsuiters, Ivy League collegians, western collegians, workers, bankers, advertising men, etc.) setting its own standards and often prescribing within fairly narrow limits what those who feel related to these groups can wear. Similarly, though not quite as dramatically, articles like furniture, magazines, refrigerators and toilet soap are seen in almost all homes, causing their purchase in general to fall outside of the orbit of reference group influence. The visibility of these items, however, coupled with the wide variety of styles and types among them make the selection of particular kinds highly susceptible to reference group influence.

d. "Product minus, brand minus" items. Purchasing behavior in this class of items is governed largely by product attributes rather than by the nature of the presumed users. In this group neither the products nor the brands tend to be socially conspicuous. This is not to say that personal influence cannot operate with respect to purchasing the kind of items included in this group. As with all products, some people tend to exert personal influence and others tend to be influenced by individual persons. Reference groups as such, however, exert relatively little influence on buying behavior in this class of items. Examples of items in this category are salt, canned peaches, laundry soap and radios. It is apparent that placement in this category is not *necessarily* inherent in the product itself and hence is not a static placement. Items can move in and out of this category.

While it is true that items which are essential socially inconspicuous, like salt and laundry soap, are natural candidates for this category, it is not entirely out of the realm of possibility that through considerable large scale advertising and other promotional efforts images of the kind of people who use certain brands of salt or laundry soap could be built up so as to bring reference group influence into play on such items, much as has been the case with cigarettes. The task here would be more difficult, however, since the cigarette is already socially visible. On the other hand, items such as radios and refrigerators which are conspicuously visible and whose purchase was once subject to considerable reference group influence have now slipped into this category through near saturation in ownership.

Implications of Strong and Weak Reference Group Influence for Advertising and Marketing

It should be stressed again that this scheme of analysis is introduced to show how reference group influence might enter into purchasing behavior in certain cases. It cannot be regarded as generally applicable to marketing problems on all levels. There is still a need to know more precisely where many different products or brands fit into this scheme. Attempts to fit products and brands into the classification above suggest research that needs to be done to obtain more relevant information about each product.

Assuming, however, that a product or brand has been correctly placed with respect to the part played by reference groups in influencing its purchase, how can this help in marketing the product in question?

Where neither product nor brand appear to be associated strongly with reference group influence, advertising should emphasize the product's attributes, intrinsic qualities, price, and advantages over competing products.

Where reference group influence is operative, the advertiser should stress the kinds of people who buy the product, reinforcing and broadening where possible the existing stereotypes of users. This involves learning what the stereotypes are and what specific reference groups enter into the picture, so that appeals can be "tailored" to each major group reached by the different media employed.

Although it is important to see that the "right" kind of people use a product, a crucial problem is to make sure that the popular image of the product's users is as broad as possible without alienating any important part of the product's present or potential market in the process. Creating or reinforcing a stereotype of consumers which is too small and exclusive for a mass-produced item may exclude a significant portion of the potential market. On the other hand, some attempts to appeal to new groups through advertising in mass media have resulted in the loss of existing groups of purchasers whose previous (favorable) image of the product-user was adversely affected. One possible means for increasing the base of the market for a product by enlarging the image of its users is to use separate advertising media through which a new group can be reached without reducing the product's appeal to the original group of users. Another method might be to appeal to a new group through cooperative advertising by a number of companies producing the product, possibly through a trade association. This would minimize the risk to an individual producer who, trying to reach a new group of users through his own advertising (women as opposed to men or wealthy as opposed to average people, for example), might antagonize people who had a strong need to identify with the *original* image of the product's kind of user.

Product Attributes Versus Reference Group Influence

A technique which could serve to assess the relative influence of reference groups, as compared with product attributes, on the purchase of any given product was employed in research on a food product which will be referred to as product "X."

A cross-section of "X" users was asked several questions relating to particular attributes of "X," such as whether it was more harmful or beneficial for one's health, whether or not it was considered fattening, whether it was considered extravagant or economical, whether or not it tasted good, and so on. These same people were also asked a reference group-oriented question about "X," to determine whether or not "X" was popular with most of their friends. It was found that there was usually more "X" eating among people who reacted negatively to "X" 's attributes but admitted to its popularity among most of their friends, than among those who reacted positively to "X" 's attributes but indicated that it was not popular with their friends.

These relationships are shown in Table 1 on the next page.

TABLE 1. *Relation Between Reference Group and Attribute Influence in Use of Food Product "X"*

| | + Reference Group – With most of respondent's friends "X" is: | |
Product Attribute	Very Popular	Not Very Popular
Effects of "X" on health	Index of Frequency of Eating "X"*	
+ more good than harm	(.41)	-.10
− more harm than good	.08	(-.51)
+ do not avoid fattening food and/or feel "X" is not really or a little fattening	(.30)	-.21
− try to avoid fattening food and feel "X" is really or a little fattening	.14	(-.29)
Economic Value Judgment		
+ fairly economical	(.29)	-.20
− sort of an extravagance	.11	(-.33)
Taste Judgment		
+ tastes good	(.42)	.05
− no reference to good taste**	.09	(-.38)

*All scores in the above table constitue an index of the frequency of "X" eating among respondents falling into the given cell. The scoring procedure used was:

Frequent "X" users—score + 1
Medium "X" users—score 0
Occasional "X" users—score −1

The final score is derived by subtracting the number of occasional "X" users in a given cell from the number of frequent users and dividing the remainder by the total number of respondents in the cell.

For example, the index score .41 was obtained as follows:

329 respondents felt that a moderate amount of "X" does more good than harm AND report that "X" is very popular with most of their friends.

Of these 329 respondents 178 are frequent "X" users, 97 are medium "X" users, and 43 are occasional "X" users.

The score: 178 − 43 = 135   The Index value: 135/329 = 41

**"Tastes good" represents the selection of this phrase from a word list of various attributes that might be applied to "X". "No Reference to Good Taste" refers to those respondents who did not select "Tastes Good" from the word list.

Source: Bureau of Applied Social Research, Columbia University. Reprinted with permission.

In this table, the scores in parentheses are those of people whose replies showed both attribute influence and reference group influence exerting pressure in the same direction.

Special attention should be directed towards the other scores. These represent situations in which people are under cross-pressures. For each of the four attributes considered, the reference group influence is stronger than the attribute influence, in the use of "X." This is brought out by the arrows, which point toward the cross-pressure situations where the reference group influence is adverse. In all of these, consumption frequency is less than where attribute influence alone is negative. Or, put another way, positive perception of reference group behavior with respect to the food product ("X" is very popular) coupled with negative perception of its actual attribute value ("X" does more harm than good, is fattening, etc.) leads to more consumption than negative perception of reference group behavior ("X" not very popular) coupled with positive perception of actual attribute value ("X" does more good than harm, not fattening, economical).

As can be seen from the comparisons indicated by the arrows, reference group influence is markedly stronger than attribute influence for three of the four attributes. Only for "taste" does the attribute influence come close to competing with reference group influence in determining consumption of "X."

One implication of this finding would be that advertising by the "X" industry might stress the variables that are related to the products' *social* utility for its consumers, rather than base its advertising solely on the *physical* attributes of the product.

In a study of a beverage, it was found that, of those who drank the beverage in question, 95% claimed that their friends also drank it, while of those who did not drink this beverage 85% also claimed that their friends did *not* drink it.

Some products, then, must be sold to whole social groups rather than primarily to individuals.

16

The Adoption Process

Foundation for Research on Human Behavior

For many products, the process of adoption follows a rather uniform pattern, from the time the new product is developed until it is widely accepted by the ultimate consumers. More is known about the adoption of agricultural products and practices than about others. Rural sociologists have been concerned with the introduction of new practices and with new product adoption in agriculture for a number of years, and they have systematically studied the process by which change takes place. In addition, some studies have been made of other kinds of innovation, including the adoption by doctors of new wonder drugs for treatment,[1] the adoption of new educational practices by school systems,[2] and the adoption of color television.[3] The process of adoption in all these cases has been quite similar. There are exceptions to the pattern; for example, black and white television. The general pattern appears so widely, however, that it is the central theme of this report.

Researchers have charted the course of a new product by determining *when* people adopt it. The curve which results is a simple one, the well known probability curve, in cumulative form.[4] A few

Reprinted from *The Adoption of New Products* (Ann Arbor: Foundation for Research on Human Behavior, 1959), pp. 1–8.

The Foundation for Research on Human Behavior is a nonprofit organization with headquarters at Ann Arbor, Michigan. The Foundation exists for the purpose of making grants for scientifically worthy and potentially practical research at institutions across the nation. Grants are made in consultation with a Research Advisory Committee drawn largely from contributing companies.

[1] E. Katz, "The Two-step Flow of Communication: An Up-to-date Report on an Hypothesis," *Public Opinion Quarterly* (1957), pp. 61–78 [see pp. 182–201 of this anthology—eds.] ; and H. Menzel and E. Katz, "Social Relations and Innovation in the Medical Profession: The Epidemiology of a New Drug," *Public Opinion Quarterly* (1955–56), pp. 337–352.

[2] P. R. Mort and T. M. Pierce, *A Time Scale for Measuring the Adaptability of School Systems* (New York: Metropolitan School Study Council, 1947).

[3] Batton, Barton, Durstine and Osborn, *Colortown.*

[4] North Central Rural Sociology Committee, *The Diffusion Process* (Ames: Agricultural Extension Service, Iowa State College, Special Report No. 18, 1957).

people adopt a product at first, then a few more, followed by a rather sharp increase and finally a leveling off when most of the potential consumers have adopted the product.

Such a curve is presented in general form in Figure 1. No scale is given for the time dimension, because this differs from product to product. A number of studies indicate, however, the *form* of the curve remains constant, and therefore that knowledge of the time required for a first relatively small group to adopt a new product will, by establishing the time scale for that product, make possible fairly accurate prediction of the rate of adoption by the rest of the applicable universe.

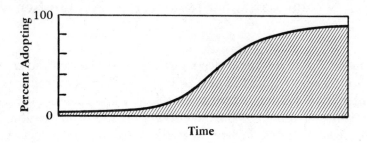

FIGURE 1.

THE KIND OF CHANGE

The time it takes from introduction to wide-spread acceptance depends, in part at least, on the kind of change involved. The adoption of a new product can be viewed as a special case of attitude change. Almost by definition, such a change encounters resistance. The new product or method usually alters or replaces something which is already part of the individual's pattern of thought. If the change under consideration is a really major one, it is quite likely that the attitudes and feelings associated with the old way are strongly held and will account for a great deal of resistance. On the other hand, if the change is trivial, the associated attitudes may be taken on easily. (They may also be cast off easily, of course.) Most new products or practices probably encounter resistance somewhere between these two extremes.

When new products are being adopted, there are different levels of *complexity* of change. The greater the complexity, the more resistance is aroused, and the longer the period required for adoption. Researchers have listed four levels of complexity in the changes usually confronting farmers who are adopting new products or practices.[5]

---

[5] E. A. Wilkening, "The Role of Communicating Agents in Technological Change in Agriculture," *Social Forces* (1956), pp. 361–367.

Least complex is a simple change in materials or equipment. Such a change might be the decision to try another brand of fertilizer or to increase the amount already being used. A change in technique is slightly more complex. The farmer must learn to use the new method and this may involve more risk. An example might be applying fertilizer along planted rows, instead of broadcast over the field. The third level involves both a change in materials and a change in technique. A farmer who has never used fertilizer faces such a change. He must adopt the new material, acquire the equipment to apply it, and learn how to use the equipment. The most complex change is a change of enterprise; for example, a change from cotton growing to dairying.

Obviously there are shadings in complexity among these four types of change, and other kinds of new products may involve a wider range of complexities than do farming practices. However, the level of complexity is an important factor in determining the time it takes for a new product to be adopted. Fifteen years elapsed between the introduction of hybrid seed corn and its adoption by almost 98 per cent of the farmers.[6] Other changes take longer. The adoption of new educational practices by school systems took 50 years.[7] Some changes take place quickly.

It is not always easy to tell how complex a change is involved in a new product. Hybrid corn is one example. Initially, this seemed like a simple change in materials. Actually, it was a far more complex change. Farmers feared the total reliance on commercial sources for seed corn, something they had previously produced for themselves. Furthermore, many farmers took pride in their ability to select good seed corn from their own crop, and they were accorded status for this skill. The new hybrid corn not only made the farmer feel more dependent, it also did away with an important source of prestige. A large majority of farmers had probably adopted hybrid corn within five years of the initial distribution, but it took fifteen years before almost all farmers were using it. Now, when a new hybrid variety of anything is introduced, it is adopted much more quickly. Examples are hybrid chickens and hybrid hogs.

The complexity of the change is only one important factor in determining the time required for adoption. There are others. For instance, *cost* is important. The more costly the item, the longer it takes before it is widely adopted. *Rate of return* and *visibility of return*

---

[6] B. Ryan and N. C. Gross, "The Diffusion of Hybrid Seed Corn in Two Iowa Communities," *Rural Sociology* (1943), pp. 15–24; and B. Ryan and N. C. Gross, *Acceptance and Diffusion of Hybrid Seed Corn in Two Iowa Communities* (Ames: Iowa Agricultural Experiment Station, Research Bulletin 372, 1950).

[7] P. R. Mort and T. M. Pierce, *op. cit.*

are also important. A change which has rapid and obvious results is adopted more quickly than a change with slower, less visible results. In the long run, of course, the change which produces slower results may return more, but it still is not adopted as quickly. A new fertilizer is likely to be adopted more quickly, for example, than soil conservation practices.

THE INDIVIDUAL ADOPTION PROCESS

The decision to adopt a new product is not simply a "yes" or "no" decision, nor is it something that happens all at once. When an individual is confronted with the possibility of change, he goes through several mental stages before he finally makes up his mind to adopt or not to adopt. Five stages in the decision-making process may be distinguished. Farmers readily recognized these stages when questioned regarding their decisions to make changes and adopt new products.

Awareness comes first. At this point, the farmer learns about the new product. He knows it exists, but he has only general information about it. The *interest or information* stage follows. If interested, the farmer begins to collect more specific information about the new product. If his interest continues to grow, he wants to know the potentialities of the new product for him; whether or not it will increase his income or contribute to other ends considered by him to be important. The next step is the mental application or evaluation stage. The farmer goes through the change mentally and asks himself, "How would I do it? Can I do it? If I do it, will I be better off?" The final stage before adoption is the *trial* stage. At this point the farmer tries the product out on a small scale if this is possible. Many farmers purchased a small can of weed spray and used it on their gardens before they used it on their crops on a large scale. A great many farmers planted six acres of hybrid seed corn the first year, the acreage one bushel of the new seed would sow. Some products cannot be tried out on a small scale, and it seems quite reasonable to expect such products to require a longer adoption time. However, people seem to be quite ingenious at finding ways to try new ideas. Some housewives prepared small amounts of food for freezing, and either rented locker space or used a neighbor's freezer before they gave up traditional canning methods and bought the necessary equipment for themselves. Marketing people have been aware of the value of free trials for many years. The trial stage appears to play a crucial role in the decision-making process. However, the other stages are important too, and probably give meaning to this final step before adoption. They should not be ignored.

The last stage is the *adoption* stage. At this point the farmer decides to adopt the new product and begins using it on a full scale. Presumably he is a "satisfied customer," at least until some other product comes along to replace it and the adoption process starts again.

ADOPTER CATEGORIES

Obviously, not all people adopt a new product at the same time. The adoption curve illustrates this point and suggests that some people arrive at a decision more quickly than others. Some people adopt very quickly. Others wait a long time before they take up the new product, and still others never adopt. There has been a great deal of interest in these individual differences and a great deal of speculation about "innovators," those who are first in a community to adopt a new product. To explore these individual differences, the Iowa State researchers took the data from a number of independent studies of new product adoption by farmers. They divided people into groups according to time of adoption,[8] and then studied each group. Significant differences appeared among them. These were the groups they distinguished and studied:

"Innovators" are arbitrarily defined here as the first 2.5 per cent to adopt the new product. Based on the data compiled, these generalizations appear for farm innovators.[9]

They have larger than average farms, are well educated and usually come from well established families. They usually have a relatively high net worth

People Adopting		Cumulative Total Adopting	
First	2.5%	Innovators	2.5%
Next	13.5%	Early adopters	16.0%
Next	34.0%	Early majority	50.0%
Next	34.0%	Late majority	84.0%
Last	16.0%	Laggards	100.0%

---

[8] For convenience in making comparative studies, researchers used standard deviations of a normal distribution to establish the percentage breaks between categories. People who fall within one standard deviation above the mean are considered in the early majority; people who are between one and two standard deviations above the mean are early adopters. Similarly, people within one standard deviation below the mean are late majority, etc.

[9] North Central Rural Sociology Committee, *How Farm People Accept New Ideas* (Ames: Iowa Agricultural Extension Service, Iowa State College, Special Report No. 15, 1955); and E. M. Rogers, "Categorizing the Adopters of Agricultural practices," *Rural Sociology* (1943), pp. 15–24. Used with permission, Cooperative Extension Service and *Rural Sociology*.

and—probably more important—a large amount of risk capital. They can afford and do take calculated risks on new products. They are respected for being successful, but ordinarily do not enjoy the highest prestige in the community. Because innovators adopt new ideas so much sooner than the average farmer, they are sometimes ridiculed by their conservative neighbors. This neighborhood group pressure is largely ignored by the innovators, however. The innovators are watched by their neighbors, but they are not followed immediately in new practices.

The activities of innovators often transcend local community boundaries. Rural innovators frequently belong to formal organizations at the county, regional, state, or national level. In addition, they are likely to have many informal contacts outside the community; they may visit with others many miles away who are also trying a new technique or product, or who are technical experts.

The "early adopters" are defined as the next 13.5 per cent of the people who adopt the new product. According to the researchers, early adopter farmers have the following characteristics.

They are younger than the average farmer, but not necessarily younger than the innovators. They also have a higher than average education, and participate more in the formal activities of the community through such organizations as churches, the PTA, and farm organizations. They participate more than the average in agricultural cooperatives and in government agency programs in the community (such as Extension Service or Soil Conservation). In fact, there is some evidence that this group furnishes a disproportionate amount of the formal leadership (elected officers) in the community. The early adopters are also respected as good sources of new farm information by their neighbors.

The third category of adopters is the "early majority," the 34 per cent of people who bring the total adoption to 50 percent. The number of adoptions increases rapidly after this group begins to adopt.

The early majority are slightly above average in age, education, and farming experience. They have medium high social and economic status. They are less active in formal groups than innovators or early adopters, but more active than those who adopt later. In many cases they are not formal leaders in the community organizations, but they are active members in these organizations. They also attend Extension meetings and farm demonstrations.

The people in this category are most likely to be informal rather than elected leaders. They have a following insofar as people respect their opinions, their "high morality and sound judgment." They are "just like their following, only more so." They must be sure an idea will work before they adopt it. If the informal leader fails two or three times, his following looks elsewhere for information and guidance. Because the informal leader has more limited resources than the early adopters and innovators, he cannot afford to make poor decisions; the social and economic costs are too high.

These people tend to associate mainly in their own community. When people in the community are asked to name neighbors and friends with whom they talk over ideas, these early majority are named disproportionally frequently. On their part, they value highly the opinions their neighbors and friends hold about them, for this is their main source of status and prestige. The early majority may look to the early adopters for their new farm information.

The "late majority" are the fourth category. These are the 34 per cent of farmers who have adopted the new product after the average farmer is already using it.

Those in this group have less education and are older than the average farmer. While they participate less actively in formal groups, they probably form the bulk of the membership in these formal organizations. Individually they belong to fewer organizations, are less active in organizational work, and take fewer leadership roles than the earlier adopters. They do not participate in as many activities outside the community as do people who adopt earlier.

The last category, the final 16 per cent of those who adopt a new idea, are the "laggards." This group may include the "non-adopters" as well if the new product is not used by everyone.

They have the least education and are the oldest. They participate least in formal organizations, cooperatives, and government agency programs. They have the smallest farms and the least capital. Many are suspicious of county Extension agents and agricultural salesmen.

These are some of the important differences among the adopter categories. They may provide useful guidelines for further exploration. For example, each of these categories plays an important role for the others in the adoption process. Innovators are the pioneers, and early adopters wait to see the innovators' results before trying the new product themselves. The early adopters, in turn, often influence the early majority. In addition, each of these categories seems to rely on different sources of information and influence, other than the sources already described.

PART
III

MARKET
ANALYSIS

In addition to understanding consumer behavior, the marketing manager must be cognizant of factors that influence such behavior in particular markets. Consumer purchasing patterns in a given market are shaped by the dynamic interactions of demand conditions, the institutional arrangement of firms, and the marketing strategies adopted by the firms. Systematic research is necessary to assess the effect of these three forces on consumers so that the firm then can take advantage of these opportunities in the market.

The Cox and Good article keynotes Part III. It proposes an organizational unit within the marketing department that has overall responsibility for market analysis and decision-making support. This article is closely complemented by Borden's concept of the marketing mix. Borden enumerates the major factors about which marketing managers must have information in order to make competent decisions.

The following two articles present the discipline's most significant strategic concept: market segmentation. Smith provides the clssic discussion of marketing segmentation in terms of economic theory. Haley presents a modern example using sophisticated research procedures.

The remaining four articles in Part III analyze various aspects of market conditions. Bucklin reviews Copeland's original classification of goods theory and subsequent refinements, then combines them with patronage motives to form a basis for marketing strategy at the retail level. Aspinwall's first paper describes his "color spectrum" method of classifying products. His second paper relates the categories to complementary distribution and promotion plans. Hollander examines the dynamic nature of the distribution function. He discusses the institutional structure of retailing, using examples from various countries.

17

How to Build a Marketing Information System

Donald F. Cox
Robert E. Good

Recently the marketing vice president of a company whose sales volume is $350 million asked, "How should we go about developing a marketing information system? I don't mean one that will keep track of orders and shipments, but a system giving our marketing managers information that will help them make better decisions about pricing, advertising, promotion, product policy, sales force effort, and so forth."

He asked the question of us because, since early 1966, we have been studying the attempts of 15 major U.S. corporations to develop a sophisticated marketing information system, or MIS. We have talked with executives at companies such as Chemstrand, Coca Cola, General Electric, General Foods, IBM, Lever Brothers, Pillsbury, Schenley, and Westinghouse.

Although this field is relatively new, most of the technical aspects of developing an MIS are no longer an obstacle. Nevertheless, few companies are very far along in taking advantage of an approach which, its users agree, has great potential.

In this article we will attempt to provide some guidelines which

Reprinted from *Harvard Business Review*, Vol. 45 (May–June 1967), pp. 145–154. Copyright © 1967 by the President and Fellows of Harvard College; all rights reserved.

Donald F. Cox is executive vice president, Coca Cola Bottling Company of California; his former positions include vice president, director of planning, Coca Cola U.S.A., and assistant professor, Harvard Business School. He holds a Harvard D.B.A. He is co-author of *Marketing Research and Information Systems.*

Robert E. Good is professor of marketing at Portland State University. He earned a D.B.A. at the Harvard Business School and has published several articles in the area of information systems.

might help answer the inquiring marketing vice president—and others with similar questions. First we will present a brief review of some of the characteristics and advantages of a sophisticated MIS, and of the current "state of the art." Then we will identify some of the key decisions which must be made by top management in the MIS development process. In each case we will present a distillation of the experience of the companies studied as an aid in making these critical management decisions.

WHAT IT IS AND CAN DO

An MIS may be defined as a set of procedures and methods for the regular, planned collection, analysis, and presentation of information for use in making marketing decisions. This of course is a step beyond logistics systems, which handle inventory control, orders, and so forth.

It is desirable first to differentiate between the two major components of such systems—*support systems* and *operating systems*. Support systems include those activities required to generate and manipulate data—i.e., market research and other data gathering, programming, and data processing. Operating systems are those that use the data as an aid to planning and controlling marketing activities.

This article is concerned mainly with the development of three types of marketing operating systems—those designed for control, for planning, and for basic research. In Exhibit I we summarize some of the applications and probable benefits of each type of system (assuming increasing degrees of sophistication) and present examples of systems now operating. The following are examples of marketing systems we have observed, with some of the advantages the companies claim for them.

1. Control Systems

These provide continuous monitoring (sometimes through exception reporting) and rapid spotting of trends, problems, and marketing opportunities. They allow better anticipation of problems, more detailed and comprehensive review of performance against plans, and greater speed of response. For instance:

IBM's Data Processing Division has developed an MIS which district sales managers can interrogate through a time-sharing computer

	TYPICAL APPLICATIONS	BENEFITS	EXAMPLES
CONTROL SYSTEMS	1. Control of marketing costs.	1. More timely computerized reports.	1. Undesirable cost trends are spotted more quickly so that corrective action may be taken sooner.
	2. Diagnosis of poor sales performance.	2. Flexible on-line retrieval of data	2. Executives can ask supplementary questions of the computer to help pinpoint reasons for a sales decline and reach an action decision more quickly.
	3. Management of fashion goods.	3. Automatic spotting of problems and opportunities.	3. Fast-moving fashion items are reported daily for quick reorder, and slow-moving items are also reported for fast price reductions.
	4. Flexible promotion strategy.	4. Cheaper, more detailed, and more frequent reports.	4. On-going evaluation of a promotional campaign permits reallocation of funds to areas behind target.
PLANNING SYSTEMS	1. Forecasting.	1. Automatic translation of terms and classifications between departments.	1. Survey-based forecasts of demand for complex industrial goods can be automatically translated into parts requirements and production schedules.
	2. Promotional planning and corporate long-range planning.	2. Systematic testing of alternative promotional plans and compatibility testing of various divisional plans.	2. Complex simulation models both developed and operated with the help of data bank information can be used for promotional planning by product managers and for strategic planning by top management.
	3. Credit management.	3. Programmed executive decision rules can operate on data bank information.	3. Credit decisions are automatically made as each order is processed.
	4. Purchasing.	4. Detailed sales reporting permits automation of management decisions.	4. Computer automatically repurchases standard items on the basis of correlation of sales data with programmed decision rules.
RESEARCH SYSTEMS	1. Advertising strategy.	1. Additional manipulation of data is possible when stored for computers in an unaggregated file.	1. Sales analysis is possible by new market segment breakdowns.
	2. Pricing strategy	2. Improved storage and retrieval capability allows new types of data to be collected and used.	2. Systematic recording of information about past R & D contract bidding situations allows improved bidding strategies.
	3. Evaluation of advertising expenditures.	3. Well-designed data banks permit integration and comparison of different sets of data.	3. Advertising expenditures are compared to shipments by county to provide information about advertising effectiveness.
	4. Continuous experiments.	4. Comprehensive monitoring of input and performance variables yields information when changes are made.	4. Changes in promotional strategy by type of customer are matched against sales results on a continuous basis.

EXHIBIT I. Benefits Possible with a Sophisticated MIS   239

terminal located in an executive's office. A manager punches a type-writer-like keyboard and receives an immediate print-out of information such as:

Sales (or rentals) to date—broken down by product code, type of customer, and branch making the sale.

Sales in relation to goals.

Combinations of information which relate to sales, customer classifications, product codes, and so forth.

The data are current to within three or four days, allowing the manager to keep up to date on marketing problems and opportunities and on progress in relation to goals.

Schenley has installed the so-called SIMR (Schenley Instant Market Reports) system which allows key executives to retrieve (via video display desk consoles and printers) current and past sales and inventory figures for any brand and package size (or combination) for each of 400 distributors. SIMR furnishes information in less than one second after a query, compared with many minutes or even hours under its former computer and manual system. Furthermore, since the computer does the calculations, managers have great flexibility and near-instant speed of response in making many types of comparisons of sales and inventory positions, such as:

How a brand is doing in any size or in all sizes in any market or in all markets.

How a distributor is doing with a particular brand.

How a bottle size is doing by distributor, state, or region.

How a market is doing by month or has done since the end of the previous fiscal year.

"We can get answers literally while we are still formulating the questions," states Bernard Goldberg, president of Schenley's marketing subsidiary. "Needed information is available so quickly that it helps us think."[1]

2. Planning Systems

These furnish, in convenient form, information the marketing executive requires for planning marketing and sales programs. At least three major consumer goods producers, for example, are developing "data books" for product managers. The books bring together the basic

---

[1] *Industrial Data Processing Applications Report* (S_3), Business Publications International, Division of OA Business Publications, Inc., 1965.

information a product manager needs to formulate annual marketing plans and to "replan" during the course of the year. Putting the information into one book, rather than in a welter of reports, not only saves time, but it also enables all product managers in a group or division to base their plans on the same data. Consequently, their superiors are able to review comparable information quickly when considering the plans for approval.

At a more sophisticated level, planning systems allow simulation of the effects of alternate plans so that the manager can make a better decision. For instance:

Pillsbury's system enables marketing managers to obtain sales forecasts for each of 39 sales branches, supported by varying levels of trade promotion. The marketing manager asks the question, "What will sales be in each branch if we spend x dollars on trade promotions in comparison with .75x dollars and with 1.2x dollars?" Pillsbury does not claim that the system is perfect—it is obviously no better than the assumptions on which the simulation is based—but it has had a surprisingly good "batting average" in accuracy. It has great value to marketing managers because it allows them to look at alternate plans in each of the 39 sales branches; this was never feasible before.

A large pharmaceutical company has developed an even more complex model. The company has programmed an artificial panel representing the nation's population of doctors. Every week the company simulates each doctor's prescription decision for every patient he "sees." (Commercial research services are available which provide information on the incidence of symptoms of illness and the "patient mix" of the various medical specialists.) The doctor considers the symptoms "presented" by each patient and decides whether to prescribe a drug and, if so, which type and brand. His decision is based on factors such as his experience with the drug, current attitudes, exposure to the advertising of various brands, exposure to detail men, and word-of-mouth information from other doctors. The simulation even includes a "forgetting routine" which causes a doctor to forget from time to time some of the information he has acquired.

While the company does not disclose how the simulation model is being used, it certainly is capable of generating extremely sophisticated marketing planning. For example, marketing managers can test the effects on share of market and sales of variations in amount, type, and timing of advertising and simultaneously test the effects of variations in frequency of detail men's calls. On a broader basis, the system can be used to screen a number of alternative marketing programs to select the most promising ones to be actually test marketed.

Perhaps the ultimate in sophistication is a marketing planning system which reviews alternatives, then actually makes decisions and takes action. Thus, several large retailing organizations have developed systems that review sales trends and inventories and then place orders for merchandise.

The most advanced unit of this type we have seen is not a marketing system; rather, it buys and sells securities in a stock brokerage house. Still in the future are marketing systems that decide the amount and timing of advertising and price promotions in each of several dozen sales districts.

3. Basic Research Systems

These systems are used to develop and test sophisticated decision rules and cause-and-effect hypotheses which should improve ability to assess affects of actions and permit greater learning from experience. For instance:

> A large consumer goods company is developing an MIS which, among other things, stores in computer memory the characteristics of each advertisement run (color versus black and white, nature of illustration, amount of copy, and so forth) and readership and attitude change scores for each ad. The purpose is to be able to relate ad characteristics to effectiveness measurements under different conditions and with different types of consumers by systematically studying "experience."
>
> Most companies find it difficult to relate advertising to sales because there are so many important "uncontrollable" variables which are nearly impossible to take into account in an unsophisticated MIS. One large consumer goods producer has developed an MIS which for the first time allows the company to collect, store, and retrieve advertising, sales, and other marketing data at a level of detail which makes possible much better controlled studies of the relationship of advertising to sales.

CURRENT PROGRESS

The examples which we have presented probably represent the most sophisticated types of MIS now in existence. While we have not surveyed the 500 largest corporations in the country, we have screened more than 50 companies and have reviewed more than 100 current articles on information systems. As far as we have been able to determine, the current state of the art is something like this:

> Very few companies have developed advanced systems, and not all of these are in operation. Some might even best be classified as sub-systems, since they relate to only a portion of the marketing decisions made.
>
> Some companies, perhaps 15, are actively upgrading their systems to a high level. Of these, about half seem to be progressing well; the others have been much less successful.
>
> Many other companies are contemplating plans to develop sophisticated systems.

The reasons why marketing systems have not developed to the same extent as, say, production, logistics, or financial systems are not "technical." Marketing research technology (data gathering), computer technology (data handling), and analytical procedures (e.g., mathematical model building) are all sufficiently advanced to permit companies to build effective marketing systems.

Although insufficient time has elapsed since the installation of most advanced marketing information systems to allow a precise assessment of benefits, the users of sophisticated systems with whom we have talked are virtually all very enthusiastic about their systems, even though many see room for improvement.

DEVELOPING THE SYSTEM

Because many of the technical problems of developing sophisticated support systems have been solved and many users are gratified over the results, why are there so few advanced marketing information systems in operation? And why have some companies succeeded more than others in realizing the potentials of the MIS?

One characteristic of the more successful companies is striking. In every case, at least some members of top management have seen the promise of the technique and have viewed its development as a top management responsibility. They have devoted a great deal of time, thought, and effort to guiding (and sometimes actually protecting) the development process. Unfortunately, it is widely believed that the job of building an MIS can be turned over to a technical staff group. This has not proved to be the case. Information systems are not merely technical appendages (developed by technical people) that are easily meshed with most existing marketing planning and control systems.

The best way to show why participation of top management is necessary is to pose five key questions which must be answered in the process of instituting a sophisticated MIS. In our opinion, each is a management question:

1. How should we organize to develop a better MIS?
2. How sophisticated should our marketing systems be?
3. What development strategy should we follow—do we attempt to build a "total" system in one move, or in stages?
4. What should be the major characteristics ("macro specifications") of our system?
5. How much should we spend on developing and operating an MIS?

While the field is too new to permit comprehensive and conclusive statements about all its aspects, we can present some guidelines and working hypotheses that are worthy of management's consideration.

Readying the Organization

The starting point in organizing for MIS development is not the establishment of a marketing systems group. The starting point is a review and appraisal of the entire marketing organization and of the policies that direct it. As James Peterson, vice president–grocery products marketing at The Pillsbury Company, pointed out to us:

"We realized we couldn't develop a marketing control system until we had clearly and sharply defined the responsibilities of our marketing managers. If the system was to measure their performance against plans, we had to specify precisely what each man was accountable for."

Some companies, for instance, have failed to decide whether a product manager is accountable for unit sales and market share, for sales revenue, for marketing profit, or for net profit. Until responsibilities and spheres of activity are clearly defined, it is virtually impossible to build a marketing control system. In fact, specification of who is accountable for what automatically determines many of the control system's characteristics.

Management must next decide how to organize MIS development activities. Our observations show that this is a much more complex problem than might be assumed. Sophisticated systems require the coordinated efforts of many departments and individuals, including:

Top management.
Marketing management, brand management.
Sales management.
New products groups.
Market research personnel.
Control and finance departments.
Systems analysts and designers.
Operations researchers, statisticians, and model builders.
Programmers.
Computer equipment experts and suppliers.

The contribution of each group of course depends on its specialized talents and interests in the system. Programmers cannot define managers' information needs, and managers usually cannot program. No one person knows enough to accomplish all phases of MIS development.

Furthermore, sophisticated systems do not fall into a company's traditional data handling domains, such as the market research department or the accounting and control department, because an essential feature of a good MIS is that it integrates and correlates marketing and financial data.

Many companies we have observed have not really come to grips with the difficult problem of providing the organizational arrangements and leadership necessary for successful MIS development. They have not answered the question of who is responsible for MIS design, planning, and development. Why is there a leadership vacuum? Partly because top management does not fully appreciate the requirements and implications of the MIS, and partly because it has an understandable reluctance to disturb entrenched and powerful departments.

The approaches which have been tried in an attempt to solve the problems of organization and leadership can be characterized as:

"Clean piece of paper" approach.

Committee approach.

Low-level approach.

Information "coordinator" approach.

"Clean Piece of Paper" Approach. This involves drawing a new organization chart. The argument goes that the financial and accounting departments and market research departments have developed as much from growing data gathering and processing capability as in response to management information needs. In the pre-computer era, it was rarely possible to correlate marketing and accounting data in a sophisticated manner and on a regular basis for presentation to management. Now it is possible, but the marketing data are supplied by one set of departments and the accounting data by another. In the absence of coordination and compatibility, line management must often do its own correlating. Therefore the "ideal" procedure is to abolish the traditional information gathering and processing departments and establish a management information department.

While this may represent an "ideal" solution, it is not feasible in most companies. Traditions and positions are too well entrenched. Furthermore, it would not solve all the problems. For one thing, it would not ensure the development of an MIS geared to management needs. For another, no management information department could supply all of the data the system needed, such as reports from the field sales organization.

Committee Approach. Some companies have established MIS committees. They are excellent vehicles for communicating points of view and for joint learning and sharing in the experience of developing an MIS. They can create shared awareness of compatibility and coordination problems and of the need to resolve them.

The committee approach alone, however, is not the answer. Because meetings and committee assignments consume time, it is difficult to involve busy line managers. Furthermore, it is not easy to get anyone to carry out assignments in addition to his regular job. Finally, a committee of peers, chaired by a peer, is not always able to exert the leadership which may be required. Committees of this kind simply lack "clout." And at times clout may be the only thing that will accomplish necessary changes.

Low-level Approach. Some companies have assigned the task of MIS development to a junior member of the market research department— often as a part-time assignment. This reflects a total lack of understanding of the difficulty of the task, and the outcome is predictable. The man, no matter how clever he is, lacks the time and the clout to overcome the organizational and psychological barriers he encounters. Such an assignment has led to the resignation of more than one bright young research man.

Information "Coordinator" Approach. Some companies, while retaining traditional departmental boundaries, have appointed a top-level executive to the post of information czar or "coordinator," sometimes called "director of marketing systems." We have observed that men who are capable of understanding both management information needs and systems problems can make substantial progress in MIS development in this position—*when* they enjoy top management support. But it is a delicate position; one coordinator we know preferred not to have any formal title until, after a year, he had established good working relationships with the various departments. Furthermore, even a sensible and sensitive information manager must establish organizational lines that encourage the coordinated efforts of the affected departments and divisions of the company in the design and the accomplishment of the MIS plan.

For many companies this approach has the best chance of success. We suggest that management designate the director of marketing systems as a "prime contractor" who develops MIS plans and specifications, and coordinates and reviews the work of the various "subcontractors" or suppliers contributing to the program. Such a prime contractor-subcontractor approach has proved in military and civilian applications to be effective in handling projects or tasks that require the utilization of many talents and capabilities, not all of which exist in the department or organization directly involved.

For the prime contractor to be effective he must have cost control. It is therefore advisable to use an interdepartmental billing system. The prime contractor is responsible for the overall budget, and negotiates with users (marketing managers) to determine their information needs and to obtain from them the funds required to develop and operate an MIS that would meet these needs. He also arranges to compensate the various supplying departments, such as the systems group for programming, for their services.

Management must also determine the prime contractor's organizational location. It is essential that he represent the department or division which will use (and pay for) the MIS. For a variety of reasons, not one of the companies studied having a central or corporate systems department (responsible for support systems) has designated that group as the "prime contractor" for operating its MIS. They view the corporate systems group as an important supplier of technical advice and of programming and data processing services for the marketing departments. But in the large companies, at least, final authority and responsibility for MIS development, where such authority has been designated, generally rests with the marketing department.

Of the several arguments for this practice, the most important is that the expertise of corporate systems groups is usually in support systems (programming and data processing). Effective development of marketing planning and control systems requires a management, rather than a technical support systems, orientation. Furthermore, effective MIS can be developed only by people who understand users' problems and who can be responsive to users' needs.

How Sophisticated?

Someone must decide on the level of sophistication of the MIS to be developed. This decision should, of course, be based on a review of the company's needs and the costs of meeting them.

Equally important, the abilities of managers must be considered. To develop and use effectively some of the more sophisticated systems that have been described, managers must be able to:

Define specific information needs.

Develop analytical approaches and models.

Make explicit their planning, decision-making, and control processes and procedures.

Interpret and use sophisticated information.

One of the characteristics of the more advanced MIS is automation of certain aspects of the marketing management process. But it is first necessary to make the process explicit. For instance, to develop exception-reporting systems, managers' exception or "control" criteria must be articulated. Simulation models cannot be built into the system until managers have spelled out the characteristics of the different elements of the company's marketing system (consumers, distributors, competitors, and so forth) and have attempted to define how these elements interact.

If a company already has a well-articulated set of decision rules as to what constitutes an "exception," it would not be difficult to build an automated exception reporting system. Such a system could be developed for the marketing manager who says,

> I always like to know about all situations in which sales, profits, or market share are running 4% or more behind plan. Furthermore, in any exceptional cases I also require the following diagnostic information: prices, distribution levels, advertising, and consumer attitudes.

The problem is, as has been well documented in a Marketing Science Institute study,[2] that many marketing managers, particularly those at the operating level, do not use explicit planning and control systems. They do not make their decision rules and exception criteria explicit. In short, they are not equipped to contribute to the development of a sophisticated MIS, nor are they comfortable with it once it is operating. Though related to research information, their decisions often are highly intuitive. The problem seems less severe at higher management levels, partly because top management control systems are more explicitly articulated than those at the operating level.

System-Manager Balance

It is important that a balance be maintained between management sophistication and MIS sophistication. As a company upgrades the latter, so must it raise the former.

In a "steady state" (before anyone tinkers with the marketing system) there usually seems to be a correspondence between management sophistication and information quality. Managers usually get the quality of information they ask for. Though they may complain of a lack of good information and blame one or more of the information supplying departments, questioning often reveals that in most cases they have not been asking for better information in any specific way.

---

[2] D. J. Luck and Patrick J. Robinson, *Promotional Decision Making* (New York, McGraw-Hill Book Company, Inc., 1964).

If, as we have suggested, the two "quality levels" are roughly in balance, what happens when only the level of information quality is raised significantly? Our prediction is that this would not lead to better decisions. In fact, the reverse may be true, as the result of the confusion and resentment generated by the manager's inability to deal with the more sophisticated information.

Information quality can be upgraded much more rapidly than management quality. It is easy to throw the management system out of balance by installing a sophisticated MIS, but there seems to be little point in doing so. A more positive approach is to develop a master plan for improving the system, but make the improvements gradually—say, over several years. Marketing control systems like Schenley's or IBM's, described earlier, are easier to develop and use than those like the pharmaceutical company's simulation-based planning system. So a company might first install a marketing control system and subsequently, as managers gained experience in using it, develop advanced planning systems.

"Complete" Systems

While an attempt to develop a highly sophisticated "total" marketing system at the outset has a high probability of failure, it *is* desirable to build a complete subsystem at one time—even if it is only a part of what will eventually be the company's total system. To illustrate:

A company develops a first-rate exception reporting system that will quickly present "exceptional" sales results to the marketing manager. Very likely he will be faced with more problems than ever before, because of the system's ability to monitor large amounts of detailed information. It will be difficult (and dangerous), however, for the manager to act on this information. Before he can take intelligent action, he must also know whether the deviations from plan are the result of deviations in sales effort, of unusual competitive activities, or of other factors. To be complete, therefore, the system must also include a diagnostic procedure.

"Macro" Specifications. Apart from decisions on the general characteristics of the system to be used, the company must determine the overall or "macro" MIS specifications. Besides the type of system to be developed, the most important considerations are the nature of the data bank, the form and the method of data display and presentation, and computer selection.

We should, however, underscore here the necessity of ensuring the participation in these decisions not only of top management but also of the line managers. In most cases we have studied, and in all of the least successful instances, the marketing systems developers have failed to involve line managers in the process of developing macro specifications. In many cases where systems developers have made the effort, they have found it difficult to elicit the views of busy line managers in the brief periods available in typical interviews or meetings. The systems developers subsequently present the managers with a fait accompli—which may or may not work.

A more effective approach is to involve the managers in an extended session, lasting days if necessary, in which a consensus on overall MIS specifications can be reached. In these sessions the group should develop flow charts of the "system"—or total environment in which the company operates—and designate critical decision points, identify the information they require for planning and controlling marketing (or other management) activities, and make cost/benefit analyses of alternative designs before agreeing on one design. This approach not only helps ensure a system that is keyed to management's needs, but also allows management to defer a decision on the size of the MIS development budget until it has assessed the alternative systems.

"Micro" Data Bank. Perhaps the most essential element in upgrading a system is a bank or file based on disaggregated or "micro" data. These are data recorded and stored in the lowest level of aggregation and detail—such as the size, price, time, and location of a single purchase of a product.

As Professor Arnold E. Amstutz of M.I T. has commented:

> At the heart of every successful information system is a disaggregated data file. . . . As new inputs are received they are maintained along with existing data rather than replacing or being combined with existing information. . . . The existence of a disaggregated data file facilitates system evaluation. . . . In the first stages of system development it is simply impossible to anticipate the direction of later advancement. Aggregate data files may preclude highly profitable system modifications. The disaggregated data file provides the flexibility which is the prerequisite of intelligent system evolution.[3]

In designing the data bank it is important to provide for common denominators in different sets of data, so that the correlation and analysis potential of the MIS can be realized. This means that such elements as the geographic, time, and responsibility boundaries of different types of data must be compatible to permit meaningful comparisons.

---

[3]"The Marketing Executive and Management Information Systems," in *Science, Technology and Marketing,* 1966 Fall Conference Proceedings of the American Marketing Association, p. 76.

A disaggregated data bank gives the system the flexibility required for future upgrading. The alternative is to try to anticipate all possible future uses of the system and to agree on aggregated units (like aggregating all package sizes of a brand), aggregated time periods (a week, month, or quarter), and aggregated geographical areas (sales territories or regions).

Management must weigh the greater cost of a disaggregated data bank against the possibility that future conditions or new insights may call for analyses which are precluded because the data have been aggregated. Since most people who have participated in MIS development admit that they are unable to foresee all important management information needs, and since most current systems are likely to evolve to increasing stages of sophistication, the prudent decision would be to develop a disaggregated data bank—*if* the company can afford it.

Presentation and Format. Developing a sophisticated MIS involves resolving the matters of what information should be presented, how it should be presented, and to whom.

One important aspect of this question is the degree of executive-system interaction desired. At the extreme of "distance," executives receive information in the form of regular reports. With somewhat closer but not complete interaction, the manager can make special requests for information from the data bank. At the extreme of "closeness," the manager can obtain almost instantaneous computer response with a time-sharing or on-line system. Consider Schenley's experience.

> Schenley has installed a video display and retrieval system. Of interest is the fact that the new system carries little new information; indeed, the same data were generated previously in the form of computer print-out. The information in paper form, however, was too voluminous and unwieldy to use. What the new retrieval and presentation system has achieved is simply to make data much more usable for management.

On-line systems such as Schenley's have a tremendous advantage in speed of access to information. Critics of these systems argue that managers do not need to know what happened as of the close of business yesterday.[4] This may be true. But there are benefits in being able to receive split-second responses. A manager's willingness to formulate questions and get data on which to base decisions may depend on the ease and speed with which he can retrieve answers from the computer. Although it is too early to tell whether the cost of this capability can be justified, large companies should seriously consider experimenting with this type of system.

---

[4] See John Dearden, "Myth of Real-Time Management Information," *Harvard Business Review* (May–June 1966), p. 123.

Computer Selection. The computer requirement for a company's MIS will, of course, depend on the system's performance specifications and the decisions management has made on each of the preceding design problems. While technical help is necessary in the decisions on equipment, management has the responsibility for making certain that the hardware chosen will meet the MIS needs and specifications at the time of installation, which may be some years away. In this respect, managers should recognize that they probably will learn many new ways to use the computer, such as new marketing planning, control, decision, and research applications, given some experience with an improved MIS. So even with the most careful planning, demands for computer capacity are likely to expand faster than anticipated.

Cost and Value

It is difficult to generalize about how much an MIS will cost—or how much it will be worth. Usually there is not a large increase in data gathering costs, since many companies now have available to them much of the raw data required. Cost increases result from data storage and transforming the raw data into useful information. It is extremely difficult to determine MIS development costs, since many companies lack accounting arrangements, like interdepartmental billing, which allow them to keep track of the total cost of the manpower contributing to the program.

On a "best estimate" basis, we are aware of simple or partial systems which have cost only a few thousand dollars. At the other extreme, one complex marketing system we know of must have cost several million dollars. A large company with sales in the $500 million range should expect to invest several hundred thousand dollars (plus equipment charges) to develop a relatively sophisticated, computer-based MIS. And development costs will not end there, since after the first stage is operational, it is probable that management will want to upgrade the system continually.

If top executives authorize expenditures of this magnitude, they are likely to want a justification of the value of the system. Usually, computer-based information systems, such as those used for accounting, have been justified mainly on the ground that they reduce personnel and other administrative costs. Few advanced marketing information systems could be justified on the basis of cost reduction.

However, that test alone is not appropriate for an MIS. The main purpose of an MIS is to help the marketing manager make more profitable decisions, not to reduce data handling and paperwork costs. So an MIS should be evaluated in terms of its estimated effects on marketing efficiency.

Determining how much an MIS could increase marketing effectiveness is not an easy task. The involvement of management in developing overall specifications should help in making an estimate, however imprecise, of system benefits. In addition, the decision on a budget for MIS development need not be made in a single giant step. Rather, it is possible to attain system sophistication in discrete increments, involving a series of smaller budgeting decisions and cost-benefit evaluations.

CONCLUSION

Marketing men in many of the large corporations we studied are almost uniformly enthusiastic about the promise of the computer-based, advanced MIS. Relatively few such systems are now operating, however, and many companies have had indifferent success in deriving benefits from them.

In the more successful companies, the following patterns have been evident:

The development of the MIS has been viewed as a management responsibility, including both top management and operating line management.

Formal organizational lines have been drawn to provide leadership in use of the technique—usually including the appointment of a high-level information coordinator or "prime contractor" who develops plans and coordinates the efforts of the departments involved.

The prime contractor reports to the user group, such as the marketing department, rather than to the central systems group.

Line managers participate in developing overall specifications for the MIS.

The sophistication of the system is balanced with that of the managers who use it.

Systems development typically proceeds in manageable stages, rather than in attempts to develop "total" systems at once.

The system is based on a disaggregated data bank which allows managers to retrieve analyses in the form they want without having to specify all their information needs in advance.

Investments in systems development and operation are justified not on the basis of cost reduction, which is often irrelevant with the MIS, but on an estimate of the system's ability to help managers make more profitable marketing decisions.

It is evident that a good deal of faith is required to make substantial investments in the MIS—whose benefits by and large are still unproven. Yet more and more companies are demonstrating their faith. And some of the pioneers already claim their faith is justified.

18

The Concept of the
Marketing Mix

Neil H. Borden

I have always found it interesting to observe how an apt or colorful term may catch on, gain wide usage, and help to further understanding of a concept that has already been expressed in less appealing and communicative terms. Such has been true of the phrase "marketing mix," which I began to use in my teaching and writing some 15 years ago. In a relatively short time it has come to have wide usage. This note tells of the evolution of the marketing mix concept.

The phrase was suggested to me by a paragraph in a research bulletin on the management of marketing costs, written by my associate, Professor James Culliton.[1] In this study of manufacturers' marketing costs he described the business executive as a

> "decider," an "artist"—a "mixer of ingredients," who sometimes follows a recipe as he goes along, sometimes adapts a recipe to the ingredients immediately available, and sometimes experiments with or invents ingredients no one else has tried.

I liked his idea of calling a marketing executive a "mixer of ingredients," one who is constantly engaged in fashioning creatively a mix of marketing procedures and policies in his efforts to produce a profitable enterprise.

Reprinted from *Journal of Advertising Research*, © Advertising Research Foundation, Inc. (June, 1964), pp. 2–7.

Neil H. Borden, Professor Emeritus of Advertising at Harvard, spent a summer lecturing in Australia, served for three years as a consultant in India, and lectured on management in Singapore. His M.B.A. degree is from Harvard, where he has taught since 1922. He is a past president of the American Marketing Association and has published work on many phases of advertising. His 1942 study, *The Economic Effects of Advertising*, is still recognized as a definitive work.

[1] James W. Culliton, *The Management of Marketing Costs* (Boston: Division of Research, Graduate School of Business Administration, Harvard University, 1948).

For many years previous to Culliton's cost study the wide variations in the procedures and policies employed by managements of manufacturing firms in their marketing programs and the correspondingly wide variation in the costs of these marketing functions, which Culliton aptly ascribed to the varied "mixing of ingredients," had become increasingly evident as we had gathered marketing cases at the Harvard Business School. The marked differences in the patterns or formulae of the marketing programs not only were evident through facts disclosed in case histories, but also were reflected clearly in the figures of a cost study of food manufacturers made by the Harvard Bureau of Business Research in 1929. The primary objective of this study was to determine common figures of expenses for various marketing functions among food manufacturing companies, similar to the common cost figures which had been determined in previous years for various kinds of retail and wholesale businesses. In this manufacturer's study we were unable, however, with the data gathered to determine common expense figures that had much significance as standards by which to guide management, such as had been possible in the studies of retail and wholesale trades, where the methods of operation tended toward uniformity. Instead, among food manufacturers the ratios of sales devoted to the various functions of marketing such as advertising, personal selling, packaging, and so on, were found to be widely divergent, no matter how we grouped our respondents. Each respondent gave data that tended to uniqueness.

Culliton's study of marketing costs in 1947–48 was a second effort to find out, among other objectives, whether a bigger sample and a more careful classification of companies would produce evidence of operating uniformities that would give helpful common expense figures. But the result was the same as in our early study: there was wide diversity in cost ratios among any classifications of firms which were set up, and no common figures were found that had much value. This was true whether companies were grouped according to similarity in product lines, amount of sales, territorial extent of operations, or other bases of classification.

Relatively early in my study of advertising, it had become evident that understanding of advertising usage by manufacturers in any case had to come from an analysis of advertising's place as one element in the total marketing program of the firm. I came to realize that it is essential always to ask: what overall marketing strategy has been or might be employed to bring about a profitable operation in light of the circumstances faced by the management? What combination of marketing procedures and policies has been or might be adopted to bring about desired behavior of trade and consumers at costs that will permit a profit? Specifically, how can advertising, personal selling, pricing, packaging, channels, warehousing, and the other elements of a marketing program be manipulated and fitted together in a way that will give a profitable operation? In short, I saw that every advertising management case called for a consideration of the strategy to be adopted for the total marketing program, with advertising recognized as only one element whose form and extent depended on its careful adjustment to the other parts of the program.

The soundness of this viewpoint was supported by case histories throughout my volume, *The Economic Effects of Advertising.*[2] In the chapters devoted to the utilization of advertising by business, I had pointed out the innumerable combinations of marketing methods and policies that might be adopted by a manager in arriving at a marketing plan. For instance, in the area of branding, he might elect to adopt an individualized brand or a family brand. Or he might decide to sell his product unbranded or under private label. Any decision in the area of brand policy in turn has immediate implications that bear on his selection of channels of distribution, sales force methods, packaging, promotional procedure, and advertising. Throughout the volume the case materials cited show that the way in which any marketing function is designed and the burden placed upon the function are determined largely by the overall marketing strategy adopted by managements to meet the market conditions under which they operate. The forces met by different firms vary widely. Accordingly, the programs fashioned differ widely.

Regarding advertising, which was the function under focus in the economic effects volume, I said at one point:

> In all the above illustrative situations it should be recognized that advertising is not an operating method to be considered as something apart, as something whose profit value is to be judged alone. An able management does not ask, "Shall we use or not use advertising," without consideration of the product and of other management procedures to be employed. Rather the question is always one of finding a management formula giving advertising its due place in the combination of manufacturing methods, product form, pricing, promotion and selling methods, and distribution methods. As previously pointed out different formulae, i.e., different combinations of methods, may be profitably employed by competing manufacturers.

From the above it can be seen why Culliton's description of a marketing manager as a "mixer of ingredients" immediately appealed to me as an apt and easily understandable phrase, far better than

---

[2]Neil H. Borden, *The Economic Effects of Advertising* (Homewood, Illinois: Richard D. Irwin, 1942).

my previous references to the marketing man as an empiricist seeking in any situation to devise a profitable "pattern" or "formula" of marketing operations from among the many procedures and policies that were open to him. If he was a "mixer of ingredients," what he designed was a "marketing mix."

It was logical to proceed from a realization of the existence of a variety of "marketing mixes" to the development of a concept that would comprehend not only this variety, but also the market forces that cause managements to produce a variety of mixes. It is the problems raised by these forces that lead marketing managers to exercise their wits in devising mixes or programs which they hope will give a profitable business operation.

To portray this broadened concept in a visual presentation requires merely:

1. A list of the important elements or ingredients that make up marketing programs.
2. A list of the forces that bear on the marketing operation of a firm and to which the marketing manager must adjust in his search for a mix or program that can be successful.

The list of elements of the marketing mix in such a visual presentation can be long or short, depending on how far one wishes to go in his classification and sub-classification of the marketing procedures and policies with which marketing managements deal when devising marketing programs. The list of elements which I have employed in my teaching and consulting work covers the principal areas of marketing activities which call for management decisions as revealed by case histories. I realize others might build a different list. Mine is as follows:

Elements of the Marketing Mix of Manufacturers

1. *Product Planning*—policies and procedures relating to:
   a. Product lines to be offered—qualities, design, etc.
   b. Markets to sell—whom, where, when, and in what quantity.
   c. New product policy—research and development program.
2. *Pricing*—policies and procedures relating to:
   a. Price level to adopt.
   b. Specific prices to adopt—odd-even, etc.
   c. Price policy—one-price or varying price, price maintenance, use of list prices, etc.
   d. Margins to adopt—for company, for the trade.
3. *Branding*—policies and procedures relating to:
   a. Selection of trade marks.
   b. Brand policy—individualized or family brand.
   c. Sale under private label or unbranded.

4. *Channels of Distribution*—policies and procedures relating to:
   a. Channels to use between plant and consumer.
   b. Degree of selectivity among wholesalers and retailers.
   c. Efforts to gain cooperation of the trade.
5. *Personal Selling*—policies and procedures relating to:
   a. Burden to be placed on personal selling and the methods to be employed in:
      1. Manufacturer's organization.
      2. Wholesale segment of the trade.
      3. Retail segment of the trade.
6. *Advertising*—policies and procedures relating to:
   a. Amount to spend—i.e., the burden to be placed on advertising.
   b. Copy platform to adopt:
      1. Product image desired.
      2. Corporate image desired.
   c. Mix of advertising—to the trade, through the trade, to consumers.
7. *Promotions*—policies and procedures relating to:
   a. Burden to place on special selling plans or devices directed at or through the trade.
   b. Form of these devices for consumer promotions, for trade promotions.
8. *Packaging*—policies and procedures relating to:
   a. Formulation of package and label.
9. *Display*—policies and procedures relating to:
   a. Burden to be put on display to help effect sale.
   b. Methods to adopt to secure display.
10. *Servicing*—policies and procedures relating to:
    a. Providing service needed.
11. *Physical Handling*—policies and procedures relating to:
    a. Warehousing.
    b. Transportation.
    c. Inventories.
12. *Fact Finding and Analysis*—policies and procedures relating to:
    a. Securing, analysis, and the use of facts in marketing operations.

Also, if one were to make a list of all the forces which managements weigh at one time or another when formulating their marketing mixes, it would be very long indeed, for the behavior of individuals and groups in all spheres of life has a bearing, first, on what goods and services are produced and consumed, and second, on the procedures that may be employed in bringing about exchange of these goods and services. However, the important forces which bear on marketers, all arising from the behavior of individuals or groups, may readily be listed under four heads, namely, the behavior of consumers, the trade, competitors, and government.

The next outline contains these four behavior forces with notations of some of the important behavioral determinants within each force. These must be studied and understood by the marketer, if his marketing mix is to be successful. The great quest of marketing management is to understand the behavior of humans in response to the stimuli to which they are subjected. The skillful marketer is one who is a perceptive and practical psychologist and sociologist, who has keen insight into individual and group behavior, who can foresee changes in behavior that develop in a dynamic world, who has creative ability for building well-knit programs because he has the capacity to visualize the probable response of consumers, trade, and competitors to his moves. His skill in forecasting response to his marketing moves should well be supplemented by a further skill in devising and using tests and measurements to check consumer or trade response to his program or parts thereof, for no marketer has so much prescience that he can proceed without empirical check.

Here, then, is the suggested outline of forces which govern the mixing of marketing elements. This list and that of the elements taken together provide a visual presentation of the concept of the marketing mix.

Market Forces Bearing on the Marketing Mix

1. *Consumers' Buying Behavior*—as determined by their:
   a. Motivation in purchasing.
   b. Buying habits.
   c. Living habits.
   d. Environment (present and future, as revealed by trends, for environment influences consumers' attitudes toward products and their use of them).
   e. Buying power.
   f. Number (i.e., how many).
2. *The Trade's Behavior*—wholesalers' and retailers' behavior, as influenced by:
   a. Their motivations.
   b. Their structure, practices, and attitudes.
   c. Trends in structure and procedures that portend change.
3. *Competitors' Position and Behavior*—as influenced by:
   a. Industry structure and the firm's relation thereto.
      1. Size and strength of competitors.
      2. Number of competitors and degree of industry concentration.
      3. Indirect competition—i.e., from other products.
   b. Relation of supply to demand—oversupply or undersupply.
   c. Product choices offered consumers by the industry—i.e., quality, price, service.

d. Degree to which competitors compete on price vs. nonprice bases.
e. Competitors' motivations and attitudes—their likely response to the actions of other firms.
f. Trends technological and social, portending change in supply and demand.

4. *Government Behavior*—controls over marketing:
    a. Regulations over products.
    b. Regulations over pricing.
    c. Regulations over competitive practices.
    d. Regulations over advertising and promotion.

When building a marketing program to fit the needs of his firm, the marketing manager has to weigh the behavioral forces and then juggle marketing elements in his mix with a keen eye on the resources with which he has to work. His firm is but one small organism in a large universe of complex forces. His firm is only a part of an industry that is competing with many other industries. What does the firm have in terms of money, product line, organization, and reputation with which to work? The manager must devise a mix of procedures that fit these resources. If his firm is small, he must judge the response of consumers, trade, and competition in light of his position and resources and the influence that he can exert in the market. He must look for special opportunities in product or method of operation. The small firm cannot employ the procedures of the big firm. Though he may sell the same kind of product as the big firm, his marketing strategy is likely to be widely different in many respects. Innumerable instances of this fact might be cited. For example, in the industrial goods field, small firms often seek to build sales on a limited and highly specialized line, whereas industry leaders seek patronage for full lines. Small firms often elect to go in for regional sales rather than attempt the national distribution practiced by larger companies. Again, the company of limited resources often elects to limit its production and sales to products whose potential is too small to attract the big fellows. Still again, companies with small resources in the cosmetic field not infrequently have set up introductory marketing programs employing aggressive personal selling and a "push" strategy with distribution limited to leading department stores. Their initially small advertising funds have been directed through these selected retail outlets, with the offering of the products and their story told over the signatures of the stores. The strategy has been to borrow kudos for their products from the leading stores' reputations and to gain a gradual radiation of distribution to smaller stores in all types of channels, such as often comes from the trade's follow-the-leader behavior. Only after resources have grown from mounting sales has a dense retail distribution been aggressively sought and a shift made to place the selling burden more and more on company-signed advertising.

The above strategy was employed for Toni products and Stoppette deodorant in their early marketing stages when the resources of their producers were limited (cf. case of Jules Montenier, Inc. in Borden and Marshall).[3] In contrast, cosmetic manufacturers with large resources have generally followed a "pull" strategy for the introduction of new products, relying on heavy campaigns of advertising in a rapid succession of area introductions to induce a hoped-for, complete retail coverage from the start (cf. case of Bristol-Meyers Company in Borden and Marshall).[4] These introductory campaigns have been undertaken only after careful programs of product development and test marketing have given assurance that product and selling plans had high promise of success.

Many additional instances of the varying strategy employed by small versus large enterprises might be cited. But those given serve to illustrate the point that managements must fashion their mixes to fit their resources. Their objectives must be realistic.

LONG VS. SHORT TERM ASPECTS OF MARKETING MIX

The marketing mix of a firm in a large part is the product of the evolution that comes from day-to-day marketing. At any time the mix represents the program that a management has evolved to meet the problems with which it is constantly faced in an ever-changing, ever-challenging market. There are continuous tactical maneuvers: a new product, aggressive promotion, or price-change initiated by a competitor must be considered and met; the failure of the trade to provide adequate market coverage or display must be remedied; a faltering sales force must be reorganized and stimulated; a decline in sales share must be diagnosed and remedied; an advertising approach that has lost effectiveness must be replaced; a general business decline must be countered. All such problems call for a management's maintaining effective channels of information relative to its own operations and to the day-to-day behavior of consumers, competitors, and the trade. Thus, we may observe that short-range forces play a large part in the fashioning of the mix to be used at any time and in determining the

[3] Neil H. Borden and M. V. Marshall, *Advertising Management: Text and Cases* (Homewood, Illinois: Richard D. Irwin, 1959), pp. 498–518.
[4] *Ibid.*, pp. 518–33.

allocation of expenditures among the various functional accounts of the operating statement.

But the overall strategy employed in a marketing mix is the product of longer-range plans and procedures dictated in part by past empiricism and in part, if the management is a good one, by management foresight as to what needs to be done to keep the firm successful in a changing world. As the world has become more and more dynamic, blessed is that corporation which has managers who have foresight, who can study trends of all kinds—natural, economic, social, and technological—and, guided by these, devise long-range plans that give promise of keeping their corporations afloat and successful in the turbulent sea of market change. Accordingly, when we think of the marketing mix, we need to give particular heed today to devising a mix based on long-range planning that promises to fit the world of five or ten or more years hence. Provision for effective long-range planning in corporate organization and procedure has become more and more recognized as the earmark of good management in a world that has become increasingly subject to rapid change.

To cite an instance among American marketing organizations which have shown foresight in adjusting the marketing mix to meet social and economic change, I look upon Sears Roebuck and Company as an outstanding example. After building an unusually successful mail order business to meet the needs of a rural America, Sears management foresaw the need to depart from its marketing pattern as a mail order company catering primarily to farmers. The trend from a rural to an urban United States was going on apace. The automobile and good roads promised to make town and city stores increasingly available to those who continued to be farmers. Relatively early, Sears launched a chain of stores across the land, each easily accessible by highway to both farmer and city resident, and with adequate parking space for customers. In time there followed the remarkable telephone and mail order plan directed at urban residents to make buying easy for Americans when congested city streets and highways made shopping increasingly distasteful. Similarly, in the areas of planning products which would meet the desires of consumers in a fast-changing world, of shaping its servicing to meet the needs of a wide variety of mechanical products, of pricing procedures to meet the challenging competition that came with the advent of discount retailers, the Sears organization has shown a foresight, adaptability, and creative ability worthy of emulation. The amazing growth and profitability of the company attest to the foresight and skill of its managements. Its history shows the wisdom of careful attention to market forces and their impending change in devising marketing mixes that may assure growth.

Like many concepts, the marketing mix concept seems relatively simple, once it has been expressed. I know that before they were ever tagged with the nomenclature of "concept," the ideas involved were widely understood among marketers as a result of the growing knowledge about marketing and marketing procedures that came during the preceding half century. But I have found for myself that once the ideas were reduced to a formal statement with an accompanying visual presentation, the concept of the mix has proved a helpful device in teaching, in business problem solving, and, generally, as an aid to thinking about marketing. First of all, it is helpful in giving an answer to the question often raised as to "what is marketing?" A chart which shows the elements of the mix and the forces that bear on the mix helps to bring understanding of what marketing is. It helps to explain why in our dynamic world the thinking of management in all its functional areas must be oriented to the market.

In recent years I have kept an abbreviated chart showing the elements and the forces of the marketing mix in front of my classes at all times. In case discussion it has proved a handy device by which to raise queries as to whether the student has recognized the implications of any recommendation he might have made in the areas of the several elements of the mix. Or, referring to the forces, we can question whether all the pertinent market forces have been given due consideration. Continual reference to the mix chart leads me to feel that the students' understanding of "what marketing is" is strengthened. The constant presence and use of the chart leaves a deeper understanding that marketing is the devising of programs that successfully meet the forces of the market.

In problem solving the marketing mix chart is a constant reminder of:

1. The fact that a problem seemingly lying in one segment of the mix must be deliberated with constant thought regarding the effect of any change in that sector on the other areas of marketing operations. The necessity of integration in marketing thinking is ever present.
2. The need of careful study of the market forces as they might bear on problems in hand.

In short, the mix chart provides an ever-ready checklist as to areas into which to guide thinking when considering marketing questions or dealing with marketing problems.

MARKETING: SCIENCE OR ART?

The quest for a "science of marketing" is hard upon us. If science is in part a systematic formulation and arrangement of facts in a way to help understanding, then the concept of the marketing mix may possibly be considered a small contribution in the search for a science of marketing. If we think of a marketing science as involving the observation and classification of facts and the establishment of verifiable laws that can be used by the marketer as a guide to action with assurance that predicted results will ensue, then we cannot be said to have gotten far toward establishing a science. The concept of the mix lays out the areas in which facts should be assembled, these to serve as a guide to management judgment in building marketing mixes. In the last few decades American marketers have made substantial progress in adopting the scientific method in assembling facts. They have sharpened the tools of fact finding—both those arising within the business and those external to it. Aided by these facts and by the skills developed through careful observation and experience, marketers are better fitted to practice the art of designing marketing mixes than would be the case had not the techniques of gathering facts been advanced as they have been in recent decades. Moreover, marketers have made progress in the use of the scientific method in designing tests whereby the results from mixes or parts of mixes can be measured. Thereby marketers have been learning how to subject the hypotheses of their mix artists to empirical check.

With continued improvement in the search for and the recording of facts pertinent to marketing, with further application of the controlled experiment, and with an extension and careful recording of case histories, we may hope for a gradual formulation of clearly defined and helpful marketing laws. Until then, and even then, marketing and the building of marketing mixes will largely lie in the realm of art.

19

Product Differentiation and Market Segmentation as Alternative Marketing Strategies

Wendell R. Smith

During the decade of the 1930's, the work of Robinson and Chamberlin resulted in a revitalization of economic theory. While classical and neoclassical theory provided a useful framework for economic analysis, the theories of perfect competition and pure monopoly had become inadequate as explanations of the contemporary business scene. The theory of perfect competition assumes homogeneity among the components of both the demand and supply sides of the market, but diversity or heterogeneity had come to be the rule rather than the exception. This analysis reviews major marketing strategy alternatives that are available to planners and merchandisers of products in an environment characterized by imperfect competition.

DIVERSITY IN SUPPLY

That there is a lack of homogeneity or close similarity among the items offered to the market by individual manufacturers of various products

Reprinted from the *Journal of Marketing,* published by the American Marketing Association (July, 1956), pp. 3–8. This article won the 1956 Alpha Kappa Psi Award as best article of the year.

Wendell R. Smith is professor of marketing at the School of Business Administration at the University of Massachusetts. He has been chairman of the national marketing advisory committee of the U.S. Department of Commerce and president of the American Marketing Association. For three years, he was staff vice president for market development for Radio Corporation of America, and he was the first director of the Marketing Science Institute. He holds three degrees from the University of Iowa.

is obvious in any variety store, department store, or shopping center. In many cases the impact of this diversity is amplified by advertising and promotional activities. Today's advertising and promotion tends to emphasize appeals to *selective* rather than *primary* buying motives and to point out the distinctive or differentiating features of the advertiser's product or service offer.

The presence of differences in the sales offers made by competing suppliers produces a diversity in supply that is inconsistent with the assumptions of earlier theory. The reasons for the presence of diversity in specific markets are many and include the following:

1. Variations in the production equipment and methods or processes used by different manufacturers of products designed for the same or similar uses.
2. Specialized or superior resources enjoyed by favorably situated manufacturers.
3. Unequal progress among competitors in design, development, and improvement of products.
4. The inability of manufacturers in some industries to eliminate product variations even through the application of quality control techniques.
5. Variations in producers' estimates of the nature of market demand with reference to such matters as price sensitivity, color, material, or package size.

Because of these and other factors, both planned and uncontrollable differences exist in the products of an industry. As a result, sellers make different appeals in support of their marketing efforts.

DIVERSITY OR VARIATIONS IN CONSUMER DEMAND

Under present-day conditions of imperfect competition, marketing managers are generally responsible for selecting the over-all marketing strategy or combination of strategies best suited to a firm's requirements at any particular point in time. The strategy selected may consist of a program designed to bring about the *convergence* of individual market demands for a variety of products upon a single or limited offering to the market. This is often accomplished by the achievement of product differentiation through advertising and promotion. In this way, variations in the demands of individual consumers are minimized or brought into line by means of effective use of appealing product claims designed to make a satisfactory volume of demand *converge* upon the product or product line being promoted. This strategy was once believed to be essential as the marketing counterpart to standardization and mass production in manufacturing because of the rigidities imposed by production cost considerations.

In some cases, however, the marketer may determine that it is better to accept *divergent* demand as a market characteristic and to adjust product lines and marketing strategy accordingly. This implies ability to merchandise to a heterogeneous market by emphasizing the precision with which a firm's products can satisfy the requirements of one or more distinguishable market segments. The strategy of product differentiation here gives way to marketing programs based upon measurement and definition of market differences.

Lack of homogeneity on the demand side may be based upon different customs, desire for variety, or desire for exclusiveness or may arise from basic differences in user needs. Some divergence in demand is the result of shopping errors in the market. Not all consumers have the desire or the ability to shop in a sufficiently efficient or rational manner as to bring about selection of the most needed or most wanted goods or services.

Diversity on the demand side of the market is nothing new to sales management. It has always been accepted as a fact to be dealt with in industrial markets where production to order rather than for the market is common. Here, however, the loss of precision in the satisfying of customer requirements that would be necessitated by attempts to bring about convergence of demand is often impractical and, in some cases, impossible. However, even in industrial marketing, the strategy of product differentiation should be considered in cases where products are applicable to several industries and may have horizontal markets of substantial size.

LONG-TERM IMPLICATIONS

While contemporary economic theory deals with the nature of product differentiation and its effects upon the operation of the total economy, the alternative strategies of product differentiation and market segmentation have received less attention. Empirical analysis of contemporary marketing activity supports the hypothesis that, while product differentiation and market segmentation are closely related (perhaps even inseparable) concepts, attempts to distinguish between these approaches may be productive of clarity in theory as well as greater precision in the planning of marketing operations. Not only do strategies of differentiation and segmentation call for differing systems of action at any point in time, but the dynamics of markets and marketing underscore the importance of varying degrees of diversity *through time* and suggest that the rational selection of marketing strategies is a requirement for the achievement of maximum functional effectiveness in the economy as a whole.

If a rational selection of strategies is to be made, an integrated approach to the minimizing of total costs must take precedence over separate approaches to minimization of production costs on the one hand and marketing costs on the other. Strategy determination must be regarded as an over-all management decision which will influence and require facilitating policies affecting both production and marketing activities.

DIFFERENCES BETWEEN STRATEGIES OF DIFFERENTIATION AND SEGMENTATION

Product differentiation and market segmentation are both consistent with the framework of imperfect competition.[1] In its simplest terms, *product differentiation* is concerned with the bending of demand to the will of supply. It is an attempt to shift or to change the slope of the demand curve for the market offering of an individual supplier. This strategy may also be employed by a group of suppliers such as a farm cooperative, the members of which have agreed to act together. It results from the desire to establish a kind of equilibrium in the market by bringing about adjustment of market demand to supply conditions favorable to the seller.

Segmentation is based upon developments on the demand side of the market and represents a rational and more precise adjustment of product and marketing effort to consumer or user requirements. In the language of the economist, segmentation is *disaggregative* in its effects and tends to bring about recognition of several demand schedules where only one was recognized before.

Attention has been drawn to this area of analysis by the increasing number of cases in which business problems have become soluble by doing something about marketing programs and product policies that overgeneralize both markets and marketing effort. These are situations where intensive promotion designed to differentiate the company's products was not accomplishing its objective—cases where failure to recognize the reality of market segments was resulting in loss of market position.

---

[1] Imperfect competition assumes lack of uniformity in the size and influence of the firms or individuals that comprise the demand or supply sides of a market.

While successful product differentiation will result in giving the marketer a horizontal share of a broad and generalized market, equally successful application of the strategy of market segmentation tends to produce depth of market position in the segments that are effectively defined and penetrated. The differentiator seeks to secure a layer of the market cake, whereas one who employs market segmentation strives to secure one or more wedge-shaped pieces.

Many examples of market segmentation can be cited; the cigarette and automobile industries are well-known illustrations. Similar developments exist in greater or lesser degree in almost all product areas. Recent introduction of a refrigerator with no storage compartment for frozen foods was in response to the distinguishable preferences of the segment of the refrigerator market made up of home freezer owners whose frozen food storage needs had already been met.

Strategies of segmentation and differentiation may be employed simultaneously, but more commonly they are applied in sequence in response to changing market conditions. In one sense, segmentation is a momentary or short-term phenomenon in that effective use of this strategy may lead to more formal recognition of the reality of market segments through redefinition of the segments as individual markets. Redefinition may result in a swing back to differentiation.

The literature of both economics and marketing abounds in formal definitions of product differentiation. *From a strategy viewpoint,* product differentiation is securing a measure of control over the demand for a product by advertising or promoting differences between a product and the products of competing sellers. It is basically the result of sellers' desires to establish firm market positions and/or to insulate their business against price competition. Differentiation tends to be characterized by heavy use of advertising and promotion and to result in prices that are somewhat above the equilibrium levels associated with perfectly competitive market conditions. It may be classified as a *promotional* strategy or approach to marketing.

Market segmentation, on the other hand, consists of viewing a heterogeneous market (one characterized by divergent demand) as a number of smaller homogeneous markets in response to differing product preferences among important market segments. It is attributable to the desires of consumers or users for more precise satisfaction of their varying wants. Like differentiation, segmentation often involves substantial use of advertising and promotion. This is to inform market segments of the availability of goods or services produced for or presented as meeting their needs with precision. Under these circumstances, prices tend to be somewhat closer to perfectly competitive equilibrium. Market segmentation is essentially a *merchandising* strategy, merchandising being used here in its technical sense as representing the adjustment of market offerings to consumer or user requirements.

THE EMERGENCE OF THE SEGMENTATION STRATEGY

To a certain extent, market segmentation may be regarded as a force in the market that will not be denied. It may result from trial and error in the sense that generalized programs of product differentiation may turn out to be effective in some segments of the market and ineffective in others. Recognition of, and intelligent response to, such a situation necessarily involves a shift in emphasis. On the other hand, it may develop that products involved in marketing programs designed for particular market segments may achieve a broader acceptance than originally planned, thus revealing a basis for convergence of demand and a more generalized marketing approach. The challenge to planning arises from the importance of determining, preferably in advance, the level or degree of segmentation that can be exploited with profit.

There appear to be many reasons why formal recognition of market segmentation as a strategy is beginning to emerge. One of the most important of these is decrease in the size of the minimum efficient producing or manufacturing unit required in some product areas. American industry has also established the technical base for product diversity by gaining release from some of the rigidities imposed by earlier approaches to mass production. Hence, there is less need today for generalization of markets in response to the necessity for long production runs of identical items.

Present emphasis upon the minimizing of marketing costs through self-service and similar developments tends to impose a requirement for better adjustment of products to consumer demand. The retailing structure, in its efforts to achieve improved efficiency, is providing less and less sales push at point of sale. This increases the premium placed by retailers upon products that are presold by their producers and are readily recognized by consumers as meeting their requirements as measured by satisfactory rates of stock turnover.

It has been suggested that the present level of discretionary buying power is productive of sharper shopping comparisons, particularly for items that are above the need level. General prosperity also creates increased willingness "to pay a little more" to get "just what I wanted."

Attention to market segmentation has also been enhanced by the recent ascendancy of product competition to a position of great economic importance. An expanded array of goods and services is competing for the consumer's dollar. More specifically, advancing technology is creating competition between new and traditional materials with reference to metals, construction materials, textile products, and in many other areas. While such competition is confusing and difficult to analyze in its early stages, it tends to achieve a kind of balance as various competing materials find their markets of maximum potential as a result of recognition of differences in the requirements of market segments.

Many companies are reaching the stage in their development where attention to market segmentation may be regarded as a condition or cost of growth. Their *core* markets have already been developed on a generalized basis to the point where additional advertising and selling expenditures are yielding diminishing returns. Attention to smaller or *fringe* market segments, which may have small potentials individually but are of crucial importance in the aggregate, may be indicated.

Finally, some business firms are beginning to regard an increasing share of their total costs of operation as being fixed in character. The higher costs of maintaining market position in the channels of distribution illustrate this change. Total reliance upon a strategy of product differentiation under such circumstances is undesirable, since market share available as a result of such a promotion-oriented approach tends to be variable over time. Much may hinge, for example, upon week-to-week audience ratings of the television shows of competitors who seek to outdifferentiate each other. Exploitation of market segments, which provides for greater maximization of consumer or user satisfactions, tends to build a more secure market position and to lead to greater over-all stability. While traditionally, high fixed costs (regarded primarily from the production viewpoint) have created pressures for expanded sale of standardized items through differentiation, the possible shifting of certain marketing costs into the fixed area of the total cost structure tends to minimize this pressure.

CONCLUSION

Success in planning marketing activities requires precise utilization of both product differentiation and market segmentation as components of marketing strategy. It is fortunate that available techniques of marketing research make unplanned market exploration largely unnecessary. It is the obligation of those responsible for sales and marketing administration to keep the strategy mix in adjustment with market structure at any given point in time and to produce in marketing strategy at least as much dynamism as is present in the market.

The ability of business to plan in this way is dependent upon the maintenance of a flow of market information that can be provided by marketing research as well as the full utilization of available techniques of cost accounting and cost analysis.

Cost information is critical because the upper limit to which market segmentation can be carried is largely defined by production cost considerations. There is a limit to which diversity in market offerings can be carried without driving production costs beyond practical limits. Similarly, the employment of product differentiation as a strategy tends to be restricted by the achievement of levels of marketing costs that are untenable. These cost factors tend to define the limits of the zone within which the employment of marketing strategies or a strategy mix dictated by the nature of the market is permissive.

It should be emphasized that while we have here been concerned with the differences between product differentiation and market segmentation as marketing strategies, they are closely related concepts in the setting of an imperfectly competitive market. The differences have been highlighted in the interest of enhancing clarity in theory and precision in practice. The emergence of market segmentation as a strategy once again provides evidence of the consumer's preeminence in the contemporary American economy and the richness of the rewards that can result from the application of science to marketing problems.

20

Benefit Segmentation: A Decision-Oriented Research Tool

Russell I. Haley

Market segmentation has been steadily moving toward center stage as a topic of discussion in marketing and research circles. Hardly a conference passes without at least one session devoted to it. Moreover, in March the American Management Association held a three-day conference entirely concerned with various aspects of the segmentation problem.

According to Wendell Smith, "segmentation is based upon developments on the demand side of the market and represents a rational and more precise adjustment of product and marketing effort to consumer or user requirements."[1] The idea that all markets can be profitably segmented has now received almost as widespread acceptance as the marketing concept itself. However, problems remain. In the extreme, a marketer can divide up his market in as many ways as he can describe his prospects. If he wishes, he can define a left-handed segment, or a blue-eyed segment, or a German-speaking segment. Consequently, current discussion revolves largely around which of the virtually limitless alternatives is likely to be most productive.

Reprinted from the *Journal of Marketing*, published by the American Marketing Association. Russell I. Haley, "Benefit Segmentation: A Decision-Oriented Research Tool," *Journal of Marketing*, Vol. 32, pp. 30–35, July 1968.

Russell I. Haley is president of Haley, Oberholtser and Associates, specialists in marketing research and advertising. He has long been associated with attitude research and market segmentation studies. Mr. Haley received his M.B.A. from Columbia University in statistics.

[1] Wendell R. Smith, "Product Differentiation and Market Segmentation as Alternative Product Strategies," *Journal of Marketing*, Vol. XXI (July, 1956), pp. 3–8.

Several varieties of market segmentation have been popular in the recent past. At least three kinds have achieved some degree of prominence. Historically, perhaps the first type to exist was geographic segmentation. Small manufacturers who wished to limit their investments, or whose distribution channels were not large enough to cover the entire country, segmented the U.S. market, in effect, by selling their products only in certain areas.

However, as more and more brands became national, the second major system of segmentation—demographic segmentation—became popular. Under this philosophy targets were defined as younger people, men, or families with children. Unfortunately, a number of recent studies have shown that demographic variables such as age, sex, income, occupation and race are, in general, poor predictors of behavior and, consequently, less than optimum bases for segmentation strategies.[2]

More recently, a third type of segmentation has come into increasing favor—volume segmentation. The so-called "heavy half" theory, popularized by Dik Twedt of the Oscar Mayer Company,[3] points out that in most product categories one-half of the consumers account for around 80% of the consumption. If this is true, the argument goes, shouldn't knowledgeable marketers concentrate their efforts on these high-volume consumers? Certainly they are the most *valuable* consumers.

The trouble with this line of reasoning is that not all heavy consumers are usually available to the same brand—because they are not all seeking the same kinds of benefits from a product. For example, heavy coffee drinkers consist of two types of consumers—those who drink chain store brands and those who drink premium brands. The chain store customers feel that all coffees are basically alike and, because they drink so much coffee, they feel it is sensible to buy a relatively inexpensive brand. The premium brand buyers, on the other hand, feel that the few added pennies which coffees like Yuban, Martinson's, Chock Full O'Nuts, and Savarin cost are more than justified by their fuller taste. Obviously, these two groups of people, although they are both members of the "heavy half" segment, are not equally good

---

[2] Ronald E. Frank, "Correlates of Buying Behavior for Grocery Products," *Journal of Marketing*, Vol. 31 (October, 1967), pp. 48–53; Ronald E. Frank, William Massey, and Harper W. Boyd, Jr., "Correlates of Grocery Product Consumption Rates," *Journal of Marketing Research*, Vol. 4 (May, 1968), pp. 184–190; and Clark Wilson, "Homemaker Living Patterns and Marketplace Behavior—A Psychometric Approach," in John S. Wright and Jac L. Goldstucker, Editors, *New Ideas for Successful Marketing*, Proceedings of 1966 World Congress (Chicago: American Marketing Association, June, 1966), pp. 305–331.

[3] Dik Warren Twedt, "Some Practical Applications of the 'Heavy Half' Theory" (New York: Advertising Research Foundation 10th Annual Conference, October 6, 1964).

prospects for any one brand, nor can they be expected to respond to the same advertising claims.

These three systems of segmentation have been used because they provide helpful guidance in the use of certain marketing tools. For example, geographic segmentation, because it describes the market in a discrete way, provides definite direction in media purchases. Spot TV, spot radio, and newspapers can be bought for the geographical segment selected for concentrated effort. Similarly, demographic segmentation allows media to be bought more efficiently since demographic data on readers, viewers, and listeners are readily available for most media vehicles. Also, in some product categories demographic variables are extremely helpful in differentiating users from non-users, although they are typically less helpful in distinguishing between the users of various brands. The heavy-half philosophy is especially effective in directing dollars toward the most important parts of the market.

However, each of these three systems of segmentation is handicapped by an underlying disadvantage inherent in its nature. All are based on an ex post facto analysis of the kinds of people who make up various segments of a market. They rely on *descriptive* factors rather than *causal* factors. For this reason they are not efficient predictors of future buying behavior, and it is future buying behavior that is of central interest to marketers.

BENEFIT SEGMENTATION

An approach to market segmentation whereby it is possible to identify market segments by causal factors rather than descriptive factors, might be called "benefit segmentation." The belief underlying this segmentation strategy is that the benefits which people are seeking in consuming a given product are the basic reasons for the existence of true market segments. Experience with this approach has shown that benefits sought by consumers determine their behavior much more accurately than do demographic characteristics or volume of consumption.

This does not mean that the kinds of data gathered in more traditional types of segmentation are not useful. Once people have been classified into segments in accordance with the benefits they are seeking, each segment is contrasted with all of the other segments in terms of its demography, its volume of consumption, its brand perceptions, its media habits, its personality and life-style, and so forth. In this way, a reasonably deep understanding of the people who make up each segment can be obtained. And by capitalizing on this understanding, it is possible to reach them, to talk to them in their own terms, and to present a product in the most favorable light possible.

The benefit segmentation approach is not new. It has been employed by a number of America's largest corporations since it was introduced in 1961.[4] However, case histories have been notably absent from the literature because most studies have been contracted for privately, and have been treated confidentially.

The benefit segmentation approach is based upon being able to measure consumer value systems in detail, together with what the consumer thinks about various brands in the product category of interest. While this concept seems simple enough, operationally it is very complex. There is no simple straightforward way of handling the volumes of data that have to be generated. Computers and sophisticated multivariate attitude measurement techniques are a necessity.

Several alternative statistical approaches can be employed, among them the so-called "Q" technique of factor analysis, multi-dimensional scaling, and other distance measures.[5] All of these methods relate the ratings of each respondent to those of every other respondent and then seek clusters of individuals with similar rating patterns. If the items rated are potential consumer benefits, the clusters that emerge will be groups of people who attach similar degrees of importance to the various benefits. Whatever the statistical approach selected, the end result of the analysis is likely to be between three and seven consumer segments, each representing a potentially productive focal point for marketing efforts.

Each segment is identified by the benefits it is seeking. However, it is the *total configuration* of the benefits sought which differentiates one segment from another, rather than the fact that one segment is seeking one particular benefit and another a quite different benefit. Individual benefits are likely to have appeal for several segments. In fact, the research that has been done thus far suggests that most people would like as many benefits as possible. However, the *relative* importance they attach to individual benefits can differ importantly and, accordingly, can be used as an effective lever in segmenting markets.

Of course, it is possible to determine benefit segments intuitively as well as with computers and sophisticated research methods. The kinds of brilliant insights which produced the Mustang and the first 100-millimeter cigarette have a good chance of succeeding whenever marketers are able to tap an existing benefit segment.

[4] Russell I. Haley, "Experimental Research on Attitudes Toward Shampoos," an unpublished paper (February, 1961).
[5] Ronald E. Frank and Paul E. Green, "Numerical Taxonomy in Marketing Analysis: A Review Article," *Journal of Marketing Research*, Vol. V (February, 1968), pp. 83–98.

However, intuition can be very expensive when it is mistaken. Marketing history is replete with examples of products which someone felt could not miss. Over the longer term, systematic benefit segmentation research is likely to have a higher proportion of successes.

But is benefit segmentation practical? And is it truly operational? The answer to both of these questions is "yes." In effect, the crux of the problem of choosing the best segmentation system is to determine which has the greatest number of practical marketing implications. An example should show that benefit segmentation has a much wider range of implications than alternative forms of segmentation.

An Example of Benefit Segmentation

While the material presented here is purely illustrative to protect the competitive edge of companies who have invested in studies of this kind, it is based on actual segmentation studies. Consequently, it is quite typical of the kinds of things which are normally learned in the course of a benefit segmentation study.

The toothpaste market has been chosen as an example because it is one with which everyone is familiar. Let us assume that a benefit segmentation study has been done and four major segments have been identified—one particularly concerned with decay prevention, one with brightness of teeth, one with the flavor and appearance of the product, and one with price. A relatively large amount of supplementary information has also been gathered (Table 1) about the people in each of these segments.

The decay prevention segment, it has been found, contains a disproportionately large number of families with children. They are seriously concerned about the possibility of cavities and show a definite preference for fluoride toothpaste. This is reinforced by their personalities. They tend to be a little hypochondriacal and, in their life-styles, they are less socially-oriented than some of the other groups. This segment has been named The Worriers.

The second segment, comprised of people who show concern for the brightness of their teeth, is quite different. It includes a relatively large group of young marrieds. They smoke more than average. This is where the swingers are. They are strongly social and their life-style patterns are very active. This is probably the group to which toothpastes such as Macleans or Plus White or Ultra Brite would appeal. This segment has been named The Sociables.

In the third segment, the one which is particularly concerned with the flavor and appearance of the product, a large portion of the brand deciders are children. Their use of spearmint toothpaste is well

TABLE 1. *Toothpaste market segment description*

Segment name:	The Sensory Segment	The Sociables	The Worriers	The Independent Segment
Principal benefit sought:	Flavor, product appearance	Brightness of teeth	Decay prevention	Price
Demographic strengths:	Children	Teens, young people	Large families	Men
Special behavioral characteristics:	Users of spearmint-flavored toothpaste	Smokers	Heavy users	Heavy users
Brands disproportionately favored:	Colgate, Stripe	Macleans, Plus White, Ultra Brite	Crest	Brands on sale
Personality characteristics:	High self-involvement	High sociability	High hypochondriasis	High autonomy
Life-style characteristics:	Hedonistic	Active	Conservative	Value-oriented

above average. Stripe has done relatively well in this segment. They are more ego-centered than other segments, and their life-style is outgoing but not to the extent of the swingers. They will be called The Sensory Segment.

The fourth segment, the price-oriented segment, shows a predominance of men. It tends to be above average in terms of toothpaste usage. People in this segment see very few meaningful differences between brands. They switch more frequently than people in other segments and tend to buy a brand on sale. In terms of personality, they are cognitive and they are independent. They like to think for themselves and make brand choices on the basis of their judgment. They will be called The Independent Segment.

Marketing Implications of Benefit Segmentation Studies

Both copy directions and media choices will show sharp differences depending upon which of these segments is chosen as the target—The Worriers, The Sociables, The Sensory Segment, or The Independent Segment. For example, the tonality of the copy will be light if The Sociable Segment or The Sensory Segment is to be addressed. It will be more serious if the copy is aimed at The Worriers. And if The Independent Segment is selected, it will probably be desirable to use rational, two-sided arguments. Of course, to talk to this group at all it will be necessary to have either a price edge or some kind of demonstrable product superiority.

The depth-of-sell reflected by the copy will also vary, depending upon the segment which is of interest. It will be fairly intensive for The Worrier Segment and for The Independent Segment, but much more superficial and mood-oriented for The Sociable and Sensory Segments.

Likewise, the setting will vary. It will focus on the product for The Sensory Group, on socially-oriented situations for The Sociable Group, and perhaps on demonstration or on competitive comparisons for The Independent Group.

Media environments will also be tailored to the segments chosen as targets. Those with serious environments will be used for The Worrier and Independent Segments, and those with youthful, modern and active environments for The Sociable and The Sensory Groups. For example, it might be logical to use a larger proportion of television for The Sociable and Sensory Groups, while The Worriers and Independents might have heavier print schedules.

The depth-of-sell needed will also be reflected in the media choices. For The Worrier and Rational Segments longer commercials— perhaps 60-second commercials—would be indicated, while for the other two groups shorter commercials and higher frequency would be desirable.

Of course, in media selection the facts that have been gathered about the demographic characteristics of the segment chosen as the target would also be taken into consideration.

The information in Table 1 also has packaging implications. For example, it might be appropriate to have colorful packages for The Sensory Segment, perhaps aqua (to indicate fluoride) for The Worrier Group, and gleaming white for The Sociable Segment because of their interest in bright white teeth.

It should be readily apparent that the kinds of information normally obtained in the course of a benefit segmentation study have a wide range of marketing implications. Sometimes they are useful in suggesting physical changes in a product. For example, one manufacturer discovered that his product was well suited to the needs of his chosen target with a single exception in the area of flavor. He was able to make a relatively inexpensive modification in his product and thereby strengthen his market position.

The new product implications of benefit segmentation studies are equally apparent. Once a marketer understands the kinds of segments that exist in his market, he is often able to see new product opportunities or particularly effective ways of positioning the products emerging from his research and development operation.

Similarly, benefit segmentation information has been found helpful in providing direction in the choice of compatible point-of-purchase materials and in the selection of the kinds of sales promotions which are most likely to be effective for any given market target.

Generalizations from Benefit Segmentation Studies

A number of generalizations are possible on the basis of the major benefit segmentation studies which have been conducted thus far. For example, the following general rules of thumb have become apparent:

- It is easier to take advantage of market segments that already exist than to attempt to create new ones. Some time ago the strategy of product differentiation was heavily emphasized in marketing textbooks. Under this philosophy it was believed that a manufacturer was more or less able to create new market segments at will by making his product somewhat different from those of his competitors. Now it is generally recognized that fewer costly errors will be made if money is first invested in consumer research aimed at determining the present contours of the market. Once this knowledge is available, it is usually most efficient to tailor marketing strategies to existing consumer-need patterns.

- No brand can expect to appeal to all consumers. The very act of attracting one segment may automatically alienate others. A corollary to this principle is that any marketer who wishes to cover a market fully must offer consumers more than a single brand. The flood of new brands which have recently appeared on the market is concrete recognition of this principle.

- A company's brands can sometimes cannibalize each other but need not necessarily do so. It depends on whether or not they are positioned against the same segment of the market. Ivory Snow sharply reduced Ivory Flakes' share of market, and the Ford Falcon cut deeply into the sales of the standard size Ford because, in each case, the products were competing in the same segments. Later on, for the same companies, the Mustang was successfully introduced with comparatively little damage to Ford; and the success of Crest did not have a disproportionately adverse effect on Gleem's market position because, in these cases, the segments to which the products appealed were different.

- New and old products alike should be designed to fit *exactly* the needs of some segment of the market. In other words, they should be aimed at people seeking a specific combination of benefits. It is a marketing truism that you sell people one at a time—that you have to get *someone* to buy your product before you get *anyone* to buy it. A substantial group of people must be interested in your specific set of benefits before you can make progress in a market. Yet, many products attempt to aim at two or more segments simultaneously. As a result, they are not able to maximize their appeal to any segment of the market, and they run the risk of ending up with a dangerously fuzzy brand image.

· Marketers who adopt a benefit segmentation strategy have a distinct competitive edge. If a benefit segment can be located which is seeking exactly the kinds of satisfactions that one marketer's brand can offer better than any other brand, the marketer can almost certainly dominate the purchases of that segment. Furthermore, if his competitors are looking at the market in terms of traditional types of segments, they may not even be aware of the existence of the benefit segment which he has chosen as his market target. If they are ignorant in this sense, they will be at a loss to explain the success of his brand. And it naturally follows that if they do not understand the reasons for his success, the kinds of people buying his brand, and the benefits they are obtaining from it, his competitors will find it very difficult to successfully attack the marketer's position.

· An understanding of the benefit segments which exist within a market can be used to advantage when competitors introduce new products. Once the way in which consumers are positioning the new product has been determined, the likelihood that it will make major inroads into segments of interest can be assessed, and a decision can be made on whether or not counteractions of any kind are required. If the new product appears to be assuming an ambiguous position, no money need be invested in defensive measures. However, if it appears that the new product is ideally suited to the needs of an important segment of the market, the manufacturer in question can introduce a new competitive product of his own, modify the physical properties of existing brands, change his advertising strategy, or take whatever steps appear appropriate.

Types of Segments Uncovered Through Benefit Segmentation Studies

It is difficult to generalize about the types of segments which are apt to be discovered in the course of a benefit segmentation study. To a large extent, the segments which have been found have been unique to the product categories being analyzed. However, a few types of segments have appeared in two or more private studies. Among them are the following:

The Status Seeker	. . . a group which is very much concerned with the prestige of the brands purchased.
The Swinger	. . . a group which tries to be modern and up to date in all of its activities. Brand choices reflect this orientation.
The Conservative	. . . a group which prefers to stick to large successful companies and popular brands.
The Rational Man	. . . a group which looks for benefits such as economy, value, durability, etc.
The Inner-Directed Man	. . . a group which is especially concerned with self-concept. Members consider themselves to have a sense of humor, to be independent and/or honest.
The Hedonist	. . . a group which is concerned primarily with sensory benefits.

Some of these segments appear among the customers of almost all products and services. However, there is no guarantee that a majority of them or, for that matter, any of them exist in any given product category. Finding out whether they do and, if so, what should be done about them is the purpose of benefit segmentation research.

CONCLUSION

The benefit segmentation approach is of particular interest because it never fails to provide fresh insight into markets. As was indicated in the toothpaste example cited earlier, the marketing implications of this analytical research tool are limited only by the imagination of the person using the information a segmentation study provides. In effect, when segmentation studies are conducted, a number of smaller markets emerge instead of one large one. Moreover, each of these smaller markets can be subjected to the same kinds of thorough analyses to which total markets have been subjected in the past. The only difference— a crucial one—is that the total market was a heterogeneous conglomeration of sub-groups. The so-called average consumer existed only in the minds of some marketing people. When benefit segmentation is used, a number of relatively homogeneous segments are uncovered. And, because they are homogeneous, descriptions of them in terms of averages are much more appropriate and meaningful as marketing guides.

21

Retail Strategy and the Classification of Consumer Goods

Louis P. Bucklin

When Melvin T. Copeland published his famous discussion of the classification of consumer goods, shopping, convenience, and specialty goods, his intent was clearly to create a guide for the development of marketing strategies by manufacturers.[1] Although his discussion involved retailers and retailing, his purpose was to show how consumer buying habits affected the type of channel of distribution and promotional strategy that a manufacturer should adopt. Despite the controversy which still surrounds his classification, his success in creating such a guide may be judged by the fact that through the years few marketing texts have failed to make use of his ideas.

The purpose of this article is to attempt to clarify some of the issues that exist with respect to the classification, and to extend the concept to include the retailer and the study of retail strategy.

CONTROVERSY OVER THE CLASSIFICATION SYSTEM

The starting point for the discussion lies with the definitions adopted by the American Marketing Association's Committee

Reprinted from the *Journal of Marketing*, published by the American Marketing Association (January, 1963), pp. 51–56.

Louis P. Bucklin has taught in business schools at the University of Colorado and Northwestern University, and is now professor of marketing at the University of California at Berkeley. He received his bachelor's degree from Dartmouth, his M.B.A. from Harvard, and his Ph.D. from Northwestern. He is an authority on marketing channels and channel management.

[1] Melvin T. Copeland, "Relation of Consumers' Buying Habits to Marketing Methods," *Harvard Business Review* (April, 1923), pp. 282–289.

on Definitions for the classification system in 1948.[2] These are:

Convenience Goods: Those consumers' goods which the customer purchases frequently, immediately, and with the minimum of effort.

Shopping Goods: Those consumers' goods which the customer in the process of selection and purchase characteristically compares on such bases as suitability, quality, price and style.

Specialty Goods: Those consumers' goods on which a significant group of buyers are habitually willing to make a special purchasing effort.

This set of definitions was retained in virtually the same form by the Committee on Definitions in its latest publication.[3]

Opposing these accepted definitions stands a critique by Richard H. Holton.[4] Finding the Committee's definitions too imprecise to be able to measure consumer buying behavior, he suggested that the following definitions not only would represent the essence of Copeland's original idea, but be operationally more useful as well.

Convenience Goods: Those goods for which the consumer regards the probable gain from making price and quality comparisons as small compared to the cost of making such comparisons.

Shopping Goods: Those goods for which the consumer regards the probable gain from making price and quality comparisons as large relative to the cost of making such comparisons.

Specialty Goods: Those convenience or shopping goods, which have such a limited market as to require the consumer to make a special effort to purchase them.

Holton's definitions have particular merit because they make explicit the underlying conditions that control the extent of a consumer's shopping activities. They show that a consumer's buying behavior will be determined not only by the strength of his desire to secure some good, but by his perception of the cost of shopping to obtain it. In other words, the consumer continues to shop *for all goods* so long as he feels that the additional satisfactions from further comparisons are at least equal to the cost of making the additional effort. The distinction between shopping and convenience goods lies principally in the degree of satisfaction to be secured from further comparisons.

The Specialty Good Issue

While Holton's conceptualization makes an important contribution, he has sacrificed some of the richness of Copeland's original ideas.

---

[2] Definitions Committee, American Marketing Association, "Report of the Definitions Committee," *Journal of Marketing* (October, 1948), pp. 202–217, at p. 206, p. 215.

[3] Definitions Committee, American Marketing Association, *Marketing Definitions*, (Chicago: American Marketing Association, 1960), pp. 11, 21, 22.

[4] Richard H. Holton, "The Distinction Between Convenience Goods, Shopping Goods, and Specialty Goods," *Journal of Marketing* (July, 1958), pp. 53–56.

This is essentially David J. Luck's complaint in a criticism of Holton's proposal.[5] Luck objected to the abandonment of the *willingness* of consumers to make a special effort to buy as the rationale for the concept of specialty goods. He regarded this type of consumer behavior as based upon unique consumer attitudes toward certain goods and not the density of distribution of those goods. Holton, in a reply, rejected Luck's point; he remained convinced that the real meaning of specialty goods could be derived from his convenience goods, shopping goods continuum, and market conditions.[6]

The root of the matter appears to be that insufficient attention has been paid to the fact that the consumer, once embarked upon some buying expedition, may have only one of two possible objectives in mind. A discussion of this aspect of consumer behavior will make possible a closer synthesis of Holton's contributions with the more traditional point of view.

A Forgotten Idea

The basis for this discussion is afforded by certain statements, which the marketing profession has largely ignored over the years, in Copeland's original presentation of his ideas. These have regard to the extent of the consumer's awareness of the precise nature of the item he wishes to buy, *before* he starts his shopping trip. Copeland stated that the consumer, in both the case of convenience goods and specialty goods, has full knowledge of the particular good, or its acceptable substitutes, that he will buy before he commences his buying trip. The consumer, however, lacks this knowledge in the case of a shopping good.[7] This means that the buying trip must not only serve the objective of purchasing the good, but must enable the consumer to discover which item he wants to buy.

The behavior of the consumer during any shopping expedition may, as a result, be regarded as heavily dependent upon the state of his decision as to what he wants to buy. If the consumer knows precisely what he wants, he needs only to undertake communication activities sufficient to take title to the desired product. He may also undertake ancillary physical activities involving the handling of the product and delivery. If the consumer is uncertain as to what he wants to buy, then an additional activity will have to be performed. This involves the work of making comparisons between possible alternative purchases, or simply search.

---

[5] David J. Luck, "On the Nature of Specialty Goods," *Journal of Marketing* (July, 1959), pp. 61–64.

[6] Richard H. Holton, "What Is Really Meant by 'Specialty' Goods?" *Journal of Marketing* (July, 1959), pp. 64–67.

[7] Melvin T. Copeland, same reference as footnote 1, pp. 283–284.

There would be little point, with respect to the problem of classifying consumer goods, in distinguishing between the activity of search and that of making a commitment to buy, if a consumer always performed both before purchasing a good. The crucial point is that he does not. While most of the items that a consumer buys have probably been subjected to comparison at some point in his life, he does not make a search before each purchase. Instead, a past solution to the need is frequently remembered and, if satisfactory, is implemented.[8] Use of these past decisions for many products quickly moves the consumer past any perceived necessity of undertaking new comparisons and leaves only the task of exchange to be discharged.

REDEFINITION OF THE SYSTEM

Use of this concept of problem solving permits one to classify consumer buying efforts into two broad categories which may be called shopping and nonshopping goods.

Shopping Goods

Shopping goods are those for which the consumer *regularly* formulates a new solution to his need each time it is aroused. They are goods whose suitability is determined through search before the consumer commits himself to each purchase.

The motivation behind this behavior stems from circumstances which tend to perpetuate a lack of complete consumer knowledge about the nature of the product that he would like to buy.[9] Frequent changes in price, style, or product technology cause consumer information to become obsolete. The greater the time lapse between purchases, the more obsolete will his information be. The consumer's needs are also subject to change, or he may seek variety in his purchases as an actual goal. These forces will tend to make past information inappropriate. New search, due to forces internal and external to the consumer, is continuously required for products with purchase determinants which the consumer regards as both important and subject to change.[10]

---

[8] George Katona, *Psychological Analysis of Economic Behavior* (New York: McGraw-Hill Book Co., Inc. 1951), p. 47.

[9] Same reference, pp. 67–68.

[10] George Katona and Eva Mueller, "A Study of Purchase Decisions in Consumer Behavior," Lincoln Clark, editor, *Consumer Behavior* (New York: University Press, 1954), pp. 30–87.

The number of comparisons that the consumer will make in purchasing a shopping good may be determined by use of Holton's hypothesis on effort. The consumer, in other words, will undertake search for a product until the perceived value to be secured through additional comparisons is less than the estimated cost of making those comparisons. Thus, shopping effort will vary according to the intensity of the desire of the consumer to find the right product, the type of product and the availability of retail facilities. Whether the consumer searches diligently, superficially, or even buys at the first opportunity, however, does not alter the shopping nature of the product.

Nonshopping Goods

Turning now to nonshopping goods, one may define these as products for which the consumer is both willing and able to use stored solutions to the problem of finding a product to answer a need. From the remarks on shopping goods it may be generalized that nonshopping goods have purchase determinants which do not change, or which are perceived as changing inconsequentially, between purchases.[11] The consumer, for example, may assume that price for some product never changes or that price is unimportant. It may be unimportant because either the price is low, or the consumer is very wealthy.

Nonshopping goods may be divided into convenience and specialty goods by means of the concept of a preference map. Bayton introduces this concept as the means to show how the consumer stores information about products.[12] It is a rough ranking of the relative desirability of the different kinds of products that the consumer sees as possible satisfiers for his needs. For present purposes, two basic types of preference maps may be envisaged. One type ranks all known product alternatives equally in terms of desirability. The other ranks one particular product as so superior to all others that the consumer, in effect, believes this product is the only answer to his need.

Distinguishing the Specialty Good

This distinction in preference maps creates the basis for discriminating between a convenience good and a specialty good. Clearly, where the consumer is indifferent to the precise item among a number of substitutes which he could buy, he will purchase the most accessible

---

[11] Katona, same reference as footnote 8, p. 68.

[12] James A. Bayton, "Motivation, Cognition, Learning–Basic Factors in Consumer Behavior," *Journal of Marketing* (January, 1958), pp. 282–289, at p. 287. [See pp. 132–142 of this anthology–eds.] .

one and look no further. This is a convenience good. On the other hand, where the consumer recognizes only one brand of a product as capable of satisfying his needs, he will be willing to bypass more readily accessible substitutes in order to secure the wanted item. This is a specialty good.

However, most nonshopping goods will probably fall in between these two polar extremes. Preference maps will exist where the differences between the relative desirability of substitutes may range from the slim to the well marked. In order to distinguish between convenience goods and specialty goods in these cases, Holton's hypothesis regarding consumer effort may be employed again. A convenience good, in these terms, becomes one for which the consumer has such little preference among his perceived choices that he buys the item which is most readily available. A specialty good is one for which consumer preference is so strong that he bypasses, or would be willing to bypass, the purchase of more accessible substitutes in order to secure his most wanted item.

It should be noted that this decision on the part of the consumer as to how much effort he should expend takes place under somewhat different conditions than the one for shopping goods. In the non-shopping good instance the consumer has a reasonably good estimate of the additional value to be achieved by purchasing his preferred item. The estimate of the additional cost required to make this purchase may also be made fairly accurately. Consequently, the consumer will be in a much better position to justify the expenditure of additional effort here than in the case of shopping goods where much uncertainty must exist with regard to both of these factors.

The New Classification

The classification of consumer goods that results from the analysis is as follows:

Convenience Goods: Those goods for which the consumer, before his need arises, possesses a preference map that indicates a willingness to purchase any of a number of known substitutes rather than to make the additional effort required to buy a particular item.

Shopping Goods: Those goods for which the consumer has not developed a complete preference map before the need arises, requiring him to undertake search to construct such a map before purchase.

Specialty Goods: Those goods for which the consumer, before his need arises, possesses a preference map that indicates a willingness to expend the additional effort required to purchase the most preferred item rather than to buy a more readily accessible substitute.

The classification of the goods concept developed above may now be extended to retailing. As the concept now stands, it is derived from consumer attitudes or motives toward a *product*. These attitudes, or product motives, are based upon the consumer's interpretation of a product's styling, special features, quality, and social status of its brand name, if any. Occasionally the price may also be closely associated with the product by the consumer.

Classification of Patronage Motives

The extension of the concept to retailing may be made through the notion of patronage motives, a term long used in marketing. Patronage motives are derived from consumer attitudes concerning the retail establishment. They are related to factors which the consumer is likely to regard as controlled by the retailer. These will include assortment, credit, service, guarantee, shopping ease and enjoyment, and usually price. Patronage motives, however, have never been systematically categorized. It is proposed that the procedure developed above to discriminate among product motives be used to classify consumer buying motives with respect to retail stores as well.

This will provide the basis for the consideration of retail marketing strategy and will aid in clearing up certain ambiguities that would otherwise exist if consumer buying motives were solely classified by product factors. These ambiguities appear, for example, when the consumer has a strong affinity for some particular brand of a product, but little interest in where he buys it. The manufacturer of the product, as a result, would be correct in defining the product as a specialty item if the consumer's preferences were so strong as to cause him to eschew more readily available substitutes. The retailer may regard it as a convenience good, however, since the consumer will make no special effort to purchase the good from any particular store. This problem is clearly avoided by separately classifying product and patronage motives.

The categorization of patronage motives by the above procedure results in the following three definitions. These are:

Convenience Stores: Those stores for which the consumer, before his need for some product arises, possesses a preference map that indicates a willingness to buy from the most accessible store.

Shopping Stores: Those stores for which the consumer has not developed a complete preference map relative to the product he wishes to buy, requiring him to undertake a search to construct such a map before purchase.

Specialty Stores: Those stores for which the consumer, before his need for some product arises, possesses a preference map that indicates a willingness to buy the item from a particular establishment even though it may not be the most accessible.

The Product-Patronage Matrix

Although this basis will now afford the retailer a means to consider alternative strategies, a finer classification system may be obtained by relating consumer product motives to consumer patronage motives. By cross-classifying each product motive with each patronage motive, one creates a three-by-three matrix, representing nine possible types of consumer buying behavior. Each of the nine cells in the matrix may be described as follows:

1. *Convenience Store—Convenience Good:* The consumer, represented by this category, prefers to buy the most readily available brand of product at the most accessible store.
2. *Convenience Store—Shopping Good:* The consumer selects his purchase from among the assortment carried by the most accessible store.
3. *Convenience Store—Specialty Good:* The consumer purchases his favored brand from the most accessible store which has the item in stock.
4. *Shopping Store—Convenience Good:* The consumer is indifferent to the brand of product he buys, but shops among different stores in order to secure better retail service and/or lower retail price.
5. *Shopping Store—Shopping Good:* The consumer makes comparisons among both retail controlled factors and factors associated with the product (brand).
6. *Shopping Store—Specialty Good:* The consumer has a strong preference with respect to the brand of the product, but shops among a number of stores in order to secure the best retail and/or price for this brand.
7. *Specialty Store—Convenience Good:* The consumer prefers to trade at a specific store, but is indifferent to the brand of product purchased.
8. *Specialty Store—Shopping Good:* The consumer prefers to trade at a certain store, but is uncertain as to which product he wishes to buy and examines the store's assortment for the best purchase.
9. *Specialty Store—Specialty Good:* The consumer has both a preference for a particular store and a specific brand.

Conceivably, each of these nine types of behavior might characterize the buying patterns of some consumers for a given product.

It seems more likely, however, that the behavior of consumers toward a product could be represented by only three or four of the categories. The remaining cells would be empty, indicating that no consumers bought the product by these methods. Different cells, of course, would be empty for different products.

THE FORMATION OF RETAIL STRATEGY

The extended classification system developed above clearly provides additional information important to the manufacturer in the planning of his marketing strategy. Of principal interest here, however, is the means by which the retailer might use the classification system in planning his marketing strategy.

Three Basic Steps

The procedure involves three steps. The first is the classification of the retailer's potential customers for some product by market segment, using the nine categories in the consumer buying habit matrix to define the principal segments. The second requires the retailer to determine the nature of the marketing strategies necessary to appeal to each market segment. The final step is the retailer's selection of the market segment, and the strategy associated with it, to which he will sell. A simplified, hypothetical example may help to clarify this process.

A former buyer of dresses for a department store decided to open her own dress shop. She rented a small store in the downtown area of a city of 50,000, ten miles distant from a metropolitan center of several hundred thousand population. In contemplating her marketing strategy, she was certain that the different incomes, educational backgrounds, and tastes of the potential customers in her city meant that various groups of these women were using sharply different buying methods for dresses. Her initial problem was to determine, by use of the consumer buying habit matrix, what proportion of her potential market bought dresses in what manner.

By drawing on her own experience, discussions with other retailers in the area, census and other market data, the former buyer estimated that her potential market was divided, according to the matrix, in the proportions [shown in Table 1].

This analysis revealed four market segments that she believed were worth further consideration. (In an actual situation, each of

TABLE 1 *Proportion of Potential Dress Market in Each Matrix Cell*

Buying habit	% of market
Convenience store—convenience good	0
Convenience store—shopping good	3
Convenience store—specialty good	20
Shopping store—convenience good	0
Shopping store—shopping good	35
Shopping store—specialty good	2
Specialty store—convenience good	0
Specialty store—shopping good	25
Specialty store—specialty good	15
	100

these four should be further divided into submarket segments according to other possible factors such as age, income, dress size required, location of residence, etc.) Her next task was to determine the type of marketing mix which would most effectively appeal to each of these segments. The information for these decisions was derived from the characteristics of consumer behavior associated with each of the defined segments. The following is a brief description of her assessment of how elements of the marketing mix ought to be weighted in order to formulate a strategy for each segment.

A Strategy for Each Segment

To appeal to the convenience store-specialty good segment she felt that the two most important elements in the mix should be a highly accessible location and selection of widely-accepted brand merchandise. Of somewhat lesser importance, she found, were depth of assortment, personal selling, and price. Minimal emphasis should be given to store promotion and facilities.

She reasoned that the shopping store-shopping good requires a good central location, emphasis on price, and a broad assortment. She ranked store promotion, accepted brand names and personal selling as secondary. Store facilities would, once again, receive minor emphasis.

The specialty store-shopping good market would, she believed, have to be catered to with an exceptionally strong assortment, a high level of personal selling and more elaborate store facilities. Less emphasis would be needed upon prominent brand names, store promotions, and price. Location was of minor importance.

The specialty store-specialty good category, she thought, would require a marketing mix heavily emphasizing personal selling and highly elaborate store facilities and service. She also felt that prominent brand names would be required, but that these would probably have to include the top names in fashion, including labels from Paris. Depth of assortment would be secondary, while least emphasis would be placed upon store promotion, price, and location.

Evaluation of Alternatives

The final step in the analysis required the former dress buyer to assess her abilities to implement any one of these strategies, given the degree of competition existing in each segment. Her considerations were as follows. With regard to the specialty store–specialty good market, she was unprepared to make the investment in store facilities and services that she felt would be necessary. She also thought, since a considerable period of time would probably be required for her to build up the necessary reputation, that this strategy involved substantial risk. Lastly, she believed that her experience in buying high fashion was somewhat limited and that trips to European fashion centers would prove burdensome.

She also doubted her ability to cater to the specialty store–shopping good market, principally because she knew that her store would not be large enough to carry the necessary assortment depth. She felt that this same factor would limit her in attempting to sell to the shopping store–shopping good market as well. Despite the presence of the large market in this segment, she believed that she would not be able to create sufficient volume in her proposed quarters to enable her to compete effectively with the local department store and several large department stores in the neighboring city.

The former buyer believed her best opportunity was in selling to the convenience store–specialty good segment. While there were already two other stores in her city which were serving this segment, she believed that a number of important brands were still not represented. Her past contacts with resources led her to believe that she would stand an excellent chance of securing a number of these lines. By stocking these brands, she thought that she could capture a considerable number of local customers who currently were purchasing them in the large city. In this way, she believed, she would avoid the full force of local competition.

Decision

The conclusion of the former buyer to use her store to appeal to the convenience store–specialty good segment represents the culmination to the process of analysis suggested here. It shows how the use of the three-by-three matrix of consumer buying habits may aid the retailer in developing his marketing strategy. It is a device which can isolate the important market segments. It provides further help in enabling the retailer to associate the various types of consumer behavior with those elements of the marketing mix to which they are sensitive. Finally, the analysis forces the retailer to assess the probability of his success in attempting to use the necessary strategy in order to sell each possible market.

22

The Marketing Characteristics of Goods

Leo V. Aspinwall

The characteristics of goods theory attempts to arrange all marketable goods in systematic and useful fashion. It has been tested both in the classroom and in application to business problems. It provides a perspective and frame of reference for organizing marketing facts and for weighing marketing decisions. Previous efforts included the three-way classification of products as convenience goods, shopping goods, and specialty goods. The characteristics of goods theory sets up a continuous scale rather than discrete classes and defines the criteria by which any product can be assigned to an appropriate place on the scale. All of these criteria lend themselves to objective measurement, at least potentially. By contrast, it would be rather difficult to distinguish a shopping good from a convenience good in positive, quantitative terms.

The marketing characteristics of a product determine the most appropriate and economical method for distributing it. To fix its position on the scale, representing the variation in these characteristics, is to take the first major step toward understanding its marketing requirements. To know these characteristics is to be able to predict with a high degree of reliability how a product will be distributed, since most products conform to the pattern. Serious departure from the theoretical expectations will almost certainly indicate the need

Reprinted from Leo V. Aspinwall, *Four Marketing Theories* (Boulder, Colorado: University of Colorado, 1961), by permission of the author.

Leo V. Aspinwall is professor emeritus at the University of Colorado, having headed the marketing and real estate division for 27 years. Before teaching, he served in the Bureau of Business Research at that university. Professor Aspinwall received his B.A. degree from the University of South Dakota and his M.B.A. at the University of Colorado. He is noted for his perceptive analyses of marketing phenomena.

for change and improvement in distribution methods. These considerations apply both to physical distribution and to the parallel problem of communications including the choice of promotional media and appeals. It follows also that goods having similar characteristics call for similar handling. Finally, if precise weights or values could be assigned to each characteristic, their combination would determine the unique position of a product on the marketing scale.

CHARACTERISTICS OF GOODS THEORY

The problem-solving process often leads into totally unfamiliar areas which sometimes bring us to a dead end. Only occasionally do these probing excursions uncover new combinations of old ideas that have some relevance to the problem in hand. When such combinations prove to be useful the mind is quick to employ such combinations again for problems of the same general type, so that repeated use tends to formulate a framework of reference which can be readily used for problem solving. Into the framework thus formulated the problem can be fitted so that the relationship of the integral parts can be observed. This may well be a mental sorting operation which seeks to classify problems into similar groups for greater efficiency in the unending task of problem solving.

The characteristics of goods theory is the result of one of these mental excursions, and its repeated use has had the effect of crystalizing the combination of old ideas into a fairly stabilized form. The theory has been revised from time to time through the constructive criticism of my colleagues, but whether it will ever be in final form is doubtful, since the dynamic character of all marketing activity is such that changes are more likely than anything else. Somehow the thought of achieving a final state of equilibrium is rather frightening.

CHARACTERISTICS OF GOODS

The problem of weights or values being assigned to these individual characteristics has been one of the real difficulties in giving the theory a mathematical setting. So far that objective has not been fully achieved. We have been obliged to deal with relative values which might be considered as an intermediary stage in the theory's development. The analogy of an electric circuit may eventually prove useful in formulating

CHART I *Characteristics of Goods Theory*

	Color Classification		
Characteristics	Red Goods	Orange Goods	Yellow Goods
Replacement Rate	High	Medium	Low
Gross Margin	Low	Medium	High
Adjustment	Low	Medium	High
Time of Consumption	Low	Medium	High
Searching Time	Low	Medium	High

a mathematical approach. Getting goods distributed is not unlike moving an electric current through resistance factors, each of which takes a part of the gross margin. When the good finally reaches the consumer's hands, ready for consumption, all of the gross margin has been used. Looking at this idea from the consumer end, the amount of the gross margin the consumer has given up in order to enjoy the utilities the good provides is, in fact, the voltage that the electric current must have in order to pass through the resistance factors and finally reach the consumer.

The decision as to the number and kinds of characteristics to be used was approached by setting up tests which these characteristics should meet. These criteria are:

1. Every characteristic selected must be applicable to every good.
2. Every characteristic selected must be relatively measurable in terms of its relationship to every good.
3. Every characteristic must be logically related to all the other characteristics.

This brings us to the point of defining a characteristic. A characteristic is a distinguishing quality of a good relative to its stable performance in a market and its relationship to the consumers for whom it has want-satisfying capacity. Under this definition five characteristics have been selected, each of which must in turn be defined. These are:

1. Replacement rate.—This characteristic is defined as *the rate at which a good is purchased and consumed by users in order to provide the satisfaction a consumer expects from the product.* The replacement rate is associated with the concept of a flow or movement of units of a good from producer to ultimate consumer. The idea is somewhat akin to a turnover rate, except that our understanding of turnover is related to the number of times per year that an average stock of goods is bought and sold. Replacement rate as used here is consumer-oriented. It asks how often the consumer buys shoes—once each month,

once each six months, or once each year? It does not ask whether or not the shoes have been consumed, but only how often the market must be ready to make shoes available for consumers. This characteristic differentiates the rate or flow of different goods and attempts to envision the market mechanism that will meet the aggregate needs of consumers. This is marketing in motion as dictated by consumer purchasing power.

It may be helpful to introduce a few illustrative cases and at the same time show how the idea of relative measurement is used. Loaves of bread, cigarettes, packets of matches all have high replacement rates in terms of relative measurement. Some people consume bread more often than others, yet the average frequency of all bread eaters in a consumption area determines the replacement rate for bread. In comparison with grand pianos, bread has a high replacement rate and grand pianos have a low replacement rate. Men's shirts and ready-to-wear have medium replacement rates when compared to bread and grand pianos. Here we can visualize fast moving streams, slow moving streams and moderately moving streams of different kinds of goods, each with its characteristically different rate of replacement.

2. Gross margin.—The definition of gross margin as used here is not different from its use in marketing generally. *The money sum which is the difference between the laid in cost and the final realized sales price* is the gross margin. It is brought to mind at once that there are several gross margins involved in moving goods from factory gates to final consumer. What is meant here is the summation of all the gross margins involved. It is that total money sum necessary to move a good from point of origin to final consumer. It might be thought of as channel costs or as the fare a good must pay to reach its destination. If the amount of gross margin is less than the fare needed, the good will not reach destination. The calculation of the gross margin is a market-oriented function which is based, in the final analysis, on the amount of money a consumer will exchange for a particular good. If the consumer elects to pay a money fund which is less than the production cost and the necessary marketing costs, the good will not be marketed because the gross margin is too low in relation with the other characteristics. The availability of gross margin is the force that operates our marketing system. Suppose a consumer wishes to procure a pack of cigarettes from a vending machine and the machine is set to operate when a twenty-five cent piece is inserted in the slot. Nothing would happen if a ten-cent piece were dropped into the slot, except that the ten-cent piece would be returned to the customer. The gross

margin contained in the twenty-five-cent piece was large enough to bring the consumer the cigarettes he needed.

This may be the appropriate place to call attention to the fact that whenever the flow of goods is arrested for whatever reason, costs begin to take a larger share of the planned gross margin and may actually prevent a good from reaching the final market. Such losses as may have been incurred in the stoppage must be borne by someone, and the calculations made by marketing men are such that loss situations cannot be tolerated, and the flow of goods will be stopped. The secondary action in such a case is that a money flow back to the producer also stops, which in turn closes down production. While this may be oversimplified, it does emphasize the importance of gross margin to the whole economic process.

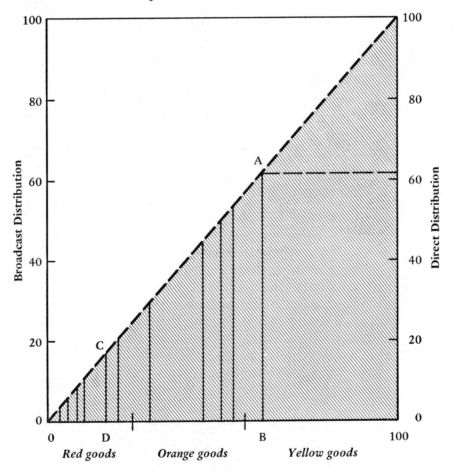

CHART II *Schematic Array of a Few Selected Goods (Plotted in terms of yellow goods)*

Certain types of goods are necessarily involved in storage by reason of their seasonal production. Storage assumes the availability of the needed amount of gross margin to pay these costs, otherwise such goods would not be stored. Whatever takes place during the movement of goods from producer to consumer affects gross margin.

This is the first opportunity to test these characteristics against the criteria set up for their selection. It has been shown that the replacement rate is applicable to all goods and that the replacement rate is relatively measurable. Lastly the question must be asked: Is the replacement rate related to gross margin? This is without doubt the most important relationship of all those needing demonstration in this theory. The relationship is inverse. Whenever replacement rate is high gross margin is low and, conversely, when replacement rate is low then gross margin is high. Thus, when goods move along at a lively clip the costs of moving them are decreased. This relationship brings to mind some economic laws which bear on the situation. The theory of decreasing costs seems to apply here to show that marketing is a decreasing-cost industry. This might be stated as follows: As the number of units distributed increases, the cost per unit distributed tends to decrease up to the optimum point. Mass distribution insofar as marketing is concerned has important possibilities. This is amply demonstrated in modern marketing operations. Goods handling in modern warehouses has been studied in this light and warehousing costs have been decreased, which in turn has expedited the flow of goods into consumer's hands. Here again, economic laws operate to induce the seller to pass on savings in marketing costs. Small decreases in gross margin tend to bring forth a disproportionately larger market response.

The relationship of replacement rate and gross margin has thus far been concerned with the increasing side of the relationship. When replacement rate is low and gross margin is relatively higher, it is not difficult to envision higher marketing costs. Almost at once it can be seen that selling costs will be relatively higher per unit. The gross margin on the individual sale of a grand piano or major appliance must bear the cost of direct sales, including salaries and commissions for salesmen who negotiate with prospective buyers and very often make home demonstrations. The fact that shipping costs are higher in moving pianos is well known. If car-lot shipments are used there are likely to be some storage costs involved, and this additional cost must come out of gross margin. It can be shown that high-value goods such as jewelry and silverware reflect this relationship in much the same way. This inverse relationship between replacement rate and gross margin strikes a balance when goods with a medium rate of replacement are involved.

3. Adjustment.—An important characteristic which pertains to all goods and which has been named "adjustment" is defined as *services applied to goods in order to meet the exact needs of the consumer.* These services may be performed as the goods are being produced or at any intermediate point in the channel of distribution or at the point of sale. Adjustment as a characteristic of all goods reflects the meticulous demands of consumers that must be met in the market. Even in such goods as quarts of milk there is evidence of adjustment. Some consumers demand milk with low fat content, others require milk with high fat content, to name but one of the items of adjustment which pertains to milk. The matter of size of package, homogenized or regular, and even the matter of added vitamins come under adjustment. The services applied to milk are performed in the processing plant in anticipation of the adjustments the consumer may require. Here slight changes in the form or in size of package are adjustments performed in advance of the sale of the product. This type of adjustment imposes additional costs involving somewhat larger inventories and the use of a greater amount of space, with all that this implies. It can be easily understood that costs are involved whenever adjustments are performed, so that additional amounts of gross margin are necessary. Adjustments made at the point of production become manufacturing costs which only mildly affect the marketing operation, so that the measured amount of adjustment in the marketing channel is relatively low.

Goods with a high replacement rate have low adjustment, but the reverse is true when goods have low replacement rates. Goods with a medium replacement rate have a medium amount of adjustment. Here the inverse relationship between replacement rate and adjustment has been demonstrated, as well as the direct relationship between gross margin and adjustment.

4. Time of consumption.—Time of consumption as a characteristic of goods can be defined as *the measured time of consumption during which the good gives up the utility desired.* This characteristic is related to the replacement rate to a considerable degree, since goods with a low time of consumption are likely to have a high rate of replacement. The inverse relationship is true, but a low time of consumption does not mean that a repetitive purchasing program is maintained by the same consumer. Aspirin gives up its utility in the short period of time during which it is being consumed, but a purchase replacement may not occur until another headache needs attention. The idea of consumption time is more closely related to non-durable goods both in the consumer and industrial classes.

The time of consumption characteristic pertains to all goods, and the amount of this time is relatively measurable, which satisfies the criterion of relationship to all goods and the criterion of relative measurability. The final criterion of relationship to all other characteristics is also met in that low time of consumption is directly related to adjustment and gross margin and inversely related to the rate of replacement.

5. Searching time.—The characteristic of searching time can be defined as *the measure of average time and distance from the retail store* and hence convenience the consumer is afforded by market facilities. Suppose the need to purchase a package of cigarettes comes up for immediate attention for a consumer. The amount of effort exerted on his part to procure the needed cigarettes is correlated with the amount of searching time. In this case the amount of inconvenience suffered is usually very low since the market has reacted to the fact that there is a wide and insistent demand for cigarettes. To meet this demand, points of purchase are established wherever large numbers of potential customers are to be found. The result of such market action is that cigarettes can be purchased at many different places and in many different institutions, and the searching time is low. The old idea expressed in another way: consumers are motivated by a drive for convenience. Out of these relationships we have come to recognize "the span of convenience" for each product. Consumers cannot easily be forced to expend an amount of time and energy that is disproportionate to the satisfaction they expect to receive from the goods in question.

It can easily be seen that for certain goods the searching time will be low, while for certain other goods the searching time will be much larger. The amount of time and energy expended by a customer in the process of furnishing a new home would be very great and therefore, searching time would be correspondingly high. There is the need for examining the offerings of many stores, and even though these stores may be located fairly close to each other, in all probability, they will be located at some distance from the consumer's home. The reality of this situation is expressed in the characteristics of the goods. Searching time can be readily envisioned by the fact that we have many more market outlets for cigarettes than we do for grand pianos or furniture and, therefore, market availability for cigarettes is low and for pianos it is high.

Searching time is directly related to gross margin, adjustment, and time of consumption, and is inversely related to replacement rate. Searching time as a characteristic of goods pertains to all goods and for each and every good it is relatively measurable.

This information can now be fitted into a chart which will keep the relationships of the characteristics of goods in position as they pertain to all goods. This chart will show that goods with the same relative amounts of these five characteristics fall into the same broad classifications. Arbitrary names can be fitted to these broad classifications for greater convenience in conveying ideas about goods and the various ways in which they are distributed.

COLOR CONCEPT

This chart introduces an additional element into the characteristics of good theory: the color classification. The idea that goods with similar characteristics are similar to each other lends itself to the establishment of three large classes of goods that can be named in such a manner as to convey the idea of an array of goods. The choice of color names may be inept in some respects, but the idea of an array of goods, based upon the sum of the relative values of characteristics of goods, is important. The length of light rays for red, orange, and yellow, in that order, is an array of light rays representing a portion of the spectrum. For our present purpose it is more convenient to use the three colors only, rather than the seven of the full spectrum. The idea of an infinite graduation of values can be envisioned by blending these colors from red to yellow with orange in between. This is the idea we wish to convey as concerning all goods.

The sum of the characteristics for each and every good is different, and the sum of characteristics for red goods is lower than the sum of the characteristics for yellow goods. The chart shows red goods to have four low values and one of a high value, while yellow goods have four high values and one low.

It is useful to stress this tension between replacement rate and the other four marketing characteristics, since they all tend to decrease as replacement rate increases. That is equivalent to saying that as demand for a product increases, marketing methods tend to develop which reflect economies in the various aspects of marketing costs. It is easily possible, of course, to transform replacement rate into its inverse for use in arriving at a weighted index of the five characteristics. If replacement rate were expressed as the average number of purchases in a year, the inverse measure would be the average number of days between purchases. This measure would be low for red goods and high for yellow, like all of the other characteristics.

A schematic diagram can now be set up which represents all

possible graduations in goods from red through orange to yellow. As shown in Chart II, page [299], a simple percentage scale from 0 to 100 is laid out on both coordinates. It is true that the weighted value for any product could be laid out on a single line. Yet there is an advantage in the two-dimensional chart for the purpose of visualizing an array of goods. The scale of values thus really consists of all the points on the diagonal line in the accompanying chart. Since there is an infinite number of points on any line segment, the scale provides for an infinite array of goods. If the chart were large enough, vertical lines could be drawn with each line representing a product now on the market. Even after these lines were drawn there would still remain an infinite number of positions in between. Many of these positions might serve to identify goods which have been withdrawn from the market or others which might be introduced in the future.

Line AB represents a good having an ordinate value of 63, indicating the sum of the characteristics of this good. In the general classification it has 63 percent yellow characteristics and 37 percent red characteristics. Translated into marketing terms, this good might be ladies' ready-to-wear dresses sold through department stores and shipped directly from the factory to these stores in the larger cities. The smaller cities are served by wholesalers who carry small stocks of these goods along with other dry goods items. Thus the marketing channels utilized for distributing this good would be direct to large department store accounts and semi-broadcast through specialty wholesalers serving smaller city accounts.

Line CD in its position near the red end of the scale has a yellow characteristics value of 15 and a red value of 85, which puts this good in the large classification as a red good. The sum of the characteristics value in the scale 0 to 100 is 85 percent red. This might well be a soap product which is sold mainly by broadcast distribution using a broker, wholesaler, retailer channel. The 15 percent yellow characteristic might indicate specialty salesmen's activity involving factory drop shipments. The latter type of distribution is more direct and might account for the 15 percent of direct distribution from the factory to the retailer.

The position of a good on the color scale is not static. Most products fall in the yellow classification when they are first introduced. As they become better known and come to satisfy a wider segment of consumer demand, the replacement rate increases and the good shifts toward the red end of the scale. Thus there is a red shift in marketing which offers a rather far-fetched analogy to the red shift in astronomy which is associated with the increasing speed of movement of heavenly bodies. There is also an opposing tendency in marketing, however, resulting from the constant shrinking of gross margin as a good moves toward the red end of the scale. Marketing organizations, in the effort to maintain their gross margin, may improve or differentiate a good which has moved into the red category, so that some of these new varieties swing all the way back into yellow. Thereafter the competitive drive for volume serves to accelerate the movement toward the red end of the scale again.

CONCLUSION

The characteristics of goods theory provides a basis for making marketing policy decisions concerning goods of all kinds and gives an insight into the way in which marketing channels can be used. The use of the broad color classification provides a basis for more exact communication in dealing with marketing problems.

23

Parallel Systems of Promotion and Distribution

Leo V. Aspinwall

The sponsor of a product must decide how it is to be promoted and what channels to use for its physical distribution. He is confronted with a variety of possibilities both for stimulating demand and for moving his product to the consumer. It turns out that there is a parallel relationship between these two aspects of the marketing problem with a distribution system and its appropriate counterpart in promotion usually occurring together. This pairing of systems occurs because the promotion and distribution requirements of a product are both dependent on the marketing characteristics of the goods. [Article 22 in this book] explained how goods might be arrayed according to their marketing characteristics into groups designated as red, orange, and yellow. It was further shown that this array could be translated into a numerical scale and presented in simple graphic form. The purpose of the present article is to indicate how the position of a product on this scale can be used to identify the parallel systems of promotion and distribution which should be used in marketing the product.

THE PARALLEL SYSTEMS THEORY

This set of ideas has come to be designated as the parallel systems theory. It is the kind of theory which is intended to be helpful in

Reprinted from Leo V. Aspinwall, *Four Marketing Theories* (Boulder, Colorado: University of Colorado, 1961) by permission of the author.

Leo V. Aspinwall is professor emeritus at the University of Colorado, having headed the marketing and real estate division for 27 years. Before teaching, he served in the Bureau of Business Research at that university. Professor Aspinwall received his B.A. degree from the University of South Dakota and his M.B.A. at the University of Colorado. He is noted for his perceptive analyses of marketing phenomena.

resolving fundamental practical issues in marketing. Theory alone cannot settle all the details of a marketing plan. It may save much time and effort by indicating the starting point for planning and the appropriate matching of systems of promotion and distribution. The gross margin earned on a product provides the fund which must cover the costs of marketing distribution and marketing promotion. The management of this fund involves many of the most critical decisions with which marketing executives have to deal. Even slight errors of judgment in this regard may spell the difference between profit and loss.

The parallel systems theory begins with a simple thesis which may be stated as follows: The characteristics of goods indicate the manner of their physical distribution and the manner of promotion must parallel that physical distribution. Thus, we have parallel systems, one for physical distribution and one for promotion. The movement of goods and the movement of information are obviously quite different processes. It was to be expected that specialized facilities would be developed for each function. The fact that these developments take place along parallel lines is fundamental to an understanding of marketing. A few special terms must be introduced at this point for use in discussing parallel systems.

A channel for the physical distribution of goods may be either a short channel or a long channel. The shortest channel, of course, is represented by the transaction in which the producer delivers the product directly to its ultimate user. A long channel is one in which the product moves through several stages of location and ownership as from the factory to a regional warehouse, to the wholesaler's warehouse, to a retail store, and finally to the consumer. The parallel concepts in promotion may be compared to contrasting situations in electronic communication. On the one hand there is the closed circuit through which two people can carry on a direct and exclusive conversation with each other. On the other hand there is broadcast communication such as radio and television whereby the same message can be communicated to many people simultaneously.

In general, long channels and broadcast promotion are found together in marketing while short channels and closed circuit or direct promotion are found together. The parallel systems theory attempts to show how these relationships arise naturally out of the marketing characteristics of the goods.

CHARACTERISTICS OF GOODS AND MARKETING SYSTEMS

It will be remembered from the preceding article that goods were arrayed according to their marketing characteristics as red, orange, and yellow. Marketing systems can be arrayed in similar and parallel fashion. Red goods call for long channels and broadcast promotion. Yellow goods call for short channels and closed circuit promotion. Orange goods are intermediate as to their marketing characteristics and, hence, are intermediate as to the kind of distribution and promotion systems which they require. There is a continuous gradation from red to yellow and from broadcast to direct methods of marketing.

One of the fundamental marketing characteristics of goods is replacement rate. That is the frequency with which the average consumer in the market buys the product or replenishes the supply of it carried in his household inventory. Red goods are goods with a high replacement rate. A market transaction which occurs with high frequency lends itself to standardization and specialization of function. The movement of goods and the movement of information each becomes clearly marked and separate. Opportunity arises for a number of specialized marketing agencies to participate in distribution, and the result is what has been called the "long channel." Messages to the ultimate user become as standardized as the product itself. This type of information and persuasion does not need to follow the long distribution channel from step to step in its transmission from producer to consumer. Such messages are broadcast to consumers through both electronic and printed advertising media which provide a more appropriate channel.

Yellow goods are low in replacement rate and high in other marketing characteristics such as adjustment. Requirements for this class of goods tend to vary from one user to another. Adjustment embraces a variety of means by which goods are fitted to individual requirements. The marketing process remains relatively costly and a large percentage of gross margin necessarily goes along with high adjustment. The opportunity for standardization and specialization is slight compared to that of red goods. Physical movement and promotion remain more closely associated, with a two-way communication concerning what is available and what is needed finally resulting in the delivery of the custom-made product. A transaction between a man and his tailor would illustrate this type of marketing. Many kinds of industrial equipment are specially designed for the given user and would also be at the extreme yellow end of the scale. The short channel is prevalent in such situations and all promotion or related communication moves through a closed circuit.

Many products lie in the middle range which has been designated as orange goods. They have been produced to standard specifications but with the knowledge that they will have to be adapted in greater or less degree in each individual installation. The replacement rate is high enough to offer moderate opportunity for standardization and specialization. At least one intermediary is likely to enter the picture, such as an automobile dealer buying from the manufacturer and selling to the consumer or an industrial distributor serving as a channel between two manufacturers. The car sold to customers may be of the same model and yet be substantially differentiated to meet individual preferences as to color and accessories. Broadcast media are used in promotion but not on the same scale relatively as for soaps or cigarettes. The industrial distributor is often supported in his efforts by specialty salesmen or sales engineers employed by the manufacturer. Advertising of a semi-broadcast character is likely to be used. That is to say that messages are specially prepared for various segments of the market for which the appeal of the product is expected to be somewhat different. This approach lies between the standardized message to all users on the one hand and the individualized closed circuit negotiation on the other.

One qualification which may properly be suggested at this point is that marketing systems are not quite so flexible as this discussion suggests, but must conform to one type or another. Thus a channel for physical distribution could have two steps or three steps but not two and a half. Nevertheless the picture of continuous variation along a scale is generally valid because of the combinations which are possible. A producer may sell part of his output through wholesalers who service retailers and sell the remainder direct to retailers. The proportions may vary over time so that one channel presently becomes dominant rather than the other. Similarly broadcast promotion may gradually assume greater importance in the marketing mix even though a large but declining amount of adjustment is involved in some individual sales.

MOVEMENT OF GOODS AND MOVEMENT
OF INFORMATION

The schematic relationship between goods and marketing systems is shown in Chart I. This simple diagram depicts the parallels which have been discussed. It will be noted that the segment of the line allowed is greater for orange goods than for red goods and greater for yellow than for orange. It is a readily observable fact that the number of separate and distinct items in any stock of goods increases as replacement rate decreases. A drug store, for example, has to sell more separate items to achieve the same volume of sales as a grocery store. An exclusive dress shop will need more variation in styles and

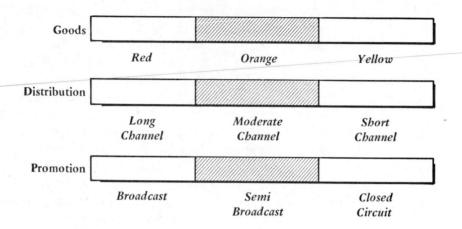

CHART 1 *Relationship Between Goods and Marketing Systems*

models than a store operating in the popular price range. Paint brushes, files, or grinding wheels will be made up in a great multiplicity of specifications to serve the industrial market as compared to the few numbers which suffice for the household user. Red goods by their very nature are those in which a single item is bought frequently because it meets the requirements of many occasions for use while in the yellow goods more numerous items with less frequent sales are required for a more accurate matching of diverse and differentiated use situations.

The second chart is intended to demonstrate the relationship between goods and the methods of distribution and promotion. It is not intended to show an accurate mathematical relationship since the data from which it is constructed are not mathematically accurate, but it does implement understanding of the problems with which marketing executives must deal. The reasoning is deductive, moving from the general to the specific and provides a quick basis for reaching an answer which can readily be adjusted to a specific case. The readings from the diagram are in complementary percentages that must be accepted as rough measurements of the kinds and amounts of distribution and promotion. Long channel distribution and broadcast promotion are grouped together as related elements of the marketing mix and designated as "broadcast" for the sake of simplicity. The line representing these two elements in combination slopes downward to the right since this type of expenditure can be expected to be relatively high for red goods and relatively low for yellow goods. Similarly short channel distribution and closed circuit communication are thrown together under the designation of "direct." The line representing direct promotion and distribution slopes upward from left to right.

APPLICATION TO A MANAGEMENT PROBLEM

A short time ago a project was undertaken for a well-known manufacturer whose operation is such that the range of products his company manufactures covers the scale from red goods to yellow goods. In following the reasoning of the characteristics of goods theory and the parallel systems theory he was able to locate a certain product in its position on the base line. He drew the ordinate representing this product and found from the diagram that the distribution indicated was a modified direct distribution and that accordingly a considerable amount

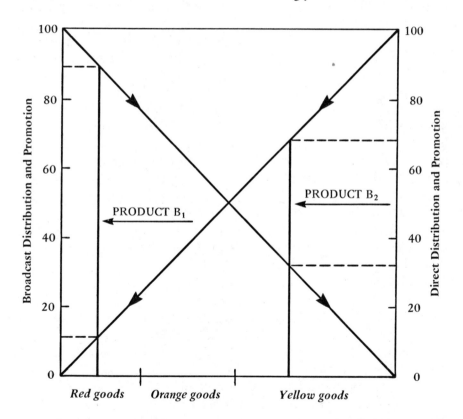

CHART 2 Parallel Systems Theory

of direct promotion should be used. In reviewing what actually was being done with this product he knew that promotion was mostly broadcast while the distribution was a modified direct. Thus, promotion and distribution were not running parallel and such a finding for this product provided a substantial explanation of the poor performance this product was making. Research had confirmed that it was an excellent product and that it was priced correctly so that a reasonable volume of sales should have been expected. The planned sales for the product were not realized and to correct this situation a more extensive broadcast promotion program was launched, but from this program little or no increase in sales was realized. At this point the manufacturer decided that it would be worth a try to follow out the indicated promotional and distributional plan shown in the parallel systems theory analysis. A program of direct promotion was initiated and results were immediately forthcoming. The full sales expectations were realized and the manufacturer decided to establish a special division to handle the product which since that time has produced even more sales at costs considerably below the estimated costs.

A somewhat closer look at this case revealed that broadcast promotion was reaching thousands of people who were in no way qualified users of the product and that the type of advertising message was such that qualified users were unable to specify the product even if they wished to do so. A careful study of the problem showed that the direct promotion had produced all of the sales results. Thus the cost of the broadcast promotion had to be borne by qualified users and the result was a higher price than would have been needed if direct promotional means had been employed. The final result of this operation was that prices were lowered and the profit position for the manufacturer and all institutions in the distribution channel was improved.

Product B_2 in the diagram represents the product discussed in the case above located in its correct position. Reading the ordinate value in the vertical scale shows that the product it represents should be distributed 69 percent direct and that promotion should also be 69 percent direct. The complementary 31 percent reading shown indicates that 31 percent of the distribution should be broadcast and 31 percent of the promotion should be of the broadcast type. Product B_1 shown on the diagram is product B_2 as it was incorrectly located on the base line array of goods. The incorrect location was based on a measurement of the method of promotion that was being used. Actually this product was being distributed correctly by a modified direct method, and consequently consumers who might have been influenced to use the product had no means by which to exercise their wishes; the product was not available in retail stores in such a way as to make it readily available to qualified customers.

By making analyses of products and their distribution and promotional programs, it will be found that many products are not in conformity with the parallel systems theory, and yet seem to be successful products. This would not of itself disprove the theory. Such results might indicate that better results might be had if the programs were modified in the direction indicated by the theory. This can often be done at a comparatively small cost by using test sales areas in which the adjustment can be made without affecting the national system in which the product may be operating. The results from such experimentation should confirm the analysis made under the parallel systems theory. A large amount of case material has been collected on the parallel systems theory but there seems to be an almost endless variety of cases and there is a need for constantly studying the problem in the light of the improvements in communications and distribution.

CONCLUSION

A further definition for broadcast promotion seems to be needed as well as for direct promotion. Whenever promotional means are used, without knowledge in advance of the identity of prospective users, the promotional means is considered to be broadcast. The firm employing broadcast promotional means relies upon the chance contact with potential customers for the product or service. The broadcast distributional means for such a product are so arranged that the customer for the product who has been reached by this type of promotion can exercise his choice conveniently and quickly. Retail stores are available within a short radius of the consumer who may wish to purchase the product. Thus, the sales gap is shortened both as to time and distance and the effectiveness of the broadcast means of promotion is enhanced. The key fact that makes this type of marketing economical is that while the prospective users are unidentified, they represent a large proportion of the general public which will be exposed to the broadcast message. The opposite of broadcast promotion is direct promotion. The definition of direct promotion turns on the fact that the recipient of the direct communication is known in advance, so that the message reaches the intended purchaser by name and address or by advance qualification of the prospect as to his need and ability to purchase the product. The most direct means would be a salesman who calls upon a selected prospect whose address and name is known in advance, and where judgment has been passed upon his need for the product, and whose ability to pay for the product has been ascertained. The next in order might be a direct first-class letter or telegram sent to a prospect. Then perhaps door-to-door selling or mailing to persons found on selected mailing lists. These selected means of direct promotion used show a widening sales gap between the customer and the product. It is readily seen that broadcast promotion creates the widest sales gap. At the same time it can readily be seen that the marketing radius over which the customer may have to search for the product is increased. Compensating for this increased radius are the more intensive means of promotion that result from direct promotion, which will induce the customer willingly to undertake greater inconveniences of time and distance in order to procure the product.

These definitions relate directly back to the characteristics of goods theory. Whenever a high replacement is involved it becomes physically impossible to effect distribution by direct means. Such a situation calls for mass selling and mass movement of goods wherein all economies of volume selling and goods handling are brought into play. The low gross margin on the individual transaction requires that the aggregate gross margin resulting from mass selling be ample to get the job done. It seems ludicrous to think of fashioning cigarettes to the consumers' needs at the point of sale, putting on filters and adjusting lengths to king size. The gross margin required to do such a job would put cigarettes in the price class of silverware and the number of people who could purchase on that basis would be very small. But mounting a diamond in a special setting is not at all ludicrous, because the gross margin available is large enough to undertake such adjustment. It would be redundant to go through the whole list of characteristics since it is perfectly clear what the relationships would be.

These two theories are excellent marketing tools and aid materially in understanding the marketing processes and their interactions. At the same time they may become dangerous tools in the hands of those who are not skilled in marketing. Even the experienced practitioners need to be fully cognizant of the technological advances as they occur and how these advances affect marketing processes. Skill in use of these tools should increase with experience in applying them to actual marketing situations.

24

The Wheel of Retailing

Stanley C. Hollander

"The wheel of retailing" is the name Professor Malcolm P. McNair has suggested for a major hypothesis concerning patterns of retail development. This hypothesis holds that new types of retailers usually enter the market as low-status, low-margin, low-price operators. Gradually they acquire more elaborate establishments and facilities, with both increased investments and higher operating costs. Finally they mature as high-cost, high-price merchants, vulnerable to newer types who, in turn, go through the same pattern. Department-store merchants, who originally appeared as vigorous competitors to the smaller retailers and who have now become vulnerable to discount house and supermarket competition, are often cited as prime examples of the wheel pattern.[1]

Many examples of conformity to this pattern can be found. Nevertheless, we may ask: (1) Is this hypothesis valid for all retailing under all conditions? (2) How accurately does it describe total American retail development? (3) What factors cause wheel-pattern changes in retail institutions?

The following discussion assembles some of the slender empirical evidence available that might shed some light on these three questions: In attempting to answer the third question, a number of hypotheses

Reprinted from the *Journal of Marketing,* published by the American Marketing Association (July, 1960), pp. 37-42.

Stanley C. Hollander is professor of marketing at Michigan State University. He has been an analyst for a chain of retail stores and has taught at the Universities of Buffalo, Pennsylvania, and Minnesota. His published work is in the field of retailing, and he holds a B.S. from New York University, an M.A. from the American University, and a Ph.D. in economics from the University of Pennsylvania. *Explorations in Retailing,* which Professor Hollander edited, is a milestone in the academic progress of the retailing field.

[1]M. P. McNair, "Significant Trends and Developments in the Postwar Period," in A. B. Smith (editor), *Competitive Distribution in a Free, High-Level Economy and Its Implications for the University* (Pittsburgh: University of Pittsburgh Press, 1958), pp. 1-25, at pp. 17-18.

should be considered that marketing students have advanced concerning the forces that have shaped retail development.

TENTATIVE EXPLANATIONS OF THE WHEEL

(A) Retail Personalities. New types of retail institutions are often established by highly aggressive, cost-conscious entrepreneurs who make every penny count and who have no interest in unprofitable frills. But, as P. D. Converse has suggested, these men may relax their vigilance and control over costs as they acquire age and wealth. Their successors may be less competent. Either the innovators or their successors may be unwilling, or unable, to adjust to changing conditions. Consequently, according to this view, deterioration in management causes movement along the wheel.[2]

(B) Misguidance. Hermann Levy has advanced the ingenious, if implausible, explanation that retail trade journals, seduced by profitable advertising from the store equipment and supply industry, coax merchants into superfluous "modernization" and into the installation of overly elaborate facilities.[3]

(C) Imperfect Competition. Although retail trade is often cited as the one type of business that approaches the Adam Smith concept of perfect competition, some economists have argued that retailing actually is a good example of imperfect competition. These economists believe that most retailers avoid direct price competition because of several forces, including resale price maintenance, trade association rules in some countries, and, most important, the fear of immediate retaliation. Contrariwise, the same retailers feel that service improvements, including improvements in location, are not susceptible to direct retaliation by competitors. Hence, through a ratchet process, merchants in any established branch of trade tend to provide increasingly elaborate services at increasingly higher margins.[4]

(D) Excess Capacity. McNair attributes much of the wheel effect to the development of excess capacity, as more and more dealers enter any branch of retail trade.[5] This hypothesis rests upon a imperfect competition assumption, since, under perfect competition excess capacity

---

[2]P. D. Converse, "Mediocrity in Retailing," *Journal of Marketing* (April, 1959), pp. 419–420.

[3]Hermann Levy, *The Shops of Britain* (London: Kegan Paul, Trench, Trubner & Co., 1947), pp. 210–211.

[4]D. L. Shawver, *The Development of Theories of Retail Price Determination* (Urbana: University of Illinois Press, 1956), p. 92.

[5]Same reference as footnote 1.

would simply reduce margins until the excess vendors were eliminated.

(E) Secular Trend. J. B. Jefferys has pointed out that a general, but uneven, long-run increase in the British standard of living provided established merchants with profitable opportunities for trading up. Jefferys thus credits adjustments to changing and wealthier market segments as causing some movement along the wheel. At the same time, pockets of opportunity have remained for new, low-margin operations because of the uneven distribution of living-standard increases.[6]

(F) Illusion. Professor B. Holdren has suggested in a recent letter that present tendencies toward scrambled merchandising may create totally illusory impressions of the wheel phenomenon. Store-wide average margins may increase as new, high-markup lines are added to the product mix, even though the margins charged on the original components of that mix remain unchanged.

DIFFICULTIES OF ANALYSIS

An examination of the actual development of retail institutions here and abroad does shed some light on both the wheel hypothesis and its various explanations. However, a number of significant difficulties hinder the process.

(1) Statements concerning changes in retail margins and expenses are the central core of the wheel hypothesis. Yet valid information on historical retail expense rates is very scarce. Long-run changes in percentage margins probably do furnish fairly reliable clues to expense changes, but this is not true over short or intermediate periods. For example, 1957 furniture-store expense rates were about 5 percentage points higher than their 1949–1951 average, yet gross margins actually declined slightly over the same period.[7]

(2) Historical margin data are somewhat more plentiful, but these also have to be dredged up from fragmentary sources.[8]

(3) Available series on both expenses and margins merely note changes in retailers' outlays and receipts. They do not indicate what caused those changes and they do not report changes in the costs borne by suppliers, consumers, or the community at large.

---

[6] J. B. Jefferys, *Retail Trading in Great Britain*, 1850–1950 (Cambridge: Cambridge University Press, 1954), various pages, especially p. 96.

[7] Cited in Fabian Linden, "Department Store Operations," *Conference Board Business Record* (October, 1958), pp. 410–414, at p. 411.

[8] See Harold Barger, *Distribution's Place in the American Economy Since 1869* (Princeton: Princeton University Press, 1955).

(4) Margin data are usually published as averages that may, and frequently do, mask highly divergent tendencies.

(5) A conceptual difficulty presents an even more serious problem than the paucity of statistics. When we talk about "types" of retailers, we think of classifications based upon ways of doing business and upon differences in price policy. Yet census categories and other systems for reporting retail statistics are usually based upon major differences in commodity lines. For example, the "pineboard" druggists who appeared in the 1930s are a "type" of retailing for our purposes. Those dealers had cruder fixtures, charged lower prices, carried smaller assortments, gave more attention to turnover, and had less interest in prescriptions than did conventional druggists. Yet census reports for drugstores necessarily included all of the pineboards that maintained any sort of prescription department.

Discount houses provide another example of an important, but amorphous, category not reflected in census classifications. The label "discount house" covers a variety of retailers. Some carry stocks, others do not. Some have conventional store facilities, whereas others operate in office buildings, lofts, and warehouses. Some feature electrical appliances and hard goods, while others emphasize soft goods. Some pose as wholesalers, and others are practically indistinguishable from all other popular priced retailers in their fields. Consequently discount dealers' operating figures are likely to be merged into the statistics reported for other appliance, hardware, or apparel merchants.

EXAMPLES OF CONFORMITY

British

British retailing provides several examples of conformity to the wheel pattern. The grocery trade has gone through several wheel-like evolutions, according to a detailed analysis made by F. G. Pennance and B. S. Yamey.[9] Established firms did initiate some changes and some margin reductions, so that the pattern is obscured by many cross currents. But the major changes seem to have been due to the appearance and then the maturation, first, of department-store food counters; then of chain stores; and finally, of cut-price and cash-and-carry stores. Now supermarkets seem to be carrying the pattern through another evolution.[10]

---

[9] F. G. Pennance and B. S. Yamey, "Competition in the Retail Grocery Trade, 1850–1939," *Economica* (March, 1955), pp. 303–317.

[10] "La Methode Americaine," *Time* (November 16, 1959), pp. 105–106.

Jefferys also has noted a general long-run upgrading in both British department stores and chains.[11] Vague complaints in the co-operative press and a decline in consumer dividend rates suggest that wheel-like changes may have occurred in the British co-operative movement.[12]

American

Very little is known about retail margins in this country before the Civil War. Our early retail history seems to have involved the appearance, first, of hawkers, walkers, and peddlers; then, of general stores; next, of specialty stores; and finally, of department stores. Each of these types apparently came in as a lower-margin, lower-price competitor to the established outlets, and thus was consistent with the wheel pattern. We do not know, however, whether there was simply a long-run decline in retail margins through successive improvements in retail efficiency from one type to another (contrary to the wheel pattern), or whether each of the early types was started on a low-margin basis, gradually "up-graded," and so provided room for the next entrant (in accordance with the pattern).

The trends toward increasing margins can be more easily discerned in many branches of retailing after the Civil War. Barger has described increases over the years 1869–1947 among important retail segments, including department stores, mail-order firms, variety stores, and jewelry dealers. He attributes much of the pre–World War I rise in department-store margins to the absorption of wholesaling functions. Changes in merchandise mix, such as the addition of soda fountains and cafeterias to variety stores and the upgrading of mail-order merchandise, seem to have caused some of the other increases. Finally, he believes changes in customer services have been a major force in raising margins.[13] Fabian Linden has extended Barger's observations to note similar 1949–1957 margin increases for department stores, variety chains, and appliance dealers.[14]

Some other examples of at least partial conformity to the wheel pattern may be cited. Many observers feel that both discount-house services and margins have increased substantially in recent years.[15]

[11] Same reference as footnote 6.

[12] "Battle of the Dividend," *Co-operative Review* (August, 1956), p. 183; "Independent Commission's Report," *Co-operative Review* (April, 1958), pp. 84–89; "£52 Million Dividend in 1957," *Co-operative Review* (August, 1958), pp. 171–172.

[13] Same reference as footnote 8, p. 82.

[14] See footnote 7.

[15] D. A. Loehwing, "Resourceful Merchants," *Barron's* (November 17, 1958), p. 3.

One major discount-house operator has stated that he has been able to keep his average markup below 12%, in spite of considerable expansion in his facilities and commodity mix.[16] However, the concensus seems to be that this probably is an exception to the general rule.

A study of gasoline pricing has pointed out how many of the so-called "off-brand" outlets have changed from the "trackside" stations of pre-war days. The trackside dealers typically maintained unattractive and poorly equipped installations, at out-of-the-way locations where unbranded gasoline was sold on a price basis. Today many of them sell well-promoted regional and local brands, maintain attractive, efficient stations, and provide prompt and courteous service. Some still offer cut prices, but many have raised their prices and margins up to or above national brand levels.[17] Over time, many of the pineboard druggists also seem to have become converted to fairly conventional operations.[18]

NON-CONFORMING EXAMPLES

Foreign

In underdeveloped countries, the relatively small middle- and upper-income groups have formed the major markets for "modern" types of retailing. Supermarkets and other modern stores have been introduced in those countries largely at the top of the social and price scales, contrary to the wheel pattern.[19] Some non-conforming examples may also be found in somewhat more industrialized environments. The vigorous price competition that developed among Japanese department stores during the first three decades of this century seems directly contrary to the wheel hypothesis.[20] B. S. Yamey's history of resale price maintenance also reports some price-cutting by traditional, well-established British merchants who departed from the wheel pattern in

[16] S. Masters, quoted in "Three Concepts of Retail Service," *Stores* (July-August, 1959), pp. 18–21.

[17] S. M. Livingston and T. Levitt, "Competition and Retail Gasoline Prices," *The Review of Economics and Statistics* (May, 1959), pp. 119–132, at p. 132.

[18] Paul C. Olsen, *The Marketing of Drug Products* (New Brunswick: Rutgers University Press, 1948), pp. 130–132.

[19] H. S. Hettinger, "Marketing in Persia," *Journal of Marketing* (January, 1951), pp. 289–297; H. W. Boyd, Jr., R. M. Clewett, & R. L. Westfall, "The Marketing Structure of Venezuela," *Journal of Marketing* (April, 1958), pp. 391–397; D. A. Taylor, "Retailing in Brazil," *Journal of Marketing* (July, 1959), pp. 54–58; J. K. Galbraith and R. Holton, *Marketing Efficiency in Puerto Rico* (Cambridge: Harvard University Press, 1955), p. 35.

[20] G. Fukami, "Japanese Department Stores," *Journal of Marketing* (July, 1953), pp. 41–49, at p. 42.

the 1880s and 1890s.[21] Unfortunately, our ignorance of foreign retail history hinders any judgment of the representatives of these examples.

American

Automatic merchandising, perhaps the most "modern" of all American retail institutions, departed from the wheel pattern by starting as a high-cost, high-margin, high-convenience type of retailing.[22] The department-store branch movement and the concomitant rise of planned shopping centers also has progressed directly contrary to the wheel pattern. The early department-store branches consisted of a few stores in exclusive suburbs and some equally high-fashion college and resort shops.

Only in relatively recent years have the branches been adjusted to the changing and more democratic characteristics of the contemporary dormitory suburbs. Suburban shopping centers, too, seem to have appeared first as "Manhasset Miracle Miles" and "Ardmores" before reaching out to the popular price customers. In fact, complaints are still heard that the regional shopping centers have displayed excessive resistance to the entry of really aggressive, low-margin outlets.[23] E. R. A. Seligman and R. A. Love's study of retail pricing in the 1930s suggests that pressures on prices and margins were generated by all types of retailers. The mass retailing institutions, such as the department and chain stores, that had existed as types for many decades were responsible for a goodly portion of the price cutting.[24] As McNair has pointed out, the wheel operated very slowly in the case of department stores.

Finally, Harold Barger has described the remarkable stability of overall distributive margins during the years 1919–1947.[25] Some shifting of distributive work from wholesalers to retailers apparently affected their relative shares of the total margins during this period, but this is not the type of change contemplated by the wheel pattern. Of course, the stability Barger notes conceivably could have been

---

[21] "The Origins of Resale Price Maintenance," *The Economic Journal* (September, 1952), pp. 522–545.

[22] W. S. Fishman, "Sense Makes Dollars," *1959 Directory of Automatic Merchandising* (Chicago: National Automatic Merchandising Association, 1959), p. 52; M. V. Marshall, *Automatic Merchandising* (Boston: Graduate School of Business Administration, Harvard University, 1954), pp. 108–109, 122.

[23] P. E. Smith, *Shopping Centers* (New York: National Retail Merchants' Association, 1956), pp. 11–12; M. L. Sweet, "Tenant-Selection Policies of Regional Shopping Centers," *Journal of Marketing* (April, 1959), pp. 399–404.

[24] E. R. A. Seligman and R. A. Love, *Price Cutting and Price Maintenance* (New York: Harper & Brothers, 1932).

[25] Same reference as footnote 8, pp. ix, x.

the result of a perfectly smooth functioning of the pattern, with the entrance of low-margin innovators providing exactly the right balance for the upcreep of margins in the longer established types. But economic changes do not come in smooth and synchronized fashion, and Barger's data probably should indicate considerably wider oscillations if the wheel really set the mold for all retailing in the post-war period.

CONCLUSIONS

The number of non-conforming examples suggests that the wheel hypothesis is not valid for all retailing. The hypothesis, however, does seem to describe a fairly common pattern in industrialized, expanding economies. Moreover, the wheel is not simply an illusion created by scrambled merchandising, as Holdren suggests. Undoubtedly some of the recent "upcreep" in supermarket average margins is due to the addition of nonfood and other high margin lines. But in recent years the wheel pattern has also been characteristic of department-store retailing, a field that has been relatively unreceptive to new commodity groups.[26]

In some ways, Jefferys' secular trend explanation appears most reasonable. The tendency of many established retailers to reduce prices and margins during depressions suggests also that increases may be a result of generally prospering environments. This explanation helps to resolve an apparent paradox inherent in the wheel concept. Why should reasonably skilled businessmen make decisions that consistently lead their firms along seemingly profitable routes to positions of vulnerability? Jefferys sees movement along the wheel as the result of sensible, business-like decisions to change with prospering market segments and to leave the poorer customers to low-margin innovators. His explanation is supported by the fact that the vulnerability contemplated by the wheel hypothesis usually means only a loss of market share, not a loss of absolute volume. At least in the United States, though, this explanation is partially contradicted by studies showing that prosperous consumers are especially prone to patronize discount houses. Also they are equally as likely to shop in supermarkets as are poorer consumers.[27]

---

[26] R. D. Entenberg, *The Changing Competitive Position of Department Stores in the United States by Merchandise Lines* (Pittsburgh: University of Pittsburgh Press, 1957), p. 52.

[27] R. Holton, *The Supply and Demand Structure of Food Retailing Services, A Case Study* (Cambridge: Harvard University Press, 1954).

The imperfect competition and excess capacity hypotheses also appear highly plausible. Considerably more investigation is needed before their validity can be appraised properly. The wheel pattern developed very slowly, and very recently in the department-store field. Yet market imperfections in that field probably were greater before the automobile gave the consumer shopping mobility. Major portions of the supermarket growth in food retailing and discount-house growth in appliance distribution occurred during periods of vastly expanding consumption, when excess capacity probably was at relatively low levels. At the moment there is little evidence to suggest any clear-cut correlation between the degree of market imperfection and the appearance of the wheel pattern. However, this lack may well be the result of the scarcity of empirical studies of retail competition.

Managerial deterioration certainly must explain some manifestations of the wheel, but not all. Empires rise and fall with changes in the quality of their leadership, and the same thing seems true in business. But the wheel hypothesis is a hypothesis concerning types of retailing and not merely individual firms. Consequently, the managerial-deterioration explanation holds true only if it is assumed that new people entering any established type of retailing as the heads of both old and new companies are consistently less competent than the first generation. Again, the fact that the wheel has operated very slowly in some fields suggests that several successive managerial generations can avoid wheel-like maturation and decay.

PART
IV

MARKETING STRATEGY

Once the marketing manager has analyzed consumers and market forces, he or she can design a marketing strategy to take advantage of the opportunities revealed by the analysis. The development of marketing strategy begins with Adler's vivid exposition of the systems concept as it applies to marketing strategy. The remaining articles in Part IV focus on strategic aspects of the various decision elements of marketing (product, distribution, promotion, and price).

Alexander vividly underscores the need in today's dynamic marketing environment for flexibility and change in a firm's product policy. McVey sketches and then questions the channels-of-distribution concept as a basis of marketing strategy. Mallen, on the other hand, points out that channels provide opportunities for both conflict and cooperation among the firms that constitute the marketing channels.

Lavidge and Steiner present a model of consumer behavior (which can be related to the more sophisticated Howard and Sheth model), and then show how advertising strategy can be based on this model. Dean shows how institutional forces—in this case, tax laws—can affect marketing strategy. Institutional structures and practices with respect to pricing policies are discussed by Lanzillotti. Although his specific data are somewhat out of date, Lanzillotti's article remains the discipline's landmark study of pricing strategies. The final article, by Green, applies modern decision theory to the problems of setting prices for products.

25

Systems Approach to Marketing

Lee Adler

More and more businessmen today recognize that corporate success is, in most cases, synonymous with marketing success and with the coming of age of a new breed of professional managers. They find it increasingly important not only to pay lip service to the marketing concept but to do something about it in terms of (a) customer orientation, rather than navel-gazing in the factory, (b) organizational revisions to implement the marketing concept, and (c) a more orderly approach to problem solving.

In an increasing number of companies we see more conscious and formal efforts to apply rational, fact-based methods for solving marketing problems, and greater recognition of the benefits these methods offer. While these benefits may be newly realized, there is nothing new about the underlying philosophy; in the parlance of military men and engineers, it is the systems approach. For, whether we like it or not, marketing is, by definition, a system, if we accept Webster's definition of systems as "an assemblage of objects united by some form of regular interaction or interdependence." Certainly, the interaction of such "objects" as product, pricing, promotion, sales calls, distribution, and so on fits the definition.

There is an expanding list of sophisticated applications of systems theory—and not in one but in many sectors of the marketing

Reprinted from *Harvard Business Review*, Vol. 45 (May-June, 1967), pp. 105-118. Copyright © 1967 by the President and Fellows of Harvard College; all rights reserved.

Lee Adler, associate professor of marketing at Farleigh Dickinson University, holds an M.B.A. from New York University. He has extensive experience in marketing research and management positions, and he is a frequent contributor of provocative articles to the marketing literature. Formerly he was director of marketing research for RCA Corporation, and is also a sculptor of some renown.

front. The construction of mathematical and/or logical models to describe, quantify, and evaluate alternate marketing strategies and mixes is an obvious case in point. So, too, is the formulation of management information systems[1] and of marketing plans with built-in performance measurements of predetermined goals. But no less vital is the role of the systems approach in the design and sale of products and services. When J. P. Stevens Company color-harmonizes lines and bedspreads, and towels and bath mats, it is creating a product system. And when Avco Corporation sells systems management to the space exploration field, involving the marriage of many scientific disciplines as well as adherence to budgetary constraints, on-time performance, and quality control, it is creating a *service* system.

In this article I shall discuss the utilization of the systems concept in marketing in both quantitative and qualitative ways with case histories drawn from various industries. In doing so, my focus will be more managerial and philosophical than technical, and I will seek to dissipate some of the hocus-pocus, glamour, mystery, and fear which pervade the field. The systems concept is not esoteric or "science fiction" in nature (although it sometimes *sounds* that way in promotional descriptions). Its advantages are not subtle or indirect; as we shall see, they are as real and immediate as decision making itself. The limitations are also real, and these, too, will be discussed.

(Readers interested in a brief summary of the background and the conceptual development of the systems approach may wish to turn to the box on pages 330 and 331.)

PROMISING APPLICATIONS

Now let us look at some examples of corporate application of the systems approach. Here we will deal with specific parts or "subsystems" of the total marketing system. Exhibit I is a schematic portrayal of these relationships.

Products and Services

The objective of the systems approach in product management is to provide a complete "offering" to the market rather than merely a product. If the purpose of business is to create a customer at a profit,

---

[1] See, for example, Donald F. Cox and Robert E. Good, "How to Build a Marketing Information System," *Harvard Business Review* (May-June 1967); pp. 145-54. [See selection no. 17 in this anthology—eds.]

then the needs of the customer must be carefully attended to; we must, in short, study what the customer is buying or wants to buy, rather than what we are trying to sell.

In the consumer products field we have forged ahead in understanding that the customer buys nutrition (not bread), beauty (not cosmetics), warmth (not fuel oil). But in industrial products this concept has been slower in gaining a foothold. Where it has gained a foothold, it expresses itself in two ways: the creation of a complete product system sold (1) as a unit, or (2) as a component or components which are part of a larger consumption system.

Perhaps the most eloquent testimony to the workability and value of the systems approach comes from companies that have actually used it. For a good example let us turn to the case of The Carborundum Company. This experience is especially noteworthy because it comes from industrial marketing, where, as just indicated, progress with the systems concept has generally been slow.

EXHIBIT 1. *Marketing Subsystems and the Total System*

WHAT IS THE SYSTEMS APPROACH?

There seems to be agreement that the systems approach sprang to life as a semantically identifiable term sometime during World War II. It was associated with the problem of how to bomb targets deep in Germany more effectively from British bases, with the Manhattan Project, and with studies of optimum search patterns for destroyers to use in locating U-boats during the Battle of the North Atlantic.[1] Subsequently, it was utilized in the defeat of the Berlin blockade. It has reached its present culmination in the success of great military systems such as Polaris and Minuteman.

Not surprisingly, the parallels between military and marketing strategies being what they are, the definition of the systems approach propounded by The RAND Corporation for the U.S. Air Force is perfectly apt for marketers:

> An inquiry to aid a decision-maker choose a course of action by systematically investigating his proper objectives, comparing quantitatively where possible the costs, effectiveness, and risks associated with the alternative policies or strategies for achieving them and *formulating additional alternatives if those examined are found wanting.*[2]

The systems approach is thus an orderly, "architectural" discipline for dealing with complex problems of choice under uncertainty.

Typically, in such problems, multiple and possibly conflicting objectives exist. The task of the systems analyst is to specify a closed operating network in which the components will work together so as to yield the optimum balance of economy, efficiency, and risk minimization. Put more broadly, the systems approach attempts to apply the "scientific method" to complex marketing problems studied *as a whole;* it seeks to discipline marketing.

---

[1] See Glen McDaniel, "The Meaning of The Systems Movement to the Acceleration and Direction of the American Economy," in *Proceedings of the 1964 Systems Engineering Conference* (New York, Clapp & Poliak, Inc., 1964), p. 1; see also E. S. Quade, editor, *Analysis for Military Decisions* (Santa Monica, California, The RAND Corporation, 1964), p. 6.

[2] Quade, *op. cit.,* p. 4.

But disciplining marketing is no easy matter. Marketing must be perceived as a *process* rather than as a series of isolated, discrete actions; competitors must be viewed as components of each marketer's own system. The process must also be comprehended as involving a flow and counterflow of information and behavior between marketers and customers. Some years ago, Marion Harper, Jr., now chairman of The Interpublic Group of Companies, Inc., referred to the flow of information in marketing communications as the cycle of "listen (i.e., marketing research), publish (messages, media), listen (more marketing research), revise, publish, listen. . . ." More recently, Raymond A. Bauer referred to the "transactional" nature of communications as a factor in the motivations, frames of reference, needs, and so forth of recipients of messages. The desires of the communicator alone are but part of the picture.[3]

Pushing this new awareness of the intricacies of marketing communications still further, Theodore Levitt identified the interactions between five different forces—source effect (i.e., the reputation or credibility of the sponsor of the message), sleeper effect (the declining influence of source credibility with the passage of time), message effect (the character and quality of the message), communicator effect (the impact of the transmitter—e.g., a salesman), and audience effect (the competence and responsibility of the audience).[4] Casting a still broader net are efforts to model the entire purchasing process, and perhaps the ultimate application of the systems concept is attempts to make mathematical models of the entire marketing process.

Mounting recognition of the almost countless elements involved in marketing and of the mind-boggling complexity of their interactions is a wholesome (though painful) experience. Nevertheless, I believe we must not ignore other ramifications of the systems approach which are qualitative in nature. For the world of marketing offers a vast panorama of non- or part-mathematical systems and opportunities to apply systems thinking. We must not become so bedazzled by the brouhaha of the operations research experts as to lose sight of the larger picture.

---

[3] "Communications as a Transaction," *Public Opinion Quarterly*, Spring 1963, p. 83.
[4] See Theodore Levitt, *Industrial Purchasing Behavior* (Boston, Division of Research, Harvard Business School, 1965), p. 25ff.

Birth of the Concept. Founded in 1894, the company was content for many years to sell abrasives. It offered an extremely broad line of grinding wheels, coated abrasives, and abrasive grain, with a reputed capacity for 200,000 different products of varying type, grade, and formulation. But the focus was on the product.

In the mid-1950s, Carborundum perceived that the market for abrasives could be broadened considerably if—looking at abrasives through customers' eyes—it would see the product as fitting into *metal polishing, cleaning,* or *removal systems.* Now Carborundum is concerned with all aspects of abrading—the machine, the contact wheel, the workpiece, the labor cost, the overhead rate, the abrasive, and, above all, the customer's objective. In the words of Carborundum's president, W. H. Wendel:

> That objective is never the abrasive per se, but rather the creation of a certain dimension, a type of finish, or a required shape, always related to a minimum cost. Since there are many variables to consider, just one can be misleading. To render maximum service, Carborundum (must offer) a complete system.[2]

Organizational Overhaul. To offer such a system, management had to overhaul important parts of the organization:

(1) The company needed to enhance its knowledge of the total system. As Wendel explains:

> We felt we had excellent knowledge of coated abrasive products, but that we didn't have the application and machine know-how in depth. To be really successful in the business, we had to know as much about the machine tools as we did the abrasives.[3]

To fill this need, Carborundum made three acquisitions—The Tysaman Machine Company, which builds heavy-duty snagging, billet grinding, and abrasive cut-off machines; Curtis Machine Company, a maker of belt sanders; and Pangborn Corporation, which supplied systems capability in abrasive blast cleaning and finishing.

(2) The company's abrasive divisions were reorganized, and the management of them was realigned to accommodate the new philosophy and its application. The company found that *centering responsibility for the full system in one profit center* proved to be the most effective method of coordinating approaches in application engineering, choice of distribution channels, brand identification, field sales operations, and so forth. This method was particularly valuable for integrating the acquisitions into the new program.

---

[2] "Abrasive Maker's Systems Approach Opens New Markets," *Steel*, December 27, 1965, p. 38.
[3] *Ibid.*

(3) An Abrasives Systems Center was established to handle development work and to solve customer problems.

(4) Technical conferences and seminars were held to educate customers on the new developments.

(5) Salesmen were trained in machine and application knowledge.

Planning. A key tool in the systems approach is planning—in particular, the use of what I like to call "total business plans." (This term emphasizes the contrast with company plans that cover only limited functions.) At Carborundum, total business plans are developed with extreme care by the operating companies and divisions. Very specific objectives are established, and then detailed action programs are outlined to achieve these objectives. The action programs extend throughout the organization, including the manufacturing and development branches of the operating unit. Management sets specific dates for the completion of action steps and defines who is responsible for them. Also, it carefully measures results against established objectives. This is done both in the financial reporting system and in various marketing committees.

Quantitative Methods. Carborundum has utilized various operations research techniques, like decision tree analysis and PERT, to aid in molding plans and strategies. For example, one analysis, which concerned itself with determining the necessity for plant expansion, was based on different possible levels of success for the marketing plan. In addition, the computer has been used for inventory management, evaluation of alternate pricing strategies for systems selling, and the measurement of marketing achievements against goals.

It should be noted, though, that these quantitative techniques are management tools only and that much of the application of systems thinking to the redeployment of Carborundum's business is qualitative in nature.

Gains Achieved. As a consequence of these developments, the company has opened up vast new markets. To quote Carborundum's president again:

> Customers don't want a grinding wheel, they want metal removed. . . . The U.S. and Canadian market for abrasives amounts to $700 million a year. But what companies spend on stock removal—to bore, grind, cut, shape, and finish metal—amounts to $30 billion a year."[4]

---

[4]"Carborundum Grinds at Faster Clip," *Business Week,* July 23, 1966, pp. 58, 60.

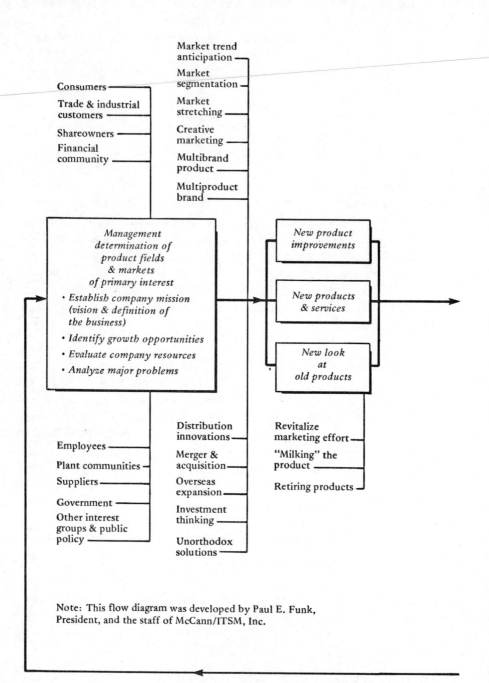

Market trend
anticipation

Market
segmentation

Market
stretching

Creative
marketing

Multibrand
product

Multiproduct
brand

Consumers

Trade & industrial
customers

Shareowners

Financial
community

*Management
determination of
product fields
& markets
of primary interest*

• *Establish company mission
(vision & definition of
the business)*

• *Identify growth opportunities*

• *Evaluate company resources*

• *Analyze major problems*

*New product
improvements*

*New products
& services*

*New look
at
old products*

Employees

Plant communities

Suppliers

Government

Other interest
groups & public
policy

Distribution
innovations

Merger &
acquisition

Overseas
expansion

Investment
thinking

Unorthodox
solutions

Revitalize
marketing effort

"Milking" the
product

Retiring products

Note: This flow diagram was developed by Paul E. Funk,
President, and the staff of McCann/ITSM, Inc.

EXHIBIT II. *Work Flow and Systems Chart for Management of*
New Products (continues through page 337).

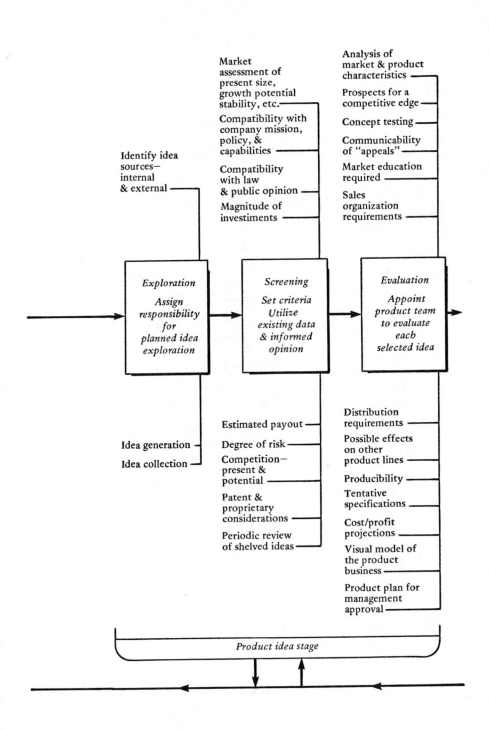

Market
assessment of
present size,
growth potential
stability, etc.——

Analysis of
market & product
characteristics ———

Compatibility with
company mission,
policy, &
capabilities ———

Prospects for a
competitive edge——

Concept testing ———

Communicability
of "appeals" ———

Identify idea
sources—
internal
& external ———

Compatibility
with law
& public opinion ———

Market education
required ———

Magnitude of
investiments ———

Sales
organization
requirements ———

Exploration	Screening	Evaluation
Assign responsibility for planned idea exploration	*Set criteria Utilize existing data & informed opinion*	*Appoint product team to evaluate each selected idea*

Distribution
requirements ———

Idea generation –

Estimated payout —

Possible effects
on other
product lines ———

Degree of risk——

Idea collection –

Competition—
present &
potential ———

Producibility ———

Patent &
proprietary
considerations ———

Tentative
specifications ———

Cost/profit
projections ———

Periodic review
of shelved ideas———

Visual model of
the product
business———

Product plan for
management
approval ———

Product idea stage

EXHIBIT II. Part 2

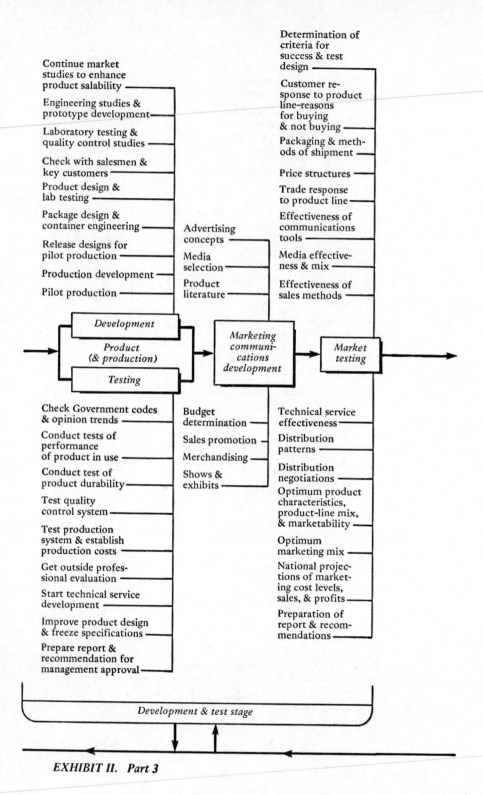

Continue market
studies to enhance
product salability

Engineering studies &
prototype development

Laboratory testing &
quality control studies

Check with salesmen &
key customers

Product design &
lab testing

Package design &
container engineering

Release designs for
pilot production

Production development

Pilot production

Advertising
concepts

Media
selection

Product
literature

Determination of
criteria for
success & test
design

Customer re-
sponse to product
line–reasons
for buying
& not buying

Packaging & meth-
ods of shipment

Price structures

Trade response
to product line

Effectiveness of
communications
tools

Media effective-
ness & mix

Effectiveness of
sales methods

Development

**Product
(& production)**

Testing

**Marketing
communi-
cations
development**

**Market
testing**

Check Government codes
& opinion trends

Conduct tests of
performance
of product in use

Conduct test of
product durability

Test quality
control system

Test production
system & establish
production costs

Get outside profes-
sional evaluation

Start technical service
development

Improve product design
& freeze specifications

Prepare report &
recommendation for
management approval

Budget
determination

Sales promotion

Merchandising

Shows &
exhibits

Technical service
effectiveness

Distribution
patterns

Distribution
negotiations

Optimum product
characteristics,
product-line mix,
& marketability

Optimum
marketing mix

National projec-
tions of market-
ing cost levels,
sales, & profits

Preparation of
report & recom-
mendations

Development & test stage

EXHIBIT II. Part 3

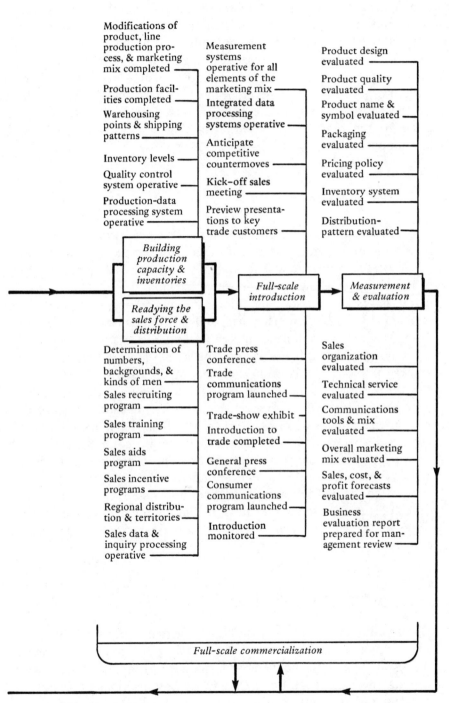

Modifications of
product, line
production pro-
cess, & marketing
mix completed ⎯

Production facil-
ities completed ⎯

Warehousing
points & shipping
patterns ⎯⎯

Inventory levels ⎯

Quality control
system operative ⎯

Production-data
processing system
operative ⎯⎯

Measurement
systems
operative for all
elements of the
marketing mix ⎯

Integrated data
processing
systems operative ⎯

Anticipate
competitive
countermoves ⎯

Kick–off sales
meeting ⎯

Preview presenta-
tions to key
trade customers ⎯

Product design
evaluated ⎯⎯

Product quality
evaluated ⎯⎯

Product name &
symbol evaluated ⎯

Packaging
evaluated ⎯⎯

Pricing policy
evaluated ⎯⎯

Inventory system
evaluated ⎯⎯

Distribution-
pattern evaluated ⎯

**Building
production
capacity &
inventories**

**Full-scale
introduction**

**Measurement
& evaluation**

**Readying the
sales force &
distribution**

Determination of
numbers,
backgrounds, &
kinds of men ⎯

Sales recruiting
program ⎯⎯

Sales training
program ⎯⎯

Sales aids
program ⎯

Sales incentive
programs ⎯

Regional distribu-
tion & territories ⎯

Sales data &
inquiry processing
operative ⎯

Trade press
conference ⎯

Trade
communications
program launched ⎯

Trade-show exhibit ⎯

Introduction to
trade completed ⎯

General press
conference ⎯

Consumer
communications
program launched ⎯

Introduction
monitored ⎯

Sales
organization
evaluated ⎯

Technical service
evaluated ⎯

Communications
tools & mix
evaluated ⎯

Overall marketing
mix evaluated ⎯

Sales, cost, &
profit forecasts
evaluated ⎯

Business
evaluation report
prepared for man-
agement review ⎯

Full-scale commercialization

EXHIBIT II. Part 4

Illustrating this market expansion in the steel industry is Carborundum's commercial success with three new developments—hot grinding, an arborless wheel to speed metal removal and cut grinding costs, and high-speed conditioning of carbon steel billets. All represent conversions from non-abrasive methods. Carborundum now also finds that the close relationship with customers gives it a competitive edge, opens top customer management doors, gains entree for salesmen with prospects they had never been able to "crack" before. Perhaps the ultimate accolade is the company's report that customers even come to the organization itself, regarding it as a consultant as well as a supplier.

Profitable Innovation

The intense pressure to originate successful new products cannot be met without methodologies calculated to enhance the probabilities of profitable innovation. The systems approach has a bearing here, too. Exhibit II shows a model for "tracking" products through the many stages of ideation, development, and testing to ultimate full-scale commercialization. This diagram is in effect a larger version of the "New Product Development" box in Exhibit I.

Observe that this is a logical (specifically, sequential), rather than numerical, model. While some elements of the total system (e.g., alternate distribution channels and various media mixes) can be analyzed by means of operations research techniques, the model has not been cast in mathematical terms. Rather, the flow diagram as a whole is used as a checklist to make sure "all bases are covered" and to help organize the chronological sequence of steps in new product development. It also serves as a conceptual foundation for formal PERT application, should management desire such a step, and for the gradual development of a series of equations linking together elements in the diagrams, should it seem useful to experiment with mathematical models.

Marketing Intelligence

The traditional notion of marketing research is fast becoming antiquated. For it leads to dreary chronicles of the past rather than focusing on the present and shedding light on the future. It is particularistic, tending to concentrate on the study of tiny fractions of a marketing problem rather than on the problem as a whole. It lends itself to assuaging the curiosity of the moment, to fire-fighting, to resolving internecine disputes. It is a slave to technique. I shall not, therefore, relate the term *marketing research* to the systems approach—although I recognize, of course, that some leading businessmen and writers are breathing new life and scope into the ideas referred to by that term.

The role of the systems approach is to help evolve a *marketing intelligence* system tailored to the needs of each marketer. Such a system would serve as the ever-alert nerve center of the marketing operation. It would have these major characteristics:

Continuous surveillance of the market.

A team of research techniques used in tandem.

A network of data sources.

Integrated analysis of data from the various sources.

Effective utilization of automatic data-processing equipment to distill mountains of raw information speedily.

Strong concentration not just on reporting findings but also on practical, action-oriented recommendations.

Concept in Use. A practical instance of the use of such an intelligence system is supplied by Mead Johnson Nutritionals (division of Mead Johnson & Company), manufacturers of Metrecal, Pablum, Bib, Nutrament, and other nutritional specialties. As Exhibit III shows, the company's Marketing Intelligence Department has provided information from these sources:

A continuing large-scale consumer market study covering attitudinal and behavioral data dealing with weight control.

Nielsen store audit data, on a bimonthly basis.

A monthly sales audit conducted among a panel of 100 high-volume food stores in 20 markets to provide advance indications of brand share shifts.

Supermarket warehouse withdrawal figures from Time, Inc.'s new service, Selling Areas–Marketing, Inc.

Salesmen's weekly reports (which, in addition to serving the purposes of sales management control, call for reconnaissance on competitive promotions, new product launches, price changes, and so forth).

Advertising expenditure data, by media class, from the company's accounting department.

Figures on sales and related topics from company factories.

Competitive advertising expenditure and exposure data supplied by the division's advertising agencies at periodic intervals.

A panel of weight-conscious women.

To exemplify the type of outputs possible from this system, Mead Johnson will be able, with the help of analyses of factory sales data, warehouse withdrawal information, and consumer purchases from Nielsen, to monitor transactions at each stage of the flow of goods through the distribution channel and to detect accumulations or developing shortages. Management will also be able to spot sources of potential problems in time to deal with them effectively. For example, if factory sales exceed consumer purchases, more promotional pressure is required. By contrast, if factory sales lag behind consumer purchases, sales effort must be further stimulated.

Similarly, the company has been able to devise a practical measurement of advertising's effectiveness in stimulating sales—a measurement that is particularly appropriate to fast-moving packaged goods. By relating advertising outlays and exposure data to the number of prospects trying out a product during a campaign (the number is obtained from the continuing consumer survey), it is possible to calculate the advertising cost of recruiting such a prospect. By persisting in such analyses during several campaigns, the relative value of alternative advertising approaches can be weighed. Since measurement of the sales, as opposed to the communications, effects of promotion is a horrendously difficult, costly, and chancy process, the full significance of this achievement is difficult to exaggerate.

Benefits Realized. Mead Johnson's marketing intelligence system has been helpful to management in a number of ways. In addition to giving executive early warning of new trends and problems, and valuable insights into future conditions, it is leading to a systematic *body* of knowledge about company markets rather than to isolated scraps of information. This knowledge in turn should lead ultimately to a theory of marketing in each field that will explain the mysteries that baffle marketers today. What is more, the company expects that the system will help to free its marketing intelligence people from fire-fighting projects so that they can concentrate on long-term factors and eventually be more consistently creative.

Despite these gains, it is important to note that Mead Johnson feels it has a long road still to travel. More work is needed in linking individual data banks. Conceptual schemes must be proved out in practice; ways must still be found to reduce an awesome volume of data, swelled periodically by new information from improved sources, so as to make intelligence more immediately accessible to decision makers. And perhaps the biggest problem of the movement, one underlying some of the others, is the difficulty in finding qualified marketing-oriented programmers.

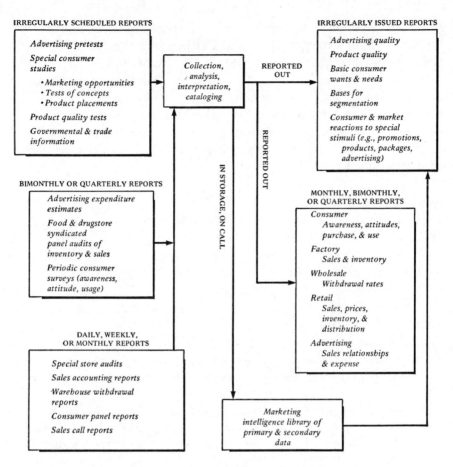

IRREGULARLY SCHEDULED REPORTS

Advertising pretests

Special consumer studies
- *Marketing opportunities*
- *Tests of concepts*
- *Product placements*

Product quality tests

Governmental & trade information

BIMONTHLY OR QUARTERLY REPORTS

Advertising expenditure estimates

Food & drugstore syndicated panel audits of inventory & sales

Periodic consumer surveys (awareness, attitude, usage)

DAILY, WEEKLY, OR MONTHLY REPORTS

Special store audits

Sales accounting reports

Warehouse withdrawal reports

Consumer panel reports

Sales call reports

Collection, analysis, interpretation, cataloging

REPORTED OUT

REPORTED OUT

IN STORAGE, ON CALL

IRREGULARLY ISSUED REPORTS

Advertising quality

Product quality

Basic consumer wants & needs

Bases for segmentation

Consumer & market reactions to special stimuli (e.g., promotions, products, packages, advertising)

MONTHLY, BIMONTHLY, OR QUARTERLY REPORTS

Consumer
  Awareness, attitudes, purchase, & use

Factory
  Sales & inventory

Wholesale
  Withdrawal rates

Retail
  Sales, prices, inventory, & distribution

Advertising
  Sales relationships & expense

Marketing intelligence library of primary & secondary data

EXHIBIT III. Mead Johnson's Marketing Intelligence System

Physical Distribution

A veritable revolution is now taking place in physical distribution. Total systems are being evolved out of the former hodgepodge of separate responsibilites, which were typically scattered among different departments of the same company. These systems include traffic and transportation, warehousing, materials handling, protective packaging, order processing, production planning, inventory control, customer service, market forecasting, and plant and warehouse site selection. Motivating this revolution are the computer, company drives to reduce distribution costs, and innovations in transportation, such as jet air freight, container ships, the interstate highway network, and larger and more versatile freight cars.

Distribution is one area of marketing where the "bread-and-butter" uses of the computer are relatively easily deployed for such functions as order processing, real-time inventory level reports, and tracking the movements of goods. Further into the future lie mathematical models which will include every factor bearing on distribution. Not only will packaging, materials handling, transportation and warehouse, order processing, and related costs be considered in such models; also included will be sales forecasts by product, production rates by factory, warehouse locations and capacities, speeds of different carriers, etc. In short, a complete picture will be developed for management.

Program in Action. The experiences of the Norge Division of Borg-Warner Corporation point up the values of the systems approach in physical distribution. The firm was confronted externally with complaints from its dealers and distributors, who were trying to cope with swollen inventories and the pressures of "loading deals." Internally, because coordination of effort between the six departments involved in distribution was at a minimum, distribution costs and accounts receivable were mounting persistently.

To grapple with this situation, Norge undertook a comprehensive analysis of its distribution system. Out of this grew a new philosophy. A company executive has described the philosophy to me as follows:

> An effective system of physical distribution cannot begin at the end of the production line. It must also apply at the very beginning of the production process—at the planning, scheduling, and forecasting stages. Logistics, in short, is part of a larger marketing system, not just an evaluation of freight rates. We must worry not only about finished refrigerators, but also about the motors coming from another manufacturer, and even about where the copper that goes into those motors will come from. We must be concerned with *total* flow.

To implement this philosophy, the appliance manufacturer took the following steps:

(1) It reorganized the forecasting, production scheduling, warehousing, order processing, and shipping functions into *one* department headed by a director of physical distribution.

(2) The management information system was improved with the help of EDP equipment tied into the communications network. This step made it possible to process and report data more speedily on orders received, inventory levels, and the actual movement of goods.

(3) Management used a combination of computer and manual techniques to weigh trade-offs among increased costs of multiple warehousing, reduced long-haul freight and local drayage costs,

reduced inventory pipeline, and the sales value of an improved "total" product offering. Also assessed were trade-offs between shorter production runs and higher inventory levels, thereby challenging the traditional "wisdom" of production-oriented managers that the longer the run, the better.

(4) The company is setting up new regional warehouses.

As a result of these moves, Norge has been able to lower inventories throughout its sales channels and to reduce accounts receivable. These gains have led, in turn, to a reduction of the company's overall investment and a concomitant increase in profitability.

It is essential to note that even though Norge has used operations research as part of its systems approach, many aspects of the program are qualitative. Thus far, the company has found that the development of an all-encompassing model is not warranted because of (a) the time and cost involved, (b) the probability that the situation will change before the model is completed, (c) a concern that such a model would be so complex as to be unworkable, and (d) the difficulty of testing many of the assumptions used. In addition, management has not tried to quantify the impact of its actions on distributor and retailer attitudes and behavior, possible competitive countermoves, and numerous other factors contributing to results.

Toward Total Integration

The integration of systems developed for product management, product innovation, marketing intelligence, physical distribution, and the other functions or "subsystems" embraced by the term *marketing* creates a total marketing system. Thus, marketing plans composed according to a step-by-step outline, ranging from enunciation of objectives and implementational steps to audit and adjustment to environmental changes, constitute a complete application of systems theory. Further, as the various subsystems of the overall system are linked quantitatively, so that the effect of modifications in one element can be detected in other elements, and as the influences of competitive moves on each element are analyzed numerically, then the total scheme becomes truly sophisticated.

PLUSES AND MINUSES

Two elements underlie the use and benefits of systems theory—order and knowledge. The first is a homely virtue, the second a lofty goal.

Marketing is obviously not alone among all human pursuits in needing them; but, compared with its business neighbors, production and finance, marketing's need is acute indeed. The application of the systems concept can bring considerable advantages. It offers:

A methodical problem-solving orientation—with a broader frame of reference so that all aspects of a problem are examined.

Coordinated deployment of all appropiate tools of marketing.

Greater efficiency and economy of marketing operations.

Quicker recognition of impending problems, made possible by better understanding of the complex interplay of many trends and forces.

A stimulus to innovation.

A means of quantitatively verifying results.

These functional benefits in turn yield rich rewards in the marketplace. The most important gains are:

A deeper penetation of existing markets—As an illustration, the Advanced Data Division of Litton Industries has become a leader in the automatic revenue control business by designing systems meshing together "hardware" and "software."

A broadening of markets—For example, the tourist industry has attracted millions of additional travelers by creating packaged tours that are really product-service systems. These systems are far more convenient and economical than anything the consumer could assemble himself.

An extension of product lines—Systems management makes it more feasible to seek out compatibilities among independently developed systems. Evidence of this idea is the work of automatic control system specialists since the early 1950's.[5] Now similar signs are apparent in marketing. For example, Acme Visible Records is currently dovetailing the design and sale of its record-keeping systems with data-processing machines and forms.

A lessening of competition or a strengthened capacity to cope with competition—The systems approach tends to make a company's product line more unique and attractive. Carborundum's innovation in metal-removal systems is a perfect illustration of this.

Problems in Practice

Having just enumerated in glowing terms the benefits of the systems approach, realism demands that I give "equal time" to the awesome

---

[5] See *Automatic and Manual Control: Papers Contributed to the Conference at Cranford, 1951*, edited by A. Tustin (London, Butterworth's Scientific Publications, 1952).

difficulties its utilization presents. There is no better evidence of this than the gulf between the elegant and sophisticated models with which recent marketing literature abounds and the actual number of situations in which those models really work. For the truth of the matter is that we are still in the foothills of this development, despite the advances of a few leaders. Let us consider some of the obstacles.

Time and Manpower Costs. First of all, the systems approach requires considerable time to implement; it took one company over a year to portray its physical distribution system in a mathematical model before it could even begin to solve its problems. RCA's Electronic Data Processing Division reports models taking three to five years to build, after which holes in the data network have to be filled and the model tested against history. Add to this the need for manpower of exceptional intellectual ability, conceptual skills, and specialized education—manpower that is in exceedingly short supply. Because the problems are complex and involve all elements of the business, one man alone cannot solve them. He lacks the knowledge, tools, and controls. And so many people must be involved. It follows that the activation of systems theory can be very costly.

Absence of "Canned" Solutions. Unlike other business functions where standardized approaches to problem solving are available, systems must be tailored to the individual situation of each firm. Even the same problem in different companies in the same industry will frequently lead to different solutions because of the impact of other inputs, unique perceptions of the environment, and varying corporate missions. These factors, too, compound time and expense demands.

"Net Uncertainties." Even after exhaustive analysis, full optimization of a total problem cannot be obtained. Some uncertainty will always remain and must be dealt with on the basis of judgment and experience.

Lack of Hard Data. In the world of engineering, the systems evolved to date have consisted all or mostly of machines. Systems engineers have been wise enough to avoid the irrationalities of man until they master control of machines. Marketing model-builders, however, have not been able to choose, for the distributor, salesman, customer, and competitor are central to marketing. We must, therefore, incorporate not only quantitative measures of the dimensions of things and processes (e.g., market potential, media outlays, and shipping rates), but also psychological measures of comprehension, attitudes, motivations, intentions, needs—yes, even psychological measures of physical behavior.

What is needed is a marriage of the physical and behavioral sciences—and we are about as advanced in this blending of disciplines as astronomy was in the Middle Ages.

Consider the advertising media fields as an instance of the problem:

A number of advertising agencies have evolved linear programming or simulation techniques to assess alternate media schedules. One of the key sets of data used covers the probabilities of exposure to all or part of the audience of a TV program, magazine, or radio station. But what is exposure, and how do you measure it? What is optimum frequency of exposure, and how do you measure it? How does advertising prevail on the predispositions and perceptions of a potential customer? Is it better to judge advertising effects on the basis of exposure opportunity, "impact" (whatever that is), messages retained, message comprehension, or attitude shifts or uptrends in purchase intentions? We do not have these answers yet.

Even assuming precise knowledge of market dimensions, product performance, competitive standing, weights of marketing pressure exerted by direct selling, advertising and promotion, and so on, most marketers do not yet know, except in isolated cases, how one force will affect another. For instance, how does a company "image" affect the setting in which its salesmen work? How does a company's reputation for service affect customer buying behavior?

Nature of Marketing Men. Man is an actor on this stage in another role. A good many marketing executives, in the deepest recesses of their psyches, are artists, not analysts. For them, marketing is an art form, and, in my opinion, they really do not want it to be any other way. Their temperament is antipathetic to system, order, knowledge. They enjoy flying by the seat of their pants—though you will never get them to admit it. They revel in chaos, abhor facts, and fear research. They hate to be trammeled by written plans. And they love to spend, but are loath to assess the results of their spending.

Obviously, such men cannot be sold readily on the value and practicality of the systems approach! It takes time, experience, and many facts to influence their thinking.

Surmounting the Barriers

All is not gloom, however. The barriers described are being overcome in various ways. While operations research techniques have not yet made much headway in evolving total marketing systems and in areas where man is emotionally engaged, their accomplishments in solving inventory control problems, in sales analysis, in site selection, and in other areas have made many businessmen more sympathetic and open-minded to them.

Also, mathematical models—even the ones that do not work well yet—serve to bolster comprehension of the need for system as well as to clarify the intricacies among subsystems. Many models are in this sense learning models; they teach us how to ask more insightful questions. Moreover, they pinpoint data gaps and invite a more systematized method for reaching judgments where complete information does not exist. Because the computer abhors vague generalities, it forces managers to analyze their roles, objectives, and criteria more concretely. Paradoxically, it demands more, not less, of its human masters.

Of course, resistance to mathematical models by no means makes resistance to the systems approach necessary. There are many cases where no need may ever arise to use mathematics or computers. For the essence of the systems approach is not its techniques, but the enumeration of options and their implications. A simple checklist may be the only tool needed. I would even argue that some hard thinking in a quiet room may be enough. This being the case, the whole trend to more analysis and logic in management thinking, as reflected in business periodicals, business schools, and the practices of many companies, will work in favor of the development of the systems approach.

It is important to note at this juncture that not all marketers need the systems approach in its formal, elaborate sense. The success of some companies is rooted in other than marketing talents; their expertise may lie in finance, technology, administration, or even in personnel—as in the case of holding companies having an almost uncanny ability to hire brilliant operating managers and the self-control to leave them alone. In addition, a very simple marketing operation—for example, a company marketing one product through one distribution channel—may have no use for the systems concept.

APPLYING THE APPROACH

Not illogically, there is a system for applying the systems approach. It may be outlined as a sequence of steps:

1. *Define the problem and clarify objectives.* Care must be exercised not to accept the view of the propounder of the problem lest the analyst be defeated at the outset.

2. *Test the definition of the problem.* Expand its parameters to the limit. For example, to solve physical distribution problems it is necessary to study the marketplace (customer preferences, usage rates, market size, and so forth), as well as the production process (which plants produce which items most efficiently, what the interplant movements of raw materials are, and so forth). Delineate the extremes of these factors, their changeability, and the limitations on management's ability to work with them.

3. *Build a model.* Portray all factors graphically, indicating logical and chronological sequences—the dynamic flow of information, decisions, and events. "Closed circuits" should be used where there is information feedback or go, no-go and recycle signals (see Exhibit II).

4. *Set concrete objectives.* For example, if a firm wants to make daily deliveries to every customer, prohibitive as the cost may be, manipulation of the model will yield one set of answers. But if the desire is to optimize service at lowest cost, then another set of answers will be needed. The more crisply and precisely targets are stated, the more specific the results will be.

5. *Develop alternative solutions.* It is crucial to be as open-minded as possible at this stage. The analyst must seek to expand the list of options rather than merely assess those given to him, then reduce the list to a smaller number of practical or relevant ones.

6. *Set up criteria or tests of relative value.*

7. *Quantify some or all of the factors or "variables."* The extent to which this is done depends, of course, on management's inclinations and the "state of the art."

8. *Manipulate the model.* That is, weigh the costs, effectiveness, profitability, and risks of each alternative.

9. *Interpret the results, and choose one or more courses of action.*

10. *Verify the results.* Do they make sense when viewed against the world as executives know it? Can their validity be tested by experiments and investigations?

Forethought and Perspective

Successful systems do not blossom overnight. From primitive beginnings, they evolve over a period of time as managers and systems specialists learn to understand each other better, and learn how to structure problems and how to push out the frontiers of the "universe" with which they are dealing. Companies must be prepared to invest time, money, and energy in making systems management feasible.

This entails a solid foundation of historical data even before the conceptual framework for the system can be constructed. Accordingly, considerable time should be invested at the outset in *thinking* about the problem, its appropriate scope, options, and criteria of choice before plunging into analysis.

Not only technicians, but most of us have a way of falling in love with techniques. We hail each one that comes along—*deus ex machina.* Historically, commercial research has wallowed in several such passions (e.g., probability sampling, motivation research, and semantic scaling), and now operations research appears to be doing the same thing. Significantly, each technique has come, in the fullness of time, to take its place as one, but only one, instrument in the research tool chest. We must therefore have a broad and dispassionate perspective on the systems approach at this juncture. We must recognize that the computer does not possess greater magical properties than the abacus. It, too, is a tool, albeit a brilliant one.

Put another way, executives must continue to exercise their judgment and experience. Systems analysis is no substitute for common sense. The computer must adapt itself to their styles, personalities, and modes of problem solving. It is an aid to management, not a surrogate. Businessmen may be slow, but the good ones are bright; the electronic monster, by contrast, is a speedy idiot. It demands great acuity of wit from its human managers lest they be deluged in an avalanche of useless paper. (The story is told of a sales manager who had just found out about the impressive capabilities of his company's computer and called for a detailed sales analysis of all products. The report was duly prepared and wheeled into his office on a dolly.)

Systems users must be prepared to revise continually. There are two reasons for this. First, the boundaries of systems keep changing; constraints are modified; competition makes fresh incursions; variables, being what they are, vary, and new ones crop up. Second, the analytical process is iterative. Usually, one "pass" at problem formulation and searches for solutions will not suffice, and it will be necessary to "recycle" as early hypotheses are challenged and new, more fruitful insights are stimulated by the inquiry. Moreover, it is impossible to select objectives without knowledge of their effects and costs. That knowledge can come only from analysis, and it frequently requires review and revision.

Despite all the efforts at quantification, systems analysis is still largely an art. It relies frequently on inputs based on human judgment; even when the inputs are numerical, they are determined, at least in part, by judgment. Similarly, the outputs must pass through the sieve of human interpretation. Hence, there is a positive correlation between the pay-off from a system and the managerial level involved in its design. The higher the level, the more rewarding the results.

Finally, let me observe that marketing people merit their own access to computers as well as programmers who understand marketing. Left in the hands of accountants, the timing, content, and format of output are often out of phase with marketing needs.

CONCLUSION

Nearly 800 years ago a monk wrote the following about St. Godric, a merchant later turned hermit:

> He laboured not only as a merchant but also as a shipman . . . to Denmark, Flanders, and Scotland; in which lands he found certain rare, and therefore more precious, wares, which he carried to other parts wherein he knew them to be least familiar, and coveted by the inhabitants beyond the price of gold itself, wherefore he exchanged these wares for others coveted by men of other lands. . . .[6]

How St. Godric "knew" about his markets we are not told, marketing having been in a primitive state in 1170. How some of us marketers today "know" is, in my opinion, sometimes no less mysterious than it was eight centuries ago. But we are trying to change that, and I will hazard the not very venturesome forecast that the era of "by guess and by gosh" marketing is drawing to a close. One evidence of this trend is marketers' intensified search for knowledge that will improve their command over their destinies. This search is being spurred on by a number of powerful developments. To describe them briefly:

> The growing complexity of technology and the accelerating pace of technological innovation.
>
> The advent of the computer, inspiring and making possible analysis of the relationships between systems components.
>
> The intensification of competition, lent impetus by the extraordinary velocity of new product development and the tendency of diversification to thrust everybody into everybody else's business.
>
> The preference of buyers for purchasing from as few sources as possible, thereby avoiding the problems of assembling bits and pieces themselves and achieving greater reliability, economy, and administrative convenience. (Mrs. Jones would rather buy a complete vacuum cleaner from one source than the housing from one manufacturer, the hose from another, and the attachments from still another. And industrial buyers are not much different from Mrs. Jones. They would rather buy an automated machine tool from one

---

[6] *Life of St. Godric*, by Reginald, a monk of Durham, c. 1170.

manufacturer than design and assemble the components themselves. Not to be overlooked in this connection, is the tremendous influence of the U.S. government in buying systems for its military and aerospace programs.)

The further development and application of the systems approach to marketing represents, in my judgment, the leading edge in both marketing theory and practice. At the moment, we are still much closer to St. Godric than to the millenium, and the road will be rocky and tortuous. But if we are ever to convert marketing into a more scientific pursuit, this is the road we must travel. The systems concept can teach us how our businesses really behave in the marketing arena, thereby extending managerial leverage and control. It can help us to confront more intelligently the awesome complexity of marketing, to deal with the hazards and opportunities of technological change, and to cope with the intensification of competition. And in the process, the concept will help us to feed the hungry maws of our expensive computers with more satisfying fare.

26

The Death and Burial of "Sick" Products

R. S. Alexander

Euthanasia applied to human beings is criminal; but aging products enjoy or suffer no such legal protection. This is a sad fact of business life.

The word "product" is used here not in its broad economic sense of anything produced—such as wheat, coal, a car, or a chair—but in its narrower meaning of an article made to distinct specifications and intended for sale under a separate brand or catalogue number. In the broader sense of the word, certain products may last as long as industrial civilization endures; in the narrow sense, most of them are playthings of change.

Much has been written about managing the development and marketing of new products, but business literature is largely devoid of material on product deletion.

This is not surprising. New products have glamour. Their management is fraught with great risks. Their successful introduction promises growth in sales and profits that may be fantastic.

But putting products to death—or letting them die—is a drab business, and often engenders much of the sadness of a final parting with

R. S. Alexander, "The Death and Burial of 'Sick' Products." Reprinted from the *Journal of Marketing*, published by the American Marketing Association (April 1964), pp. 1-7. This article won the 1964 Alpha Kappa Psi Award as best article of the year.

Ralph S. Alexander is professor emeritus of marketing, Graduate School of Business, Columbia University. He received his Ph.D. from the University of Chicago in 1925. During World War II he was director of the Wholesale and Retail Division of the War Production Board. He served as chairman of the Committee on Definitions of the American Marketing Association which produced *Marketing Definitions: A Glossary of Marketing Terms* (Chicago: American Marketing Association, 1960). This pamphlet is still the definitive work. Since his retirement, Professor Alexander has remained active in marketing, serving as a visiting faculty memeber at several schools and as a consultant to various firms.

old and tried friends. "The portable 6-sided, pretzel polisher was the first product The Company ever made. Our line will no longer be our line without it."

But while deletion is an uninspiring and depressing process, in a changing market it is almost as vital as the addition of new products. The old product that is a "football" of competition or has lost much of its market appeal is likely to generate more than its share of small unprofitable orders; to make necessary short, costly production runs; to demand an exorbitant amount of executive attention; and to tie up capital that could be used more profitably in other ventures.

Just as a crust of barnacles on the hold of a ship retards the vessel's movement, so do a number of worn-out items in a company's product mix affect the company's progress.

Most of the costs that result from the lack of an effective deletion system are hidden and become apparent only after careful analysis. As a result, management often overlooks them. The need for examining the product line to discover outworn members, and for analysis to arrive at intelligent decisions to discard or to keep them, very rarely assumes the urgency of a crisis. Too often, management thinks of this as something that should be done but that can wait until tomorrow.

This is why a definite procedure for deletion of products should be set up, and why the authority and responsibility for the various activities involved should be clearly and definitely assigned. This is especially important because this work usually requires the cooperation of several functional groups within the business firm, including at least marketing, production, finance, and sometimes personnel.

Definite responsibility should be assigned for at least the following activities involved in the process: (1) selecting products which are candidates for elimination; (2) gathering information about them and analyzing the infomation; (3) making decisions about elimination; and (4) if necessary, removing the doomed products from the line.

SELECTION OF PRODUCTS FOR POSSIBLE ELIMINATION

As a first step, we are not seeking the factors on which the final decision to delete or to retain turns, but merely those which indicate that the product's continuation in the product mix should be considered carefully with elimination as a possibility. Although removal from the product line may seem to be the prime aim, the result is not inevitably deletion from the line; instead, careful analysis may lead to changes in the product itself or in the methods of making or marketing it.

Sales Trend. If the trend of a product's sales is downward over a time period that is significant in relation to the normal life of others like it, its continuation in the mix deserves careful examination. There may be many reasons for such a decline that in no way point toward deletion; but when decline continues over a period of time the situation needs to be studied.

Price Trend. A downward trend in the price of a new product may be expected if the firm introducing it pursues a skimming-price policy, or if all firms making it realize substantial cost savings as a result of volume production and increased processing know-how. But when the price of an established product whose competitive pattern has been relatively stabilized shows a downward trend over a significant period of time, the future of that product should receive attention.

Profit Trend. A declining profit either in dollars or as a per cent of sales or investment should raise questions about a product's continued place in the product line. Such a trend usually is the result of a price-factory cost squeeze, although it may be the outcome of a loss in market appeal or a change in the method of customer purchase which forces higher marketing expenditures.

Substitute Products. When a substitute article appears on the market, especially if it represents an improvement over an old product, management must face the question of whether to retain or discard the old product. This is true regardless of who introduces the substitute. The problem is especially difficult when the new product serves the same general purpose as the old one but is not an exact substitute for it.

Product Effectiveness. Certain products may lose some of their effectiveness for the purposes they serve. For example, disease germs may develop strains that are resistant to a certain antibiotic. When this happens, the question of whether to keep or delete the drug involves issues not only of the interests of the firm but of the public welfare.

Executive Time. A possible tipoff as to the location of "illness" in a product mix lies in a study of the amount of executive time and attention devoted to each of the items in the product line. Sick products, like sick people, demand a lot of care; but one must be careful to distinguish the "growing pains" of a new product from the more serious disorders of one that has matured and is now declining.

The six indicators mentioned do not of themselves provide evidence justifying deletion. But they can help management to single out from a line of products those upon which it can profitably spend time and money in analyzing them, with elimination from the line as a *possibility*.

ANALYSIS AND DECISION-MAKING
ABOUT "SICK" PRODUCTS

Although the work of analyzing a sick or decrepit product is usually done by people other than the management executives who decide what to do about it, the two processes are interdependent. Unless the right factors are chosen for analysis and unless the work is properly done, the decision is not likely to be an intelligent one. Accordingly, these two factors will be discussed together.

What information does a decision-maker need about a product, and what sort of analysis of it should he have in order to render a sound verdict as to its future? The deletion decision should not turn on the sole issue of profitability. Profit is the most important objective of a business; but individual firms often seek to achieve both long-run and short-run objectives other than profit.

So, in any individual case the critical factors and the weights assigned them in making a decision must be chosen in the light of the situation of the firm and the management objectives.

Profits

Profit management in a firm with a multi-product line (the usual situation in our economy) is not the simple operation generally contemplated in economic theory. Such a firm usually has in its product mix (1) items in various stages of introduction and development, some of which may be fantastically profitable and others deep "in the red"; (2) items which are mature but not "superannuated," whose profit rate is likely to be satisfactory; and (3) declining items which may yield a net profit somewhat less than adequate or may show heavy losses.

The task is to manage the whole line or mix so that it will show a satisfactory profit for the company. In this process, two questions are vital: What is a profit? How much profit is satisfactory?

Operating-statement accounting makes it possible to determine with reasonable accuracy the total amount of net profit a company earns on an overall basis. But when the management of a multi-product firm seeks to determine how much of this total is generated by its activities in making and marketing each product in its mix, the process is almost incredibly complex; and the results are almost certain to be conditioned on a tissue of assumptions which are so debatable that no management can feel entirely comfortable in basing decisions on them.

This is because such a large portion of the costs of the average multi-product firm are or behave like overhead or joint expense. Almost inevitably several of the items in the product mix are made of common materials, with the same equipment, and by manpower which is interchangeable. Most of the company's marketing efforts and expenses are devoted to selling and distributing the mix or a line within the mix, rather than individual items.

In general, the more varied the product mix of a firm, the greater is the portion of its total expense that must be classified as joint or overhead. In such a company, many types of cost which ordinarily can be considered direct tend to behave like overhead or joint expenses. This is particularly true of marketing costs such as advertising that does not feature specific items; personal selling; order handling; and delivery.

This means that a large part of a company's costs must be assigned to products on some arbitrary basis and that however logical this basis may be, it is subject to considerable reasonable doubt in specific cases. It also means that if one product is removed from the mix, many of these costs remain to be reassigned to the items that stay in the line. As a result, any attempt to "prune" the product mix entirely on the basis of the profit contribution, or lack of it, of specific items is almost certain to be disappointing and in some cases disastrous.

But if a multi-product firm could allocate costs to individual items in the mix on some basis recognized as sound and thus compute product-profit accurately, what standard of profit should be set up, the failure to meet which would justify deletion?

Probably most managements either formally or unconsciously set overall company profit targets. Such targets may be expressed in terms of dollars, although to be most useful in product management they usually must be translated into percentages on investment, or money used. As an example, a company may have as its profit target 15% on investment before taxes.

Certainly *every* product in the mix should not be required to achieve the target, which really amounts to an average. To do so would be to deny the inevitable variations in profit potential among products.

Probably a practical minimum standard can be worked out, below which a product should be eliminated unless other considerations demand its retention. Such a standard can be derived from a balancing out of the profit rates among products in the mix, so as to arrive at the overall company target as an average. The minimum standard thenrepresents a figure that would tip the balance enough to endanger the overall target.

What role, then, should considerations of product profit play in managerial decisions as to deletion or retention?

1. Management probably will be wise to recognize an overall company target profit in dollars or rate on investment, and to set in relation to it a minimum below which the profit on an individual product should not fall without marking that item for deletion (unless other special considerations demand its retention).
2. Management should cast a "bilious eye" on all arguments that a questionable product be kept in the mix because it helps to defray overhead and joint costs. Down that road, at the end of a series of decisions to retain such products lies a mix entirely or largely composed of items each busily "sopping up" overhead, but few or none contributing anything to net profit.
3. This does not mean that management should ignore the effect of a product deletion on overhead or joint costs. Decision-makers must be keenly aware of the fact that the total of such costs borne by a sick product must, after it is deleted, be reallocated to other products, and with the result that they may become of doubtful profitability. A detailed examination of the joint or overhead costs charged against an ailing product may indicate that some of them can be eliminated in whole or in part if it is eliminated. Such costs are notoriously "sticky" and difficult to get rid of; but every pretext should be used to try to find ways to reduce them.
4. If a deletion decision involves a product or a group of products responsible for a significant portion of a firm's total sales volume, decision-makers can assess the effects of overhead and joint costs on the problem, by compiling an estimated company operating statement after the deletion and comparing it with the current one. Such a forecasted statement should include expected net income from the use of the capital and facilities released by deletion if an opportunity for their use is ready to hand. Surviving joint and overhead expenses can even be reallocated to the remaining products, in order to arrive at an estimate of the effect that deletion might have, not only on the total company net income but on the profitability of each of the remaining products as well. Obviously such a cost analysis is likely to be expensive, and so is not justified unless the sales volume stakes are high.

Financial Considerations

Deletion is likely not only to affect the profit performance of a firm but to modify its financial structure as well.

To make and sell a product, a company must invest some of its capital. In considering its deletion, the decision-makers must estimate what will happen to the capital funds presently used in making and marketing it.

When a product is dropped from the mix, most or all of the circulating capital invested in it—such as inventories of materials, goods in process, and finished goods and accounts receivable—should drain back into the cash account; and if carried out in an orderly fashion, deletion will not disturb this part of the capital structure except to increase the ratio of cash to other assets.

This will be true, unless the deletion decision is deferred until product deterioration has gone so far that the decision assumes the aspect of a crisis and its execution that of a catastrophe.

The funds invested in the equipment and other facilities needed to make and market the "sick" product are a different matter. If the equipment is versatile and standard, it may be diverted to other uses. If the firm has no need of it and if the equipment has been properly depreciated, management may find a market for it at a price approaching or even exceeding its book value.

In either case, the capital structure of the company is not disturbed except by a shift from equipment to cash in the case of sale. In such a case management would be wise, before making a deletion decision, to determine how much cash this action promises to release as well as the chances for its reinvestment.

If the equipment is suited for only one purpose, it is highly unlikely that management can either find another use for it or sell it on favorable terms. If it is old and almost completely depreciated, it can probably be scrapped and its remaining value "written off" without serious impairment of the firm's capital structure.

But if it is only partly depreciated, the decision-makers must weigh the relative desirability of two possible courses of action: (1) to delete immediately, hoping that the ensuing improvement in the firm's operating results will more than offset the impairment in capital structure that deletion will cause; or (2) to seek to recapture as much as possible of its value, by continuing to make and market the product as long as its price is enough to cover out-of-pocket costs and leave something over to apply to depreciation.

This choice depends largely on two things: the relation between the amount of fixed and circulating capital that is involved; and the opportunities available to use the funds, executive abilities, manpower, and transferable facilities released by deletion for making profits in other ventures.

This matter of opportunity costs is a factor in every deletion decision. The dropping of a product is almost certain to release some capital, facilities, manpower skills, and executive abilities. If opportunities can be found in which these assets can be invested without undue risk and with promise of attractive profits, it may be good management to absorb considerable immediate loss in deleting a sick product.

If no such opportunities can be found, it is probably wise to retain the product so long as the cash inflow from its sales covers out-of-pocket costs and contributes something to depreciation and other overhead expenses. In such a case, however, it is the part of good management to seek actively for new ventures which promise satisfactory profits, and to be ready to delete promptly when such an opportunity is found.

Employee Relations

The effect which product elimination may have on the employees of a firm is often an important factor in decisions either to drop or to retain products.

This is not likely to be a deciding factor if new product projects are under development to which the people employed in making and marketing the doubtful product can be transferred, unless such transfer would deprive them of the earning power of special skills. But when deletion of a product means discharging or transferring unionized employees, the decision-makers must give careful thought to the effect their action is likely to have on company-union relations.

Even in the absence of union pressure, management usually feels a strong sense of responsibility for the people in its employ. Just how far management can go in conserving specific jobs at the expense of deferring or foregoing necessary deletions before it endangers the livelihood of all the employees of the firm is a nice question of balance.

Marketing Factors

Many multi-product firms retain in their marketing mixes one or more items which, on the basis of profits and the company financial structure, should be deleted. To continue to make and market a losing product is no managerial crime. It is reprehensible only when management does not know the product is a losing one or, knowing the facts, does not have sound reasons for retaining it. Such reasons are very likely to lie in the marketing area.

Deletions of products are often deferred or neglected because of management's desire to carry a "full line," whatever that means. This desire may be grounded on sound reasons of consumer patronage or on a dubious yearning for the "prestige" that a full line is supposed to engender. But there is no magic about a full line or the prestige that is supposed to flow from it. Both should be evaluated on the basis of their effects on the firm's sales volume, profits, and capacity to survive and grow.

Products are often associated in the marketing process. The sale of one is helped by the presence of another in the product mix.

When elimination of a product forces a customer who buys all or a large part of his requirements of a group of profitable items from the firm to turn to another supplier for his needs of the dropped product, he might shift some or all of his other patronage as well. Accordingly, it is sometimes wise for management to retain in its mix a no-profit item, in order to hold sales volume of highly profitable products. But this should not be done blindly without analysis.

Rarely can management tell ahead of time exactly how much other business will be lost by deleting a product, or in what proportions the losses will fall among the remaining items. But in many cases the amount of sales volume can be computed that will be *hazarded* by such action; what other products will be subject to that hazard; and what portion of their volume will be involved. When this marketing interdependence exists in a deletion problem, the decision-makers should seek to discover the customers who buy the sick product; what other items in the mix they buy; in what quantities; and how much profit they contribute.

The firm using direct marketing channels can do this with precision and at relatively little cost. The firm marketing through indirect channels will find it more difficult, and the information will be less exact; but it still may be worthwhile. If the stakes are high enough, marketing research may be conducted to discover the extent to which the customer purchases of profitable items actually are associated with that of the sick product. Although the results may not be precise, they may supply an order-of-magnitude idea of the interlocking patronage situation.

Product interrelationships in marketing constitute a significant factor in making deletion decisions, but should never be accepted as the deciding factor without careful study to disclose at least the extent of the hazards they involve.

Other Possibilities

The fact that a product's market is declining or that its profit performance is substandard does not mean that deletion is the *only* remedy.

Profits can be made in a shrinking market. There are things other than elimination of a product that can be done about deteriorating profit performance. They tend to fall into four categories.

(1) Costs. A careful study may uncover ways of reducing factory costs. This may result from improved processes that either eliminate manpower or equipment time or else increase yield; or from the elimination of forms or features that once were necessary or worthwhile but are no longer needed. The natural first recourse of allocating joint and overhead costs on a basis that is "kinder" to the doubtful product is not to be viewed with enthusiasm. After reallocation, these costs still remain in the business; and the general profit picture has not been improved in the least.

(2) Marketing. Before deleting a product, management will be wise to examine the methods of marketing it, to see if they can be changed to improve its profit picture.

Can advertising and sales effort be reduced without serious loss of volume? A holding operation requires much less effort and money than a promotional one.

Are services being given that the product no longer needs?

Can savings be made in order handling and delivery, even at some loss of customer satisfaction? For example, customers may be buying the product in small orders that are expensive to handle.

On the other hand, by spending more marketing effort, can volume be increased so as to bring about a reduction in factory cost greater than the added marketing expense? In this attempt, an unexpected "assist" may come from competititors who delete the product and leave more of the field to the firm.

By remodeling the product, "dressing it up," and using a new marketing approach, can it be brought back to a state of health and profit? Here the decision-makers must be careful not to use funds and facilities that could be more profitably invested in developing and marketing new products.

(3) Price. It is natural to assume that the price of a failing product cannot be raised. At least in part, its plight is probably due to the fact that it is "kicked around" by competition, and thus that competition will not allow any increases.

But competitors may be tired of the game, too. One company that tried increasing prices found that wholesalers and retailers did not resent a larger cost-of-goods-sold base on which to apply their customary gross profit rates, and that consumers continued to buy and competitors soon followed suit.

Although a price rise will not usually add to the sum total of user happiness, it may not subtract materially from total purchases. The decision-makers should not ignore the possibility of using a price reduction to gain enough physical volume to bring about a more-than-offsetting decline in unit costs, although at this stage the success of such a gambit is not likely.

(4) Cross Production. In the materials field, when small production runs make costs prohibitive, arrangements may sometimes be made for Firm A to make the *entire* supply of Product X for itself and Competitor B. Then B reciprocates with another similar product. Such "trades," for instance, are to be found in the chemical business.

SUMMATION FOR DECISION

In solving deletion problems, the decision-makers must draw together into a single pattern the results of the analysis of all the factors bearing on the matter. Although this is probably most often done on an intangible, subjective basis, some firms have experimented with the formula method.

For example, a manufacturer of electric motors included in its formula the following factors:

Profitability
Position on growth curve
Product leadership
Market position
Marketing dependence of other products

Each factor was assigned a weight in terms of possible "counts" against the product. For instance, if the doubtful item promised no profits for the next three years, it had a count of 50 points against it, while more promising prospects were assigned lesser counts. A critical total for all factors was set in advance which would automatically doom a product. Such a system can include other factors—such as recapturability of invested capital, alternate available uses of facilities, effects on labor force, or other variables peculiar to the individual case.

The use of a formula lends an aura of precision to the act of decision-making and assures a degree of uniformity in it. But obviously the weights assigned to different factors cannot be the same in all cases. For example, if the deletion of a doubtful product endangers a large volume of sales of other highly profitable items, that alone should probably decide the matter.

The same thing is true if deletion will force so heavy a writeoff of invested funds as to impair the firm's capital structure. Certainly this will be true if all or most of the investment can be recaptured by the depreciation route if the product stays in the mix.

This kind of decision requires that the factors be weighted differently in each case. But when managers are given a formula, they may tend to quit thinking and do too much "weighing."

The Deletion of a Product

Once the decision to eliminate a product is made, plans must be drawn for its death and burial with the least disturbance of customer relations and of the other operations of the firm.

Such plans must deal with a variety of detailed problems. Probably the most important fall into four categories: timing; parts and replacements; stocks; and holdover demand.

Timing. It is desirable that deletion be timed so as to dovetail with the financial, manpower, and facilities needs for new products. As manpower and facilities are released from the dying product and as the capital devoted to it flows back into the cash account, it is ideal if these can be immediately used in a new venture. Although this can never be completely achieved, it may be approximated.

The death of a product should be timed so as to cause the least disturbance to customers. They should be informed about the elimination of the product far enough in advance so they can make arrangements for replacement, if any are available, but not so far in advance that they will switch to new suppliers before the deleting firm's inventories of the product are sold. Deletion at the beginning of a selling season or in the middle of it probably will create maximum customer inconvenience. whereas at the end of the season it will be the least disturbing.

Parts and Replacements. If the product to be killed off is a durable one, probably the deleting firm will find it necessary to maintain stocks of repair parts for about the expected life of the units most recently sold. The firm that leaves a trail of uncared-for "orphan" products cannot expect to engender much good will from dealers or users. Provision for the care and maintenance of the orphan is a necessary cost of deletion.

This problem is much more widespread than is commonly understood. The woman who buys a set of china or silverware and finds that she cannot replace broken or lost pieces does not entertain an affectionate regard for the maker. The same sort of thing is true if she installs draperies and later, when one of them is damaged, finds that the pattern is no longer available.

Stocks. The deletion plan should provide for clearing out the stocks of the dying product and materials used in its production, so as to recover the maximum amount of the working capital invested in it. This is very largely a matter of timing—the tapering off of purchase, production, and selling activities. However, this objective may conflict with those of minimizing inconvenience to customers and servicing the orphan units in use after deletion.

Holdover Demand. However much the demand for a product may decline, it probably will retain some following of devoted users. They are bound to be disturbed by its deletion and are likely to be vocal about it; and usually there is little that management can do to mitigate this situation.

Sometimes a firm can avoid all these difficulties by finding another firm to purchase the product. This should usually be tried before any other deletion steps are taken. A product with a volume too small for a big firm to handle profitably may be a money-maker for a smaller one with less overhead and more flexibility.

NEGLECT OR ACTION?

The process of product deletion is important. The more dynamic the business, the more important it is.

But it is something that most company executives prefer not to do; and therefore it will not get done unless management establishes definite, clearcut policies to guide it, sets up carefully articulated procedures for doing it, and makes a positive and unmistakable assignment of authority and responsibility for it.

Exactly what these policies should be, what form these procedures should take, and to whom the job should be assigned are matters that must vary with the structure and operating methods of the firm and with its postiion in the industry and the market.

In any case, though, the need for managerial attention, planning, and supervision of the deletion function cannot be overemphasized. Many business firms are paying dearly for their neglect of this problem, but unfortunately do not realize how much this is costing them.

27

Are Channels of Distribution What the Textbooks Say?

Phillip McVey

Perhaps Wroe Alderson said as much as is safe to say when he described a marketing channel as a group of firms which "constitute a loose coalition engaged in exploiting joint opportunity in the market."[1]

THEORY AND ACTUALITY

Certainly too much is said about channel relationships in many published textbooks for businessmen and students, if one is to look for proof in current marketing practice. The picture usually given is one of long lists of various types of middlemen and facilitating agencies, which differ minutely but precisely in functions performed. Alignments of particular types are presented as "right" or "customary" for a given commodity or type of producer. Furthermore, it is often implied that it is the producer who selects all the links in the channel and establishes the working arrangements with them, down to and including the outlet which sells his goods to the final user.

Reprinted from the *Journal of Marketing*, published by the American Marketing Association (January, 1960), pp. 61–64.

Phillip McVey is professor and chairman of marketing at the University of Nebraska. He received an M.B.A. from Harvard and Ph.D. in marketing from Ohio State University, where he later taught. He has also taught engineering administration at Case-Western Reserve University.

[1] Wroe Alderson, "The Development of Marketing Channels," in Richard M. Clewett (editor), *Marketing Channels for Manufactured Products* (Homewood, Illinois; Richard D. Irwin, Inc., 1954), p. 30.

Several popular college textbooks in marketing illustrate this manufacturer-oriented approach to channel planning.[2] One reason for fairly standard treatment of channel-building is that the growth of marketing knowledge has proceeded from a description of the activities of existing business firms, leaning heavily on data provided by the U.S. Censuses of Wholesale and Retail Trade. The framework appears orderly and well planned. But little recognition is given to the probability that some channel sequences "just grew" like Topsy, without direction or intent of known parents.

The Census method of counting, whereby each separate establishment is assigned to a single traditional category on the basis of a *major-portion-of-dollar-volume* rule, tends to produce more orderliness in the picture than probably exists. It tends to obscure a great deal of "promiscuous distribution" and channel-jumping. The Census rule, like the Procrustean bed of Greek mythology, effectively reduces the number of categories into which firms are sorted, and avoids hybrid, nondescript classifications.

Yet hybridity is too common among marketing firms to be ignored. For example, almost any wholesaler will do some business at retail; similarly, it is not uncommon for a broker to find himself holding title to a given lot of goods, thus becoming temporarily a merchant middleman. A realistic classification may require the use of relative terms to identify types of operation, according to a range of variables—for example, the *degree* to which a firm caters to a given customer group, or the *frequency* with which a function is performed.

Further study of marketing textbooks may lead a reader to conclude that: (a) middlemen of many types are available to any manufacturer in any market to which he wishes to sell, and within each type there is an ample selection of individual firms; (b) the manufacturer habitually controls the selection and operation of individual firms in his channel; and (c) middlemen respond willingly as *selling agents* for the manufacturer rather than as *purchasing agents* for a coveted group of customers to whom the middlemen sell.

Yet none of these conclusions is entirely valid.

In a product line such as fashion apparel, a garment maker may have an extremely limited choice of types of middlemen: the selling agent, the broker, and direct-buying retailer, or the chain store buying office. The general absence of service wholesalers from this line of trade is not correctible by manufacturers' *fiat*.

---

[2] Examples are found in: T. N. Beckman, H. H. Maynard, and W. R. Davidson, *Principles of Marketing*, sixth edition (New York, The Ronald Press Company, 1957), pp. 44–45. C. F. Phillips and D. J. Duncan, *Marketing Principles and Methods*, third edition (Homewood, Illinois; Richard D. Irwin, Inc., 1956), p. 562. M. P. McNair, M. P. Brown, D. S. R. Leighton, and W. B. England, *Problems in Marketing*, second edition (New York, McGraw-Hill Book Company, Inc., 1957), p. 66.

In a particular market area, the choice may be even more limited. Of individual firms of a given type, there may be no choice at all. These limitations arise, of course, because of the free choices made by the middlemen as to locations, customer groups, and product assortments they elect to sell.

IS THE "CHANNEL" AN ACADEMIC CONCEPT?

Integrated action up and down a channel is a rare luxury in marketing. Why? It may be that the "channel of distribution" is a concept that is principally academic in usage and unfamiliar to many firms selling to and through these channels.

Instead of a channel, a businessman is likely to concern himself merely with suppliers and customers. His dealings are not with all of the links in the channel but only with those immediately adjacent to him, from which he buys and to which he sells. He may little know nor care what becomes of his products after they leave the hands of some merchant middleman who has paid him for them and released him to return to problems involving his special functions. A manufacturer may not even consider himself as standing at the head of a channel, but only as occupying a link in a channel that begins with his suppliers.

Policies

Choice of a channel is not open to any firm unless it has considerable freedom of action in matters of marketing policy. Other areas of policy seem to be treated with more respect. For example, it is well recognized that a *price* policy is an authoritarian privilege open only to those sellers who possess power to withhold goods from the market in considerable quantities, or who have the choice of alternative markets and the means to solicit them. Usually a differentiated product is necessary. Therefore, a wheat farmer can seldom have anything resembling a price policy.

Likewise, a *design* policy is meaningful only when variations in product characteristics have been understood and accepted by customers to be of significance. Manufacturers of semi-finished or component parts, or of textile "gray goods" cannot enjoy this luxury in most cases.

Similarly, the selection of a multi-stage channel is not the prerogative of a manufacturer unless his franchise is coveted by the middlemen he seeks, as being more valuable to them than their franchise would be to him.

Names such as Sears Roebuck & Company, Macy's, or Kroger mean a great deal more to the customers of these retailers than do the brand names of most of the items sold in their stores. These firms control the channels for many products, even to the point of bringing into existence some manufacturing firms needed to fill gaps in their assortments. In the same manner some national wholesalers, holding the reins of a huge distributive system, are more powerful than either their suppliers or their customers. In such extreme cases the power position is obvious. The big company, regardless of its position in the channel, tries to make its plans and policies effective by taking the initiative for co-ordinated action.

UNCERTAINTY AMONG SMALLER FIRMS

As to the many thousands of middlesize and small companies that truly characterize American marketing, the power position is speculative, vacillating, and ephemeral. Strength in certain market areas, the temporary success of a product, ability to perform a certain needed type of financing or promotional effort—these and similar factors enable companies to assume power.

On the other hand, financial reverses, an unfortunate sales campaign, or even the lack of accurate market news—these factors can shift power elsewhere, possibly to another link in the channel or to another firm in the same link. In any case, the opportunity of any firm is contingent upon the willingness of others to use it as a link in the channel.

Comparison with Advertising Media

Selection of middlemen has been likened to the selection of advertising media. In both instances the task is to find a vehicle which has an existing coverage (or circulation) which coincides with the market desired. A region blanketed with a neat mosaic of distributors' territories will appear on a map much like the same region covered by television stations.

However, there is an important difference. Seldom does an advertising medium restrict its availability. The advertiser's product need not be sold first to the medium on the grounds of self-interest. Only occasionally will a middleman accept any product he is offered. The requirement that he invest his own money and effort forces him to be selective in terms of probable outcome or profit. No seller can afford to neglect the task of selling *to* the middlemen he seeks, as well as *through* them. Nearly every comprehensive campaign of consumer advertising allots substantial effort to dealer promotion and distributor promotion. Indeed, much consumer advertising is undertaken primarily for the stimulating effect it will have upon middlemen.

Middlemen's Reactions

Middlemen's reactions to new-product offerings probably deserve more attention from manufacturers than usual. Wholesalers and re-tailers, as well as agent middlemen, enjoy an excellent position from which to make keen judgments of a product's probable successes within local markets. Free from the manufacturer's proclivity to "fall in love with the product," but not primarily concerned with its ultimate usage characteristics, middlemen who are alert merchandisers can look at the product with an eye to salability alone.

Yet it is common practice for manufacturers to force acceptance with a heavy barrage of consumer advertising, introductory high-markup offers, free merchandise, combination deals, co-operative advertising schemes, and the like. These may have the effect of "mesmerizing" middlemen, and clouding the issue of the product's own rate of initial acceptance.

Lack of effective vertical communication in most channels is a serious deterrent. Possibly no other proof of the weakness of manufacturers' control over channels is so convincing as their inability to obtain facts from their own ultimate and intermediate markets. Information that could be used in product development, pricing, packaging, or promotion-planning is buried in non-standard records of middlemen, and sometimes purposely secreted from suppliers.

Channels research is one of the most frustrating areas of marketing investigation, since it requires access to data collected by firms which are independent, remotely situated, and suspicious. Unless given incentive to do so, middlemen will not maintain separate sales records by brands sold. Extracting the needed figures by preferred units of measure is often a hopeless task. To get such data, one producer of pipe tools adopted a device commonly used with electric appliances: a "warranty registration" questionnaire attached to the tools. Ostensibly designed to validate users' damage claims, its true purpose was to discover where, when, how, and by whom the tools had been sold.

Communication downward from the manufacturer is also faulty, placing in doubt the claim that all links in the channel are bound together by common objectives. For example, it is seldom practical to disclose a forthcoming promotional plan in all its details and to ask the middlemen whether the plan will be timely, acceptable, and supportable by their efforts. To do so would jeopardize the advantage of surprise, usually a significant competitive stratagem. Yet the value of synchronized, co-ordinated action on any new plan by all firms in the channel is obvious.

MIDDLEMEN'S VIEWS

Channel Building

To the extent that any middleman can do so, he should think of himself primarily as a purchasing agent for his customers, and only secondarily as a selling agent for his suppliers. The planning of his product line will proceed from an analysis of a finite customer group in which he is interested . . . to the selection of goods capable of satisfying those needs . . . and then to the choice of available suppliers who can provide those goods. Of course, he may actually begin his assortment with one or more basic products, chosen by him as a way of defining the area of customer needs in which he elects to deal.

From that point on, however, his chief stock in trade becomes not the franchises of important suppliers, but rather his customer group. He is interested in selling any product which these customers desire to buy from him. The attractiveness of any new offering by a supplier is not to be judged by the size of the markup or commission, nor the unusual nature of the product, nor details of its manufacture, nor the promises of manufacturer's advertising support.

The key question is: Does it fit the line? That is, does it complement the other products that he sells, in terms of salability to precisely the same group of buyers? His list of customers is probably less subject to intentional revision than are many other aspects of his business. Is it not at this point, then, that channel building starts?

Some unusual product combinations may result from this approach. A manufacturers' agent selling baby garments in the Southwest took on a line of printed business forms, which the small retailers on whom he called were seeking. An Omaha wholesaler successfully added grocery products to his liquor business. A Cleveland distributor of welding equipment rejected a portable farm welder offered by his principal supplier, since he had no contact with farmers, but was interested in carrying a line of warehouse tractors and lift trucks.

Approach to New Prospects

In some cases a middleman may deem it worthwhile to shift from his current customer group to a new list of prospects, in order to find a market for a particularly promising new product. In the main, however, he will not do so. His approach to new prospects is based on their close similarity to those now on his customer list. To all these persons he attempts to become known as a helpful specialist in a well-defined set of recurring needs. The scope of his line, and the interrelation of products in it, must be known to the bulk of his customers. Scrambled merchandising, or stocking of unrelated items, will tend to split his market into many small groups.

Assortment Sales

Furthermore, the middleman attempts to weld all of his offerings into a family of items which he can sell in combination, as a packaged assortment, to individual customers. His selling efforts are directed primarily at obtaining orders for the assortment, rather than for individual items. Naturally the greatest *numbers* of his transactions will seldom be made in this way; but often his greatest volume and more profitable sales to "blue-chip" accounts will be assortment sales.

Catering to assortment sales has considerable significance to channel operation, because the kind of sales service which a middleman can offer a single-product supplier is affected thereby. Since he is relatively disinterested in pushing individual items, the middleman is criticized for failure to stress a given brand, or for the poor quality of his salesmen's product knowledge, his disuse of suppliers' advertising materials, his neglect of certain customers (who may be good prospects for individual items but not for the assortment), and even for his unrefined systems of record keeping, in which brand designations may be lost.

THE MIDDLEMAN AS AN INDEPENDENT MARKET

The middleman is not a hired link in a chain forged by a manufacturer, but rather an independent market, the focus of a large group of customers for whom he buys. Subsequent to some market analysis of his own, he selects products and suppliers, thereby setting at least one link in the channel.

· After some experimentation, he settles upon a method of operation, performing those functions he deems inescapable in the light of his own objectives, forming policies for himself wherever he has freedom to do so. Perhaps these methods and policies conform closely to those of a Census category of middleman, but perhaps they do not.

It is true that his choices are in many instances tentative proposals. He is subject to much influence from competitors, from aggressive suppliers, from inadequate finances and faulty information, as well as from habit. Nonetheless, many of his choices are independent.

As he grows and builds a following, he may find that his prestige in his market is greater than that of the suppliers whose goods he sells. In some instances his local strength is so great that a manufacturer is virtually unable to tap that market, except through him. In such a case the manufacturer can have no channel policy with respect to that market.

28

Conflict and Cooperation in Marketing Channels

Bruce Mallen

The purpose of this paper is to advance the hypotheses that between member firms of a marketing channel there exists a dynamic field of conflicting and cooperating objectives; that if the conflicting objectives outweigh the cooperating ones, the effectiveness of the channel will be reduced and efficient distribution impeded; and that implementation of certain methods of cooperation will lead to increased channel efficiency.

DEFINITION OF CHANNEL

The concept of a marketing channel is slightly more involved than expected on initial study. One author in a recent paper[1] has identified "trading" channels, "non-trading" channels, "type" channels, "enterprise" channels, and "business-unit" channels. Another source[2] refers to channels as all the flows extending from the producer to the user.

Reprinted from L. George Smith (ed.) *Reflections on Progress in Marketing,* published by the American Marketing Association in 1964, pp. 65–85.

Bruce Mallen is professor of marketing at Sir George Williams University in Montreal. He is an international authority in the field of distribution channels. He has contributed widely to scholarly publications and formerly headed his own firm, Bruce Mallen and Associates, Inc., a marketing consulting firm.

[1] Ralph F. Breyer, "Some Observations on Structural Formation and The Growth of Marketing Channels," in *Theory in Marketing,* Reavis Cox, Wroe Alderson, Stanley J. Shapiro, Editors. (Homewood, Ill.: Richard D. Irwin, 1964), pp. 163–175.

[2] Ronald S. Vaile, E. T. Grether, and Reavis Cox, *Marketing in the American Economy* (New York: Ronald Press, 1952), pp. 121 and 124.

These include the flows of physical possession, ownership, promotion, negotiation, financing, risking, ordering, and payment.

The concept of channels to be used here involves only two of the above-mentioned flows: ownership and negotiation. The first draws merchants, both wholesalers and retailers, into the channel definition, and the second draws in agent middlemen. Both, of course, include producers and consumers. This definition roughly corresponds to Professor Breyer's "trading channel," though the latter does not restrict (nor will this paper) the definition to actual flows but to "flow-capacity." "A trading channel is formed when trading relations, making possible the passage of title and/or possession (usually both) of goods from the producer to the ultimate consumer, are consummated by the component trading concerns of the system."[3] In addition, this paper will deal with trading channels in the broadest manner and so will be concentrating on "type-trading" channels rather than "enterprise" or "business-unit" channels. This means that there will be little discussion of problems peculiar to integrated or semi-integrated channels, or peculiar to specific channels and firms.

CONFLICT

Palamountain isolated three forms of distributive conflict.[4]

1. Horizontal competition—this is competition between middlemen of the same type; for example, discount store *versus* discount store.
2. Intertype competition—this is competition between middlemen of different types in the same channel sector; for example, discount store *versus* department store.
3. Vertical conflict—this is conflict between channel members of different levels; for example, discount store *versus* manufacturer.

The first form horizontal competition, is well covered in traditional economic analysis and is usually referred to simply as "competition." However, both intertype competition and vertical conflict, particularly the latter, are neglected in the usual micro-economic discussion.

The concepts of "intertype competition" and "distributive innovation" are closely related and require some discussion. Intertype competition will be divided into two categories: (a) "traditional intertype competition" and (b) "innovative intertype competition." The first category includes the usual price and promotional competition

---

[3] Breyer, *op. cit.*, p. 165.

[4] Joseph C. Palamountain, *The Politics of Distribution* (Cambridge: Harvard University Press, 1955).

between two or more different types of channel members at the same channel level. The second category involves the action on the part of traditional channel members to prevent channel innovators from establishing themselves. For example, in Canada there is a strong campaign, on the part of traditional department stores, to prevent the discount operation from taking a firm hold on the Canadian market.[5]

Distributive innovation will also be divided into two categories: (a) "intrafirm innovative conflict" and (b) "innovative intertype competition." The first category involves the action of channel member firms to prevent sweeping changes within their own companies. The second category, "innovative intertype competition," is identical to the second category of intertype competition.

Thus the concepts of intertype competition and distributive innovation give rise to three forms of conflict, the second of which is a combination of both: 1. traditional intertype competition, 2. innovative intertype competition, and 3. intrafirm innovative conflict.

It is to this second form that this paper now turns before going on to vertical conflict.

Innovative Intertype Competition

Professor McCammon has identified several sources, both intrafirm and intertype, of innovative conflict in distribution, i.e., where there are barriers to change within the marketing structure.[6]

Traditional members of a channel have several motives for maintaining the channel status quo against outside innovators. The traditional members are particularly strong in this conflict when they can band together in some formal or informal manner—when there is strong reseller solidarity.

Both entrepreneurs and professional managers may resist outside innovators, not only for economic reasons, but because change "violates group norms, creates uncertainty, and results in a loss of status." The traditional channel members (the insiders) and their affiliated members (the strivers and complementors) are emotionally and financially committed to the dominant channel and are interested in perpetuating it against the minor irritations of the "transient" channel members and the major attacks of the "outside innovators."

---

[5] Isaiah A. Litvak and Bruce E. Mallen, *Marketing: Canada* (Toronto: McGraw-Hill of Canada, Limited, 1964), pp. 196-197.

[6] This section is based on Bert C. McCammon, Jr., "Alternative Explanations of Institutional Change and Channel Evolution," in *Toward Scientific Marketing.* Stephen A. Greyser, Editor. (Chicago: American Marketing Association, 1963), pp. 477-490.

Thus, against a background of horizontal and intertype channel conflict, this paper now moves to its area of major concern: vertical conflict and cooperation.

Vertical Conflict—Price

The Exchange Act. The act of exchange is composed of two elements: a sale and a purchase. It is to the advantage of the seller to obtain the highest return possible from such an exchange and the exact opposite is the desire of the buyer. This exchange act takes place between any kind of buyer and seller. If the consumer is the buyer, then that side of the act is termed shopping; if the manufacturer, purchasing; if the government, procurement; and if a retailer, buying. Thus, between each level in the channel an exchange will take place (except if a channel member is an agent rather than a merchant).

One must look to the process of the exchange act for the basic source of conflict between channel members. This is not to say the exchange act itself is a conflict. Indeed, the act or transaction is a sign that the element of price conflict has been resolved to the mutual satisfaction of both principals. Only along the road to this mutual satisfaction point or exchange price do the principals have opposing interests. This is no less true even if they work out the exchange price together, as in mass retailers' specification-buying programs.

It is quite natural for the selling member in an exchange to want a higher price than the buying member. The conflict is subdued through persuasion or force by one member over the other, or it is subdued by the fact that the exchange act or transaction does not take place, or finally, as mentioned above, it is eliminated if the act does take place.

Suppliers may emphasize the customer aspect of a reseller rather than the channel member aspect. As a customer the reseller is somebody to persuade, manipulate, or even fool. Conversely, under the marketing concept, the view of the reseller as a customer or channel member is identical. Under this philosophy he is somebody to aid, help, and serve. However, it is by no means certain that even a large minority of suppliers have accepted the marketing concept.

To view the reseller as simply the opposing principal in the act of exchange may be channel myopia, but this view exists. On the other hand, failure to recognize this basic opposing interest is also a conceptual fault.

When the opposite principals in an exchange act are of unequal strength, the stronger is very likely to force or persuade the weaker to adhere to the former's desires. However, when they are of equal strength, the basic conflict cannot so easily be resolved. Hence, the growth of big retailers who can match the power of big producers has possibly led to greater open conflict between channel members, not only with regard to exchange, but also to other conflict sources.

There are other sources of conflict within the pricing area outside of the basic one discussed above.

A supplier may force a product onto its resellers, who dare not oppose, but who retaliate in other ways, such as using it as a loss leader. Large manufacturers may try to dictate the resale price of their merchandise; this may be less or more than the price at which resellers wish to sell it. Occasionally, a local market may be more competitive for a reseller than is true nationally. The manufacturer may not recognize the difference in competition and refuse to help this channel member.

Resellers complain of manufacturers' special price concessions to competitors and rebel at the attempt of manufacturers to control resale prices. Manufacturers complain of resellers' deceptive and misleading price advertising, nonadherence to resale price suggestions, bootlegging to unauthorized outlets, seeking special price concessions by unfair methods, and misrepresenting offers by competitive suppliers.

Other points of price conflict are the paperwork aspects of pricing. Resellers complain of delays in price change notices and complicated price sheets.

Price Theory. If one looks upon a channel as a series of markets or as the vertical exchange mechanism between buyers and sellers, one can adapt several theories and concepts to the channel situation which can aid marketing theory in this important area of channel conflict.[7]

Vertical Conflict—Non-Price

Channel conflict not only finds its source in the exchange act and pricing, but it permeates all areas of marketing. Thus, a manufacturer may wish to promote a product in one manner or to a certain degree while his resellers oppose this. Another manufacturer may wish to get information from his resellers on a certain aspect relating to his product, but his resellers may refuse to provide this information. A producer may want to distribute his product extensively, but his resellers may demand exclusives.

---

[7] Bruce Mallen, "Introducing The Marketing Channel To Price Theory," *Journal of Marketing,* July, 1964, pp. 29–33.

There is also conflict because of the tendency for both manufacturers and retailers to want the elimination of the wholesaler.

One very basic source of channel conflict is the possible difference in the primary business philosophy of channel members. Writing in the *Harvard Business Review*, Wittreich says:

> In essence, then, the key to understanding management's problem of crossed purpose is the recognition that the fundamental (philosophy) in life of the high-level corporate manager and the typical (small) retailer dealer in the distribution system are quite different. The former's (philosophy) can be characterized as being essentially dynamic in nature, continuously evolving and emerging; the latter, which is in sharp contrast, can be characterized as being essentially static in nature, reaching a point and leveling off into a continuously satisfying plateau.[8]

While the big members of the channel may want growth, the small retail members may be satisfied with stability and a "good living."

ANARCHY[9]

The channel can adjust to its conflicting–cooperating environment in three distinct ways. *First,* it can have a leader (one of the channel members) who "forces" members to cooperate; this is an autocratic relationship. *Second,* it can have a leader who "helps" members to cooperate, creating a democratic relationship. *Finally,* it can do nothing, and so have an anarchistic relationship. Lewis B. Sappington and C. G. Browne, writing on the problems of internal company organizations, state:

> The first classification may be called "autocracy." In this approach to the group the leader determines the policy and dictates or assigns the work tasks. There are no group deliberations, no group decisions. . . .
> The second classification may be called "democracy." In this approach the leader allows all policies to be decided by the group with his participation. The group members work with each other as they wish. The group determines the division and assignment of tasks. . . .
> The third classification may be called "anarchy." In anarchy there is complete freedom of the group or the individual regarding policies or task assignments, without leader participation.[10]

---

[8]Warren J. Wittreich, "Misunderstanding The Retailers," *Harvard Business Review,* May–June, 1962, p. 149.

[9]The term "anarchy" as used in this paper connotes "no leadership" and nothing more.

[10]Lewis B. Sappington and C. G. Browne, "The Skills of Creative Leadership," in *Managerial Marketing,* rev. ed., William Lazer and Eugene J. Kelley, Editors (Homewood, Ill.: Richard D. Irwin, 1962), p. 350.

Advanced in this paper is the hypothesis that if anarchy exists, there is a great chance of the conflicting dynamics destroying the channel. If autocracy exists, there is less chance of this happening. However, the latter method creates a state of cooperation based on power and control. This controlled cooperation is really subdued conflict and makes for a more unstable equilibrium than does voluntary democratic cooperation.

CONTROLLED COOPERATION

The usual pattern in the establishment of channel relationships is that there is a leader, an initiator who puts structure into this relationship and who holds it together. This leader controls, whether through command or cooperation, i.e., through an autocratic or a democratic system.

Too often it is automatically assumed that the manufacturer or producer will be the channel leader and that the middlemen will be the channel followers. This has not always been so, nor will it necessarily be so in the future. The growth of mass retailers is increasingly challenging the manufacturer for channel leadership, as the manufacturer challenged the wholesaler in the early part of this century.

The following historical discussion will concentrate on the three-ring struggle between manufacturer, wholesaler, and retailer rather than on the changing patterns of distribution within a channel sector, i.e., between service wholesaler and agent middleman or discount and department store. This will lay the necessary background for a discussion of the present-day manufacturer-dominated *versus* retailer-dominated struggle.

Early History

The simple distribution system of Colonial days gave way to a more complex one. Among the forces of change were the growth of population, the long distances involved, the increasing complexity of new products, the increase of wealth, and the increase of consumption.

The United States was ready for specialists to provide a growing and widely dispersed populace with the many new goods and services required. The more primitive methods of public markets and barter could not sufficiently handle the situation. This type of system required short distances, few products, and a small population to operate properly.

In the same period that this older system was dissolving, the retailer was still a very small merchant who, especially in the West, lived in relative isolation from his supply sources. Aside from being small, he further diminished his power position by spreading himself thin over many merchandise lines. The retailer certainly was no specialist but was as general as a general store can be. His opposite channel member, the manufacturer, was also a small businessman, too concerned with production and financial problems to fuss with marketing.

Obviously, both these channel members were in no position to assume leadership. However, somebody had to perform all the various marketing functions between production and retailing if the economy was to function. The wholesaler filled this vacuum and became the channel leader of the 19th century.

The wholesaler became the selling force of the manufacturer and the latter's link to the widely scattered retailers over the nation. He became the retailer's life line to these distant domestic and even more important foreign sources of supply.

These wholesalers carried any type of product from any manufacturer and sold any type of product to the general retailers. They can be described as general merchandise wholesalers. They were concentrated at those transportation points in the country which gave them access to both the interior and its retailers, and the exterior and its foreign suppliers.

Early 20th Century

The end of the century saw the wholesaler's power on the decline. The manufacturer had grown larger and more financially secure with the shift from a foreign-oriented economy to a domestic-oriented one. He could now finance his marketing in a manner impossible to him in early times. His thoughts shifted to some extent from production problems to marketing problems.

Prodding the manufacturer on was the increased rivalry of his other domestic competitors. The increased investment in capital and inventory made it necessary that he maintain volume. He tended to locate himself in the larger market areas and thus, did not have great distances to travel to see his retail customers. In addition, he started to produce various products; and because of his new multiproduct production, he could reach—even more efficiently—these already more accessible markets.

The advent of the automobile and highways almost clinched the manufacturer's bid for power. For now he could reach a much vaster market (and they could reach him) and reap the benefits of economies of scale.

The branding of his products projected him to the channel leadership. No longer did he have as great a need for a specialist in reaching widely dispersed customers, nor did he need them to the same extent for their contacts. The market knew where the product came from. The age of wholesaler dominance declined. That of manufacturer dominance emerged.

Is it still here? What is its future? How strong is the challenge by retailers? Is one "better" than the other? These are the questions of the next section.

Disagreement Among Scholars

No topic seems to generate so much heat and bias in marketing as the question of who should be the channel leader, and more strangely, who is the channel leader. Depending on where the author sits, he can give numerous reasons why his particular choice should take the channel initiative.

Authors of sales management and general marketing books say the manufacturer is and should be the chief institution in the channel. Retailing authors feel the same way about retailers, and wholesaling authors (as few as there are), though not blinded to the fact that wholesaling is not "captain," still imply that they should be and talk about the coming resurrection of wholesalers. Yet a final and compromising view is put forth by those who believe that a balance of power, rather than a general and prolonged dominance of any channel member, is best.

The truth is that an immediate reaction would set in against any temporary dominance by a channel member. In that sense, there is a constant tendency toward the equilibrium of market forces. The present view is that public interest is served by a balance of power rather than by a general and prolonged predominance of any one level in marketing channels.[11]

John Kenneth Galbraith's concept of countervailing power also holds to this last view. For the retailer:

---

[11]Wroe Alderson, "Factors Governing the Development of Marketing Channels," in *Marketing Channels For Manufactured Products*, Richard M. Clewett, Editor. (Homewood, Ill.: Richard D. Irwin, 1954), p. 30.

In the opinion of the writer, "retailer-dominated marketing" has yielded, and will continue to yield in the future greater net benefits to consumers than "manufacturer-dominated marketing," as the central-buying mass distributor continues to play a role of ever-increasing importance in the marketing of goods in our economy. . . .

. . . In the years to come, as more and more large-scale multiple-unit retailers follow the central buying patterns set by Sears and Penney's, as leaders in their respective fields (hard lines and soft goods), ever-greater benefits should flow to consumers in the way of more goods better adjusted to their demands, at lower prices.[12]

. . . In a long-run buyer's market, such as we probably face in this country, the retailers have the inherent advantage of economy in distribution and will, therefore, become increasingly important.[13]

The retailer cannot be the selling agent of the manufacturer because he holds a higher commission; he is the purchasing agent for the public.[14]

For the wholesaler:

The wholesaling sector is, first of all, the most significant part of the entire marketing organization.[15]

. . . The orthodox wholesaler and affiliated types have had a resurgence to previous 1929 levels of sales importance.[16]

. . . Wholesalers have since made a comeback.[17] This revival of wholesaling has resulted from infusion of new management blood and the adoption of new techniques.[18]

For the manufacturer:

. . . the final decision in channel selection rests with the seller manufacturer and will continue to rest with him as long as he has the legal right to choose to sell to some potential customers and refuse to sell to others.[19]

These channel decisions are primarily problems for the manufacturer. They rarely arise for general wholesalers. . . .[20]

---

[12] Arnold Corbin, *Central Buying in Relation to the Merchandising of Multiple Retail Units* (New York, unpublished doctoral dissertation at New York University, 1954), pp. 708–709.

[13] David Craig and Werner Gabler, "The Competitive Struggle for Market Control," in *Readings in Marketing*, Howard J. Westing, Editor. (New York: Prentice-Hall, 1953), p. 46.

[14] Lew Hahn, *Stores, Merchants and Customers* (New York: Fairchild Publications, 1952), p. 12.

[15] David A. Revzan, *Wholesaling in Marketing Organization* (New York: John Wiley & Sons, 1961), p. 606.

[16] *Ibid.*, p. 202.

[17] E. Jerome McCarthy, *Basic Marketing* (Homewood, Ill.: Richard D. Irwin, 1960), p. 419.

[18] *Ibid.*, p. 420.

[19] Eli P. Cox, *Federal Quantity Discount Limitations and Its Possible Effects on Distribution Channel Dynamics* (unpublished doctoral dissertation, University of Texas, 1956), p. 12.

[20] Milton Brown, Wilbur B. England, John B. Matthews, Jr., *Problems in Marketing*, 3rd ed. (New York: McGraw-Hill, 1961), p. 239.

Of all the historical tendencies in the field of marketing, no other so distinctly apparent as the tendency for the manufacturer to assume greater control over the distribution of his product. . . .[21]

. . .Marketing policies at other levels can be viewed as extensions of policies established by marketing managers in manufacturing firms; and, furthermore, . . . the nature and function can adequately be surveyed by looking at the relationship to manufacturers.[22]

Pro-Manufacturer

The argument for manufacturer leadership is production-oriented. It claims that they must assure themselves of increasing volume. This is needed to derive the benefits of production scale economies, to spread their overhead over many units, to meet increasingly stiff competition, and to justify the investment risk they, not the retailers, are taking. Since retailers will not do this job for them properly, the manufacturer must control the channel.

Another major argumentative point for manufacturer dominance is that neither the public nor retailers can create new products even under a market-oriented system. The most the public can do is to select and choose among those that manufacturers have developed. They cannot select products that they cannot conceive. This argument would say that it is of no use to ask consumers and retailers what they want because they cannot articulate abstract needs into tangible goods; indeed, the need can be created by the goods rather than vice-versa.

This argument may hold well when applied to consumers, but a study of the specification-buying programs of the mass retailers will show that the latter can indeed create new products and need not be relegated to simply selecting among alternatives.

Pro-Retailer

This writer sees the mass retailer as the natural leader of the channel for consumer goods under the marketing concept. The retailer stands closest to the consumer; he feels the pulse of consumer wants and needs day in and day out. The retailer can easily undertake consumer research right on his own premises and can best interpret what is wanted, how much is wanted, and when it is wanted.

An equilibrium in the channel conflict may come about when small retailers join forces with big manufacturers in a manufacturer

---

[21] Maynard D. Phelps and Howard J. Westing, *Marketing Management*, rev. ed. (Homewood, Ill.: Richard D. Irwin, 1960), p. 11.

[22] Kenneth Davis, *Marketing Management* (New York: The Ronald Press Co., 1961), p. 131.

leadership channel to compete with a small manufacturer–big retailer leadership channel.

Pro-Wholesaler

It would seem that the wholesaler has a choice in this domination problem as well. Unlike the manufacturer and retailer though, his method is not mainly through a power struggle. This problem is almost settled for him once he chooses the type of wholesaling business he wishes to enter. A manufacturer's agent and purchasing agent are manufacturer-dominated, a sales agent dominates the manufacturer. A resident buyer and voluntary group wholesaler are retail-dominated.

Method of Manufacturer Domination

How does a channel leader dominate his fellow members? What are his tools in this channel power struggle? A manufacturer has many domination weapons at his disposal. His arsenal can be divided into promotional, legal, negative, suggestive, and, ironically, voluntary cooperative compartments.

Promotional. Probably the major method that the manufacturer has used is the building of a consumer franchise through advertising, sales promotion, and packaging of his branded products. When he has developed some degree of consumer loyalty, the other channel members must bow to his leadership. The more successful this identification through the promotion process, the more assured is the manufacturer of his leadership.

Legal. The legal weapon has also been a poignant force for the manufacturer. It can take many forms, such as, where permissible, resale price maintenance. Other contractual methods are franchises, where the channel members may become mere shells of legal entities. Through this weapon the automobile manufacturers have achieved an almost absolute dominance over their dealers.

Even more absolute is resort to legal ownership of channel members, called forward vertical integration. Vertical integration is the ultimate in manufacturer dominance of the channel. Another legal weapon is the use of consignment sales. Under this method the channel members must by law sell the goods as designated by the owner (manufacturer). Consignment selling is in a sense vertical integration; it is keeping legal ownership of the goods until they reach the consumer, rather than keeping legal ownership of the institutions which are involved in the process.

Negative Methods. Among the "negative" methods of dominance are refusal to sell to possibly uncooperative retailers or refusal to concentrate a large percentage of one's volume with any one customer.

A spreading of sales makes for a concentrating of manufacturer power, while a concentrating of sales may make for a thinning of manufacturer power. Of course, if a manufacturer is one of the few resources available and if there are many available retailers, then a concentrating of sales will also make for a concentrating of power.

The avoidance and refusal tactics, of course, eliminate the possibility of opposing dominating institutions.

Suggestives. A rather weak group of dominating weapons are the "suggestives." Thus, a manufacturer can issue price sheets and discounts, preticket and premark resale prices on goods, recommend, suggest, and advertise resale prices.

These methods are not powerful unless supplemented by promotional, legal, and/or negative weapons. It is common for these methods to boomerang. Thus a manufacturer pretickets or advertises resale prices, and a retailer cuts this price, pointing with pride to the manufacturer's suggested retail price.

Voluntary Cooperative Devices. There is one more group of dominating weapons, and these are really all the voluntary cooperating weapons to be mentioned later. The promise to provide these, or to withdraw, can have a "whip and carrot" effect on the channel members.

Retailers' Dominating Weapons

Retailers also have numerous dominating weapons at their disposal. As with manufacturers, their strongest weapon is the building of a consumer franchise through advertising, sales promotion, and branding. The growth of private brands is the growth of retail dominance.

Attempts at concentrating a retailer's purchasing power are a further group of weapons and are analogous to a manufacturer's attempts to disperse his volume. The more a retailer can concentrate his purchasing, the more dominating he can become; the more he spreads his purchasing, the more dominated he becomes. Again, if the resource is one of only a few, this generalization reverses itself.

Such legal contracts as specification buying, vertical integration (or the threat), and entry into manufacturing can also be effective. Even semiproduction, such as the packaging of goods received in bulk by the supermarket, can be a weapon of dominance.

Retailers can dilute the dominance of manufacturers by patronizing those with excess capacity and those who are "hungry" for the extra volume. There is also the subtlety, which retailers may recognize, that a strong manufacturer may concede to their wishes just to avoid an open conflict with a customer.

VOLUNTARY COOPERATION

But despite some of the conflict dynamics and forced cooperation, channel members usually have more harmonious and common interests than conflicting ones. A team effort to market a producer's product will probably help all involved. All members have a common interest in selling the product; only in the division of total channel profits are they in conflict. They have a singular goal to reach, and here they are allies. If any one of them fails in the team effort, this weak link in the chain can destroy them all. As such, all members are concerned with one another's welfare (unless a member can be easily replaced).

Organizational Extension Concept

This emphasis on the cooperating, rather than the conflicting objectives of channel members, has led to the concept of the channel as simply an extension of one's own internal organization. Conflict in such a system is to be expected even as it is to be expected within an organization. However, it is the common or "macro-objective" that is the center of concentration. Members are to sacrifice their selfish "micro-objectives" to this cause. By increasing the profit pie they will all be better off than squabbling over pieces of a smaller one. The goal is to minimize conflict and maximize cooperation. This view has been expounded in various articles by Peter Drucker, Ralph Alexander, and Valentine Ridgeway.

> Together, the manufacturer with his suppliers and/or dealers comprise a system in which the manufacturer may be designated the primary organization and the dealers and suppliers designated as secondary organizations. This system is in competition with similar systems in the economy; and in order

for the system to operate effectively as an integrated whole, there must be some administration of the system as a whole, not merely administration of the separate organizations within that system.[23]

Peter Drucker[24] has pleaded against the conceptual blindness that the idea of the legal entity generates. A legal entity is not a marketing entity. Since often half of the cost to the consumer is added on after the product leaves the producer, the latter should think of his channel members as part of his firm. General Motors is an example of an organization which does this.

Both businessmen and students of marketing often define too narrowly the problem of marketing channels. Many of them tend to define the term channels of distribution as a complex of relationships between the firm on the one hand, and marketing establishments exterior to the firm by which the products of the firm are moved to market, on the other. . . . A much broader more constructive concept embraces the relationships with external agents or units as part of the marketing organization of the company. From this viewpoint, the complex of external relationships may be regarded as merely an extension of the marketing organization of the firm. When we look at the problem in this way, we are much less likely to lose sight of the interdependence of the two structures and more likely to be constantly aware that they are closely related parts of the marketing machine. The fact that the internal organization structure is linked together by a system of employment contracts, while the external one is set up and maintained by a series of transactions, contracts of purchase and sale, tends to obscure their common purpose and close relationship.[25]

Cooperation Methods

But how does a supplier project its organization into the channel? How does it make organization and channel into one? It accomplishes this by doing many things for its resellers that it does for its own organization. It sells, advertises, trains, plans, and promotes for these firms. A brief elaboration of these methods follows.

Missionary salesmen aid the sales of channel members, as well as bolster the whole system's level of activity and selling effort. Training of resellers' salesmen and executives is an effective weapon of cooperation. The channels operate more efficiently when all are educated in the promotional techniques and uses of the products involved.

---

[23]Valentine F. Ridgeway, "Administration of Manufacture-Dealer Systems," in *Managerial Marketing,* rev. ed., William Lazer and Eugene J. Kelley, Editors. (Homewood, Ill.: Richard D. Irwin, 1962), p. 480.

[24]Peter Drucker, "The Economy's Dark Continent," *Fortune,* April, 1962, pp. 103 ff.

[25]Ralph S. Alexander, James S. Cross, Ross M. Cunningham, *Industrial Marketing,* rev. ed. (Homewood, Ill.: Richard D. Irwin, 1961), p. 266.

Involvement in the planning functions of its channel members could be another poignant weapon of the supplier. Helping resellers to set quotas for their customers, studying the market potential for them, forecasting a member's sales volume, inventory planning and protection, etc., are all aspects of this latter method.

Aid in promotion through the provision of advertising materials (mats, displays, commercials, literature, direct-mail pieces), ideas, funds (cooperative advertising), sales contests, store layout designs, push money (PM's or spiffs), is another form of cooperation.

The big supplier can act as management consultant to the members, dispensing advice in all areas of their business, including accounting, personnel, planning, control, finance, buying, paper systems or office procedure, and site selection. Aid in financing may include extended credit terms, consignment selling, and loans.

By no means do these methods of coordination take a one-way route. All members of the channel, including supplier and reseller, see their own organizations meshing with the others, and so provide coordinating weapons in accordance with their ability. Thus, the manufacturer would undertake a marketing research project for his channel, and also expect his resellers to keep records and vital information for the manufacturer's use. A supplier may also expect his channel members to service the product after the sale.

A useful device for fostering cooperation is a channel advisory council composed of the supplier and his resellers.

Finally, a manufacturer or reseller can avoid associations with potentially uncooperative channel members. Thus, a price-conservative manufacturer may avoid linking to a price-cutting retailer.

E. B. Weiss has developed an impressive, though admittedly incomplete list of cooperation methods (Table 1). Paradoxically, many of these instruments of cooperation are also weapons of control (forced cooperation) to be used by both middlemen and manufacturers. However, this is not so strange if one keeps in mind that control is subdued conflict and a form of cooperation—even though perhaps involuntary cooperation.

Extension Concept is The Marketing Concept

The philosophy of cooperation is described in the following quote:

> The essence of the marketing concept is of course customer orientation at all
> levels of distribution. It is particularly important that customer orientation

TABLE 1. *Methods of Cooperation as Listed*[26]

1. Cooperative advertising allowances	19. Delivery costs to individual stores of large retailers
2. Payments for interior displays including shelf-extenders, dump displays, "A" locations, aisle displays, etc.	20 Studies of innumerable types, such as studies of merchandise management accounting
3. P.M.'s for salespeople	21. Payments for mailings to store lists
4. Contests for buyers, salespeople, etc.	22. Liberal return privileges
5. Allowances for a variety of ware-housing functions	23. Contributions to favorite charities of store personnel
6. Payments for window display space, plus installation costs	24. Contributions to special store anniversaries
7. Detail men who check inventory, put up stock, set up complete promotions, etc.	25. Prizes, etc., to store buyers when visiting showrooms—plus entertainment, of course
8. Demonstrators	26. Training retail salespeople
9. On certain canned food, a "swell" allowance	27. Payments for store fixtures
10. Label allowance	28. Payments for new store costs, for more improvements, including painting
11. Coupon handling allowance	29. An infinite variety of promotion allowances
12. Free goods	30. Special payments for exclusive franchises
13. Guaranteed sales	31. Payments of part of salary of retail salespeople
14. In-store and window display material	32. Deals of innumerable types
15. Local research work	33. Time spent in actual selling floor by manufacturer, salesmen
16. Mail-in premium offers to consumer	34. Inventory price adjustments
17. Preticketing	35. Store name mention in manufacturer's advertising
18. Automatic reorder systems	

[26] Edward B. Weiss, "How Much of a Retailer Is the Manufacturer," in *Advertising Age*, July 21, 1958, p. 68. Reprinted with permission from the July 21, 1958, issue of *Advertising Age*. Copyright by Advertising Publications, Inc.

motivate all relations between a manufacturer and his customer—both immediate and ultimate. It must permeate his entire channels-of-distribution policy.[27]

This quote synthesizes the extension-of-the-organization system concept of channels with the marketing concept. Indeed, it shows that the former is, in essence, "the" marketing concept applied to the channel area in marketing. To continue:

[27] Hector Lazo and Arnold Corbin, *Management in Marketing* (New York: McGraw-Hill, 1961), p. 379.

The characteristics of the highly competitive markets of today naturally put a distinct premium on harmonious manufacturer-distributor relationships. Their very mutuality of interest demands that the manufacturer base his distribution program not only on what he would like from distributors, but perhaps more importantly, on what they would like from him. In order to get the cooperation of the best distributors, and thus maximum exposure for his line among the various market segments, he must adjust his policies to serve their best interest and, thereby, his own. In other words, he must put the principles of the marketing concept to work for him. By so doing, he will inspire in his customers a feeling of mutual interest and trust and will help convince them that they are essential members of his marketing team.[28]

SUMMARY

Figure 1 summarizes this whole paper. Each person within each department will cooperate, control, and conflict with each other (notice arrows). Together they form a department (notice department box contains person boxes) which will be best off when cooperating (or cooperation through control) forces weight heavier than conflicting forces. Now each department cooperates, controls, and conflicts with each other. Departments together also form a higher level organization— the firm (manufacturer, wholesaler, and retailer). Again, the firm will be better off if department cooperation is maximized and conflict minimized. Finally, firms standing vertically to each other cooperate, control, and conflict. Together they form a distribution channel that will be best off under conditions of optimum cooperation leading to consumer and profit satisfaction.

CONCLUSIONS AND HYPOTHESES

1. Channel relationships are set against a background of cooperation and conflict: horizontal, intertype, and vertical.

2. An autocratic relationship exists when one channel member controls conflict and forces the others to cooperate. A democratic relationship exists when all members agree to cooperate without a power play. An anarchistic relationship exists when there is open conflict, with no member able to impose his will on the others. This last form could destroy or seriously reduce the effectiveness of the channel.

3. The process of the exchange act where one member is a seller and the other is a buyer is the basic source of channel conflict. Economic

[28] Lazo and Corbin, *loc. cit.*

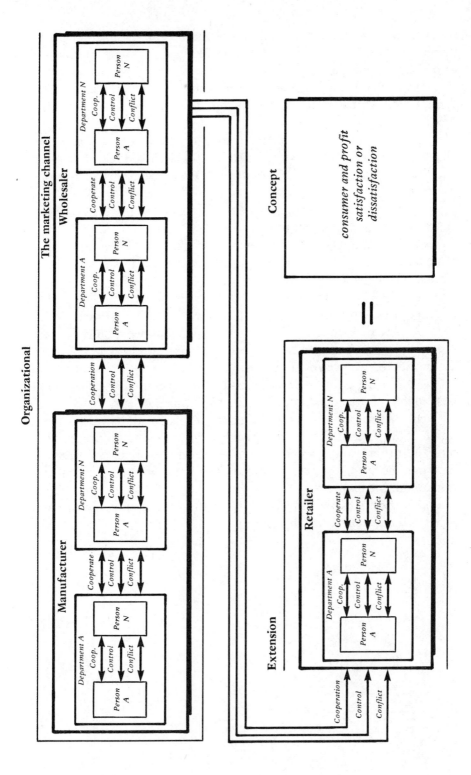

FIGURE 1.

theory can aid in comprehending this phenomenon. There are, however, many other areas of conflict, such as differences in business philosophy or primary objectives.

4. Reasons for cooperation, however, usually outweigh reasons for conflict. This has led to the concept of the channel as an extension of a firm's organization.

5. This concept drops the facade of "legal entity" and treats channel members as one great organization with the leader providing each with various forms of assistance. These are called cooperating weapons.

6. It is argued that this concept is actually the marketing concept adapted to a channel situation.

7. In an autocratic or democratic channel relationship, there must be a leader. This leadership has shifted and is shifting between the various channel levels.

8. The wholesaler was the leader in the last century, the manufacturer now, and it appears that the mass retailer is next in line.

9. There is much disagreement on the above point, however, especially on who should be the leader. Various authors have differing arguments to advance for their choice.

10. In the opinion of this writer, the mass retailer appears to be best adapted for leadership under the marketing concept.

11. As there are weapons of cooperation, so are there weapons of domination. Indeed the former paradoxically are one group of the latter. The other groups are promotional, legal, negative, and suggestive methods. Both manufacturers and retailers have at their disposal these dominating weapons.

12. *For maximization of channel profits and consumer satisfaction, the channel must act as a unit*

29

A Model for Predictive Measurements of Advertising Effectiveness

Robert J. Lavidge
Gary A. Steiner

What are the functions of advertising? Obviously the ultimate function is to help produce sales. But all advertising is not, should not, and cannot be designed to produce immediate purchases on the part of all who are exposed to it. Immediate sales results (even if measurable) are, at best, an incomplete criterion of advertising effectiveness.

In other words, the effects of much advertising are "long-term." This is sometimes taken to imply that all one can really do is wait and see—ultimately the campaign will or will not produce.

However, if something is to happen in the long run, something must be happening in the short run, something that will ultimately lead to eventual sales results. And this process must be measured in order to provide anything approaching a comprehensive evaluation of the effectiveness of the advertising.

Ultimate consumers normally do not switch from disinterested individuals to convinced purchasers in one instantaneous step. Rather, they approach the ultimate purchase through a process or series of steps in which the actual purchase is but the final threshold.

Reprinted from the *Journal of Marketing*, published by the American Marketing Association (October, 1961), pp. 59-62.

Robert J. Lavidge is president of Elrick and Lavidge, Chicago-based market research and marketing consulting firm. A faculty member in the Northwestern University Evening Division, he received his B.A. degree from DePauw and his M.B.A. from the University of Chicago. He is a past president of the American Marketing Association. He is co-editor (with R. J. Holloway) of *Marketing and Society: The Challenge*.

Gary A. Steiner was, before his death, professor of business at the University of Chicago, from which he earned an M.A. degree in sociology and a Ph.D. in psychology. He also served as a consultant in applications of psychological techniques. He was co-author (with B. L. Berenson) of *Human Behavior: An Inventory of Scientific Findings*.

SEVEN STEPS

Advertising may be thought of as a force, which must move people up a series of steps:

1. Near the bottom of the steps stand potential purchasers who are completely *unaware of the existence* of the product or service in question.
2. Closer to purchasing, but still a long way from the cash register, are those who are merely *aware of its existence.*
3. Up a step are prospects who *know what the product has to offer.*
4. Still closer to purchasing are those who have favorable attitudes toward the product—those who *like the product.*
5. Those whose favorable attitudes have developed to the point of *preference over all other possibilities are up still another step.*
6. Even closer to purchasing are consumers who couple preference with a desire to buy and the *conviction* that the purchase would be wise.
7. Finally, of course, is the step which translates this attitude into actual *purchase.*

Research to evaluate the effectiveness of advertisements can be designed to provide measures of movement on such a flight of steps.

The various steps are not necessarily equidistant. In some instances the "distance" from awareness to preference may be very slight, while the distance from preference to purchase is extremely large. In other cases, the reverse may be true. Furthermore, a potential purchaser sometimes may move up several steps simultaneously.

Consider the following hypotheses. The greater the psychological and/or economic commitement involved in the purchase of a particular product, the longer it will take to bring consumers up these steps, and the more important the individual steps will be. Contrariwise, the less serious the commitment, the more likely it is that some consumers will go almost "immediately" to the top of the steps.

An impulse purchase might be consummated with no previous awareness, knowledge, liking, or conviction with respect to the product. On the other hand, an industrial good or an important consumer product ordinarily will not be purchased in such a manner.

DIFFERENT OBJECTIVES

Products differ markedly in terms of the role of advertising as related to the various positions on the steps. A great deal of advertising is designed to move people up the final steps toward purchase. At an extreme is the "Buy Now" ad, designed to stimulate immediate overt action. Contrast this with industrial advertising, much of which is not intended to stimulate immediate purchase in and of itself. Instead, it is designed to help pave the way for the salesman by making the prospects aware of his company and products, thus giving them knowledge and favorable attitudes about the ways in which those products or services might be of value. This, of course, involves movement up the lower and intermediate steps.

Even within a particular product category, or with a specific product, different advertisements or campaigns may be aimed primarily at different steps in the purchase process—and rightly so. For example, advertising for new automobiles is likely to place considerable emphasis on the lower steps when new models are first brought out. The advertiser recognizes that his first job is to make the potential customer aware of the new product, and to give him knowledge and favorable attitudes about the product. As the year progresses, advertising emphasis tends to move up the steps. Finally, at the end of the "model year" much emphasis is placed on the final step—the attempt to stimulate immediate purchase among prospects who are assumed, by then, to have information about the car.

The simple model assumes that potential purchasers all "start from scratch." However, some may have developed negative attitudes about the product, which place them even further from purchasing the product than those completely unaware of it. The first job, then, is to get them off the negative steps—before they can move up the additional steps which lead to purchase.

THREE FUNCTIONS OF ADVERTISING

The six steps outlined, beginning with "aware," indicate three major functions of advertising. The first two, awareness and knowledge, relate to *information or ideas.* The second two steps, liking and preference, have to do with favorable *attitudes or feelings* toward the product. The final two steps, conviction and purchase, are to produce *action*—the acquisition of the product.

These three advertising functions are directly related to a classic psychological model which divides behavior into three components or dimensions:

1. The *cognitive* component—the intellectual, mental, or "rational" states.

2. The *affective* component—the "emotional" or "feeling" states.
3. The *conative or motivational* component—the "striving" states, relating to the tendency to treat objects as positive or negative goals.

This is more than a semantic issue, because the actions that need to be taken to stimulate or channel motivation may be quite different from those that produce knowledge. And these, in turn, may differ from actions designed to produce favorable attitudes toward something.

FUNCTIONS OF ADVERTISING RESEARCH

Among the first problems in any advertising evaluation program are to:

1. Determine what steps are most critical in a particular case, that is, what the steps leading to purchase are for most consumers.
2. Determine how many people are, at the moment, on which steps.
3. Determine which people on which steps it is most important to reach.

Advertising research can then be designed to evaluate the extent to which the advertising succeeds in moving the specified "target" audience(s) up the critical purchase steps.

Table 1 summarizes the stair-step model, and illustrates how several common advertising and research approaches may be organized according to their various "functions."

Over-all and Component Measurements

With regard to most any product there are an infinite number of additional "sub-flights" which can be helpful in moving a prospect up the main steps. For example, awareness, knowledge and development of favorable attitudes toward a specific product feature may be helpful in building a preference for the line of products. This leads to the concept of other steps, subdividing or "feeding" into the purchase steps, but concerned solely with more specific product features or attitudes.

Advertising effectiveness measurements may, then, be categorized into:

TABLE 1. *Advertising and Advertising Research Related to the Model*

Related Behavioral Dimensions	Movement Toward Purchase	Examples of Types of Promotion or Advertising Relevant to Various Steps	Examples of Research Approaches Related to Steps of Greatest Applicability
	PURCHASE	Point-of-purchase	Market or sales tests
CONATIVE —the realm of motives. Ads stimulate or direct desires	↑	Retail store ads Deals "Last-chance" offers Price appeals Testimonials	Split-run tests Intention to purchase Projective techniques
	CONVICTION		
	↑		
	PREFERENCE		Rank order of preference for brands
AFFECTIVE —the realm of emotions. Ads change attitudes and feelings	↑	Competitive ads Argumentative copy "Image" ads Status, glamour appeals	Rating scales Image measurements, including check lists and semantic differentials
	LIKING		Projective techniques
	↑		
	KNOWLEDGE		
COGNITIVE —the realm of thoughts. Ads provide information and facts	↑	Announcements Descriptive copy Classified ads Slogans Jingles Sky writing	Information questions Play-back analyses Brand awareness surveys
	AWARENESS	Teaser campaigns	Aided recall

1. Over-all or "global" measurements, concerned with measuring the results—the consumers' positions and movement on the purchase steps.
2. Segment or component measurements, concerned with measuring the relative effectiveness of various means of moving people up the purchase steps—the consumers' positions on ancillary flights of steps, and the relative importance of these flights.

Measuring Movement on the Steps

Many common measurements of advertising effectiveness have been concerned with movement up either the first steps or the final step on the primary purchase flight. Examples include surveys to determine the extent of brand awareness and information and measures of purchase and repeat purchase among "exposed" versus "unexposed" groups.

Self-administered instruments, such as adaptations of the "semantic differential" and adjective check lists, are particularly helpful in providing the desired measurements of movement up or down the middle steps. The semantic differential provides a means of scaling attitudes with regard to a number of different issues in a manner which facilitates gathering the information on an efficient quantitative basis. Adjective lists, used in various ways, serve the same general purpose.

Such devices can provide relatively spontaneous, rather than "considered," responses. They are also quickly administered and can contain enough elements to make recall of specific responses by the test participant difficult, especially if the order of items is changed. This helps in minimizing "consistency" biases in various comparative uses of such measurement tools.

Efficiency of these self-administered devices make it practical to obtain responses to large numbers of items. This facilitates measurement of elements or components differing only slightly, though importantly, from each other.

Carefully constructed adjective check lists, for example, have shown remarkable discrimination between terms differing only in subtle shades of meaning. One product may be seen as "rich," "plush," and "expensive," while another one is "plush," "gaudy," and "cheap."

Such instruments make it possible to secure simultaneous measurements of both *global* attitudes and *specific* image components. These can be correlated with each other and directly related to the content of the advertising messages tested.

Does the advertising change the thinking of the respondents with regard to specific product attributes, characteristics or features, including not only physical characteristics but also various image elements such as "status"? Are these changes commercially significant?

The measuring instruments mentioned are helpful in answering these questions. They provide a means for correlating changes in specific attitudes concerning image components with changes in global attitudes or position on the primary purchase steps.

Testing the Model

When groups of consumers are studied over time, do those who show more movement on the measured steps eventually purchase the product in greater proportions or quantities? Accumulation of data utilizing the stair-step model provides an opportunity to test the assumptions underlying the model by measuring this question.

THREE CONCEPTS

This approach to the measurement of advertising has evolved from three concepts:

1. Realistic measurements of advertising effectiveness must be related to an understanding of the functions of advertising. It is helpful to think in terms of a model where advertising is likened to a force which, if successful, moves people up a series of steps toward purchase.

2. Measurements of the effectiveness of the advertising should provide measurements of changes at all levels on these steps—not just at the levels of the development of product or feature awareness and the stimulation of actual purchase.

3. Changes in attitudes as to specific image components can be evaluated together with changes in over-all images, to determine the extent to which changes in the image components are related to movement on the primary purchase steps.

30

Does Advertising Belong in the Capital Budget?

Joel Dean

Should advertising be budgeted as an expense or as an investment?

Advertising is now book-kept and budgeted as though its benefits were used up immediately, like purchased electricity. Management things about advertising as it is book-kept, as a current expense. The decision as to how much a corporation should spend on persuasion is made by the same criteria as for materials used up in the factory—impact upon the current P&L. The advertising budget is part of the *operating* budget.

So far as is known, no corporation puts advertising in its capital budget. But maybe it belongs there. Several disinterested parties say so:

The stock market says it belongs there. It says the benefits derived from promotional outlays are just as capitalizable as the tangible assets that the bookkeeper does capitalize. It says this when Bristol Myers sells at ten times its book value.

Corporation presidents occasionally say it belongs there, especially when they evoke *investment* in advertising to justify poor current profits.

New entrants into an industry say advertising belongs in the capital budget. They say it by including the promotional outlays required to build brand-acceptance as an integral part of the total investment required to break into the business.

Antitrust economists say advertising belongs in the capital budget. They say it by viewing brand-acceptance, which is built up by promotion, as just

Reprinted from the *Journal of Marketing,* published by the American Marketing Association (October, 1966), pp. 15–21. This article won the 1966 Alpha Kappa Psi Award as best article of the year.

Joel Dean is professor of business economics at Columbia University. His academic degrees include a Harvard M.B.A. and a Ph.D. from the University of Chicago. He has his own consulting firm and has published books on managerial economics, budgeting, and statistical determination of costs. Professor Dean's *Capital Budgeting* is the classic work in this field.

as substantial a barrier to entry as the investment required in buildings and machinery.

It is just possible that the bookkeeper's guide to top-management thinking about advertising is wrong.

THE APPROACH

The plan of this article is, first, to find whether promotion is an investment; second, to consider how to optimize it if it is an investment; and third, to speculate on the probabilities that this novel approach, even if theoretically valid, will do any good.

The approach here to the problem of how much to invest in advertising is formal and objective, rather than intuitive. The premise is that the overriding goal of the corporation is to maximize profits. The viewpoint is that of an economist concerned with managerial finance.

This article is confined to the conceptual framework for deciding how much to invest in promotion. Measurement problems are not examined, nor the mechanics of application. The analysis is presented in terms of advertising, but is equally applicable to all forms of persuasion. Advertising is used as an example simply because it is the purest and most indisputable form of selling cost, and for many firms also the largest.

My thesis is as follows. Most advertising is, in economic essence, an investment. How much to spend on advertising is, therefore, a problem of investment economics. A new approach is required—economic and financial analysis of futurities. This approach focuses on future after-tax cash flows and centers on the profit-productivity of capital.

IS PROMOTION AN INVESTMENT?

To determine whether, as a matter of economics, outlays for advertising and other forms of promotion constitute an investment, rather than a current expense, is our first task.

So we must bravely face three basic questions concerning the economics of investment in corporate persuasion:

A. Precisely what is a business investment; how is it distinguished from a current expense?

B. Just what are promotional costs; how should they be distinguished from production costs?

C. What are the distinctive characteristics of promotional outlays; do they disqualify promotion for investment treatment?

A. Concept of Investment

What distinguishes a business investment from a current expense?

An investment is an outlay made today to achieve benefits in the future. A current expense is an outlay whose benefits are immediate. The question is not how the outlay is treated in conventional accounting, how it is taxed, or whether the asset is tangible or intangible. The hallmark of an investment is futurity.

B. Concept of Promotional Costs

Precisely what are promotional costs? How do they differ from production costs?

Promotional costs are outlays to augment the demand for the product—that is, to shift its price-quantity demand schedule upward, so that more will be sold at a given price. In contrast, production costs are all outlays required to meet this demand.

This different dividing line means that some costs which are conventionally classified as marketing costs, for example, physical distribution, are here viewed as part of production costs. It means also that some costs usually viewed as production costs, for example, inspection, are here viewed as promotional costs, even though they are incurred in the factory.

This is the cost-dichotomy needed for clear thinking about promotional investments. A clear idea of the purpose of an outlay is indispensable for a useful estimate of its effectiveness. Moreover, the criterion for optimization is quite different for production costs than for promotional costs. For production, it is sheer cost-minimization; for promotion, it is not cost-minimization but something much more intricate, as we shall see.

C. Distinctive Traits of Promotional Outlays

Do promotional investments differ from unimpeachable corporate investments in ways that make it impractical to manage them like true investments?

Promotional investments *are* different from traditional corporate investments—for example, capital tied up in machinery. The question is whether these differences call for a different intellectual apparatus for measuring productivity and rationing the firm's capital.

Promotional investments *are book-kept differently.* They are not capitalized and not depreciated. But this does not keep them from being investments. They tie up capital with equal inflexibility and do so with similar expectation of future benefits.

Promotional investments *are taxed differently.* Unlike acknowledged investments, they are deductible against income fully at the time of outlay, regardless of the delay of benefits. The fact that the tax collector is oblivious to promotional investments increases their productivity. Immediate tax write-off of the entire outlay halves the investment after tax and steps up its true rate of return.

Promotional investments *are generally spread out over time* and usually can be adjusted in amount in relatively small steps. However, this is irrelevant in determining whether or not they are true investments.

Most promotional investments *have an indeterminate economic life.* Brand-acceptance "planted in the head" of a teenager by television may influence his purchases for 50 minutes or 50 years. But uncertainty of duration of the benefits does not make the promotional outlay any less an investment. The obsolescence-life of a computer is also quite uncertain.

Promotional investments *have multiple benefits* which can be reaped in optional ways. The profitability of augmented demand may be taken out either in higher prices or in larger volume. But this is not unique to promotional investments. Usually factory modernization not only saves labor, but also increases capacity and improves product-quality and employee morale.

Promotional investments *usually have irregular and diverse time-shapes in their benefits streams.* But this is a common characteristic of many tangible investments. Some oil wells, for example, come in as gushers, have an unexpected midlife rejuvenation from repressuring, and live out a tranquil old age as pumpers.

Promotional investments *have a benefit-stream which is difficult to measure and to predict.* But they share this characteristic with many forms of outlay conventionally classified as capital expenditures. Obsolescence of chemical-processing equipment, for example, is hard to predict, yet vitally affects its rate of return.

Promotional investments *are provocative;* they may induce rivals to retaliate. This adds to the difficulty of measuring and predicting benefits. Tangible investments, however, can also provoke competitors' reactions in ways that erode their profitability (for example, retail store modernization).

All this adds up to the fact that promotional investments do have unusual characteristics, different from many other investments that now fight for funds in the capital budget. However, these traits either are not distinctive, or if they are, do not destroy the essential investment-character of the promotional outlays.

All promotional outlays are now conventionally viewed exclusively as current expenses. Some are, if the time lag of benefits is sufficiently short; but others are instead true investments, because the delay in their benefits is substantial. Most promotion is a *mixture*, and the richness of the investment-mix varies over a wide range.

HOW TO OPTIMIZE INVESTMENT IN PROMOTION

Granted that much advertising is largely an investment in economic reality, how should a corporation determine how much it should invest in promotion? To solve this problem, we need answers to the following questions:

a. Does a satisfactory solution for the problem already exist?
b. Why has such an important problem remained unsolved?
c. To what corporate goal should the solution be geared?
d. How does promotion tie into other ways of getting business?
e. What are the determinants of the productivity of capital invested in promotion?
f. What concepts of measurement are needed to calibrate productivity of capital?
g. What is the most appropriate yardstick of capital productivity for promotional investments?
h. How would rate-of-return rationing work for investments in corporate persuasion?

A. Problem Unsolved

Has the problem of how much a corporation should spend on advertising and other forms of persuasion been already satisfactorily solved?

The problem is important. The answer is crucial to the competitive success of many firms, and may involve vast expenditures.

In the future, it is likely to be even more vital. Depersonalized distribution, increased urbanization, rising consumer affluence, revolutionary advances in technology, and bigger economies of scale in some promotional media are dynamic forces which will make the decision as to how much to invest in promotion a jugular issue for many corporations in the next decade.

Surprisingly, this crucial problem is not yet solved. Despite yards of computer print-outs and millions of dollars spent on advertising research, most corporations do not really know whether their promotional outlays should be half or twice as large as they now are.

B. Reasons for Failure

Why has such an important problem remained unsolved? There are three main causes.

The first cause is *failure to acknowledge the importance of futurity*. The full impact of most promotional outlays upon demand is delayed with associated uncertainty. Hence, the conceptual framework of analysis that management needs for solving this problem is the kind that is used in modern, sophisticated management of conventional corporate capital appropriations.

A second cause is *lack of a conceptual apparatus whose orientation is economic*. The problem of optimizing promotional investment is basically a matter of managerial economics, that is, balancing incremental promotional investment against predicted benefits, so as to augment sales most profitably.

The third cause of failure is *the difficulty of measuring the effectiveness of promotional outlays*. Their impacts on demand are diffused, delayed, and intricately interwoven with other forces. To make the kind of investment approach needed to produce practical benefits will require an open mind, fresh concepts, substantial research spending, and great patience.

C. Overriding Corporate Goal

What is the corporate goal to which the solution of optimum investment in promotion should be geared?

Promotional outlays, like other expenditures, should be judged in terms of their contribution to attainment of the corporation's objectives. Most companies have several goals, some of which conflict; but the solution for the problem of how much to invest in promotion should be geared primarily to the goal of profitability.

The master goal of the modern corporation should be maximum profits in the long run. More explicitly, it should be to maximize the present worth at the corporation's cost of capital of the future stream of benefits to the stockholder.

All other objectives—such as growth or market-share or eternal life—should be either intermediate or subsidiary to this overriding corporate objective.

D. Business-getters

How does promotion relate to other ways of getting business?

A company has three ways to augment its sales: by cutting price, by spending more on promotion, and by bettering its product. The three members of the business-getting threesome pull together. But being alternatives, they are at the margin rivalrous substitutes.

The three reinforce each other in a complex symbiotic relationship. For a product that is superior to rivals in wanted ways, promotional outlays will be more effective than for an inferior product. A given amount and quality of promotion will produce more sales of a product priced in correct economic relationship to buyers' alternatives than for an overpriced product.

Each of the three business-getters can have delayed impacts and hence be a business investment. Their delayed and intertwining effects on sales, now and in the future, increase the problem of measuring the effects of promotional investment.

E. Determinants of Capital Productivity

What are the determinants of the productivity of capital invested in promotion?

These need to be identified to find out whether capital tied up in advertising will yield enough profits to earn its keep. Its yield must pay for the cost of this capital in the marketplace, or its opportunity costs in benefits passed up by not investing the money somewhere else.

The productivity of an investment in promotion is the relation of its earnings to the amount of capital tied up. This relationship requires explicit recognition of four economic determinants to be measured: (1) the amount and timing of *added investment;* (2) the amount and timing of *added earnings;* (3) the *duration of the earnings;* and (4) the *risks and imponderable benefits associated with the project.*

1. *Added Investment.* The appropriate investment base for calculating rate of return is the added outlay which will be occasioned by the adoption of a promotion project as opposed to its rejection.

The investment should include the entire amount of the original added outlay, regardless of how it is classified on the accounts. Any additional outlay for point-of-purchase displays or for distribution of samples to consumers should be included in the investment amount, as should future research expenses caused by the proposal.

The timing of these added investments has an important effect upon true profitability and should, therefore, be reflected in the rate-of-return computation.

2. *Added Earnings.* Concern with capital productivity implies, of course, that the company's goal is profits.

The productivity of the capital tied up is determined by the increase in earnings or savings, that is, net cash receipts, caused by making the investment as opposed to not making it. These earnings should be measured in terms of their after-tax cash or cash equivalents.

Only costs and revenues that will be different as a result of the adoption of the proposal should be included. The concept of earnings should be broad enough to encompass intangible and often unquantifiable benefits. When these have to be omitted from the formal earnings estimates, they should be noted for subsequent appraisal of the project.

3. *Durability of earnings.* The duration of the benefits from a promotional investment has a vital effect on its rate of return.

Economic life of promotion depends (a) on frequency of purchase; (b) on loyalty-life-expectancy, that is, longevity of customers; (3) on gestation period of the purchase decision; and (d) on erosion by the promotional efforts of rivals.

For advertising investments, durability is often the most difficult dimension of project value to quantify. But the problem cannot be avoided. Some estimate is better than none; and estimates can be improved by well-directed research.

4. *Risks and Imponderable Benefits.* Appraising the risks and uncertainties associated with a project requires a high order of judgment. It is only disparities in risk among projects which need to be allowed for, since the company's cost of capital reflects the overall risks. Although measurement of this sort of dispersion is difficult, some headway can sometimes be made by a necessarily arbitrary risk-ranking of candidate projects or categories of projects.

Most projects have some added benefits over and above the measurable ones. If excessive weight is given to those imponderables, then there is danger that rate-of-return rationing will occur. When a low rate-of-return project is preferred to a high one on the grounds of imponderable benefits, the burden of proof clearly should rest on the imponderables.

F. Concepts of Measurement

For calibrating these four determinants of return on investment, what concepts of measurement are needed? Four are particularly useful:

1. *Alternatives.* The proper benchmark for measuring added investment and the corresponding added earnings is the best alternative way to do it.
2. *Futurity.* Future earnings and future outlays of the project are all that matter.

3. *Increments.* Added earnings and added investment of the project alone are material.

4.*Cash Flows.* After-tax cash flows (or their equivalents) alone are significant for measuring capital productivity.

1. *Alternatives.* There is always an alternative to the proposed capital expenditure.

The alternative may be so catastrophic that refined measurement is unnecessary to reject it; but in any case, the proper benchmark for the proposal is the next profitable alternative way of doing it.

2. *Futurity.* The value of a proposed capital project depends on its future earnings.

The past is irrelevant, except as a benchmark for forecasting the future. Consequently, earnings estimates need to be based on the best available projections. The outlays and earnings need to be estimated year by year over the economic life of the proposed promotion, and their time shape needs to be taken into account explicitly.

3. *Increments.* A correct estimate of both earnings and investment must be based on the simple principle that the earnings from the promotional proposal are measured by the total *added* earnings by making the investment, as opposed to *not* making it . . . and that the same is true for the investment amount.

Project costs should be unaffected by allocation of existing overheads, but should reflect the changes in total overhead and other costs likely to result from the project. No costs or revenues which will be the same, regardless of whether the proposal is accepted or rejected, should be included and the same goes for investment.

4. *Cash flows.* To be economically realistic, attention should be directed exclusively at the after-tax flows of cash or cash equivalents which will result from making the promotional investment.

Book costs are confusing and immaterial. But taxes do matter, because advertising investments are favored over depreciable investments in after-tax rate of return.

G. Yardstick of Financial Worth

The productivity of capital in a business investment is the relationship between its earnings and the amount of capital tied up. To measure this productivity for promotional investments, we not only must have a correct conceptual framework of measurements, but also must choose the most appropriate yardstick of investment worth.

The concept of advertising as an investment already has some limited acceptance in new-product introduction. The measure of productivity of capital often used is the payout period—a crude yardstick. The cutoff criterion is also set rather arbitrarily to get the original outlay back in two years or three years. Such standards have no objective justification as compared with corporate cost of capital.

What is the best yardstick of economic worth for investments in persuasion? Clearly, the yardstick that is economically appropriate for investments in promotion is true profitability as measured by discounted-cash-flow analysis.

1. *Discounted-Cash-Flow Analysis.* The discounted-cash-flow (DCF) method is a new approach to measuring the productivity of capital and measuring the cost of capital.

The application is new, not the principle. Discounting has long been used in the financial community, where precision and realism are indispensable. The essential contributions of discounted-cash-flow analysis to management thinking about investment in promotion are three:

a. An explicit recognition that time has economic value—and hence, that near money is more valuable than distant money.
b. A recognition that cash flows are what matter—and hence, that book costs are irrelevant for capital-decisions except as they affect taxes.
c. A recognition that income taxes have such an important effect upon cash flows that they must be explicitly figured into project worth.

The discounted-cash-flow method has two computational variants.

The first is a rate-of-return computation, which consists essentially of finding the interest rate that discounts gross future after-tax cash earnings of a project down to a present value equal to the project cost. This interest rate is the rate of return on that particular investment.

The second variant is a present-value computation which discounts gross future after-tax cash earnings of all projects at the same rate of interest. This rate of interest is the company's minimum acceptable rate of return. This should be based on the company's cost of capital. Special risk should be reflected either by deflating project earnings or by adjusting the cutoff rate for projects of different categories of risk. The resulting present-value is then compared with the project cost investment. If the present value exceeds it, the project is acceptable. If it falls below, it is rejected.

In addition, projects can by this variant be ranked by various kinds of profitability indexes which reflect the amount or ratios of excess of present value over project cost.

Both variants of the discounted-cash-flow approach require a timetable of after-tax cash flows of investment and of gross earnings which cover the entire economic life of the project.

In practice, the timetable can be simplified by grouping years in blocks. For projects for which investment is substantially instantaneous and gross earnings are level, simple computational charts and tables can be used to estimate the discounted-cash-flow rate of return directly from estimated economic life and after-tax payback. For projects with rising or declining earnings streams, this conversion is more complex.

2. *Superiorities of DCF.* The discounted-cash-flow method of analysis is particularly needed for measuring the profitability of promotional investments, for two reasons.

First, the outlays are usually spread out. Second, benefits, mainly incremental profits from added sales in the future, are always spread out and usually have a non-level time-shape.

The superiorities of discounted-cash-flow analysis over rival yardsticks for measuring the productivity of capital in promotional investments are imposing:

a. It is economically realistic in confining the analysis to cash-flows and forgetting about book-allocations.
b. It forces guided thinking about the whole life of the project, and concentration on the lifetime earnings.
c. It weights the time-pattern of the investment outlay and the cash earnings, so as to reflect real and important differences in the value of near and distant cash-flows.
d. It reflects accurately and without ambiguity the timing of tax-savings.
e. It permits simple allowances for risks and uncertainties, and can be adapted readily to increasing the risk allowance over time.
f. It is strictly comparable to cost-of-capital, correctly measured, so that decisions can be made quickly and safely by comparing rate of return and the value of money to the firm.

H. Rate-of-return Rationing

How should rationing of capital work for persuasion-investments? Rate-of-return "battling" among capital proposals is the essence of capital rationing. The standard of minimum acceptable profitability should (after proper allowance for special risks and for imponderables) be the same for all, namely, the company's market cost-of-capital or its opportunity cost-of-capital, whichever is higher.

Market cost-of-capital is what the company probably will pay for equity and debt funds, on the average, over the future. For a large publicly-held company, this cost can be measured with adequate precision for rationing purposes. There is no better cutoff criterion.

Opportunity cost-of-capital is the sacrificed profit-yield from alternative investments. Only when a company refuses to go to market for funds can its opportunity costs stay long above market cost-of-capital.

PRACTICAL VALUES

Will putting advertising in the capital budget do any good?

Granted that as a matter of economic principle much advertising and other forms of promotional spending are investments . . . and granted also that conceptually correct and pragmatically proved techniques for optimizing investment outlays are available for promotional investment . . . the question is whether this sophisticated and powerful mechanism, applied to promotional investments, will have any practical value.

Most business investments are not made in ignorance of their probable impacts, whereas, many of the outlays for persuasion now are. Characteristically, the amount and timing of the effects of advertising are unknown. The duration of their impact on economic life is unknown, and the probabilities of effectiveness are also unknown. Quite possibly, attempting to estimate these unknowns cannot improve overall results.

The problem of how much to invest in promotion can be solved either by intuitive and perhaps artistic processes, or through a more formal and more systematic study of objective evidence. Quite possibly men of experience and good judgment can determine how much the corporation should invest in promotion by subjective judgment, regardless of whether advertising is formally put in the capital budget. This article is nevertheless confined to a consideration of ways in which sophisticated economic models and systematic quantitative study can help to find the appropriate size of the appropriation for corporate persuasion.

1. Much advertising (and other corporate persuasion) is in economic reality partly an investment. The investment-mix varies over a wide spectrum.

2. Investments in promotion are different from conventional capital expenditures, but these distinctive characteristics do not disqualify promotion for investment treatment.

3. Profitability must be the basic measurement of the productivity of capital invested in promotion. Despite the multiplicity of conflicting corporate goals, the overriding objective for decisions or investment of corporate capital should be to make money.

4. The main determinants of profitability of an advertising investment that need to be estimated are the amount and timing of added investment and of added earnings, the duration of advertising effects and risks.

5. The measurement concepts of capital productivity that must be estimated are future, time-spotted, incremental, after-tax cash flows of investment outlays and of added profits from added sales.

6. Discounted-cash Flow (DCF) analysis supplies the financial yardstick most appropriate for promotional investments. By comparison, payback period, although widely used, has no merit.

7. Advertising belongs in the capital budget. Promotional investments should be made to compete for funds on the basis of profitability, that is, DCF rate of return.

8. The criterion for rationing scarce capital among competing investment proposals should be DCF rate of return. The criterion of the minimum acceptable return should be the corporation's cost of capital—outside market-cost or internal opportunity-cost, whichever is higher.

9. Putting advertising into the capital budget will not perform a miracle. Judgment cannot be displaced by DCF analysis and computers. But judgment can be economized and improved. The most that it can do is to open the way for a research approach which is oriented to the kind of estimates that are relevant and that will permit advertising investment in promotion to fight for funds on the basis of financial merit rather than on the basis of personal persuasiveness of their sponsor.

10. An investment approach to produce practical benefits will require fresh concepts, substantial research-spending, and great patience.

31

Pricing Objectives in Large Companies

Robert F. Lanzillotti

The recent sharpened interest of the "Kefauver committee" in administered prices and inflation has focused attention once again on the inadequate state of knowledge of the price-making process.[1] In particular, more empirical information is needed with respect to (a) the motivational hypothesis of the firm, i.e., the specific objectives upon which business firms base pricing decisions, and (b) the mechanics of price formulation. This article is addressed to the first problem; it will present some data on pricing objectives of the firm which have been developed in the course of a general study of pricing policies and practices of large industrial corporations.

I. SCOPE OF PRESENT STUDY

The procedure followed involved the postprandial variety of research. Lengthy interviews were undertaken with officials of twenty companies over periods ranging up to about one week in most cases.[2]

Reprinted from *American Economic Review* (December, 1958), pp. 921–940.

Robert F. Lanzillotti is dean of the business school at the University of Florida. He received his B.A. and M.A. degrees in economics from the American University and his Ph.D. from the University of California. Professor Lanzillotti served in the U.S. Navy in World War II, rising to the rank of lieutenant commander. He is a co-author of *Pricing in Big Business* and was a member of the Price Control Board in the early '70's.

[1] See *Administered Prices*. Hearings Before the Subcommittee on Antitrust and Monopoly of the Committee on the Judiciary, United States Senate, 85th Cong., 1st Sess., Washington 1958.

[2] The companies were selected from among the largest corporations on the basis of the willingness of management to cooperate by permitting extensive interviews with top company officials: Aluminum Company of America, American Can, A & P Tea Company, du Pont, General Electric, General Foods, General Motors, Goodyear, Gulf, International Harvester, Johns-Manville, Kennecott Copper, Kroger, National Steel, Sears, Standard of Indiana, Standard Oil Company of New Jersey (ESSO), Swift, Union Carbide, and U.S. Steel.

A second set of interviews was undertaken several years later to fill in gaps in the data and to ascertain if any changes had been made in price policy since the original interviews. Pricing obviously being a sensitive area, some officials did not care to discuss their policies except in general terms, but these persons paved the way to individuals who were more willing and, in some cases, more aware of the practices employed and reasons for them.

The questions were designed to elicit information concerning: (1) whether any formal or informal commercial goals had been adopted by the corporation; (2) the procedures employed for implementing and evaluating the goal; (3) the techniques of price determination (i.e., the mechanics of pricing); and (4) the functions of pricing executives (individuals, committees, special divisions, etc.)—including extent of authority on price matters, kinds of materials utilized by them in setting prices, and relative weights given to various price-influencing factors. The portion of the information presented in this paper concerns, for each of the twenty companies, the principal and collateral objectives which are regarded as guiding pricing decisions.

The twenty corporations have one feature in common: each of them is among the 200 largest industrial corporations, and over one-half fall within the 100 largest industrials, in terms of assets. But they differ in a wide variety of ways from each other. Some, like Johns-Manville, U.S. Steel, International Harvester, and Union Carbide, dominate a whole industry and are price leaders. At the other extreme, there are companies like Swift and A & P which face so many competitors of various sizes and abilities that in spite of their absolute size they are very far from being able to make decisions for the market, and do not think of competition in terms of actions of one or a few competitors. The other companies fall between these extremes.

II. COMPANY GOALS: RATIONALIZATIONS
OF PRICING METHODS

It is important to recognize at the outset that a company statement of policy is not necessarily an accurate representation of what that policy is.[3] Also, company rationalizations of pricing do not always represent the first step in planning price policy, and not all pricing of a given company is determined by the general company objective.

---

[3] The following analysis is based upon the author's interpretations of views expressed orally by officials of the corporations concerned. Of course, neither the companies nor the author wish these views to be interpreted as necessarily the official views of the companies.

In a few cases officials insisted that there was little latitude in selecting a policy. However, for the most part, the prominence of each of the corporations in their respective industries makes most of them masters, to a significant degree, of their fates; hence, they are able to adjust pricing to the company's general goal.

Table 1 presents a summary of the principal and collateral pricing goals of the twenty companies as determined from interviews with their respective officials. The most typical pricing objectives cited were: (1) pricing to achieve a target return on investment; (2) stabilization of price and margin; (3) pricing to realize a target market share; and (4) pricing to meet or prevent competition. In most of the companies, one of the goals predominates, but as the listing of collateral objectives indicates, price-making by any one firm was not always ruled by a single policy objective.[4]

III. PRICING TO ACHIEVE A TARGET RETURN ON INVESTMENT

Target return on investment was perhaps the most frequently mentioned of pricing goals.[5] About one-half of the companies explicitly indicated that their pricing policies were based mainly upon the objective of realizing a particular rate of return on investment, in a given year, over the long haul, or both; but in most cases the target was regarded as a long-run objective. The average of the targets mentioned

---

[4] To illustrate, in U.S. Steel, out of a variety of divergent views mentioned, three rationales can be distinguished. (1) The first is the "ideal" price, i.e., pricing that is believed to be "just, fair, and economic," with reference to a general target of about 8 per cent after taxes on stockholders' investment plus long-term debt. This strand is colored by the management's concept of the corporation as the industry leader vested with the responsibilities and subject to the inhibitions of a public utility. In fact, one official said he was "unable to understand or properly describe the Corporation's pricing policy except as something like the approach of the public utilities." (2) The second rationale centers on the difference between the "ideal" system and what officials regard as the "practical exigencies of steel price-making," i.e., limitations imposed upon price policy "by followers who are disloyal and prices of competitive products that get out of hand." (3) A third policy objective is essentially a target market share and is embodied in the motto: "to obtain as a minimum that share of all markets for the products sold, product by product, and territory by territory, to which the corporation's capacity in relation to the industry as the whole entitles it, and to accomplish this participation ratio through the exercise of judgment so as to insure the maximum continuing return on investment to the Corporation."

[5] Target-return pricing is defined as the building up of a price structure designed to provide such a return on capital employed for specific products, product groups, and divisions, as to yield a predetermined corporate average return. In most cases managements referred to stockholders' equity (net worth) plus long-term debt. Usually a standard cost system is used as a means of allocating fixed cost to various product divisions, with the standards premised on an assumed rate of production, typically about 70 per cent to 80 per cent of capacity, and an assumed product-mix as "normal."

was 14 per cent (after taxes); only one was below 10 per cent; and the highest was 20 per cent.

Under this pricing system both costs and profit goals are based not upon the volume level which is necessarily expected over a short period, but rather on standard volume; and the margins added to standard costs are designed to produce the target profit rate on investment, assuming standard volume to be the long-run average rate of plant utilization. In effect, the procedure is designed to prevent cyclical or shorter-run changes in volume or product-mix from unduly affecting price, with the expectation that the averaging of fluctuations in cost and demand over the business cycle will produce a particular rate of return on investment.

Firms that were conscious of shooting for a particular target return on investment in their price policies were those that sold products in a market or markets more or less protected and in which the companies were leaders in their respective industries. In Alcoa, du Pont, Esso, General Electric, General Motors, International Harvester, Johns-Manville, Union Carbide, and U.S. Steel, the pricing of many products was hinged to this particular objective, and with the expectation of being able to reach the target return. Target-return pricing was usually tied in with a long-run view of prices, especially on new products where an "orderly" stepping down ("cascading") of prices was followed by du Pont, Union Carbide, and Alcoa.

A distinction should be made, however, between those companies that use target return on investment as a rigid and primary guide to pricing and those to whom it is more useful as a benchmark in an area where prices otherwise might be subject to wide and dangerous variations.[6]

---

[6]To illustrate, the use of rate-of-return pricing by U.S. Steel (likened by its officials to a public utility's "fair return"), apparently has not always been consistently followed. Under market pressure, U.S. Steel has at times had to accept much less than this return; when desperate for business, as in 1938, its competitors offered substantial concessions below published prices on almost every type of business. A very different situation shows up in the discussions of the target return by officials of General Motors. Instead of vainly attempting to realize its target in good years and bad, General Motors takes a long-run view and has sufficient assurance of its retention of a minimum market share to accept a diminished profit note in years when diminished output bears a heavy unallocated overhead. Du Pont seems to assume its ability to realize a target return, especially in connection with new products. The same could be said for Union Carbide, the other chemical producer in the sample. International Harvester, although as vulnerable as U.S. Steel to wide swings in volume of business, appeared to be less worried by competitors' ability to jeopardize its prices based on long-run normal cost and return. Harvester was not able to maintain its prices during the great depression, and there is no evidence that such reductions as it made correspond merely to changes in direct cost. But in spite of frank admission by Harvester's management that the company was faced by tough competition, company officials appeared to be much more independent in their pricing policy than U.S. Steel.

Columns 4 and 5 of Table 1 show the average and range of the profit rates realized by the twenty companies over the 1947–1955 period. It will be noted that the target figures are *less* than the actual returns: for the nine-year period, the target-return companies earned on the average slightly more to substantially more than their indicated profit objective (International Harvester being the only exception). Also, there is a rather wide range in the profit rates for each company.[7]

The actual profit rates may be higher than the targets for several possible reasons: (a) the targets may only be nominal or minimal goals (which is suggested by footnote 7); (b) the generally prosperous nature of the period in question in which company operations exceeded "normal" or average percentage of capacity upon which costs and prices were determined; and (c) some of the companies have found that pricing on an historical-cost basis using the company's traditional objective does not provide adequate capital for replacement and expansion at current costs, and accordingly have made allowance for this factor in their pricing formulas.[8] Thus, if actual profit rates were "adjusted" for changes in the price level, the actual profits would more closely approximate the stated targets.

Whichever of the foregoing may be the most plausible explanation of the differences between actual and target profit rates, the findings indicate that a distinction must be made between year-to-year and secular profits objectives. The evidence on actual profit rates, taken in conjunction with the targets mentioned, raises serious questions whether these companies are attempting to "maximize" profits on a year-to-year basis. Moreover, to construe the actual profit rates (as against target rates) as evidence of a long-run maximization policy would require the demonstration that the prices charged were based not upon the targets but on what the firms believed they could get as a maximum. In any event, for this sample of firms and for this time period, there are limitations upon profit maximization as an adequate explanation of the relationships between profit targets and actual profit rates.

[7]If the lowest figure for each firm is omitted, however, the low side of the range of returns approximates the target figure. This is especially true of Alcoa, du Pont, Johns-Manville, Union Carbide, and U.S. Steel.

[8]When U.S. Steel for example, announces an increase in its base prices, it usually justifies its action in terms of increased direct costs, especially labor costs. But that rising capital costs have also influenced the prices set in recent years is suggested by President Hood's announcement in connection with the $8.50 increase in 1956:

"The new prices do not provide a solution to the problem that United States Steel faces with respect to inadequate depreciation allowances for the replacement of obsolete and outworn facilities, nor do they attempt to provide a solution to the many problems attending the expansion program upon which United States Steel is currently engaged." *New York Times,* August 7, 1956, p. 10.

TABLE 1. *Pricing Goals of Twenty Large Industrial Corporations*

Company	Principal Pricing Goal	Collateral Pricing Goal		Rate of Return on Investment (After Taxes) 1947–1955 [a]		Average Market Share [b]
				Avg.	Range	
Alcoa	20% on investment (before taxes); higher on new products [about 10% effective rate after taxes]	(a)	"Promotive" policy on new products	13.8	7.8–18.7	Pig & ingot, 37%; sheet, 46%; other fabrications, 62%.[c]
		(b)	Price stabilization			
American Can	Maintenance of market share	(a)	"Meeting" competition (using cost of substitute product to determine price)	11.6	9.6–14.7	Approx. 55% of all types of cans [d]
		(b)	Price stabilization			
A & P	Increasing market share		"General promotive" (low-margin policy)	13.0	9.7–18.8	n.a.
du Pont	Target return on investment—no specific figure given	(a)	Charging what traffic will bear over long run	25.9	19.6–34.1	n.a.
		(b)	Maximum return for new products—"life cycle" pricing			
Esso (Standard Oil of N.J.)	"Fair-return" target—no specific figure given	(a)	Maintaining market share	16.0	12.0–18.9	n.a.
General Electric	20% on investment (after taxes); 7% on sales (after taxes)	(a)	Promotive policy on new products	21.4	18.4–26.6	–[e]
		(b)	Price stabilization on nationally advertised products			

[Continued on following page]

TABLE 1 (Continued)

Company	Principal Pricing Goal		Collateral Pricing Goal	Rate of Return on Investment (After Taxes) 1947-1955[a]		Average Market Share[b]
General Foods	33 1/3% gross margin ("1/3 to make, 1/3 to sell, and 1/3 for profit"); expectation of realizing target only on new products	(a)	Full line of food products and novelties	12.2	8.9–15.7	n.a.
		(b)	Maintaining market share			
General Motors	20% on investment (after taxes)		Maintaining market share	26.0	19.9–37.0	50% of passenger automobiles[f]
Goodyear	"Meeting competitors"	(a)	Maintain "position"	13.3	9.2–16.1	n.a.
		(b)	Price stabilization			
Gulf	Follow price of most important marketer in each area	(a)	Maintain market share	12.6	10.7–16.7	n.a.
		(b)	Price stabilization			
International Harvester	10% on investment (after taxes)		Market share: ceiling of "less than a dominant share of any market"	8.9	4.9–	Farm tractors, 28–30%; combines, cornpickers, tractor plows, cultivators, mowers, 20–30%; cotton pickers, 65%; light & light/heavy trucks, 5–18%; medium-heavy to heavy-heavy, 12–30%
Johns-Manville	Return on investment greater than last 15-year average (about 15% after taxes); higher target for new products	(a)	Market share not greater than 20%	14.9	10.7–19.6	n.a.
		(b)	Stabilization of prices			

[Continued on following page]

TABLE 1 (Continued)

Company	Principal Pricing Goal	Collateral Pricing Goal	Rate of Return on Investment (After Taxes) 1947–1955[a] Avg.	Range	Average Market Share[b]
Kennecott	Stabilization of prices		16.0	9.3–20.9	n.a.
Kroger	Maintaining market share	Target return of 20% on investment before taxes[g]	12.1	9.7–16.1	n.a.
National Steel	Matching the market—price follower	Increase market share	12.1	7.0–17.4	5%
Sears Roebuck	Increasing market share (8–10% regarded as satisfactory share)	(a) Realization of traditional return on investment of 10–15% (after taxes) (b) General promotive (low margin) policy	5.4	1.6–10.7	5–10% average (twice as large a share in hard goods v. soft goods)
Standard Oil (Indiana)	Maintain market share	(a) Stabilize prices (b) Target-return on investment (none specified)	10.4	7.9–14.4	n.a.
Swift	Maintenance of market share in livestock buying and meat packing		6.9	3.9–11.1	Approximately 10% nationally[h]
Union Carbide	Target return on investment[i]	Promotive policy on new product; "life cycle" pricing on chemicals generally	19.2	13.5–24.3	—[j]
U.S. Steel	8% on investment (after taxes)	(a) Target market share of 30% (b) Stable price (c) Stable margin	10.3	7.6–14.8	Ingots and steel, 30%; blast furnaces, 34%; finished hot-rolled products, 35%; other steel mill products, 37%[k]

TABLE 1 (Continued)

[a]Federal Trade Commission, *Rates of Return (After Taxes) for Identical Companies in Selected Manufacturing Industries, 1940, 1947–55,* Washington [1957], pp. 28–30, except for the following companies whose rates were computed by the author using the methods outlined in the Commission Report: A & P, General Foods, Gulf, International Harvester, Kroger, National Steel, Sears Roebuck, and Swift.

[b]As of 1955, unless otherwise indicated. Source of data is company mentioned unless noted otherwise.

[c]*U.S. v. Alcoa et al.,* "Stipulation Concerning Extension of Tables III–X," dated May 31, 1956, U.S. District Court for the Southern District of New York.

[d]As of 1939. U.S. Department of Justice, *Western Steel Plants and the Tin Plate Industry,* 79th Cong, 1st Sess., Doc. No. 95, p. L 1.

[e]The company states that on the average it aims at not more than 22 to 25 per cent of any given market. Percentages for individual markets or products were not made available, but it is estimated that in some markets, e.g., electrical turbines, General Electric has 60 per cent of the total market. *Cf.* Standard and Poor's *Industry Surveys,* "Electrical-Electronic-Basic Analysis," Aug. 9, 1956, p. E 21.

[f]Federal Trade Commission, *Industrial Concentration and Product Diversification in the 1000 Largest Manufacturing Companies: 1950,* Washington, Jan. 1957, p. 113.

[g]Target return on investment evidently characterizes company policy as much as target market share. In making investment decisions the company is quoted as follows: "The Kroger Co. normally expected a return on investment of at least 20% before taxes." See McNair, Burnham, and Hersum, *Cases in Retail Management,* New York 1957, pp. 205 ff.

[h]This represents the average share of total industry shipments of the four largest firms in 1954. *Cf. Concentration in American Industry.* Report of Subcommittee on the Judiciary, U.S. Senate, 85th Cong, 1st Sess, Washington 1957, p. 315.

[i]In discussions with management officials various profit-return figures were mentioned, with considerable variation among divisions of the company. No official profit target percentage was given, but the author estimates the *average* profit objective for the corporation to be approximately 35% before taxes, or an effective rate after taxes of about 18%.

[j]Chemicals account for 30% of Carbide's sales, most of which are petro-chemicals, a field that the company opened thirty years ago and still dominates; plastics account for 18%—the company sells 40% of the two most important plastics (vinyl and polyethylene); alloys and metals account for 26% of sales—ferroalloys (e.g., chrome, silicon, manganese), and the biggest U.S. titanium producer; gases account for 14% of sales—estimated to sell top U.S. supplier of ferroalloys (e.g., chrome, silicon, manganese), and the biggest U.S. titanium producer; gases account for 14% of sales—estimated to sell 50% of oxygen in the U.S.; carbon, electrodes, and batteries account for 12% of sales—leading U.S. producer of electrodes, refractory carbon, and flashlights and batteries; and miscellaneous—leading operator of atomic energy plants, a leading producer of uranium, the largest U.S. producer of tungsten, and a major supplier of vanadium. *Cf.* "Union Carbide Enriches the Formula," *Fortune,* Feb. 1957, pp. 123 ff.; Standard and Poor's, *Industry Surveys,* "Chemicals-Basic Analysis," Dec. 20, 1956, p. C44; and "Annual Report for 1955 of the Union Carbide and Carbon Corporation."

[k]The range of the corporation's capacity as a percentage of total industry capacity varies from 15% to 54%, as of January 1957. For more detail see *Administered Prices, Hearings Before the Subcommittee on Antitrust and Monopoly of the Senate Committee on the Judiciary,* 85th Cong. 1st Sess., Pt. 2, *Steel,* Washington 1958, pp. 335–36.

It is perhaps significant that there has been an increasing tendency in recent years for the companies in the sample to adopt some form of target-return pricing, either across-the-board or at least for particular products. In a few cases it was found that managements had developed a target-return policy between the time of the first interviews with the company and subsequent interviews several years later. The reasons for this movement toward greater use of a target-return approach are varied, but the major influences seem to have been: (a) an increasing awareness of and concern by managements for profit-capital-investment planning and capital budgeting, especially in the conglomerate company within which there is keen competition for capital funds by many units; (b) the desire for a good common denominator for evaluating the performance of divisions and product groups; (c) the wartime experiences of most of the companies with "cost-plus," "cost plus fixed fee," and other contractual arrangements with the government which focused attention on the return of investment; and (d) the emulation, by competitiors and others, of successful large companies which have followed a target-return policy for many years (several companies in the sample mentioned that they had patterned their general target-return policy after that of du Pont or General Motors).

It is not surprising that new products above all are singled out for target-return pricing. Since they have no close rivals, new products are usually expected to produce a predetermined level of profit return on the investment represented.[9] No rigid length of time after the introduction of the product was mentioned in which the target is supposed to be achieved. However, the time horizon is more short

---

[9] A good example of the kinds of data utilized in determining which new products will be added or which existing facilities will be expanded is one company's procedure for capital investment decisions. The request by a division for new funds shows (a) estimated new commitment (new fixed investment, working capital, and noncapital expenditures); (b) estimated total utilized investment (the new investment plus transfer of existing investment); (c) estimated annual operating income (i.e., income before depreciation, amortization, depletion, other income and income taxes); and (d) estimated return on investment income, which is shown both as a ratio to the new commitment and the total utilized investment. No figure was mentioned as a minimum return; normally new products were expected to return better than the corporate average, but expansions of existing facilities have been made on a projected return of no greater than 20 to 25 per cent before taxes.

An elaborate check-off list is designed to insure attention to various aspects of projected demand, supply, costs, and competition. Of particular interest are such items as: capacities, captive requirements and future expansion plans of competitors; company's estimated market share before and after expansion; degree of diversity of customers; extent to which success of venture depends upon short- or long-term contracts; the effects of changes in tariff rates on competition from abroad; selling prices used for sales to other units of the company; shape of short-run unit cost curve; comparative cost position of competitors; the degree to which an alternative exists of either making or buying important intermediates; flexibility of proposed facilities for production of other products; the probabilities of obsolescence of the process or products; and the relative position of the company with respect to research and development, technical knowledge, labor supply, patents, and raw materials.

range vis-à-vis established products in the sense that the target payout is delineated from the start.[10] Accordingly, pricing may take the form of "skimming" the market by exploiting the inelasticity of demand in different markets (maintaining a selected price as long as actual or potential competition permits), or a "penetration" price policy designed to develop mass markets via relatively low prices, provided a rapid expansion of the market and higher returns may be obtained later. This approach is most typical of du Pont, Union Carbide, Alcoa, International Harvester, and General Foods. The prescribed target for new products is usually higher than on established products, at least initially. But the target approach is not limited to unique products; it is also typical of low-unit-profit high-volume commodities (e.g., steel, aluminum, and chemicals).

Minimum target profit figures also are used by most of the companies as a basis for sloughing off products and in arriving at "make-or-buy" decisions. An exact minimum target figure was rarely mentioned, but good justifications were required of operating divisions or product departments when returns consistently fell below the corporate average. Not infrequently, officers made statements along the following lines: "If the average corporate return were, say, 20 per cent and the return on investment for a particular item kept falling below 10 per cent, it would be dropped unless (a) a good customer needs it in order to keep a full line, or (b) it is a by-product anyhow, and anything it brings in is really gravy."

A variety of explanations was given by the companies to justify the particular size of the profit target used as a guide in pricing decisions. The most frequently mentioned rationalizations included: (a) fair or reasonable return, (b) the traditional industry concept of fair return in relation to risk factors, (c) desire to equal or better the corporation average return over a recent period, (d) what the company felt it could get as a long-run matter, and (e) use of a specific profit target as a means of stabilizing industry prices. At least one of the foregoing, and most frequently the first, was mentioned by the companies interviewed, and in a few cases the entire list was offered as justification for the company profit goal.

This reinforces the observation made earlier that no one single objective or policy rules all price-making in any given company. In

[10] The problem here is not simply one of the target return and target payout period, but rather one of balancing the desire to recoup development and other investment costs as rapidly as possible against the desire to prolong the period from distinctiveness to obsolescence by discouraging potential competitors with a relatively low-price or low-profits policy. The most rapid recovery of investment mentioned was one year, with two years not infrequently mentioned, especially where the innovative monopoly was not expected to last long or process secrecy was not secure. Also, there did not appear to be any consistent relationship between the presence of patent protection and the payout period.

fact, in many companies a close interrelationship exists among target-return pricing, desire to stabilize prices, and target market-share (either a minimum or maximum objective); this is especially true of U.S. Steel, Union Carbide, and Johns-Manville. It would seem, however, that a target-return approach is ordinarily incompatible with a market-share policy; that is, if a company desires to expand its share of the market, it will be inclined to place less emphasis on rigid adherence to a predetermined target.

IV. STABILIZATION OF PRICE AND MARGIN

The drive for stabilized prices by companies like U.S. Steel, Alcoa, International Harvester, Johns-Manville, du Pont, and Union Carbide involves both expectation of proper reward for duty done, i.e., "proper" prices, and a sense of *noblesse oblige.* Having earned what is necessary during poor times to provide an adequate return, they will refrain from upping the price as high as the traffic will bear in prosperity. Likewise, in pricing different items in the product line, there will be an effort (sustained in individual cases by the pricing executive's conscience) to refrain from exploiting any item beyond the limit set by cost-plus.

The distinction between target return on investment as a pricing philosophy and cost-plus pricing in the companies surveyed is difficult to define. Some of the companies that clearly employ the target-return-on-investment procedure in pricing new products—the area of most frequent use of target-return pricing—use cost-plus pricing for other products. The difference between the two rationalizations lies in the extent to which the company is willing to push beyond the limits of a pricing method to some average-return philosophy. According to a General Motors executive, the target plays a prominent role in the formulation of the cost-plus method.[11] But in the case of International Harvester, U.S. Steel, A & P, Johns-Manville, Alcoa, or Union Carbide, it seems fair to say that the pricing executive set the prices of many products on a cost-plus basis (except where competition precludes such action) without questioning the appropriateness of the traditional mark-up.

Cost-plus, therefore, may be viewed as one step on the road to return-on-investment as a guide, or precept for price policy. But some firms never go any farther. The standard can be accepted as

[11] See Donaldson Brown, "Pricing in Relation to Financial Control," *Manag. and Admin.,* Feb. 1924, 7, 195–98, 283–86, 417–22. This may seem to be a rather old reference, but General Motors officials cited it so frequently as an accurate representation of their present-day pricing that it warrants emphasis.

self-sufficient; just as the target-return perhaps needs no modification to make it accord with profit maximization (with all the necessary qualifications). Pricing executives seldom look beyond the particular formula with which they are accustomed to justify their decisions. They differentiate between price policies according to the degree of control they exercise; but not by the gap between the price policy and an ideal of profit maximization. They appear as ready to accept cost-plus at a reasonable volume as an ultimate standard for pricing as any other principle.

V. TARGET MARKET-SHARE

A maximum or minimum share of the market as a determinant of pricing policy was listed almost as frequently, and seemed to govern policy almost to the same extent as target-return on investment. Share of the market was ordinarily thought of in terms of a maximum, bearing witness to the power of the corporations interviewed. Being giants, they were careful to limit themselves; they apparently did not wish to gobble up any market they entered, unless it was one which they had created, like nylon, asbestos pipe, aluminum screen wire, cable products, or some synthetic chemical.

Hence, the target share of the market as a guide to pricing tended to be used for those products in which the firm did not, at the outset, enjoy a patent or innovative monopoly. Du Pont made no mention of shooting for a given share of the cellophane or nylon market, nor did Union Carbide in the Prestone market; Johns-Manville set no limit to its market share in specialized insulation materials; American Can was not thinking in terms of winning against stiff competition a moderate share of the market for vacuum packed can; nor was Alcoa in the wire and cable market. But a General Electric official spoke at length of the company's policy of not exceeding 50 per cent of any given market because it then would become too vulnerable to competition.[12] Johns-Manville officials likewise indicated that product and sales development are geared to attaining a given percentage of the market for a product line. The company endeavors, executives indicated, to maintain the

[12] He stated, "The company would rather be pushing to expand a 25 per cent share than defending a 50 per cent share." As a matter of fact, he indicated, there were few instances where G.E. had more than 22 to 25 per cent of a market. In substance, this means that when G.E. enters an appliance field with a new product, it will price to match its competitors. The company believes that it has been a downward price leader on appliances generally, however, and that both its postwar attempt to lead in price reductions and its long-term reduction in margins (its over-all margins were said to be only 58 per cent as high as in 1940) demonstrates that it has not been content merely to follow the ruling price after moving into a field.

offensive, rather than to be subject to attack because of their large product share. The company felt strongly that 20 per cent of competitive markets was the maximum share in which it was interested. This policy ruled in those areas where Johns-Manville was *not* the price leader. It stresses sales, service, and superior quality of its product in order to maintain its prices somewhat above those of its competitors. Apparently the program of reaching no more than a given market-share and of moving ahead against competition does not find expression in price reductions.

It is not possible to reach any general conclusions from comparisons of target market-shares and actual share of business realized by the companies mentioning this as a policy for pricing purposes. This is due on the one hand to the unwillingness of the companies to specify in detail particular target-share percentages, and on the other to the lack of sufficiently detailed information for the companies in question, especially for the highly diversified firms. Patently, most of these companies have very significant proportions of national markets.[13]

VI. "MEETING OR MATCHING COMPETITION"

To some of the officials interviewed, the requirement that the product price "meet competition" appeared, at first glance, to preclude the existence of any pricing policy at all. Meeting competition according to their view cannot be regarded as a rationalization of action; it is the action itself.

The rationalization of this policy of meeting competition is far from elaborate; at first blush it is perhaps unnecessary. How can "meeting competition" be dignified as one out of several alternative guides

---

[13] One interesting example of the connection between pricing (livestock bidding), market share, and investment policy is found in Swift. An analysis of livestock buying raises the question whether there is something of an understanding by the major packers of what constitutes their "normal share" of the animals sold in given public stockyards, which was the essence of the Department of Justice's complaint (1948) against Armour, Swift, Cudahy, and Wilson (since dismissed). It would seem that the relative constancy of the proportions of livestock purchased by the principal meat packers is traceable in large part to the short-run fixity of plant capacity, the desire to keep that plant operating at least up to a specific minimum level of utilization (governed partly by labor commitments), and the ever present threat that another packer may secure a larger share of the animals and the market for dressed meats. In view of these considerations, the percentages of animals purchased by the major packers would logically evidence substantial constancy over periods of weeks or months in given markets. But, unless this same approach is carried over into the planning of plant sizes in new locations (or enlargement of established plants), as well as the rate of utilization of these facilities, this would seem to be an insufficient explanation for the long-run stability of shares.

to action? In chemicals du Pont seems to apply a rule of thumb of adopting the going price in the markets for many standardized products where it never had or else had lost the leadership—e.g., carbon tetrachloride, hydrogen peroxide, disodium phosphate, nitric acid, hydrochloric acid, and various rubber chemicals. Moreover, in the case of many products selling on a freight-equalization basis, prices were not set at a high executive level; the pricing in many cases had not been reviewed for years, having been established beyond the ken of anyone now in the organization. Yet, even here there is perhaps more discretion than the officials are willing or accustomed to admit. In the pricing of neozone, du Pont was forced—though it had introduced the chemical—to change its price policy because of the tactics of competitors, who shifted the basing point. But need the matter have stopped there? Was there not a decision by du Pont to go no further than matching the Akron-based price? In many other cases du Pont undoubtedly could, if it chose, have altered the basing points or other features of the marketing of chemicals of which it produced more than an inconsequential market share.

In many cases the policy of meeting competition appears to be materially influenced by market-share psychology. Esso Standard, while going to great lengths to devise a cost-plus theory, has modified it when and where it seemed necessary or desirable. Standard of Indiana was even more specific in basing its policies on "meeting"—or forestalling—competition. Esso and, to a much lesser extent, Standard of Indiana refrained from publishing or trying to reduce to definiteness the details of the policy. A number of questions related to the companies' rationalizations are basic to understanding the functioning of the policy, for clearly neither company changed prices instantaneously when facing "competition": Did they meet the exact price charged, at the refinery or to the retail dealer? How long did a substandard price have to prevail before it could undermine a cost-plus price? Whose competitive price brought action? How were competitors rated in effectiveness? Answers to these questions are basic to an understanding of the policy. But the oil companies have not divulged the facts that would permit full and consistent treatment of the theory of "meeting competition" as seen by their managements.

It seems also that in some cases the companies are not simply meeting competition—they are preventing it. This appears to have been the purpose of A & P in localizing price cuts just to make matters difficult for a competitive store on its opening day, or General Foods in reducing the price of Certo and Sur-Jell in the Northwest where rival pectins were strong.[14] Standard of Indiana, a dominant seller not overfond of price wars, may easily justify meeting competition locally on the basis that the policy offers a permanent threat to potential price-cutters.

In other cases, the companies are aware of specific competitive products whose prices must be matched by their own if volume is to be expanded. Union Carbide knew that its synthetic organic chemicals, like the various alcohols, had to meet or undersell the price of the natural products if the investment was ever to be returned. In other cases, where a standardized commodity—e.g., bakery flour, livestock feeds, and frozen fish sold by General Foods, flour by General Mills, or wholesale meat by Swift—is simply marketed at a price over which no firm, or even small group of firms, can have control, then pricing policy ceases to have meaning. The phrase "meeting competition" is either inapplicable or inaccurate, since there is no specific competition to meet—only the market price.

VII. OTHER RATIONALIZATIONS

There are other pegs on which managements hang pricing decisions. In view of American Can's undisputed (at least until 1954) leadership in the metal container industry, and its bargaining power vis-à-vis both its suppliers and customers, it is somewhat surprising that the company should not have set out an explicit pricing goal in terms of return on investment. The management seems to be more concerned with the assurance of funds for innovating research than any particular target return on investment, although the maintenance of its market share through its closing-machine leasing policy indirectly accomplishes the same objective. The company's pricing policy could be construed as "marginal" in the sense that it automatically (via its contracts) transmits to its customers increases or decreases in costs of materials (tin plate) or labor in the can factories. In turn, this adjustability in price seems to have had the effect of stabilizing American Can's margin, the price of its services as the owner of can-closing equipment and engineering services, and, at the same time, the price of cans throughout the canning season.

[14]This information was not provided by the companies when interviewed, but is based on statements in the A & P antitrust case and the General Foods F. T. C. case made by officials of the respective companies. An A & P official of the Atlantic Division, for example, said, "It might be necessary for us to operate unprofitably for several weeks . . . reducing our line of [sic] 10% several weeks prior to the time the competitor plans to open so that people in the community will be impressed with our low prices. . . ." U.S. v. New York Great Atlantic and Pacific Tea Co., Inc., 67 F. Supp. 626 (1946), p. 668; see also ibid., pp. 667, 669, and Government Brief, pp. 909, 931; and General Foods F. T. C. Docket No. 5675, Complaint, July 7, 1949.

The companies cited many instances involving the need for resolution of conflicts of interest between integrated and nonintegrated firms and between established giants and newcomers, which displaced the usual bases for their pricing decisions. The Robinson-Patman and Sherman Acts, even when they have not been the basis for actions against the companies, were used as fundamental rationalizations of policy.

VIII. A COMPOSITE VIEW OF PRICING OBJECTIVES

Because it is big the large firm envisages itself as a part of a socially integrated group, with responsibilities for the whole pipeline and production (including full-line offerings) and associated distribution. They see themselves in a continuing relationship not only with their own distributors, but even with dealers and ultimate customers, and with their suppliers—even when the latter lacked, or especially when they lacked, the bargaining power of a larger firm. The market, in effect, is regarded as a creature of the firm, and the firm has the responsibility for preserving these relationships and perpetuating its own position.

The size of these firms also makes them an obvious target for antitrust suits, legislation, Congressional investigation, and similar restraining forces. To a certain extent, size thus entails a vulnerability and generates a sense of *noblesse oblige.* This is reinforced by the disposition of the government and the community generally to look on and appeal to these firms as "pattern-setters" for industry generally; and in pricing they are expected to avoid taking full advantage of immediate profit opportunities. This attitude is perhaps most clearly expressed in the *Economic Report of the President* of January 1957, which stated:

> Specifically, business and labor leadership have the responsibility to reach agreements on wages and other labor benefits that are fair to the rest of the community as well as to those persons immediately involved. . . . *And business must recognize the broad public interest in prices set on their products and services.* (p. 3, italics added.)

From this point, it is an easy step to the position taken by the typical large firm that it is entitled to a "just price" and "fair return" on investment. In the case of some companies, like U.S. Steel, the resolution of conflicts of interest between integrated and nonintegrated firms, between established giants and newcomers, and between the pattern-setter and the community generally, has modified company price policy to a point where even the managements have come to refer to it as akin to that of a public utility. This may be a logical development in cases where unpleasant experiences of cutthroat competition—especially in fairly standardized products like steel, copper, gasoline, and aluminum—have generated a disposition by management to avoid price changes except through periodic, thoroughly considered, and well-publicized alterations in recognized base prices. By relating price revisions to changes in direct costs (especially increases in wage costs), the firm avoids the annoyance to itself and its customers (who they claim vastly prefer stable prices) of frequent changes in price structure.

This desire for stabilized pricing, oftentimes described with a blanket adjective as "administered," usually implies that the company or companies set some kind of target to which their price policies conform. The price, according to this view, is under the control of one firm acting as the price leader or a group of firms that make policy for the industry. The contention of the business executives themselves is that an administered price, like the tank-wagon price of gasoline, far from being an independent creation of the price leader, is merely a device for approximating a market equilibrium. According to this view, there are so many possibilities of substitution of one product for another, or an off-brand for a name brand, that the limits of discretion are much narrower than is generally supposed. Administration of prices, officials contend, thus merely avoids the decision to use cutthroat competition—which itself would be another form of administered pricing; it also avoids temporary exploitation of shortages. Refraining from raising prices when a higher price is necessary to equate supply with demand, is also justified by management on the grounds that over the long run higher prices would disturb equilibrium by bringing unneeded capacity into the industry. But it is impossible to accept the conventional justification for leadership. It can masquerade as resulting in a genuine "equilibrium" only if the word is made equivalent to whatever is the decision of the leading firms.

The foregoing data, above all, make it clear that management's approach to pricing is based upon *planned* profits. The company proceeds on the assumption of the need for a certain amount of capital to undertake the investment in plant expansion and new facilities which are envisaged for the long haul in order to maintain and/or improve market position. In some cases, quite in contrast to the thinking of management before the second world war, this desire to hold position and to penetrate wider markets requires that capital investment should be planned with built-in excess capacity (this is best illustrated by the fact that prices are premised on the assumption of operating at a rate of 75 to 80 per cent of capacity, which is assumed to be the long-run normal). In deciding upon which products and productive facilities will be added or expanded, the top-level corporation appropriations committee relies upon estimates of return on utilized investment. The only way in which price policy can be viewed in such companies as these, with their wide variety of products and selling in a large number of different markets, is in terms of profits-investment ratios. This criterion serves as an effective guide for pricing decisions at divisional and departmental levels. If we are to speak of "administered" decisions in the large firm, it is perhaps more accurate to speak of administered *profits* rather than administered *prices*.

IX. CONCLUSIONS

The principal purpose of this paper has been to contribute to our knowledge of the actual process by which prices are formed in industry, with the expectation that the data will help in constructing a more realistic theory of the firm capable of yielding useful predictions of industrial price behavior. The general hypothesis which emerges is that (a) the large company has a fairly well-defined pricing goal that is related to a long-range profit horizon; (b) its management seeks—especially in multiproduct multimarket operations—a simultaneous decision with respect to price, cost, and product characteristics; and (c) its pricing formulas are handy devices for checking the internal consistency of the separate decisions as against the general company objective. Under this hypothesis no single theory of the firm—and certainly no single motivational hypothesis such as profit-maximization—is likely to impose an unambiguous course of action for the firm for any given situation; nor will it provide a satisfactory basis for valid and useful predictions of price behavior.

In pursit of price policies that will yield the maximum satisfaction of the company's community of interests, the findings show that one company will prefer stability, another will seek to expand its market share, or to engage in continuous discovery and pre-emption of new fields, while others will be content to meet competition, to satisfy a set target, or to aim at combinations and variations of these goals. It seems reasonable to conclude that the pricing policies are in almost every case equivalent to a company policy that represents an order of priorities and choice from among competing objectives rather than policies tested by any simple concept of profits maximization. Managerial specialists down the line are given a framework of requirements that must be met, while managers at the top, of course, are free to and do change these requirements to meet particular situations.[15]

Another relevant aspect of the data for theoretical analysis is the conception of the market held by managements of large corporations. Individual products, markets, and pricing are not considered in isolation; the unit of decision-making is the enterprise, and pricing and marketing strategies are viewed in this global context. Because of the tremendously complex joint-cost problems and the lack of knowledge of actual relationships between costs and output or sales, on the one hand, and the joint-revenue aspects of multiproduct companies, on the other, pricing is frequently done for product groups with an eye to the over-all profit position of the company. This means that costing of products ends up as a result of price policy rather than the reverse. In view of the various external pressures on the company and the nature of the strategy of the enterprise, however, it is doubtful if prices would bear any closer relationship to actual costs were detailed cost data available to management. The incentive to realize target rates of profits for the long haul better suits the objectives of management-controlled companies than any desire to profiteer or to seek windfall profits.

It might appear that there are conflicts between the objectives of price leaders and price followers, e.g., between such companies as U.S. Steel and National Steel. Actually, however, it is a matter of leaders having fairly well-defined target objectives, whereas price followers evidently do not have independent targets. Their objective, especially where undifferentiated products make up the bulk of the product line, will be determined by the target set by the price leader. If the target is acceptable, the follower is content to hold a market share and will adjust price policy accordingly.

In more general cases, including differentiated product markets as well as undifferentiated, the extent to which companies—with the dimensions and diversification of those under discussion—serve as leaders or followers on individual products or product groups depends upon the profit-importance of a particular product in a given company's line, the nature of the product—whether a producer or a consumer good—and the size and degree of diversification of companies with which there are product overlaps. Moreover, the manner in which interfirm policies will be coordinated will depend upon the above factors as they bear upon particular products, plus the over-all objectives of the enterprise as a unit and its general market strategy.

[15]"The managerial philosophy not only calls into question the assumption of profit maximization as a workable description of entrepreneurial behavior but denies the institutional basis of the classical profit motivation." E. S. Mason. "The Apologetics of 'Managerialism'," *Journal of Business*, Volume 31 (January 1958), p. 6.

A further implication of the findings for the theory of the firm is the relationship found between price and investment decisions. The information on this aspect is limited, but nevertheless the setting of and attempt to follow specific target returns on investment are manifest at two separate levels of operations: short-run pricing and investment decisions. The investment decision presupposes a price (and usually a market-share) assumption, which, in turn, determines short-run price decisions thereafter. Thus, investment decisions in effect are themselves a form of pricing decision, and over time become an inherent part of price policy.

Finally, the general approach of these large corporations to price policy, and the attendant price behavior, raise some important issues for public policy. Their very size—both absolutely and relatively—permits the managements to select from among various alternative courses of action. This is a fairly clear manifestation of economic or market power. In partial reflection of this power, plus a variety of other reasons related to their size, vulnerability to public criticism, and potential antitrust action, these corporations tend to behave more and more like public utilities, especially the target-return-minded companies. To complicate the issue further, target-return pricing implies a policy of stable or rigid pricing, even though exceptions are found within particular product lines.

A crucial question raised by these facets of policy is: What is the net impact on economic growth and stability? More specifically, do target-return pricing, profits planning, and the attendant price behavior, tend to promote or inhibit stability and growth? Much more adequate empirical data on corporation objectives and detailed study of individual company pricing, profits, and investment planning over the course of economic fluctuations are needed before answers can be given to this question.

32

Bayesian Decision Theory in Pricing Strategy

Paul E. Green

Since the publication of Robert Schlaifer's pioneering work, *Probability and Statistics for Business Decisions*,[1] the Bayesian approach to decision-making under uncertainty has received much comment, pro and con, by theoretical and applied statisticians alike.

However, in contrast to the large number of theoretical contributions being made to decision theory in general and Bayesian statistics in particular, reported applications of these procedures to real-world problem situations have been rather meager. Applications appear especially lacking in the marketing field.

In highly oversimplified terms, the Bayesian approach to decision-making under uncertainty provides a framework for explicitly working with the economic costs of alternative courses of action, the prior knowledge or judgments of the decision maker, and formal modification of these judgments as additional data are introduced into the problem.

Paul E. Green, "Bayesian Decision Theory in Pricing Strategy." Reprinted with permission from *Journal of Marketing*, published by the American Marketing Association, January, 1963, pp. 5-14. This article was co-winner of the 1963 Alpha Kappa Psi award as best article of the year.

Paul E. Green is S. S. Kresge professor of marketing at the Wharton School of Finance and Commerce and associate director of the school's Management Science Center. He received both M.A. and Ph.D. from the Wharton School. Professor Green spent 12 years in industry with such firms as the du Pont Company and the Sun Oil Company. He is a leading proponent of Bayesian analysis in marketing; his current interests include the use of quantitative techniques in marketing planning and decision making, particularly multidimensional and non-metric scaling. He and his co-author D. S. Tull have recently revised their successful textbook *Research for Marketing Decisions*.

[1] Robert Schlaifer, *Probability and Statistics for Business Decisions* (New York: McGraw-Hill Book Company, 1959). In addition two excellent general articles dealing with the Bayesian approach are: Harry V. Roberts, "The New Business Statistics," *Journal of Business* (January, 1960, pp. 21-30) and Jack Hirshleifer, "The Bayesian Approach to Statistical Decision—An Exposition," *Journal of Business,* October, 1961, pp. 471-489.

In the du Pont Company, the decision theory approach, often augmented by computer simulation, has been used experimentally over the past few years in a variety of market planning applications, ranging from capacity expansion problems to questions concerning the introduction of new products and long-range price and promotional strategy. The application to follow concerns the use of Bayesian theory in the selection of a "best" pricing policy for a firm in an oligopolistic industry where such factors as demand elasticity, competitive retaliation, threat of future price weakness, and potential entry of new competitors influence the effectiveness of the firm's courses of action. Although the content of this case is apocryphal, its structure has been compounded from actual situations.

No attempt will be made to describe even superficially all of the many facets of the Bayesian approach to decision-making under uncertainty. The content of this article is focused on only two main considerations.

First, in dealing with actual marketing situations, for example, pricing problems, the opportunity to obtain field information may be non-existent. Second, in dealing with actual marketing problems, the complexity of the situation may force the analyst to develop a problem structure in much greater detail than has been described in the literature.

AN ILLUSTRATIVE APPLICATION

Since early 1955, the Everclear Plastics Company had been producing a resin called Kromel, basically designed for certain industrial markets. In addition to Everclear, three other firms were producing Kromel resin. Prices among all four suppliers (called here the Kromel industry) were identical: and the product quality and service among producers were comparable. Everclear's current share of Kromel industry sales amounted to 10 per cent.

Four industrial end uses comprised the principal marketing area for the Kromel industry. These market segments will be labeled A, B, C, and D. Three of the segments (B, C, and D) were functionally dependent on segment A in the sense that Kromel's *ultimate* market position and rate of approach to this level in each of these three segments was predicated on resin's making substantial inroads in segment A.

The Kromel industry's only competition in these four segments consisted of another resin called Verlon, which was produced by six other firms. Shares of the total Verlon-Kromel market (weighted sums over all four segments) currently stood at 70 per cent Verlon industry, and 30 per cent Kromel industry. Since its introduction in 1955, the superior functional characteristics per dollar cost of Kromel had enabled this newer product to displace fairly large poundages of Verlon in market segments B, C, and D.

On the other hand, the functional superiority per dollar cost of Kromel had not been sufficiently high to interest segment A consumers. While past price decreases in Kromel had been made, the cumulative effect of these reductions had still been insufficient to accomplish Kromel sales penetration in segment A. (Sales penetration is defined as a market share exceeding zero.)

In the early fall of 1960, it appeared to Everclear's management that future weakness in Kromel price might be in the offing. The anticipated capacity increases on the part of the firm's Kromel competitors suggested that in the next year or two potential industry supply of this resin might significantly exceed demand, if no substantial market participation for the Kromel industry were established in segment A. In addition, it appeared likely that potential Kromel competitors might enter the business, thus adding to the threat of oversupply in later years.

Segment A, of course, constituted the key factor. If substantial inroads could be made in this segment, it appeared likely that Kromel industry sales growth in the other segments not only could be speeded up, but that ultimate market share levels for this resin could be markedly increased from those anticipated in the absence of segment A penetration. To Everclear's sales management, a price reduction in Kromel still appeared to represent a feasible means to achieve this objective, and (even assuming similar price reductions on the part of Kromel competitors) perhaps could still be profitable to Everclear.

However, a large degree of uncertainty surrounded both the overall attractiveness of this alternative, and under this alternative the amount of the price reduction which would enable Kromel to penetrate market segment A.

PROBLEM STRUCTURING AND DEVELOPMENT
OF THE MODEL

Formulation of the problem required a certain amount of artistry and compromise toward achieving a reasonably adequate description of the problem. But it was also necessary to keep the structure simple enough so that the nature of each input would be comprehensible to the personnel responsible for supplying data for the study. Problem components had to be formulated, such as:

1. length of planning period;
2. number and nature of courses of action;
3. payoff functions; and
4. states of nature covering future growth of the total Verlon-Kromel market, inter-industry (Kromel vs. Verlon) and intra-Kromel industry effects of a Kromel price change, implications on Everclear's share of the total Kromel industry, and Everclear's production costs.

Initial discussions with sales management indicated that a planning period of five years should be considered in the study. While the selection of five years was somewhat arbitrary, sales personnel believed that some repercussions of a current price reduction might well extend over several years into the future.

A search for possible courses of action indicated that four pricing alternatives covered the range of actions under consideration:

1. maintenance of *status quo* on Kromel price, which was $1.00 per pound;
2. a price reduction to $.93 per pound within the next three months;
3. a price reduction to $.85 per pound within the next three months;
4. a price reduction to $.80 per pound within the next three months.

Inasmuch as each price action would be expected to produce a different time pattern in the flow of revenues and costs, and since no added investment in production facilities was contemplated, it was agreed that cumulative, compounded net profits over the five-year planning period would constitute a relevant payoff function. In the absence of any unanimity as to the "correct" opportunity cost of capital, it was decided to use two interest rates of 6 and 10 per cent annually in order to test the sensitivity of outcomes to the cost of the capital variable.

Another consideration came to light during initial problem discussions. Total market growth (for the Kromel or Verlon industry) over the next five years in each market segment constituted a "state of nature" which could impinge on Everclear's profit position. Accordingly, it was agreed to consider three separate forecasts of total market growth, a "most probable," "optimistic," and "pessimistic" forecast.

From these assumptions a base case was then formulated. This main case would first consider the pricing problem under the most probable forecast of total Verlon-Kromel year-by-year sales potential in each segment, using an opportunity cost of capital of 6 per cent annually. The two other total market forecasts and the other cost of capital were then to be treated as subcases, in order to test the sensitivity of the base case outcomes to variations in these particular states of nature.

However, inter- and intra-industry alternative states of nature literally abounded in the Kromel resin problem. Sales management at Everclear had to consider such factors as:

1. The possibility that Kromel resin could effect penetration of market segment A if no price decrease were made;
2. If a price decrease were made, the extent of Verlon retaliation to be anticipated;
3. Given a particular type of Verlon price retaliation, its possible impact on Kromel's penetration of segment A;
4. If segment A were penetrated, the possible market share which the Kromel industry could gain in segment A;
5. If segment A were penetrated, the possible side effects of this event on speeding up Kromel's participation in market segments B, C, and D;
6. If segment A were not penetrated, the impact which the price reduction could still have on speeding up Kromel's participation in segments B, C, and D;
7. If segment A were not penetrated, the possibility that existing Kromel competitors would initiate price reductions a year hence;
8. The possible impact of a current Kromel price reduction on the decisions of existing or potential Kromel producers to increase capacity or enter the industry.

While courses of action, length of planning period, and the payoff measure (cumulative, compounded net profits) for the base case had been fairly quickly agreed upon, the large number of inter- and intra-Kromel industry states of nature deemed relevant to the problem would require rather lengthy discussion with Everclear's sales personnel.

Accordingly, introductory sessions were held with Everclear's sales management, in order to develop a set of states of nature large enough to represent an adequate description of the real problem, yet small enough to be comprehended by the participating sales personnel. Next, separate interview sessions were held with two groups of Everclear's sales personnel; subjective probabilities regarding the occurrence of alternative states of nature under each course of action were developed in these sessions. A final session was held with all contributing personnel in attendance; each projection and/or subjective probability was gone over in detail, and a final set of ground rules for the study was agreed upon. A description of these ground rules appears in Table I.

TABLE 1: *Subjective Probabilities and Data Estimates Associated with Everclear's Pricing Problem*

1. If Kromel price remained at $1.00/pound and market segment A were not penetrated, what market share pattern for Kromel industry sales pounds would obtain in segments B, C, and D?

| | Base assumptions–Kromel industry share | | |
	Segment B	Segment C	Segment D
1961	57.0%	40.0%	42.0%
1962	65.0	50.0	44.0
1963	75.0	80.0	46.0
1964	76.0	84.0	48.0
1965	76.0	84.0	50.0

2. If Kromel price remained at $1.00/pound, what is the probability that Kromel would still penetrate market segment A?

	Probability of penetration–Segment A
1961	.05
1962	.10
1963	.20
1964	.25
1965	.40

3. Under price strategies $.93/pound, $.85/pound, and $.80/pound, what is the probability of Verlon industry price retaliation; and given the particular retaliation (shown below), what is the probability that Kromel would still penetrate market segment A?

	Pricing case (entries are probabilities)		
Verlon industry retaliation	$.93 case	$.85 case	$.80 case
Full match of Kromel price reduction	.05	.15	.38
Half match of Kromel price reduction	.60	.75	.60
Stand pat on price	.35	.10	.02

Given a particular Verlon retaliatory action, the probability that Kromel would still penetrate segment A

| | $.93 case | | | $.85 case | | | $.80 case | | |
	Full match	Half match	Stand pat	Full match	Half match	Stand pat	Full match	Half match	Stand pat
1961	.15	.20	.35	.20	.40	.80	.75	.80	.90
1962	.25	.30	.60	.30	.60	.90	.80	.85	.95
1963	.35	.40	.65	.40	.65	.95	.85	.90	1.00
1964	.60	.65	.75	.70	.75	.98	.90	.95	1.00
1965	.65	.70	.80	.75	.80	.98	.95	.98	1.00

TABLE 1. (Continued)

4. If penetration in market segment A were effected, what is the probability that Kromel would obtain the specific share of this segment (a) during the first year of penetration, and (b) during the second year of participation?

Share	First year	Second year
25%	.15	.00
50	.35	.00
75	.40	.00
100	.10	1.00

5. If Kromel penetration of market segment A were effected, what impact would this event have on speeding up Kromel industry participation in segments B, C, and D?

  Segment B—Would speed up market participation one year from base assumption shown under point 1 of this Table.

  Segment C—Would speed up market participation one year from base assumption shown under point 1 of this Table.

  Segment D—Kromel would move up to 85% of the market in the following year, and would obtain 100% of the market in the second year following penetration of segment A.

6. Under the price reduction strategies, if Kromel penetration of market segment A were *not* accomplished, what is the probability that Kromel industry participation in segments B, C, and D (considered as a group) would still be speeded up one year from the base assumption shown under point 1 of this Table?

Probability of speedup	
$.93 case	.45
$.85 case	.60
$.80 case	.80

7. If Kromel price at the end of any given year were $1.00/pound, $.93/pound, $.85/pound, or $.80/pound respectively, *and* if market segment A were not penetrated, what is the probability that present competitive Kromel producers would take the specific price action shown below?

If Kromel price	Action	Probability
@$1.00/pound	$1.00/pound	.15
	.93	.80
	.85	.05
	.80	.00
@$.93/pound	.93	.80
	.85	.20
	.80	.00
@$.85/pound	.85	1.00
	.80	.00
@ $.80/pound	.80	1.00

TABLE 1. *(continued)*

8. Under each of the four price strategies, what is the probability that competitive (present or potential) Kromel producers would add to or initiate capacity (as related to the price prevailing in mid-1961) in the years 1963 and 1964? (No capacity changes were assumed in 1965.)

Competitor	$1.00/pound	$.93/pound	$.85/pound	$.80/pound
R	.50	.20	.05	.00
S	.90	.75	.50	.20
T	.40	.10	.05	.00
U	.70	.50	.25	.00
V	.70	.50	.25	.00

	Timing and amount available beginning of year	
Competitor	1963	1964
R	10 million pounds	20 million pounds
S	12	20
T	12	20
U	6	12
V	6	6

USE OF TREE DIAGRAMS

The large number of alternative states of nature which were associated with inter- and intra-industry factors necessitated the construction of "tree diagrams" for each pricing alternative. These diagrams enabled sales management to trace the implications of their assumptions. Figure 1 shows a portion of one such tree diagram.

A word of explanation concerning interpretation of the probability tree is in order. The two principal branches underneath the *$1.00 case* refer to the event of whether or not Kromel penetrates segment A in the first year of the planning period. Sales personnel felt that a 5 per cent chance existed for penetration, hence the figure .05000 under A.

However, if A were penetrated, four market participations were deemed possible; 25, 50, 75 and 100 per cent carrying the conditional probabilities of .15, .35, .40 and .10 respectively.

Multiplication of each conditional probability, in turn, by the .05 marginal probability leads to the four joint probabilities noted in the upper left portion of the chart.

Next, if Kromel did not penetrate segment A during the first year, a probability of .80 was attached to the event that competitive

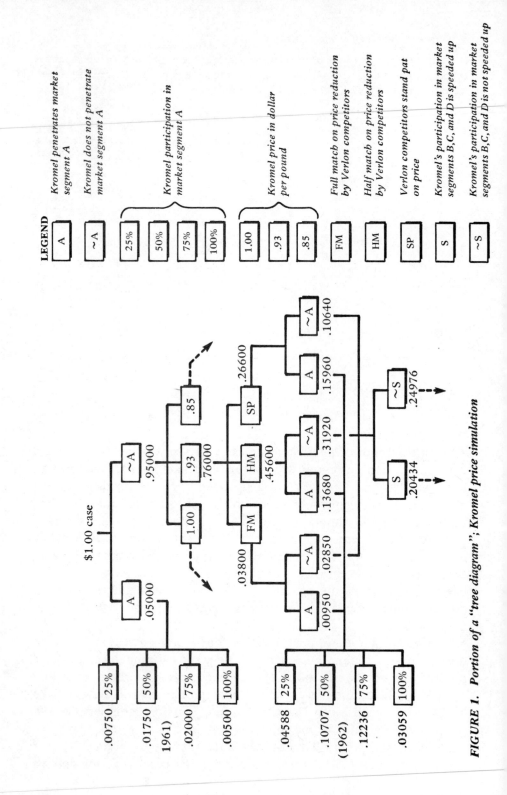

LEGEND

A	Kromel penetrates market segment A
~A	Kromel does not penetrate market segment A
25% 50% 75% 100%	Kromel participation in market segment A
1.00 .93 .85	Kromel price in dollar per pound
FM	Full match on price reduction by Verlon competitors
HM	Half match on price reduction by Verlon competitors
SP	Verlon competitors stand pat on price
S	Kromel's participation in market segments B, C, and D is speeded up
~S	Kromel's participation in market segments B, C, and D is not speeded up

FIGURE 1. Portion of a "tree diagram"; Kromel price simulation

Kromel producers would reduce price to $.93 per pound. Multiplying the conditional probability of .80 by .95 results in the .76000 probability assigned to the joint event, "did not penetrate segment A and Kromel price was reduced to $.93 per pound."

However, if Kromel price were reduced to $.93 per pound, Verlon retaliation had to be considered, leading to the joint probabilities assigned to the next set of tree branches. In this way probabilities were built up for each of the over 400 posssible outcomes of the study by appropriate application of the ground rules noted in Table 1.

A mathematical model was next constructed for determining the expected value of Everclear's cumulative, compounded net profits under each price strategy. See Table 2.

This model was then programmed for an electronic computer. The simulation was first carried out for the base case assumptions regarding total Verlon-Kromel market growth and cost of capital. Additional runs were made in which these assumptions were varied.

TABLE 2. *Kromel Model—Expected Value of Cumulative, Compounded Net Profits*

The mathematical model used to determine the expected values of Everclear's cumulative, compounded net profits was as follows:

$$CCN(X_k) = \sum_{j=1}^{n} p_j \cdot \sum_{i=1}^{m} [(1 + r)^{m-i} \, T \left\{ (D_{ij} - Z_{ij}) \, (K_{ij} \, M_{ij}) \right\}]$$

$$Z_{ij} = \phi \, (K_{ij} M_{ij})$$

$CCN(X_k)$ = Expected value of Everclear's cumulative, compounded net profits under each X_k price strategy ($k = 1, \ldots, 4$).

  p_j = Probability assigned to the j-th outcome ($j = 1, 2, \ldots, n$).

  r = Interest rate per annum, expressed decimally.

  T = Ratio of net to gross profits of Everclear's Kromel operation (assumed constant in the study).

  D_{ij} Kromel price in $/pound in the i-th year ($i = 1,2, \ldots, m$) for the j-th outcome.

  Z_{ij} = Cost in $/pound of Everclear's Kromel resin in the i-th year for the j-th outcome. (This cost is a function of the amount of Kromel pounds sold by Everclear.)

  ϕ = Function of.

  K_{ij} = Everclear's overall market share of Kromel Industry sales (in pounds) in the i-th year for the j-th outcome (expressed decimally).

  M_{ij} = Kromel Industry poundage (summed over all four market segments) in the i-th year for the j-th outcome.

The computer run for the base case showed some interesting results for the relevant variables affecting Everclear's cumulative, compounded net profits position at the end of the planning period. These results are portrayed in Figures 2 through 4.

Figure 2 summarizes the cumulative probability of Kromel's penetration of market segment A (the critical factor in the study) as a function of time, under each pricing strategy. As would be expected, the lowest price strategy, the *$.80 case,* carried the highest probability of market penetration. However, the cumulative probability approached 1, that *all* price strategies would eventually effect penetration of market segment A by the end of the simulation period. This behavior stems from the impact of price decreases assumed to be initiated by Kromel *competitors* (if penetration were not initially effected under the original price strategies) which in turn changed the probability of Kromel's penetration of segment A in later years, since this probability was related to price.

Figure 3 shows the expected incremental sales dollars (obtained by subtracting the expected outcomes of the *$1.00 case,* used as a reference base, from the expected outcomes of each of the other three cases respectively) generated for Everclear under each price strategy. While some tapering off in average sales dollars generated from the price reduction cases compared to the *$1.00 case* can be noted near the end of the simulation period, this tapering off is less pronounced than that which would be experienced by the total Kromel industry.

The reason for this different pattern is that the price reduction strategies (by reducing the probability of future capacity expansion on the part of existing and potential Kromel competitors) led to gains in Everclear's market share, relative to market share under the *$1.00 case.* These increases in Everclear's market share, under the price reduction strategies, partially offset the decline in incremental sales dollar gains (experienced by the Kromel industry near the end of the period) and thus explain the difference in sales patterns that would be observed between Everclear and the Kromel industry.

Figure 4 summarizes the behavior of Everclear's average, year-by-year (compounded) net profits performance again on an incremental basis compared to the *$1.00 case.* As would be expected, time lags in the penetration of segment A, under the price reduction strategies, result in an early profit penalty compared to the *$1.00 case.* This penalty is later overbalanced by the additional sales dollars accruing from earlier (on the average) penetration of segment A under the price reduction strategies versus the *status quo* price case.

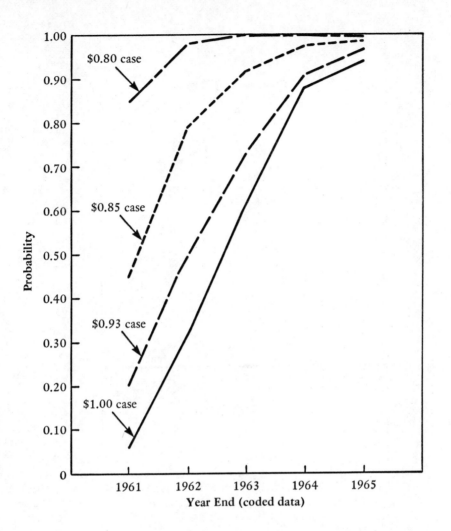

FIGURE 2. *Cumulative probability of Kromel's penetration of market segment A (As a function of time and initial price)*

The overall performance of each pricing strategy on Everclear's cumulative, compounded net profits position (expected value basis) at the *end* of the five-year planning period is shown in Table 3. These values were obtained by application of the formula shown in Table 2.

Table 3 shows that all of the price reduction strategies yield expected payoffs which exceed the *$1.00 case.* These additional profits stem from two principal sources:

1. the higher profits generated in the middle portion of the planning period, as a function of the increased probability of effecting penetration of market segment A, and its associated effect on Kromel industry sales in market segments B, C, and D; and

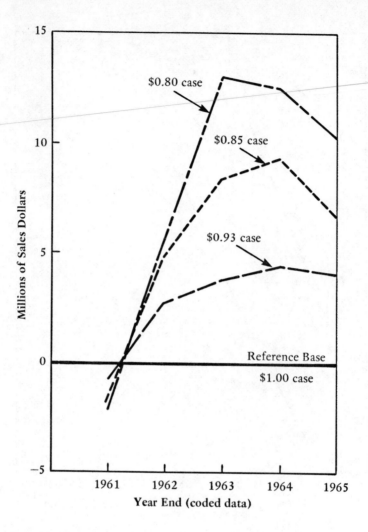

FIGURE 3. *Kromel sales volume—Everclear Plastics Co. (Incremental sales dollars generated over $1.00 case)*

2. The higher market share for Everclear, resulting from the influence of the price reduction strategies on lowering the probability of capacity expansion and/or entry by Kromel competitors (existing or potential). These combined factors overbalance the lower profit margins per pound associated with the price reduction strategies compared to the *$1.00 case.*

However, a relevant question arose concerning the influence of the more favorable market share factor (under the price reduction cases) on the outcomes of these strategies vs. the *$1.00 case.* Suppose that no favorable difference in market share were obtained under the price reduction strategies compared to the no-price reduction case. That

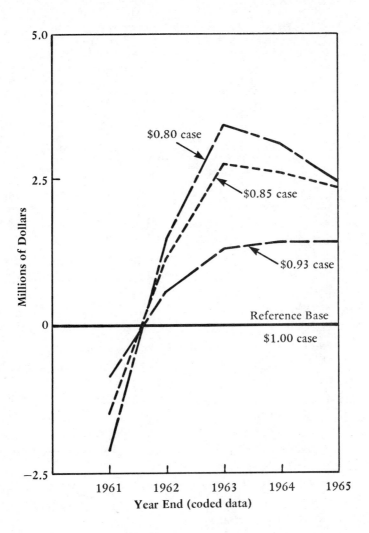

FIGURE 4. Compounded year-by-year net profits of Everclear Plastics Co. (Compound rate equals 6% annually)

is, suppose the probability that lower Kromel price would discourage future competitive expansion of Kromel industry capacity in the 1963-64 period were zero. How would this affect Everclear's profit position?

In order to test the impact of this variable on Everclear's cumulative, compounded net profits, the market share factor was held constant at the trend level estimated under the no-price reduction, or *$1.00 case* over the simulation period. This analysis resulted in the information given in Table 4.

It is clear from Table 4 that the market share factor is important in producing Everclear's higher profit position as associated with the

TABLE 3. Cumulative, Compounded Net Profits—Everclear Plastics Co. (1961-65)

Price strategy	End-of-period profit position
$1.00 case	$26.5 million
.93 case	30.3 million
.85 case	33.9 million
.80 case	34.9 million

price reduction alternatives noted in Table 3. If increased share for Everclear were *not* obtained in the 1963–65 period (relative to the share expected under the *$1.00 case*), all strategies would yield close to equal payoffs. That is, over the planning period, the increased sales volume resulting from earlier (on the average) penetration of segment A under the price reduction strategies just about balances the less favorable profit margins associated with these strategies.

However, beyond the planning period, all strategies have for all practical purposes accomplished penetration of segment A. The impact of *higher market share* for Everclear thus assumes an important role toward maintaining higher payoffs for the price reduction cases versus the *$1.00 case.*

When computer run results were analyzed for the sub-cases (varying the total market forecast and cost of capital variables), it was found that the study outcomes were not sensitive to these factors. Although the absolute levels of all payoffs changed, no appreciable change was noted in their relative standing.

In Summary. This illustration has shown two principal findings regarding the expected payoffs associated with the alternative courses of action formulated by Everclear:

1. All price reduction strategies result in higher expected payoffs than that associated with the *status quo* pricing case and of these, the *$.80 case* leads to the largest expected value.

TABLE 4. Profit Position—Market Share Help Constant (Everclear's cumulative, compounded net profits; 1961-65)

Price strategy	End-of-period profit position
$1.00 case	$26.5 million
.93 case	26.9 million
.85 case	27.4 million
.80 case	25.2 million

2. The higher payoffs associated with the price reduction strategies are quite sensitive to the assumption that Everclear's future market share would be favorably influenced by reductions in Kromel price.

Everclear's management is now at least in a position to appraise the *financial implications* of its marketing assumptions in order to arrive at a reasoned selection among alternative choices.

IMPLICATIONS

The preceding illustration indicates the extent of problem detail which can be (and frequently must be) introduced to reflect adequately the characteristics of real market situations. Nevertheless, this illustration omits some important features of Bayesian decision theory.

First, payoffs were expressed in monetary terms (cumulative, compounded net profits) rather than utility, in the von Neumann-Morgenstern sense, as discussed by Schlaifer.[2] One assumes implicitly, then, that utility is linear with money. As tempting as this assumption may be, some small-scale studies at du Pont in which attempts were made to construct empirical utility functions raise some questions regarding the assumption of linearity. However, this feature of the Bayesian approach may well take many years of further education and development before it may find regular application on the industrial scene.

Second, while a plethora of Bayesian prior probabilities were used in this problem, no mention was made of analyzing sample data and calculating *posterior* probabilities. How does one investigate states of nature in problems of this type? Certainly the problems of conducting meaningful experiments are hardly trivial in pricing problems, or the general area of market planning.

Third, just how detailed a structure can be warranted, particularly when the inputs to the problem are largely subjective in character? One may obviously over-structure as well as under-structure a problem. This *caveat*, however, applies to all model building. While sensitivity analysis may be used to shed light on which variables "make a difference," the fact remains that the model-building process is still based largely on the builder's intuitive grasp of problem essentials and the interplay between analyst and decision-maker. The structure of the problem discussed in this article turned out to be complex precisely because the variables included *were* deemed important by the decision-maker(s). And part of the analyst's job is thus to examine

---

[2] Schlaifer, *op. cit.*, chap. 2.

the impact of supposedly important variables on the relevant payoff junction and then feed back his findings to the decision-maker.

Finally, in conducting this study, realistic problems have a way of generating quite a lot of arithmetic detail, for example, a multi-stage set of alternative states of nature and payoffs. Implementation of the Bayesian approach must, therefore, frequently be aided by recourse to a high-speed computing device. Moreover, a computer model also facilitates the task of running sensitivity analyses concerning either changes in the payoff values related to any particular combination of state of nature and course of action.

Our experience has indicated that the Bayesian approach, even coupled with the ancillary techniques of computer simulation and sensitivity analysis, does not offer any foolproof procedure for "solving" market planning problems. Still, it would seem that this method *does* offer definite advantage over the more traditional techniques usually associated with market planning. Traditional techniques rarely consider *alternative* states of nature, let alone assigning prior probabilities to their occurrence. Moreover, traditional market planning techniques seldom provide for testing the sensitivity of the study's outcomes to departures in the basic assumptions.

At the very least, the Bayesian model forces a more rigorous approach to market planning problems and offers a useful device for quickly finding the financial implications of assumptions about the occurrence of alternative states of nature. In time, this procedure coupled with a more sophisticated approach to the design, collection, and interpretation of field data appears capable of providing an up-to-date and flexible means to meet the more stringent demands of dynamic decision situations, so typical in the problems faced by the marketing manager.

Index